Charlie Rael

AN INTRODUCTION TO
HOMINOLOGY

An Integrated View of Mankind and Self

By

THEODORE C. KAHN, Ph.D., Sc.D.

Professor of Behavioral Science
University of Southern Colorado

THIRD EDITION

NATIONWIDE PRESS, LTD.

Pueblo • Colorado • U.S.A.

Published and Distributed by

NATIONWIDE PRESS, LTD.

P. O. Box 1528, Pueblo, Colorado 81002

First Edition, First Printing, 1969
First Edition, Second Printing, 1970
Second Edition, 1972

Third and Revised Edition, 1976
by Nationwide Press, Ltd.

Third Edition, First Printing, 1976
Third Edition, Second Printing, 1976

Printed and manufactured in the
United States of America

PREFACE

In 1969 *An Introduction to Hominology - The Study of the Whole Man* was published (Charles C. Thomas) and in the same year the *Encyclopedia Britannica Yearbook* defined hominology as a "generalized study of mankind without regard to traditional academic disciplines." Some important changes were incorporated into the revised second edition of the book published in 1972. Three years later, the present book, *Hominology - An Integrated Study of Mankind and Self* was published (Nationwide, 1976).

In the intervening years several publications brought the study of hominology to a wider audience. Articles on hominology appeared in a number of journals. In 1969, the potentialities for hominology in the area of psychotherapy were explored in *New Frontiers in Psychiatric Technology*. An article, "Hominology — A New Dimension in Psychotherapy" was published in the *Journal of Contemporary Psychotherapy* in the Spring of 1972. The April 1973 issue of *A Forum for a Better World* (PHP Institute, Tokyo) featured an article on hominology entitled, "Who Wants to Study Fragments of Man?" "Hominology as an Aspect of Humanistic Psychology" appeared as a chapter in the book, *Essays in Humanistic Psychology* in 1973 (Shields).

Hominology - Psychiatry's Newest Frontier by C. D. Jones (Charles C. Thomas, 1975) is considered by some in the mental health field as representing a new and challenging approach to the problems of emotional adjustment and psychopathology. Dr. L. A. Ruybalid wrote in his introduction to Jones' book "The emphasis of this book is on the technique and results of encouraging the adoption of a new and vastly more therapeutic self-concept by participation in self-enhancing exercises within a new approach to human behavior called 'hominology'." In the same year another book, *Methods and Evaluation in Clinical and Counseling Psychology* (Kahn *et al*, Pergamon, General Psychology Series, 1975), included hominological therapy as one of the newer methods of dealing with human problems.

It is interesting that a course of study which had originally been devised as a method of teaching psychiatrists in a residency program how to focus on the total patient instead of fragmenting him into disease entities has become a successful academic subject with a range of students from second grade to university graduate level. Since 1965, hominology has been taught at the University of Southern Colorado. In 1966, the *Colorado School Journal* (May issue) described the teaching of hominology in "Hominology: A New Approach to Understanding Man." Other universities, colleges and community colleges have adopted hominology and made this integrated study of mankind and self a part of their regular curriculum. Additionally, hominology has been adapted for teaching in elementary and secondary schools and one of these programs, the "Conahan Experiment", is described in *Hominology - Psychiatry's Newest Frontier*. The *Directory of Teaching Innovations in Psychology* (published by the Division of the Teaching of Psychology, American Psychological Association, 1975) refers to hominology as a significant teaching innovation and mentions in its description, "The study of hominology does not indoctrinate students in any one school of thought or opinion. It provides guidelines which can help them discover what they believe, how they perceive the world around them, and why they act as they do."

After the death of Dr. C. D. Jones, the founder and first president of the American Hominological Association, Dr. L. A. Ruybalid was elected president. Upon assuming the duties of this office, he helped establish several chapters throughout the country enabling the Association to reach a larger number of people. Dr. Ruybalid joined the faculty of the University of Southern Colorado (1974) where he presently heads the Department of Behavioral Science. He has been involved in research which led to his development of the "Conglomerate Hominologram" which has proven to be a valuable addition to the materials used to explore the self-image.

After introducing a class in hominology at Hiram Scott College where he was Dean of Men, Professor S. Clay joined the staff of the University of Southern Colorado in 1971 and has contributed numerous teaching techniques which clarify the ideas inherent in hominology. Professor Clay has, also, lectured to national and local professional groups on the application of hominology to make intergroup communications more effective.

A variety of reviews of the concepts inherent in hominology have been published. John A. Callahan, M.D. with the Mayo Clinic (*Mayo Clinical Proceedings,* Vol 47, August 1972) sees hominology as leading students "towards the construction of global human models" and notes that this is done "without offering a dogmatic scheme." After reading the Second Edition to *An Introduction To Hominology*, this reviewer wrote, "I feel more than amply rewarded for the reading and the contemplation of the role of man as a student and as a subject."

An increasing number of people have found that the study of hominology has had an important impact on their thinking and their lives. In the final analysis, it is the reader and the student of hominology who will decide what this integrated view of mankind and self can do to help them obtain a clearer and more meaningful understanding of human struggles and goals.

ACKNOWLEDGMENT

I am grateful for the encouragement and support my family gave me while this book was being written. My wife, Shirley, helped me throughout in so many ways that I can not begin to enumerate. My daughter, Susan, an anthropologist, was a source of inspiration as well as an occasional consultant. My son, Steven, gave me support and contributed some important quotations I use in teaching.

The debt that the study of hominology owes to the late Dr. C. David Jones is considerable. His book, *Hominology - Psychiatry's Newest Frontier,* represents a landmark in the development of hominology as an applied science. I thank my colleagues at the University of Southern Colorado, Dr. Louis A. Ruybalid, Professor Samuel Clay and my wife, Shirley, for teaching hominology very successfully and contributing ideas that make this study more effective. I wish to acknowledge my debt to my publisher of *An Introduction to Hominology*, Charles C. Thomas Company, who saw the book through a first and second printing and a second edition (1969, 1970, 1972). I appreciate their release of their copyright so that previously published material could be incorporated in the present edition. Finally, I wish to say that I owe much to the many interested students that I have had throughout the years. Student enthusiasm for the study of hominology is responsibility for the fact that this subject is continuing to be taught.

T.C.K.

INTRODUCTION

When in 1734 Alexander Pope wrote the famous couplet, "know then thyself, presume not God to scan; the proper study of mankind is man," he put into words what many people have thought before and since his time. Even though we have had a proliferation of studies dealing with mankind, it seems that the essence of being human remains relatively unknown while more and more of the rest of nature is revealed.

Some behavioral scientists think that human beings are too self-involved to be capable of meaningful self-exploration. If true, most of us would agree that this handicap should not deter us from attempting to study ourselves as best as we can. Every student of mankind must recognize the limitations that are inherent in an evaluation of a species by its own members. In studying human nature, the observer is liable to view his species as behaving in a manner that suits his own subjective conceptions of what the human race is or should be. This danger can not be avoided but it can be recognized and precautions taken to minimize it.

The book, which is an introduction to hominology, is divided into three sections — a preparation section (Chapters 1 - 5); an information section (Chapters 6 - 10); and a section devoted to integration (Chapters 11 - 15). In the first section, the purpose and goal of the study of hominology are explained. Mankind is compared to other species and the philosophical nature of reality is probed. A hominologram is constructed to give the student an insight into his own unique view of reality and create an awareness of several different frameworks within which truth can be perceived. Improved communications and a deeper appreciation of human differences can result.

The second section, Chapters 6 - 10 begins with information on methodology, reference points and frameworks used in scientific investigations. The use of the scientific method applied to the social and behavioral sciences is discussed. In Chapter 7 the works of a number of important writers on social problems are examined. These authors expressed a variety of different opinions on what is beneficial for mankind's future development.

In the chapter that follows a representative number of more recent writings are discussed. Since these authors have different religious, national and ideological backgrounds, it is not surprising that they arrive at different conclusions about the nature of man's fate and future. The theory of organic evolution is examined in a manner that leaves the reader free to accept or reject it as an explanation of the adaptive development of living organisms. Finally, there is a chapter that explores the question of human origins in the light of paleontology. This chapter discusses how some of the human fossils have been classified. It is difficult to remain current on this interesting subject because every new discovery can change previously accepted concepts of what fossil forms belong within the hominid line. Complicating matters further is the fact that at any given time two or more contradictory theories of classification may be held by experts in the field of paleontology.

For example, when the first edition of the introduction to hominology was written (1969), *Ramapithecus* was considered to be within the human developmental line. Many anthropologists still adhere to this view. Others believe that this fossil was merely a female *Driopithecus*. Reevaluation of taxonomy is certain to continue. The purpose for including descriptions of human fossils in this book is to stimulate an awareness of the insights and challenges inherent in the attempt to explore mankind's past and to illustrate that the human race belongs to one family of mankind. This remains true even if taxonomic classifications keep changing with new discoveries.

Chapters 11 - 15 attempt to provide examples and illustrations of how concepts may be integrated when they deal with ethical values and mental health. These concepts are tied to psycho-social-cultural developmental levels representing theoretical models of the unfolding of the human moral potentiality.

Eight developmental levels are postulated and mankind's contemporary struggle is seen as a conflict stemming from the contradictory influences that these various behavioral levels exert. It is hypothesized that mankind is presently capable in several parts of the world of participating in the action theme of "Level Seven" in which there is a loss of rigid boundary in self-identity with a corresponding growth of the psyche on a different dimension.

For some readers the idea of going beyond self presents difficulty. The thought of relinquishing ego integrity is conceived by them as a loss of freedom of action. Actually, the reverse is true. Blanchard writing in *Determinism and Freedom* (Collier Books, 1961) observes:

> ". . . the moral man, like the logician and the artist, is really seeking self surrender. Through him as through others an impersonal ideal is working, and to the extent that this ideal takes possession of him and molds him according to its pattern, he feels free and is free."

Jones writing on the hominological levels in *Hominology - Psychiatry's Newest Frontier* (C. C. Thomas, 1975) views the ego structure as reaching its highest point of integration within the action theme of Level Six. Within Level Seven "the boundaries of 'I' become fuzzy and indistinct as 'you' and 'I' merge and broaden out . . ." to become "We." Thus, within Level Seven there is some ego disintegration or "loss of personal ego structure" as Jones puts it. However, this is not regarded negatively and Jones describes it as "the beginning of something different."

Level Eight represents a stage of development beyond Level Seven. In the action themes of Level Two to Seven the individual can be viewed as part of the universe. In the conceptualization of both Levels One and Eight the universe is viewed as part of the individual. Thus, in Level Eight the developmental spiral has again reached the starting point within a new dimension.

With the use of Hominologram II, the reader is aided in attempting to find his own position within the human developmental process as this is reflected in the hominological behavioral model.

Chapter 12 presents a capsule of universal moral values with an emphasis on their application in daily life. In Chapter 13 mental health is discussed within the context of moral values. In the chapter that follows some common pitfalls that can occur in problem-solving activities are described. Ten contemporary problems typical of industrialized nations are then discussed. Since students have expressed an increasing interest in the "Third World Nations," the problems currently being faced by such nations are briefly described in this introduction (see also pages 346-348).

In order to be able to discuss from personal experience some of the problems which emerging nations face, my wife, Shirley Kahn, a professor of hominology at the University of Southern Colorado, and I visited Bolivia, Ecuador, Peru, Columbia, Panama, Costa Rica, Honduras, Guatamala, Kenya and Tanzania. We wished to obtain the views of people living on two different continents and to contrast these with the opinions of contemporary problems obtained from Great Britain - a highly commercialized nation currently facing some financial problems. Kenya and Tanzania, former colonies of Great Britain are struggling to increase their commercial activities hoping, thereby, to raise the subsistence level of their people.

We devoted the summers of 1974 and 1975 to the effort of attempting to identify some of the problems of these emerging nations especially as they may parallel or contrast those of industrialized nations. The following are among those most often mentioned:

1) Overpopulation is a controversial subject when it is discussed with people in emerging nations. Some government leaders in these countries insist overpopulation does not exist and they blame "underproduction" and a lack of "exploitation of natural resources" as the real basis of their population difficulties.

2) Concern over the divided world of communism and non-communism was not often expressed. Instead we heard complaints about the "haves" and "have-nots" within national boundaries and "rich countries" versus "poor countries" internationally.

In South and Central America we found that the differences in socio-economic levels between peoples seemed very great. In Kenya and Tanzania one of the problems mentioned most consistently was the difficulty of uniting persons with different tribal loyalties into a unified nation.

3) Outside of Great Britain the idea of a dwindling need for manpower in an automated society did not apply. However, unemployment in emerging nations is not related to automation but to changes in life-styles and by the continuing shift of rural populations to urban centers.

4) People in South America suffer fears of a weakening of cultural traditions whereas in East Africa the impending loss of tribal solidarity and the extended family concept is a cause of anxiety. Geographical dislocations increased tensions and dissatisfaction on both continents. Historical developments have profoundly influenced the adjustment of people in nations that have lived under colonial rule and are presently groping for an independent national life.

5) Most people in emerging nations did not seem to be as concerned with abstractions such as freedom as are citizens of industrialized nations. However, we heard some admiration expressed for the United States because reports unfavorable to the government were able to surface in the media contrary to what is possible in most of the countries we visited. In less complex societies, freedom was often equated with the availability of sufficient food and the acquisition of a few luxuries or the opportunity to maintain religious and cultural tradition.

In East Africa we heard remarks about the need to gain freedom from the mentality of colonialism. In Tanzania the slogan *Freedom is Work* serves as an incentive for maintaining a unique combination of political Maoism with the practice of Christianity.

6) The existence of wide-spread poverty was rated as the most serious problem by many people we interviewed in South America and East Africa. In England we heard complaints of rampant inflation which was described as the cause of poverty in that country. Inflation seemed to be a problem that the emerging nations fully shared with the industrial nations of the world. This tends to remind us of the interdependence that exists among the world's nations large and small.

In much of Africa the uncertainties of the annual rainfall are major considerations affecting survival. In East Africa competition for grazing lands between domesticated animals and wild animals protected by the Government in National Parks and Reserves is destined to become an ever sharper issue in the future.

Industrial nations usually have some kind of social security in the form of employment insurance and old age pensions. In less affluent nations the burden of caring for an unemployed, ill, or old person frequently falls upon the extended family where such care is considered to be part of family responsibility. The concept of poverty differs in emerging and industrialized nations. Among the latter, poverty may be viewed as the inability to maintain a desired life-style whereas in underdeveloped nations it is equated with the lack of the bare necessities for survival.

7) In most of the countries we visited, we discovered that racial and ethnic differences did not play a role comparable to "prejudice" in certain, other nations. Instead, social and class differences were used as demarcations between people in some of the South and Central American countries, and in East Africa one could hear grumbling about "tribal discrimination."

8) Crime in the underdeveloped nations we visited can not be compared to the situation in the United States. We received many warnings that pickpockets were rampant in some of the areas we visited. Murder, vandalism, and other crimes of violence do not exist in any way comparable to the high percentage of such crimes in the United States. However, in recent years brutal crimes with political motives seem to be becoming more wide-

spread in all nations. These methods of achieving political ends are viewed by their perpetrators as "idealistic" but, in fact, they are symptoms of a social pathology that is even more dangerous because it is capable of being contagious.

9) Large segments of the indigenous people among the populations we were able to study followed their traditional way of life in the matter of sex-role identification. Often, in simple societies, the division of labor between males and females contributes to survival. Among the educated classes in the emerging nations some success is being achieved in providing women with greater occupational choice.

10) For many people living in the emerging nations, participation in religious events is the sole source of comfort and escape from the grueling routine of daily work. We found that religion often was a combination of Christianity with precolumbian (in South America) or tribal (in Africa) elements. Religion offers the people explanations and compensations for the hardships of life and the mystery of death. Many people in the countries we visited had few other means of coping with disaster.

Finally, our interviews on both continents with persons who had some education revealed that they believed that the most urgent problem existing in underdeveloped nations is the lack of education and the wide-spread presence of illiteracy. They told us that all other problems their nations faced were derived from this primary one. However, it seems likely that if education is to serve a useful purpose it will have to be geared to the specific and immediate needs of the majority of the people. Education must be designed to increase employment and it must be consistent with local and national goals for an improved standard of living. Formal education that is not oriented towards solving problems may actually increase unemployment and create a disillusioned intelligentsia.

The study of hominology encourages students to combine the effort of self-understanding with an exploration of the nature of mankind. It does this by making available models, guidelines, reference points and perspectives which may be applied to daily life. Participation in the unfolding of the human potentiality for living a moral life is seen as bestowing meaning and significance to the human existence. Students of hominology from all walks of life and of all ages are viewed as searchers for something beyond mere existence and self-gratification. It is believed that the study of hominology may be useful in this search for meaningful goals. The idea of this search encompasses the widest possible perspectives using an integrated, nondisciplinary approach. The idea of this search for meaning has been expressed in the cogent language of poetry by Steven J. Kent in 1974 when, as an undergraduate, he wrote the following lines:

> We must know purpose in life
> beyond just living.
> We must find reason for death
> besides just dying.
> There must be meaning
> which transcends both,
> for man must have reason to be
> beyond just to be or not . . .
> and so he searches.

OBJECTIVES OF THE HOMINOLOGY
TEACHING PROGRAM

Overall Objective: Expose the student to the integrated study of human behavior defined as the study of the whole Man. Help the student understand how facts from various disciplines may be used to form a unified picture of mankind evolving throughout time. Assist the student to discover his own personal role in this process, thereby enabling him to view the human situation with greater self-involvement and wider perspectives.

OBJECTIVES OF SECTION ONE

1. Give the student an understanding of what a comprehensive nondisciplinary approach to Man can offer and describe its limitations.

2. Compare Man with animals, especially with other primates and explain the significance of the differences and similarities.

3. Explore the nature of truth and assist the student to discover why he accepts or rejects certain ideas as true.

4. Assist the student in discovering how his personal concept of truth affects his outlook on life. Use a graphic method to illustrate this and create an awareness of how and why the ideas of other people may differ from his own.

OBJECTIVES OF SECTION TWO

1. Explain research methods used in the human sciences. Demonstrate how these methods may be classified. Review computerized and intuitional methods. Compare inductive and deductive reasoning.

2. Expose the student to historical perspectives pertinent to the development of becoming and being human.

3. Offer the student information about some of the contemporary writings of other authors who have attempted to use nondiscipli-

nary, integrated methods of studying Man as an individual and as a species.

4. Help the student to discover who his hominid ancestors were and to recognize the kind of changes that took place during the humanization of Man.

OBJECTIVES OF SECTION THREE

1. Offer the student developmental perspectives which may be applied to the concept of mankind evolving.

2. Acquaint the student with a behavioral science interpretation of the nature of ethics and moral values. Make this interpretation applicable to the way the student lives his daily life.

3. Use a universal framework to explore a new meaning of mental health. Tie mental health into an evolutionary concept of moral development and help the student find his own role in this developmental process.

4. Identify some of the causes of current controversies within the behavioral sciences and the pitfalls to logical analysis. Examine ten contemporary problems in the light of what has been learned in the study of hominology.

CONTENTS

SECTION ONE
PREPARATION FOR HOMINOLOGY

SECTION TWO
INFORMATION FOR HOMINOLOGY

LIST OF FIGURES

LIST OF TABLES

Contents

LIST OF TABLES

AN INTRODUCTION TO

HOMINOLOGY
An Integrated View of
Mankind and Self

SECTION ONE
PREPARATION FOR HOMINOLOGY

Chapter 1

WHAT IS HOMINOLOGY?

"It would be interesting to know what it is that men are most
afraid of. Taking a new step, uttering a new word is what they
fear most."

DOSTOEVSKI, *Crime and Punishment*

"So knowledge is a hindrance when it has become a tradition
which shapes or conditions the mind to a particular pattern because
then it not only divides people and creates enmity between them,
but it also prevents the deep discovery of what is truth, what is
life. . . ."

J. KISHNAMURTI, *This Matter of Culture*

HOMINOLOGY WAS designed to facilitate the comprehensive
study of mankind. It is not a discipline since it does not contribute an indigenous body of facts. Because it has no
disciplinary commitments, it has no well-defined boundaries.
It attempts to serve as a bridge between the various behavioral
and social sciences. It may be taught within presently established academic departments of sociology, anthropology, psychology, social work, business administration, education, or in
the medical and health specialties. Since it attempts to integrate
facts gleaned from the disciplines that deal with diverse aspects
of human nature, it searches the past, surveys the present, and
speculates about the future of mankind.

Hominology has five distinguishing characteristics: 1) It is
nondisciplinary and nonspecialized[1]; 2) Hominology explores

----

[1] Nondisciplinary differs in important respects from single disciplinary,
interdisciplinary, and cross-disciplinary. Nondisciplinary implies disciplinary
neutrality and comprehensiveness. In any given case, the others may include or
exclude any one or more of the social or behavioral sciences. Hominology,
however, cannot knowingly omit from consideration any pertinent body of facts
when a human problem is explored.

5

abstractions such as Man's ethics, his morality, values, and religions; 3) Hominology concerns itself with Man's past, present, and future; 4) As a prerequisite for understanding mankind, it suggests that the student attempt self-understanding in order to become aware of his philosophical commitments which influence the formation of his hypotheses; 5) Finally, consistent with its emphasis on neutrality, hominology does not offer any dogma or prescriptions for the student to follow. It encourages students to chart their own course in their quest for answers. Hominology provides a nondisciplinary framework within which it is hoped an impartial consideration of known pertinent facts can take place. This requires an examination of the various theories extant which attempt to account for present day human actions.

The word *hominology* is a hybrid combination of the Latin *homini* of man and the Greek *logos* knowledge. The root word of hominology is *hominidae,* the family of Man that includes all the various species which evolved during the geological period known as the Pleistocene—one to three million years in duration. A number of persons with classical orientations have objected to the hybridization of a Latin and Greek stem, but linguists who were consulted, in general, endorsed the term, citing many other similar combinations in use today, such as virology, sociology, economics, dictaphone, television, cablegram, to name but a few. Several mentioned that the term *hominidae* from which hominology was derived itself has a greco-latin suffix.

The first step in the process of studying hominology is to recognize the difficult task that the definition implies. In refusing to grasp the handles which help the specialists in various behavioral sciences organize their body of facts, the student of hominology may experience a kind of intellectual weightlessness which, initially, he may find disconcerting.

THE HOMINOLOGICAL APPROACH IS NOT A NEW ONE

Another point to mention is that hominology does not represent something which has not been thought of previously.

On the contrary, the first manuscript on hominology, *An Intro-duction to Hominology* (Kahn, 1965), states,

> Hominology does not conceive of itself as an innovation. Primitive man was probably a hominologist when he was able to take time out, after a successful hunt, to contemplate his role in the universe as he pictured it in his day. But in several respects it is new. In these days of specialization where men in the Behavioral and Social Sciences have gone their separate ways within the framework of the academic disciplines, hominology again attempts to explore the global aspect of man's nature, using the knowledge that has been gained to date, as early man may have used it, that is, to theorize where we, as a human race, have come from, where we are going. Hominology may also contribute some of its own techniques in reaching this goal. These techniques were designed to permit the broad view of the generalist but yet utilize, to the best advantage, the specialists' contributions represented by the academic disciplines.

The attempt made currently by some colleges and universities to teach broad area social or behavioral science is commendable but often these programs still evoke a fragmented picture of Man. Efforts which offer students "interdisciplinary" programs for the purpose of "cross-fertilization" fail to supply the necessary neutral structure which underlies meaningful integration. Sometimes such attempts try to combine topics as poetry and history, sciences and humanities. More conventionally, they offer behavioral or social science disciplines superimposed, one upon the other, with only a token of integration between them. There exists today no *specialists in integration.* This is the role which the advanced student of hominology envisions for himself.

Current efforts at integration of human knowledge are not always successful because of a lack of an appropriate methodology. The process of integrating knowledge requires structure which permits meaningful conceptualizations to take place. The need for integration grows greater by the year as behavioral scientists attempt to assess the seriousness of the "Information Explosion." The skills and techniques, and the wide variety of backgrounds necessary to cope with what Szent-Györgyi (1964) calls "today's exploding knowledge" in the behavioral sciences requires it.

It has been noted that a plethora of information in the fifty thousand scientific journals currently published fails to add substantially to our basic understanding of Man. Computorizing this information, as is being attempted today, may not help us arrive at any significant clarifications. Foa (1965) comments that "behavioral studies tend to become wider in scope and to include a larger number of variables as time goes on." This information, far from alleviating our difficulties, adds to them in the absence of a structure around which these facts can be meaningfully arranged. Electronic computors can greatly assist us in processing enormous numbers of facts efficiently and they can cluster them as programmed. But in the end, *meaning* must be supplied by Man, himself. In spite of technological advances, scientists, such as Bixenstine (1964), believe "there is a general feeling that we, behavioral scientists, have less confidence today about the grasp of the field than we had 20 years ago."

REASON FOR THE COINING OF A NEW TERM

Any scientist would experience considerable reluctance in coining a new term. Nevertheless, *hominology* serves a purpose which existing terms fail to satisfy. Handy (1964), in *Methodology of the Behavioral Sciences,* found the expression "social science" lacking in meaning, and used "behavioral science" . . . "reluctantly, and only in order to have a brief convenient label." Bartley (1958) writes, "Terms such as life science, behavioral science, etc. have been coined. With regard to each of these, the author suspects the inventor's lack of the appreciation for both psychology and biology." Others have expressed similar dissatisfaction with current terms.

Behavioral science fails to give any definite idea of what is included and what is not. For example, in the United States, there is an annual national "Behavioral Science Symposium" which is composed solely of psychiatrists, clinical psychologists, and psychiatric social workers. An entirely different conference consisting exclusively of anthropologists, sociologists, and geographers could also have been as correctly referred to as a "Behavioral Science Symposium." Thus, the term, *behavioral science,* is meaningless since it fails to do the very job that words were intended to do—that is, communicate information. Pfaffman (1965) is forced to ask, "What are Behavioral Sciences?" Berelson (1963) struggles to give an answer but admits that the term *social science* is vague and that "perhaps the best way of delineating the field is to say what it is not." Marshall (1966) observes that the breakdown of precise boundaries between scientific disciplines requires vocabularies that describe new conceptual frontiers, "The Behavioral Sciences in particular are hard pressed to intercommunicate with impinging disciplines, as well as among themselves."

We see, then, that confusion is inevitable since social science no longer means science of society, nor behavioral science, science of behavior. Instead, the terms refer to an ill-defined collection of separate and individual sciences rather haphazardly thrown together. Each term appears capable of excluding many essential aspects of Man's nature without loss of the integrity of its definition (Table I).

Individual disciplines were historically necessary in order that a study of mankind could evolve. They still serve an essential purpose since they afford the scientist the opportunity for specialization without which any meaningful generalization would

TABLE I

COMPONENTS OF THE SOCIAL AND BEHAVIORAL SCIENCES

Discipline	Classification	Area of Specialization
Psychology	B or S	Behavior of individuals.
Psychiatry	B	Abnormal behavior.
Sociology	S	Group behavior.
Anthropology	B or S	1) Human culture, present and past. 2) Human biological classification.
History	S	Longitudinal study of mankind.
Economics	S	Laws affecting distribution of material goods.
Political Science	S	The nature of human organization.
Geography	S	Earth and human adaptation of its conditions.
Ecology	B or S	Interaction of organisms and environments.
Ethology	B or S	Residuals in behavior, instincts.
Business Administration	S	Interpersonal relationships in commerce.
Education	B	1) Cultural indoctrination. 2) Training in adaptive skills.
Cybernetics	B	Human analogies from machine models.
Bionics	B	Human analogies from biological models.

B represents Behavioral Science; S represents Social Science

What really belongs within Behavioral and Social Sciences is controversial and there is seldom complete agreement among those who teach or work in these sciences.

be impossible. The multidisciplinary or combinatory approaches are also useful provided they claim to do only that which they are capable of doing—namely, offer a wider focus than a single discipline. Single disciplines, developing haphazardly from historical roots and having origins which gave them a circumscribed territory, cannot easily be enlarged except at the expense of another discipline. The boundaries of these disciplines crisscross the social and behavioral sciences so that the whole represents a confusing patchwork. The "interdisciplinary" or "multidisciplinary" label has failed to bind the fragments into a unified study of Man.

TWO ROADS TO UNDERSTANDING

The question which we are facing today, namely how and from which disciplinary bridgehead to approach the study of Man, was presaged by a previous problem with which Kurt Goldstein (1940) was concerned. When writing twenty-five years ago on human nature he observed, "Perhaps the most distinctive feature of the nineteenth century is the amazing increase during that period of detailed scientific knowledge acquired through the admirable use of what we may call the atomistic method." He noted that this method uses "dissection" to gain knowledge and derives laws from a study of the parts. Goldstein recognized the disadvantage of this approach in that it increased knowledge of specifics at the expense of an appreciation of wholes. Psychologists such as William James and psychiatrists such as Adolf Meyer were cited by Goldstein as showing "an increasing concern with synthesizing the diverse sciences which are concerned with the nature of man."

Today, at over the halfway mark of the twentieth century we are still aware of these two trends—the atomistic one which sharpens our focus but narrows our view and the synthesizing one which discloses broad vistas but obfuscates details. Contrary to what critics of either of these methods say, each has made contributions and has valid reasons for existing. Today, as in the nineteenth century, we require the atomistic approach which probes deeply into the molecular nature of life. On the other hand, in the last decades, notable successes have been scored in both behavioral and physical sciences by intermural teams of specialists participating in broad area government and organizationally endowed research efforts. In these cases, co-ordination and integration of specialized disciplines was achieved by utilization of administrators experienced in facilitating inter-communication between various orientations. The attempted duplication of such efforts on a smaller scale have not been as successful because of the lack of disciplinary-neutral generalists capable of creating the required fusion. Let us briefly review some characteristics of typical single disciplinary and combinatory studies which the student may encounter in his search for the broad, generalized approach to the study of total Man.

Single Disciplines Cannot Deal With Total Man

The first obstacle encountered in any comprehensive study of Man is the problem of deciding which of the disciplines has the best claim to all-inclusiveness. Thompson (1961) sees it as fitting that anthropology should represent the "unified study of mankind." However, this is contested by representatives of other disciplines. Nevertheless, it is true that anthropology can make a relatively good case for itself. I must, however, specify American anthropology since in the United States, the term *anthropology,* includes cultural, physical, ethnology, ethnography, archeology, linguistics, and social anthropology. European anthropology is limited to human evolution, primatology, human classification, and genetics.

However, anthropology, in common with psychology, sociology, history, and so on, represents only a sectional aspect of mankind, and this gives it an unremediable limitation. For all of his wide background, the anthropologist still sees himself as a specialist within the behavioral sciences. Often he may be knowledgeable in only one or two fields within the larger area of anthropology. For example, even though American anthropology includes linguistics, it is possible for an anthropologist to know less about specific aspects of this topic than a psychologist who has majored in psycholinguistics. No anthropologist would claim that the intensive study of a single person falls within the purview of his specialty. He would leave the individual to the psychologist. Yet, undeniably, there can be no genuine study of Man without a close look at the individual.[2]

Malinowski (1960) who was much concerned with the matter of a unified theory of Man writes,

> The 'study of Man' is certainly a somewhat presumptuous, not to say preposterous label when applied to academic anthropology as it now stands. A variety of disciplines, old and recent, venerable and new, deal also with inquiries into human nature, human handiwork, and into the relations of human beings. These can claim one and all, to be regarded as branches of the legitimate study of man.

In this view he supports Kroeber (1948) who declared "the word 'anthropology' literally means, study of man. This literal etymological meaning is too broad and general."[3] Handy (1964) observes,

> It seems clear that the conventional academic division of labor is neither coherent nor very helpful. The futility of trying to separate man's economic behavior, for example, hardly needs documenting. Some of the other divisions of effort also seem highly suspicious. To mention one instance, some psychologists still formally describe their field as concerning individual rather than social behavior. But if social behavior were truly excluded from psychology, the unemployment rate for psychologists would increase sharply. To study human behavior as it occurs in ongoing transactions, then, seems to offer more hope than to divide human behavior arbitrarily into categories that apparently cannot be used effectively.

------

[2] I have selected anthropology as a discipline beset by temptations to consider its content to be all, or nearly all that is important in the study of Man. However, there is, actually, not one discipline—nor even one single study of behavior—which is entirely free of such a tendency. Skinner (1966) quotes Beach as having written, "Many . . . appear to believe that in studying the rat they are studying all or nearly all that is important in behavior . . . How else are we to interpret . . . a 457 page opus which is based exclusively upon the performance of rats in bar-pressing situations but is entitled simply, *The Behavior of Organisms?*"

[3] Kroeber later viewed anthropology as an integrating science (*Anthropology Today: An Encyclopedic Inventory.* Chicago, University of Chicago Press, 1953.)

Bernard (1962) who spent many years studying the problem of higher education, notes that "a rather revolutionary shift in the study of human behavior has occurred in the past few years." He mentions the complexity of human nature and declares, "No longer can one scientific discipline be responsible for supplying answers to questions about man's behavior. . . . No longer can the individual be thought of as existing in comparative isolation." He recognizes the fact that the individual specialties make important contributions, "while pooling of information is desirable, this does not mean that fusion should be so complete that specialties will disappear. In fact it seems probable that more, rather than fewer specialties will be needed." Single disciplinary specialties must concern themselves with techniques and this is often at the expense of being problem centered as Maslow (1946) pointed out. If techniques do not develop within the individual disciplines there would be no place for them to evolve.

Though no one specialty can produce a global human model, the techniques and information they provide separately are necessary for such a model to be constructed. The key word in Bernard's position is *pooling* of information. I believe that it is important that such a "pool" be established in a non-disciplinary setting.

Yinger (1965) after discussing the individual and combined roles of psychology, anthropology, and sociology notes,

> It is scarcely surprising that strong pressure for a multilevel science should emerge from each of the three disciplines, since they share the fundamental interest in understanding human behavior. The need for both analytic disciplines *and a synthesizing discipline is clear.* The tendency to develop a kind of halfway house between them, however, leads to serious problems. [Italics are Kahn's.]

Interdisciplinary, Cross-Disciplinary and Multidisciplinary Approaches

In view of the limitations of the single disciplinary approach to the study of total Man, it has occurred to a number of people that an interdisciplinary approach may offer a solution. Let us review the effectiveness of several typical disciplinary combinations. First, there are titles that in themselves suggest a multi or cross-disciplinary method. Typical examples are *Psychological Anthropology* (Hsu, 1961); *Anthropology and Human Nature* (*Montagu, 1963*); *Philosophical Anthropology and Practical Politics* (Northrop, 1960); *The Cultural Background of Personality* (Linton, 1945); *Society, Culture, and Personality* (Sorokin, 1947); *Culture, Psychiatry, and the Written Word* (Carothers, 1959); *International Behavior, A Social-Psychological Analysis* (Kelman, 1965); *Sociologismic Psychology* (Alpert, 1939).

These titles, and many others now on the bookstands, reflect an awareness of a need to treat broad aspects of human behavior. Frequently, the idea of a combination of disciplines invokes in some writers a false image of holism. In these writings, the assumption, which is often implicitly made, that several combined disciplines can together yield a truly composite picture of important human areas is usually not substantiated. Interdisciplinary methods are not designed to avoid disciplinary partisanship or fragmentation and they lack the required safeguards. Authors of combinatory approaches may, themselves, be unaware of the fact that they have fallen short of anticipated goals. Thus Thompson (1961) believes that her anthropologically oriented approach can evolve a "mature, unified science of mankind." Readers may, along with authors of such works, be misled when terms such as *interdisciplinary* are applied to partial or disciplinary-biased treatments of human behavior.

INTERDISCIPLINARY METHODS REVIEWED

Lindesmith and Straus (1950) made an extensive review of the characteristic combinatory approach. They note that initially these contributions were hailed as promising a greatly broadened and unified view of Man. However, they found that interdisciplinary culture-personality writings which were supposed to offer composite global views represented several wings with contradictory approaches:

> One wing of movement includes psychoanalytically trained persons like Fromm, Erikson, and Kardiner. Another wing, rep-

resented by a writer like Benedict (a cultural anthropologist) places the main emphasis upon descriptive explanations or psychoanalytic concepts. Most writers fall between these extremes using a sprinkling of psychoanalytic terminology, sometimes with ideas derived from other areas.

As other critics of the combinatory approach discerned, Lindesmith and Straus conclude that

> The interdisciplinary nature of this approach is often stressed but is, in fact, sharply limited. For example, the theory and research of most psychologists, social psychologists, and sociologists who are concerned with personality and psychological processes are virtually unaffected by culture-personality writings. . . .

Anthropological writers were described as rarely making references to "research of social psychologists, psychologists other than clinicians of Freudian persuasion, and almost no references to writings of foreign psychologists." Tilden (1965) comes close to the heart of the problem when he editorialized in *Science*, "There seemed to be not one science-culture but a host of highly specialized groups that were not speaking each others' language." Handy (1964) in *Methodology of the Behavioral Sciences* is among the most explicit among critics. He observes that

> If one looks at the formal definitions workers in the various behavioral areas give their fields, the results are sometimes discouraging. Imperialistic and aggrandizing tendencies are frequent; it is amazing how many disciplines study 'all' human behavior without restriction. Indeed, if one did not already know which field was being defined, it would be impossible to guess from the definitions.

Nevertheless, the attempt to study this 'all' of human behavior of which Handy speaks, is in itself, praiseworthy and necessary. The difficulty stems from the fact that neither single disciplines nor the interdisciplinary efforts are apt to recognize the limitations inherent in their methods. Interdisciplinary scholars fail to perceive the difficulty of maintaining simultaneously a specialist's and a generalist's viewpoint. Nor may they be aware of the problem which Laumann (1966) writes about in

Current Issues in Higher Education:

> Another subvariety of research-oriented faculty is the inter-disciplinary scholar whose interests do not fall clearly within any of the traditionally recognized disciplines that have been put into concrete form as departments. This type has become increasingly frequent, particularly in the social sciences. They often suffer from problems of professional identity. These people create problems for schools that are strongly organized along departmental lines. One solution has been the ever-increasing proliferation of interdisciplinary centers or institutes. These centers only increase the number of possible points of conflicting institutional loyalty and confuse still further the complexities of administration.

While interdisciplinary approaches seem incapable of offering a practical solution to the problem of unifying the study of Man, pressure from students and faculty continues to be exerted for just this very goal. This is typically reflected in "News and Views," March-April, 1966, *Main Currents in Modern Thought* (Sellon, 1966):

> Recently an unusual request for information about the criteria and program of the Foundation for Integrative Education[4] came in from a university in the West. The inquirer, it seems is a student, but he writes on behalf of a formally organized Curriculum Committee, expressing the concern of an increasing number of students and faculty who are perplexed at the fragmentation of knowledge at this institution. . . . It seems to us that such a collaboration of students and faculty is quite remarkable, and should generate a real force for action. And the prime requirement now is action, for words alone cannot solve the escalating problems of overspecialization. What the student appears to be calling for is an entirely new kind of course, in which the study is based upon experience drawn from all fields of learning. Teacher and student alike will thus be talking not about definitions but about the meanings of concepts. . . .

The success of any program which attempts to utilize social and behavioral sciences to meet the need described in "News and Views" hinges on the structure of the entirely new kind of a course that the students appear to be "calling for." We have seen that interdisciplinary studies or symposia do not avoid

---

[4] Foundation for Integrative Education, 777 United Nations Plaza, New York, New York, 10017.

but, at most, enlarge areas of fragmentation. Nor do such studies avoid disciplinary biases. Therefore, it is unlikely that a course dealing with total Man can be effectively developed by the combined effort of a group of individual specialists. The inherent weakness of present interdisciplinary programs stems from the fact that integration cannot take place without some form of overall plan for the pooling of diverse information. A study of Man cannot take place in a methodological vacuum.

At the beginning of the chapter, the difficulty inherent in developing an approach such as hominology was mentioned. Gluckman (1964) describes the methods available for nonspecialized approaches, such as hominology, as prone to suffer from

1. "circumscribing a field,"
2. "incorporating complex facts without analysis,"
3. "abridging the conclusions of other sciences,"
4. "making naïve assumptions about aspects of reality. . . ,"
5. "simplifying events within the field under investigation."

The study of hominology by virtue of its commitment will fall prey to all of the pitfalls which Gluckman has enumerated. Though the student cannot avoid them, he may minimize their effect by frequent consultations with specialists and by a continual awareness of his own limitations and his biases. These biases and their philosophical roots in selection of criteria of reality are examined in a later chapter.

The chapter which follows begins with a brief examination of how we humans differ from nonhuman animals, particularly the apes, which are the closest animals to us in anatomy and physiology. The study of hominology starts in this manner because Man is, himself, an animal. As Russell and Russell (1961) declared, "To study human behavior, we must begin by considering how it differs most markedly from other species. Only then can we see how to foster this difference and develop it further." Comparisons are necessary in order to establish norms and perspectives. Of all the animals, the behavior of the higher Primates most closely approximates that of Man. Nevertheless, there are important differences as described in the following chapter.

SUMMARY

A discussion has pointed out that some of the terminology which deals with human behavior is vague and that important concepts are poorly defined. Behavioral and social scientists have difficulty in communicating with each other. Neither the single disciplinary approach nor combinatory methods lend themselves to a study of total Man. This is because disciplines are historically territorial in that they include certain well-defined areas within their boundaries. An integrated approach for the total study of Man is needed. Hominology, a nondisciplinary method, attempts to fill this need. The pitfalls inherent in such an effort were enumerated.

REFERENCES

ALPERT, H.: Emile Durkheim and sociologismic psychology. *Amer J Soc,* 45:64-70, July 1939.

BARTLEY, S. H.: *Principles of Perception.* New York, Harper, 1958.

BERELSON, B. (Ed.): *The Behavioral Sciences Today.* New York, Harper, 1963.

BERNARD, H. W.: *Human Development in Western Culture.* Boston, Allyn & Bacon, 1962.

BIXENSTINE, V. E.: Empiricism in later-date behavioral science. *Science,* 145:464-467, July 31, 1964.

CAROTHERS, J. C.: Culture, psychiatry and the written word. *Psychiatry,* 22:307-320, 1959.

FOA, U. G.: New developments in facet design and analysis. *Psychol Rev,* 72:262-274, 1965.

GLUCKMAN, M. (Ed.): *Closed Systems and Open Minds.* Chicago, Aldine, 1964.

GOLDSTEIN, K.: *Human Nature in the Light of Psychopathology.* Boston, Harvard U. P., 1940.

HANDY, R.: *Methodology of the Behavioral Sciences; Problems and Controversies.* Springfield, Thomas, 1964.

HSU, F. L. K. (Ed.): *Psychological Anthropology: Approaches to Culture and Personality.* Homewood, Dorsey, 1961.

KAHN, T. C.: An Introduction to Hominology. Mimeographed for limited distribution, San Antonio, Department of Psychiatry, Wilford Hall USAF Hospital, 1965.

KELMAN, H. C. (Ed.): *International Behavior, a Social-Psychological Analysis.* New York, Holt, 1965.

KROEBER, A. L.: *Anthropology: Race, Language, Culture, Psychology, Prehistory.* New York, Harcourt, 1948.

LAUMANN, E. O.: The new breed of faculty. In *Current Issues in Higher Education.* National Education Association, 1966.

LINDESMITH, A., AND STRAUS, A. L.: Critique of culture-personality writings. *Amer Soc Rev, 15*:587-609, Oct. 1950.

LINTON, R.: *The Cultural Background of Personality.* New York, Appleton, 1945.

MALINOWSKI, G.: *A Scientific Theory of Culture and Other Essays.* New York, Oxford U. P., 1960.

MARSHALL, L. H.: Behavioral sciences: vocabulary. *Science, 153*:323-324, July 15, 1966.

MASLOW, A. H.: Problem-centering vs means-centering in science. *Philosophy Sci, 13*:326-331, 1946.

MONTAGU, A.: *Anthropology and Human Nature.* New York, McGraw, 1963.

NORTHROP, F. S. C.: *Philosophical Anthropology and Practical Politics.* New York, Macmillan, 1960.

PFAFFMAN, C.: *De Gustibus. Amer Psychol, 20*:21-23, Jan. 1965.

RUSSELL, C., AND RUSSELL, W. M. S.: *Human Behavior.* Boston, Little, 1961.

SELLON, E. G. (Assoc. Ed.): News and views. *Main Currents in Modern Thought, 22*:102, March-April 1966.

SKINNER, B. F.: Phylogeny and ontogeny of behavior. *Science, 153*:1205-1213, Sept. 9, 1966.

SOROKIN, P. A.: *Society, Culture, and Personality: Their Structure and Dynamics.* New York, Harper, 1947.

SZENT-GYÖRGYI, A.: Teaching and the expanding knowledge. *Science, 145*:1278-1279, Dec. 4, 1964.

THOMPSON, L.: *Towards a Science of Mankind.* New York, McGraw, 1961.

TILDEN, F.: Not by truth alone. *Science, 148*:1415, June 11, 1965.

YINGER, J. M.: *Toward a Field Theory of Behavior.* New York, McGraw, 1965.

Chapter 2

WHAT IS HUMAN ABOUT HUMANS?

What is man that Thou art mindful of him? Thou hast made him little lower than the angels and hast given him dominion over land and sea.

PSALM 8:4,5

"The Big Baboon who lives upon
The plains of Caribou,
He goes about with nothing on
—A shocking thing to do.
But if he dressed respectably
And let his whiskers grow,
How like that Big Baboon would be
To Mister—So-and-So!"

HILAIRE BELLOC
Quoted by Julian Huxley in
Man in the Modern World

For ages the question has been asked, What is Man? No one has, as yet, produced a wholly satisfactory answer. There are at least two good reasons why this question is a particularly difficult one. First, since he is human himself, the person posing the question is involved in the answer. Ideas of what he would like himself to be may distort his ability to see himself as he is.

The second difficulty stems from the fact that there are many diverse ways in which Man can look at himself. No matter how he regards himself, he faces still a third problem—finding a suitable control group for self-comparison. Controls are necessary in a study of Man in order to gain perspectives. In his search for controls, the human investigator of human nature may look "up" or "down," so to speak. If he looks above his own level, God, gods, the angels, mythological figures, or a system of abstract values serve as reference points. If he looks below himself for self-comparison, that is, to other forms of animal life, he is confined to concrete but questionable comparisons. Between these extremes there are many intermediary points of reference, among these are machines such as the electronic computors.

Even if one attempts to take into account all the possible views of Man, one will be unsuccessful in defining him without being controversial. Biologists and clergymen have different orientations, and they probably would not agree on what is important in a definition. Sociologists may differ from both of these. Psychologists may have still another point of view. Even if different specialists could agree on the biological, psychological, sociological, and spiritual factors that comprise Man, the problem of integration would remain. These difficulties have not, however, hampered our expanding research which has enabled us to gain an understanding of an increasing number of partial aspects of Man.

Hominology begins by selecting the least controversial aspect of relating Man to nature. The observations of Breland and Breland (1966) are pertinent to this approach:

> However individual men may feel about the theory of evolution, and there are some men who have never heard of the theory . . . and others who reject it for religious and other reasons, almost all men, whatever their condition of civilization or sophistication, recognize that the behavior of animals is the closest thing to the behavior of people that a man can encounter.

We can all see that animals are like us in many respects. They have two eyes, two ears, a nose, and tend to be bilateral and symmetrical. Mammals are warm, have red blood, run when afraid, and may attack when threatened. Man and most animals share in having some form of parental responsibility for the new born. Most young animals play—human children, puppies, kittens, or monkeys. Men and animals expressively communicate pain and fright. Perhaps we are more aware of similarities between animals and ourselves than we are knowledgeable of where to draw the line which differentiates them from us. It is likely, too, that as one thinks of animals, one is apt to project human emotions, feelings, and intentions upon them. This tendency to see human attributes in animals is called to *anthropomorphize*. We must be aware of it since it is easy to fall into error if we succumb to it. Keeping the danger of anthropomorphizing in mind, Man's niche within the larger scheme of animal classification will be examined.

MAN IS A PRIMATE

Beginning with the most basic observation possible, one notes that between birth and death, Man is *alive*. Man is living, rather than inanimate or inorganic matter, and within the classification of living things, the human species represents one form of animal life. By feeling the center of our own back with our fingers, we know that Man has a backbone and that this puts us in the category of vertebrates. Mammals are higher vertebrates that nourish their young with milk secreted by mammary glands. Even though this definition does not entirely fit some modern human bottle-fed babies, Man obviously falls into the class of Mammalia. For years, people were satisfied with a description of Man's biological nature that did not go very far beyond this point.

Between 1735 and 1745, Carl von Linné (also known as Carolus Linnaeus) classified the botanical and animal world into related categories. In his monumental work, *Systema Naturae*, Linné used descriptive information of the habitat and behavior of the animals he had classified. Significantly, his only identifying diagnosis of the human species, *Homo sapiens* (Man the wise), was *Nosce te ipsum* (know thyself).

Animals were categorized into orders, suborders, super-families, families, genera, and finally, species. Species were later further divided into races, breeds, and stocks. Classificiations were made by the number of visual similarities and other characteristics a group of animals had in common. For example, one characteristic of a species is that within this population all members are potentially capable of interbreeding. Linné placed Man within the order of Primates which include tree shrews, lemurs, tarsiers, monkeys, and apes.

Washburn (1963) notes that "primates have been hard to

define and generalized features tend to be mentioned. Yet the order is characterized by the adaption of climbing by grasping which is a complex specialization, separating primates from other living mammals." The Primates share certain distinguishing characteristics which include a brain whose wrinkled cortex is large relative to the size and weight of the rest of the body, hands and feet that are adapted for grasping objects, a collarbone that permits free movement of the upper extremities, opposability of thumbs and toes, and with the exception of tree shrews, nails instead of claws.[1]

Within this large and variable order of primates, Man is further classified as belonging to the suborder of Anthropoidea. Members have in common eyes that are set in enclosed sockets and are directed for looking forward making stereoscopic vision possible. They have increased brain area devoted to seeing, in contrast with other animals whose brain favors the more primitive senses of smelling and hearing. All Anthropoidea have a relatively small lower face which has both an upper and a lower jaw with teeth consisting of two incisors, one canine, two premolars, and three (sometimes two) molars. Narrowing this suborder down, one finds that it consists of the superfamily of Hominoidea which includes Pongidae, the family of apes, and Hominidae, the family of Man.

MAN AND APE

Although there are many striking differences, the body of the anthropoid ape is generally much like that of Man. It has similar bones, nerves, muscles, and other organs. Its brain is roughly one-third human size; but, as far as known, it lacks none of the functional areas that are found in the human brain. The menstrual cycle in the female ape has the same phases as in human females, and in the chimpanzee the interval is the same. The gestation period approaches Man's and the placenta is essentially of the human type. Embryonic development is similar, and ape, as Man, can breed any time of the year. Also,

---

[1] Some lower primate species combine nails on some digits with claws on others.

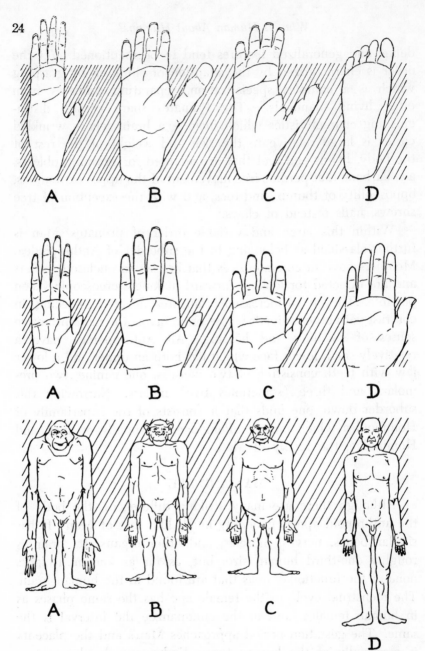

FIGURE 1. Body Proportions of Man and Ape. A, orangutan; B, chimpanzee; C, Gorilla; D, man. (Adopted from Midlo, C. and Schultz, A. H., in v. Eickstädt, E.: *Rassenkunde u. Rassengeschichte d. Menschheit*. Göttingen, Musterschmidt, 1956.)

the blood types of apes approximate those of humans. Further-more, apes' susceptibility to many human diseases to which other animals are relatively immune suggests a close parallel in the physiological and chemical composition of their bodies.

There are still other similarities which deserve a brief mention. Both Men and apes are tailless, have an absence of cheek pouches, and both have vermiform appendixes. The spinal column of apes has a suggestion of the curves seen in Man. This fact assumes importance since the curvature of the spine is associated with Man's erect posture and, therefore is a typically human characteristic. Apes, like men, are capable of a variety of facial movements for the expression of their emotions. Most zoologists would agree that Man has more anatomical charac-teristics in common with apes than apes have with monkeys. However, such comparisons are difficult to substantiate as DeVore (1963) has pointed out.

All newborn Primates, excluding Man, have similar body proportions in adulthood as in childhood. And at birth, all Primates, except Man, have reasonable control of their move-ments. Quite the opposite is true of the human infant. Although his relative weight is greater than that of his simian equivalent, the human neonate is completely helpless at birth. He has a long way to go before he can walk and does not even learn to sit up by himself until six months after birth. Creeping takes another four months, and walking is not accomplished until two additional months have passed. Complete thumb opposition, which is instantaneous to the newborn ape, usually takes humans seven months.

One of Man's unique characteristics is to be ushered into life with a helplessness and dependency which is unparalleled in all of nature. Human babies born with less than one third of their adult brain capacity would die quickly if abandoned by their mothers. But as sometimes happens, an initial dis-advantage turns out to be an advantage in the long run. Some behavioral scientists believe that Man's distinctive superiority in adaptability to the environment stems from the very fact that he is born "unripe" (Table II). Being thrust prematurely into a world of thousands of stimuli instead of remaining *in utero,*

TABLE II

DENTITION, GROWTH, AND LIFE SPAN IN PRIMATES

	Lower Primates	Apes	Man
Duration of prenatal growth	5 months	8 to 9 months	9 months
Duration of postnatal growth	3 years	11 years	20 years
Life span (optimum conditions)	14 years	35 years	75 years
Age at eruption of first dentition	birth	3 to 4 months	8 months
Age at eruption of second dentition	1 year	3 years	6 years

Adapted from Comas, J.: *Manual of Physical Anthropology.* Springfield, Thomas, 1960.

the human infant has been described by some biologists as being given a head start in life. To some extent this helplessness characterizes Man's entire life span. He is not endowed biologically with any effective, protective mechanisms—no sharp canines, claws, fangs, or armor. In order to survive he has had to develop tools and weapons from materials found in nature, and for this he requires a very unusual brain. Except for this brain, Man is one of nature's most unspecialized creatures. Species with specializations have become extinct when climatic or other environmental changes reversed the advantages achieved by their specialization. Since Man's specialization is his brain, we might ask, Will this unique human organ be the seed of Man's undoing?

Upright Gait Antedates Brain

If we were to guess about it, we might say that Man's brain came first in evolution and that his erect gait followed this development. Physical anthropologists are aware that the opposite is true, however. Impressive fossil evidence shows that Man's erect posture preceded any really significant brain increase. Among the candidates tentatively vying for the role of Man's precursors are Patterson's Kanapoi Hominoid I, earliest of the Hominidae (Patterson, 1966; Patterson and Howells, 1967) and the Australopithecines such as Dart's Taungs skull (Dart and Craig, 1959) and Leakey's Zinjanthropus (Leakey, 1963), who roamed the South African veld during the lower Pleistocene[2] (Fig. 2). The fossil remains of their frames and pelvic regions show clearly that these creatures walked erect or nearly erect.

---

[2] Leakey (1961) places these protohominids outside of Man's direct ancestry proposing instead, *Homo habilis,* almost two million years old, for this role.

Yet their brain case was not much larger than that of the modern apes. It is unlikely that without the erect gait, the human brain could have achieved its present size. Our large head with its thin skull allowing room for brain matter owes its existence to the fact that we could balance our heads on our shoulders. By substituting balance for heavy musculature, our cranium was allowed to develop an immense amount of space within which the brain could expand.

Another early disadvantage proved crucial in the making of Man. The severe climatic conditions of the early Pleistocene, the period approximately three million years before our time, destroyed the forest reserves where beings ancestral to Man had lived in relative security. With the disappearance of the forest, Man had to run instead of climb for safety. Man's life on the ground may have set the stage for the erect gait. This had survival value in that it freed his arms for defense and for carrying his food supply. In one important respect we can say, then, that climate helped make Man.

Human Foot Unique

Contrary to what we would expect, it is not Man's brain but his foot that is morphologically unique. Our brain, except in size and complexity, is similar in appearance to that of the apes. This is also true of our hands but certainly cannot be said for our feet. The musculature of the human foot more closely resembles that of baboons than apes (Straus, 1949). Without the human foot, there could be no upright gait, and without upright gait, as we have seen, there would be no human brain. Ontogenetically, Man is born into the world head first, but phylogenetically, as a species, Man entered the scene first on his feet. Even *Oreopithecus,* assigned to the Pliocene period (Table III) was thought to have already had a partially erect posture, although this ancient Primate is not now considered by most paleontologists to be a direct precursor of the hominid family (Simons, 1964).

The evolution of the human foot is an interesting development. As the great toe was no longer used for grasping, it became

TABLE III

CENOZOIC ERA

Began 70 million years ago

Period	Years Before Present	Characteristics
Holocene	10,000 to present	Modern Man: agriculture, civilization, industry, science, medicine, atomic energy, space exploration and threat of human overpopulation.
Pleistocene	3 million to 10,000	This period has recently been extended in time to 3 million years ago. During this period many areas of the earth were covered by ice. There were four ice advances with periodic recessions. Man developed many of his hominid characteristics during this period. In Chapter 10 details of this are given.
Pliocene	13 to 3 million	Rise of the hominids. Oreopithecus.
Miocene	25 to 13 million	Appearance of anthropoid apes, Ramapithecus, Dryopithecus, Proconsul.
Oligocene	36 to 25 million	Modern mammals replaced archaic types. The first anthropoids appeared: monkeys and early apes.
Eocene	58 to 36 million	Lemurs, Tarsiers, and other modern mammal types emerged including even and odd-toed hoofed mammals and advanced carnivores.
Paleocene	63 to 58 million	Mammals replaced ruling reptiles. First Primates and rodents emerged. Building continued of Rocky Mountains and coastal ranges.

stabilized to serve in helping to carry the weight of the body. Thereby, it was brought into line with the other toes, losing its opposability. The other toes became shorter and smaller. The axis of the foot shifted to a line between the great and second toe and two arches were formed—one from foot to rear and one that runs transversely. The arch ending with the heel increased in size and extended backward. The result is so characteristically human that no one would mistake its impression on sand or mud.

Bones associated with the foot continued the trend in the human direction.[3] The leg bones became longer and stronger and the attached muscles larger and more powerful, giving man a distinction between forelimbs and hindlimbs, greatly surpassing other Primates. Man's pelvis became shorter and broader and rotated forward and downward, making it possible for the body weight to be transmitted to the lower limbs. This organization of leg and pelvic structure gave man two attributes that are

----

[3] As other writers have done, I am using such description as "trend in the human direction," "increased in size," etc., merely for simplicity in communications. No teleology is implied.

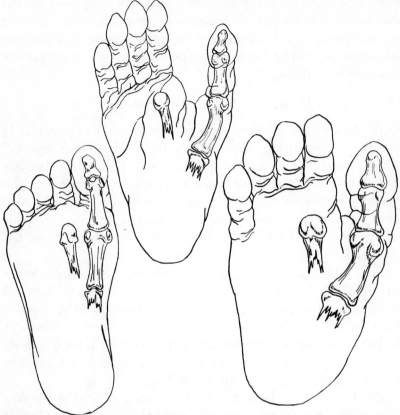

FIGURE 2. Man's Unique Foot. It is easy to recognize the human foot. (Adapted from Martin, R. and Saller, K.: *Lehrbuch der Anthropologie.* Stuttgart, Gustav Fischer Verlag, 1957.)

exclusively human—his leg calves and a padded rear on which he could sit with comfort.

The uniqueness of the human spine has already been mentioned. Its curves play an important role in keeping the head, trunk, and lower limbs in one continuous axis, and in serving as springs to provide flexibility and resiliency of movement. The chest and rib cage are round and bell-shaped in most Primates, but in Man they are relatively flat. Man's upright gait has required that strong membranes attach the internal organs to the backbone to prevent gravity from pulling them downward.

Since gravity played a major role in the development of our anatomy and in keeping it functioning properly, weightlessness as experienced by astronauts in space flights represents a problem that must be solved before long journeys of this type can be successfully undertaken.

Human Body Has Disadvantages

In the upright posture of Man, the heart is approximately four feet above the ground. When the veins of the legs fail to overcome the necessary gravitational pull, they become swollen and the condition known as varicose veins results. The tendency of the veins of the rectum to become congested may result in hemorrhoids—a condition from which quardrupeds are spared. Thanks to bipedalism, only Man suffers from flat feet and fallen arches.

Both Man and apes have relatively undifferentiated finger lengths which do not permit the flexibility of movement achieved by some of the lower primates. In this respect, Man remains closer to the reptiles than do some of the other members of the Primate order. The human forefinger however is unique in its capacity for free movement and is believed by some taxonomists to be the most adapted of all of our fingers.

The fact that the human heart has been greatly raised makes it necessary for it to overcome additional gravitational pull resulting in a strain on our entire circulatory system. There have been many explanations for the frequency of heart attacks in our species. One of these is the tensions of modern life. Another is a lack of exercise in our sedentary civilization. A third relates to diet. A variety of remedies have been suggested for each of these faults and among them have been some highly imaginative and exotic preventative measures. The upright human gait may be just as potent a factor responsible for coronaries as the others mentioned. But to my knowledge, no one has, so far, proposed that humans return to walking on all fours as a means of avoiding heart attacks. Nor is it likely that many expecting human mothers would be inclined to abandon their customary bipedal locomotion during the nine months of gestation even if they knew that female quadrupeds are spared the discomfort of the so-called milk legs of pregnancy. Apparently we have not, as yet, gone quite that far in prescribing remedies for our human ills even though a return by adults to quadrupedalism would yield the extra bonus of providing behavioral psychologists with a fascinating experimental situation.

To keep the heavy brain balanced in an upright position in the vertical axis of the body, the foramen magnum, the aperture through which the spinal cord passes to the brain, must be centrally situated at the base of the skull. The location of the foramen magnum in fossil skulls serves as an index of how erect early hominids were able to walk. Since the head is balanced on top of the spine, the size of the cervical vertebrae and the strength of the nuchal muscles required to hold the head in place are greatly reduced in Man, allowing the neck to become longer and slender compared to ape and Man's early forebearers. The maxillae and the mandible have receded dorsally and this has been accompanied by a shortening of the size of the canine teeth[4] resulting in the typical flattened human

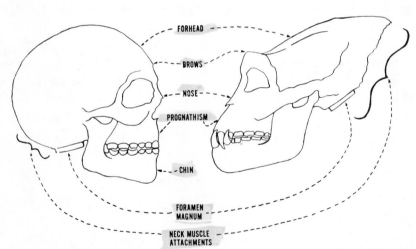

FIGURE 3. Skulls of Man and Chimpanzee. (Adapted from Howells, W. W.: *Mankind So Far*. New York, Doubleday, 1944.)

[4] The roots of the canines remain longer than those of the other teeth, suggesting that at one time canines were larger and more powerful.

profile (see Fig. 3). The development of a bony chin and prominent nose helps give the human face a straight-line facial profile.

Man shares with the apes the possession of thirty-two teeth in contrast to the sixty-six of earlier mammals. However, human teeth have not always been reduced in proportion to the facial bones and that is why some human children visit orthodontists to have their teeth straightened. Although all Hominoidea have the same dental formula, among humans the second molars erupt in the twelfth and thirteenth year while among chimpanzees dentition is completed at the age of ten.

Multiple Factors Account for Human Brain

The heavy overhanging brow ridges seen in fossils of early Man and in apes have receded. In modern Man the brain case is swollen, giving rise to a high forehead which permits, roughly, two-thirds increase in brain capacity. Other changes have taken place in skull formation on which we need not dwell here. The significant fact is that it is not mere size or weight that distinguishes the human brain. For example, the elephant has a brain that weighs 5,000 grams. It is the relative size of the brain, its specific chemistry, and its cortical convolutions that make the difference. In Table IV, we note that the whale has 1 gram of brain substance for every 15,000 grams of body substance. That weight alone is not the only factor in the development of a superior brain is illustrated by the Capuchin monkey which has 1 gram of brain substance for 17.5 grams

TABLE IV

BRAIN AND BODY WEIGHT

Species	Weight of Brain (Grams)	Ratio, Brain: Body Weight	Comparative Value*
Man	1375	1:30	27
Chimpanzee	400	1:75	5.2
Orangutan	400	1:124	3
Gorilla	425	1:231	2
Whale	7000	1:15,000	0.47
Dog	102	1:250	0.37
Chicken	3.4	1:446	0.007

Adapted from Schenck, G.: *History of Man.* Chr. Belser Verlag, 1961.
  * Comparative value is a comparable size which is obtained by squaring the value of the weight of brain and dividing by the body-weight.

TABLE V

CRANIAL CAPACITIES IN ANTHROPOIDS AND MAN

Cubic Capacity in Grams

A hospitalized idiot	241
Average gorilla	543
Australopithecus africanus	600
Anatole France	1017
Walt Whitman	1282
Australian aborigines	1338
Franz Schubert	1420
Homo sapiens (sampling of Chinese)	1467
Central Eskimos	1516
Early Neanderthals	1553
Immanuel Kant	1650
A hospitalized idiot	2850

Adapted from Montagu, A.: *An Introduction to Physical Anthropology.* Springfield, Thomas, 1960 and v. Eickstädt, E.: *Rassenkunde und Rassengeschichte der Menschheit.* Fischer Verlag, 1946.

of body substance. Some of the dwarf monkeys of South America do even better. Our former pet squirrel monkey represented a species with the largest relative brain mass in the primate world. This, however, did not make him the brightest of the Primates. Post-mortems have disclosed that there are idiots who have had unusually large brains. If we may judge brain size from cranial capacity, Neanderthal Man's brain may well have outweighted ours (Table V). It is still not understood how size and weight are related to mental qualities. Understanding how ten billion cortical synapses work to produce human thought represents one of the greatest challenges left to Man's ingenuity.

Ape With Culture and Human Child Without It

Leuba (1954), a social psychologist, wrote a pamphlet, *Natural Man,* in which he described the behavior of primitive humans and apes. Sometimes the reader of Leuba's booklet has difficulty in deciding whether a given description fits Man or chimpanzee best. The following quotations illustrate this point:

1. She learned to point to various parts of her body, such as eyes, ears, and nose, when requested to do so. She examines picture books, builds towers with blocks, and rode a kiddie car . . . laughed when tickled, played games like rolling a big ball back and forth . . . kissing and hugging members of the family and expressing a great deal of affection for them. (Description of chimpanzee.)

2. J. employed guile to lure him . . . To a much greater degree than other females, she succeeded by gentle and persuasive techniques in shaping his behavior to her desire . . . With P., she took

no liberties, claimed little by the way of right or privilege, while with B., she took endless liberties and lay claim to everything. She was the subdued, self-effacing, unassertive female in P.'s presence, but with B. she was self-confident, expressive, and certain of her ability to do as she liked . . . If one had been given a complete description of her behavior, J. would have been identified as two different personalities. (Description of chimpanzee.)

3. Living on nuts, berries, and roots . . . these were his favorite foods. He appeared shy, restless, and uneasy in civilized surroundings and sought to escape to the woods at every opportunity. He bit and scratched those who opposed his impulses. . . . He uttered only emotional cries, expressing anger, fear, pain, or sadness. He smelled almost everything. (Description of human child.)

4. He does not show an innate propensity towards any one specific way of securing food or eating it . . . When aroused or injured, or in any way excessively stimulated, he is likely to show violent emotion, especially anger or fear . . . He has no modesty nor shame of his body or of its natural functions. He is not repelled by the presence of his excrements nor by most filth. (If any attempt to clothe him is made) he tears it off at the first opportunity. He does not build any kind of shelter . . . but may use shelters afforded by nature. (Description of human child.)

The first quotation describes an ape raised as a pet in a home[5] The last two are descriptions of feral children abandoned in infancy. These children are not necessarily mental defectives and should not be classified within this group. Rather, they are children who have had no opportunity to benefit from contact with human society. A study of the behavior of such children helps us understand which human traits are inborn and which acquired. The behavioral description given represents extremes—apes in a human culture and humans developing in an environment devoid of human influence. These examples help introduce the question, What kind of behavior is really innately human? Many psychologists are becoming aware of the fact that all behavior, animal and human, is an intricate, multidimensional, complex phenomenon. Two different approaches to behavior illustrate this new awareness. One is represented by *Roots of Behavior* (Bliss, 1962), in which thirty-one authors discuss genetics, instinct, and socialization; and the other is *Exploring Behavior*

---

[5] Note possibility of anthropomorphism here.

(Candland and Campbell, 1961), which introduces such subjects as discrimination, classical and operant conditioning, and public opinion polling.

No longer is behavior explained by the simple formula, Stimulus-Response, nor does Stimulus-Organism-Response offer desired elucidation. Human actions and reactions are a complicated interdependent mosaic of external and internal pressures. From sociology and anthropology one learns that men and animals as individuals must adjust their behavior to the structure of the society of which they are a part. An animal's position within its groups allows for considerable behavioral variation but also imposes limitations. The social structure represents a synthesis of inborn characteristics of the group's members and the given environmental conditions in which the group lives. Therefore, biological, psychological, and sociological adaptations are required for survival. Among the internal biological drives are what Titiev (1963) has called the biological imperatives—hunger, propagation, and need for warmth. The complicated interaction of various kinds of required adaptations makes the study of animal behavior the great challenge that it is today.

What is Typical Behavior

We become aware of many difficulties when we attempt to compare animal with human behavior. One of the problems is finding what is "typical" in nonhuman behavior. If people wished to observe how various animals act, they would visit a zoo. Although in some cases zoos have made elaborate attempts to recreate animals' natural habitat, at best, the conditions of life there differ radically from those in nature. The cages in the experimental psychology laboratories also fail to approximate real life conditions. The fact that caged animals need not forage for food or fight natural enemies profoundly changes the psychological picture. Many animals become depressed and listless in confinement.

Not long ago, most comparisons between men and animals were, by necessity, made with animals in captivity. Lately, however, an increasing number of observers have endured the hardships of living in the field to study various species in their natural environment. Such observations have caused students of animal behavior to revise many of their former ideas. Anthropologists studying humans have also gone to where these people live and experienced many arduous days living in primitive conditions in order to discover what kinds of human behavior are basic, intrinsic, and "uncontaminated" by influences of civilization. Although such ethnographic studies have contributed to our knowledge, in order to understand total Man, civilization as well as the simple, aboriginal life of primitive peoples must be studied. In hominology it is the relationship between several different ways in which men live that is of special interest. Therefore, it is necessary to examine men in a large variety of settings in order to gain the broadest possible overview of what is human. An example of such a broad approach is offered by Opler (1959) in a cross-cultural examination of mental health. Among the different cultures examined are Zulu, Ifaluk, Iroquois, Ute, Chinese, Peruvian, Malayan, Italian, Jewish, and Spanish-American in Texas.

Difficulty in finding the "right" place or time where behavior in Man or animals may best be observed represents a major obstacle in making meaningful observations. This is illustrated by the experiences of Hediger (1955), director of the Zoological Gardens in Zurich. For example, in his attempt to study the sleeping habits of elephants, he made many carefully prepared attempts to catch his elephants sleeping in the zoo. Elephants, however, keep late hours and do not usually go to sleep before midnight. When they finally go to bed, they are light sleepers and they wake up and trumpet at the slightest disturbance or unfamiliar noise. Even when Hediger left their door unlocked to prevent any sound of lock and key, and crept into their quarters on tiptoe, the elephants were invariably already standing up clanking their chains. In the circus, however, where elephants were used to all sorts of noises at night, including the night watchman's continual visits, Hediger was able to see elephants asleep whenever he felt like it. These observations led Hediger to realize that the elephants' sensitivity to sounds depended upon what the animals had been used to. Later, in the Belgian Congo, he had a chance to observe sleeping elephants at a state-owned elephant farm. He noted that some of them made a sort of pillow out of piles of papyrus stems, lemon-scented grass, and twigs that their native keepers had heaped up in front of them for fodder. Similarly, some, but not all, of the circus elephants he had observed earlier had used hay for this same purpose.

We are apt to think of behavior which has been learned and does not occur when an animal is in its native habitat as artificial or not "typical." The truth, however, is that any potential adaptability or educability is as characteristic a part of the animal as its so-called typical behavior. An animal's complete behavioral spectrum is not visible when it is observed under a limited set of conditions, nor is Man's.

Apes in Human Homes

With this in mind, behavior observed among nonhuman Primates in human homes is instructive. Since animals do not generally pass on a learned tradition, occasional attempts have been made to bring young apes intimately into a family circle to see how well they adapt as members of a human family. I recall being present at a lecture at the University of Mainz when the behavior of Goma, a baby female gorilla raised by a family in Switzerland, was described to an audience of interested scientists.[6] Portions of Goma's reported behavior suggested that some well-established beliefs regarding the uniqueness of human characteristics might have to be revised. Goma appeared much more dependent on her human family than had been thought likely for nonhuman infants. Also her powers of abstraction and capacity to arrive at conclusions by inferences were higher than would have been expected on a nonhuman level.

W. N. Kellogg (1933), a psychologist, and his wife "adopted" a seven-month-old chimpanzee, Gua, in Florida and brought her up with their own nine-and-one-half-month-old son. The ape

----

[6] See also Lang's (1964) account of the first gorilla raised by its own mother in captivity.

and the boy ate, slept, and played together. It was observed that Gua greatly excelled her human counterpart in motor skills partly because of her faster physical development. In her ability to climb and do acrobatics, she exceeded the best that her foster brother could do. She also learned "manners" easily enough and ate with a spoon, drank out of a glass, opened doors, and skipped rope. She was less inclined to sulk and have temper tantrums than her foster brother, but she was unable to learn language. Apparently because of the ape's genetically predetermined limitations, the human child overtook and greatly outdistanced his simian stepsister within a year.

USE OF SYMBOLS MAKES HUMANS HUMAN

Chimpanzees can place poles into each other telescopically in order to make one long one out of several short ones, and they can use these to pull food into their cages. They can pile boxes on top of each other in order to reach bananas. They even can learn to use some tools. Apes have been observed unfastening locks, while others have demonstrated that they can recall where objects have been hidden and then go back to fetch them for use in solving problems. Chimpanzees have been taught to operate slot machines using tokens for money. This requires the use of concepts of size, shape, and color discrimination as well as simple reasoning. Also, apes, in a certain sense, are able to participate in a community effort. For example, they have been seen working together with a rope, pulling a heavy food box toward their cage so that all are able to reach its contents.

Various students of ape behavior report that they have observed these animals demonstrate "friendship," "sympathy," "ingenuity," and "loyalty." Nevertheless, apes share with all other nonhumans the lack of ability to use symbolic conceptions, except at a very rudimentary level. After an experiment in which a chimpanzee was raised for three years with human children in a home, it was suggested that "the species chimpanzee closely resembles our hypothetical cultureless man, with much the same individual capacities—except for language ability, the tool which man uses to build and maintain culture," (Hayes and Hayes, 1967). This lack of capacity for using verbal symbols rules out the possibility of animals developing a tradition that can be passed on to future generations. Without a verbal or written tradition, no culture or civilization could come into being.

Art is Not Unique to Man

In the many efforts made to understand Man it has been said, he can be understood through his art. He has been described as an art-creating, art-appreciating being whose aesthetic sense causes him to appreciate balance and harmony and whose capacity for artistic expression enables him to fashion objects of beauty. Yet harmony and balance in nature predate Man while rhythm, considered one of the basics of art is not the prerogative of Man.

Animals, also, are capable of creating "artistic works" of astonishingly high quality. Who has not admired a beautifully made bird's nest or beaver dam? Of course, technically we do not consider this "art" in the usual sense because these objects were created as a result of instincts.

The German animal psychologist, Rensch, (1959) states that experimental studies of three different types of Anthropoidea indicated that the same aesthetic selective factors apparent in these animals are operative in Man. Studies showed that non-human Primates preferred gay colors to gray ones, harmonizing to clashing color combinations, and rhythmic, well-balanced patterns to haphazard ones. Rensch demonstrated that even birds and fish have a sense of design and balance. When given the opportunity they will select the same patterns, Rensch claims, that humans would choose as most attractive. Unfortunately, Rensch's work in this area stands relatively alone so that needed corroboration from other researchers is lacking.

Years ago the British Institute for Modern Art held an exhibition of paintings by a three-year-old chimpanzee whose work showed such good rhythmic qualities that some art dealers (who were unaware of the identity of the artist) described them as "designs of definitely excellent artistic quality." There were some embarrassing moments when the critics were subsequently introduced to the creator of the paintings they had praised highly.

Observing animals while they are engaged in their creative endeavors can be enlightening. I recall how a nonhuman Primate with a very human name, "Johnny," was offered charcoal and cardboard through his cage. Without prompting, he filled the sheet with rhythmically arranged lines using his fingertips and wrists as would any human adult under similar circumstances. He accompanied his artistic endeavors with observable lip movements as if mumbling to himself.[7] When later he was offered five crayons, each with a different color, he carefully examined them one by one and then handed them back through his cage. The proper mood seemed not to be upon him. During a second attempt, at a later date, he immediately selected red, drew lines with his fingertips as if inspired, and at the same time gave signs of being sexually aroused. This same ape learned to draw on both sides of a sheet of cardboard with either crayons or brush and paint. Unforeseen difficulties were encountered when Johnny preferred eating the crayons to using them for creating works of art, but this is hardly a simian exclusive as every mother knows.

When comparing the artistic works of apes with that of children, two elements missing in ape drawings represent key differences between the two species. Apes do not draw diagrams, nor do they ever make pictorial representations of objects. Like very young children, apes are unable to utilize symbolic substitutes for objects external to themselves. Drawings by apes illustrate the fact that Man's capacity for making visual abstraction represents one fundamental difference between human and nonhuman behavior.

Breakdown of Configurations

The ability to break down a configuration into its component parts is related to capacity for making abstractions. If we are

_____

[7] Is this anthropomorphism?

configuration-bound, we are unable to recognize the parts that comprise the whole as entities in themselves. Among all animals, except Man, there seems to be only a limited conceptualization of things within a configuration as things-in-themselves. Schwidetsky (1959) refers to this as *Dingkonstanz* and *Dingdistanzierung,* loosely translated as stimulus-bound and stimulus-free. The ability to visualize an object as an independent entity and the capacity to disregard the ties an object has to its immediate environment are two variables upon which the building of culture depends. Thus humans can dissociate an animal skin from the animal and, seeing it as a thing in itself, it can be separated and utilized as clothing or shelter. A tree limb can be visualized as a lance or spear, a rock as an ax, and fire ignited by lightning can be conceived as a source of heat, comfort, and safety. Some of this knowledge stems from trial-and-error and some from accidental learning since both Man and animal depend on these. But in order to control, rather than merely adjust to his environment, Man must be able to break the environmental configurations he finds in nature into fragments that can be put together into new and more useful configurations. In this manner Man can create a synthetic environment by means of which he is better able to meet the demands of survival.

Lately, we have learned that the distinctions mentioned above are of degree only. Jane Goodall, the British anthropologist, studied chimpanzees in an undisturbed reserve on the western edge of Tanganyika a few years ago. A National Geographic Bulletin (Anon, 1964) reports that apes also have a rudimentary ability of abstraction:

> Already Miss Goodall's findings have forced scholars to take a new look at the definition of man. Scientists long distinguished 'man' from animals as a creature capable of making tools. But Miss Goodall saw chimps strip leaves from twigs, then use the twigs to fish for termites to eat. This, too, is tool making; so the definition of 'man' must change. She also saw chimpanzees use leaves as napkins and wadded leaves as sponges for drinking.

The article continues with the suggestion that such reports

make "scholars ponder." Obviously, differences between Man and ape are not as absolute as was once thought. Nevertheless, it is clear that only Man can fashion a synthetic environment of any complexity and pass the benefits of this on to the following generation. Man also has the advantage of being able to move this artifact-rich environment along with him when threatening situations such as hunger, adverse climate, or enemies force him to leave an accustomed area to seek a more favorable place of residence. The capacity for abstraction has enabled Man to develop a vivid sense of past and future, and he can utilize past experience to help him prepare for a future emergency. When this is coupled with the ability to dissolve natural configurations and to reconstruct them into new ones of greater utilitarian value, an immeasureable advantage over the rest of the animal world has been gained. Adding to this Man's relatively long life span for accumulation of knowledge through experience and his capacity for using verbal symbols, the fundamental requirements for the establishment of Man's uniquely human culture have been met.

TERRITORIALITY, DOMINANCE, AND SOCIALIZATION

Biologists have described many species of animals as having territorial instincts that merge with the need for social cooperation. Dominance and socialization are other characteristics often associated with the structuring of animal life. The Pongidae seem to have roughly defined home ranges rather than well-marked territories. Early humans roamed in hunting bands and the concept of territory may have been a later development, perhaps, related to the advent of agriculture. Most American sociologists and anthropologists reject the conclusions reached by Ardrey (1966) and others who found answers to the human enigma by explaining human behavior by such concepts as territoriality (see pages 334-335), establishing dominance and by genetically determined models of socialization. There is much variation among primates and for many reasons inferences based on a direct comparison between animals and humans may not be valid. This does not mean that we cannot learn about ourselves by studying animals. But applying the concept of inherited tendencies to human behavior is not accepted by many behavioral scientists and requires further research.

The identification of such characteristics as territoriality, dominance, mating patterns, imprinting, and homing instincts are studied by a limited number of scientists whose interest centers on innate and animal behavior. This interest represents a relatively recent departure from the traditional emphases within the bio-psycho-social sciences (Lorenz, [1963, 1965]; Carthy and Ebling, [1964]; see also, Geertz, [1964]; Greenfield and Lewis, [1965]; Menaker E. and Menaker W., [1965]; Klopfer and Hailman, [1967]. Ethology—the study of innate behavior — represents a controversial approach for exploring behavioral attributes in Man.

MAN CAN DELAY GRATIFICATION

As the body pays its price for its erect gait, so the psyche, too, must pay its penalty for being human. The ability to act in the present for future rewards requires the capability to maintain active psychological tensions. When any act is contemplated, a muscular and simultaneous psychological tension is set up in the organism. The completion of the act with the accompanying reward serves to reduce this tension. The capacity to delay goal achievement appears to be a function of the cortex and is related to human maturation. An infant cannot sacrifice immediate gratification for future gains. Delay in gratification enables Man to indulge in long-range planning, and this he must do in order to be fed and housed. He is not born to hibernate during the cold winter like the bear, and he is not genetically endowed with a convenient roof over his head like the turtle or even with a warm coat of fur like many of the other creatures that inhabit the earth. In searching for definitions, therefore, consideration must be given to one which describes Man as an animal gifted with a superior ability for enduring certain kinds of tensions. This gift extorts its price when tensions get out of hand.

IS MAN OFF-BALANCE?

The picture of Man as a tension enduring, tension requiring organism does not tally with the view currently held in the mental health field. Man as a creature constantly maintaining a disequilibrium while simultaneously striving for a restoration of balance is not in accord with such concepts as Coleman's (1964) that "When homeostatic mechanisms are unable to maintain or restore equilibrium, ill health or death results." More explicitly, Levitt (1967) maintains

> The maintenance of physiological equilibrium is carried out autonomically, without conscious effort or awareness on the part of the individual. The physiologist calls it *homeostasis.*
>
> The principle of homeostasis is also found in the psychological sphere. The person who is overwhelmed by anxiety is in a state of psychological disequilibrium. All or any of his behaviors may be adversely affected. His functioning is disrupted, impaired, and in extreme instances, comes to a complete halt.

Consider precisely the reverse of this. Could it be that life for Man, and to a lesser extent for animals as well, requires a constant absence of homeostasis? Does the lack of equilibrium coupled with a concomitant drive to regain it constitute a fundamental basis for human motivation? The achievement of a goal, "total adjustment homeostasis," as many psychologists view Man's ideal condition, may be something for which Man constantly strives, but will he be able to endure it once he is within sight of it or once he has it within his grasp? True equilibrium may not be established until the organism's final demise.

We talk of the "inner harmony" of being "well-balanced" as desirable ends necessary for what is considered to be "peace of mind." Could this be a fallacy? Could not the "well-balanced" person instead be one who is capable of tolerating, with reasonable endurance, the constant imbalances which life requires of him? Once homeostasis has occurred, either within an organism or within a society, history demonstrates that stagnation quickly sets in. Relief can only be obtained by upsetting this condition. Once upset, paradoxically, Man is again driven to reestablish homeostasis, using many ingenious methods to create a new balance. This leads to still another distinction between Man and animals. Man can utilize a variety of dimensions to rectify contending forces pivotal to himself. Among these are art, role playing, fantasy, crime, sports, war, religion, symptoms (both medical and psychiatric), and so on. On the other hand, animals are limited to relatively few mechanisms for achieving the same end. These consist of slight modifications of the environment, anatomical changes through mutations, physiological alterations occurring within the animal itself, and among some animals, play and socialization.

MAN AND HIS DUALITY

Returning once more to the question of homeostasis, it can be said that Man resists homeostasis more obdurately and conversely seeks to restore it with a greater tenacity and enterprise than any other creature. It seems to be a necessity that Man be constantly out of focus with himself like a person and his shadow. Man sees this theoretical "shadow" as part of himself but as he attempts to reunite himself with it, he makes certain that he fails. The resulting blurred self-image explains human motivation for achievement and accounts for progress on a higher level than a biological one. This discussion suggests that *Man is a psycho-social contradiction.* This definition may help us understand why there is so much difficulty in developing a unified, coherent description of Man. It may also explain why Man is so often viewed as struggling with duality.[8] Two-headed serpents, dragons, and mythological figures representing an externalized projection of this duality are common among art forms throughout many parts of the world. Schizophrenics, drawing upon noncultural roots within themselves, sometimes paint pictures of people with two faces.

Dualism and, occasionally, a revolt against dualism play a significant role in Man's philosophical makeup. Man visualized as enduring the stresses and conflicts of dualism may be more common to Western civilization than applicable to all mankind. Some writers view Man's conflicts and his duality as engendered by his attempt to fit his nature to social institutions and norms which are not compatible with his biological nature.

---

[8] Can our human duality be ascribed to our vegetarian Primate ancestry on the one hand and to our somewhat incompatible carniverous adaptations on the other?

The absence of complicated social institutions frees animals from such human conflicts.

The non-Western orientations of Zen Buddhism and Taoism attempt to offer methods for achieving homeostasis without requiring physical demise. In order to do this, however, they must deny the existence of an ego and emphasize that a self-concept is meaningful only to the extent that it is merged with a universal concept. The obliteration of "self" is seen as the end result of an extremely difficult process leading to *Nirvana*[9] which is equated with "blissful nonexistence." Significantly the Sanskrit derivation of the word, *Nirvana*, is *annihilation*. This is not conceived of as "death" as it might be in Western eyes but is viewed as a rebirth on a much higher level than one in which there exist self-images, egos, ambitions, conflicts, and social institutions (Watts, 1957, 1963).

In Eastern philosophical thought, dualism is conceived of as representing the passive and active principles of the universe (Yin and Yang). These two aspects are regarded as constituting a harmonious interplay of a unified single order and are not antithetical or conflicting as duality is often conceived of in Western views.[10] It has been said that Western models of successful Man have emphasized control over nature, whereas Eastern philosophical ideas have tended to recommend control over self in order to achieve harmony with nature. This basic difference between certain Eastern philosophies and Western modes of thinking is reflected in their different conceptualization of human dualism.

The idea that there is a dualistic trend in nature is reinforced by what Man observes in the world around him: summer and winter, sea and land, birth and death. But, as noted before in the discussion of homeostasis, Man as the conquerer of nature seems to require constant vacillation. In the religious sphere, monotheism might represent Man's resistance to dualistic con-

---

[9] For a more complete and a more acceptable description of *Nirvana* see Chapter 11.

[10] Western views of duality include such conflicting examples as good and evil, hot and cold, large and small.

ceptions. Yet even within monotheism a plurality arose; in Christianity there is God, Christ, and Satan; and in Mohammedism, Allah and his prophet, Mohammed, are pitted against the infidel. Children play cowboys and Indians and everywhere in the world there are the "good guys" and the "bad guys." Vacillation between duality, plurality, and singularity is seen in science and philosophy as well as elsewhere. As in Man's requirement for both homeostasis and for resistance to equilibrium, for security and a simultaneous need to jeopardize security, Man also constantly seeks unity but cannot resist duality. Perhaps, La Barre (1954) is right when he describes Man as "a shockingly new and quite revolutionary kind of animal."

Compared to animals, Man is concerned with ethics, has religion, develops culture, looks to the future, questions his origins, holds grudges, and is a relentless murderer of his own species. How does it all add up? The picture of Man as "a little lower than the angels" and a little higher than the apes does not leave us with a clear image. The examination of the biological facts fail to offer us any ready-made answers to the riddle of Man's psychological being.[11] Nor does the view of Man's behavior as stemming from conditioned influences (Skinner, 1953) or as motivated by residuals of animal heritage (Lorenz, 1963, 1965) give us genuine clarification. The inevitable conclusion is that while comparing Man with animals throws some light on how he differs from these creatures, Man's basic nature still remains unclear, controversial, and inscrutable.

SUMMARY

We have seen that Man shares with animals the long history

---

[11] A recent book by a zoologist, *The Naked Ape* (Morris, 1967) attempts to make cross-species comparisons and to explain the residuals of Man's early Primate past. Whereas the book is entertaining to read and does make some good points, it is out of focus in its emphasis on Man's animal nature. Obviously, Man is not "naked" though he may be relatively hairless. The fact that Man has learned to make clothes with which he drapes his body for warmth, appearance, and shame is a fact which is perhaps more diagnostic of Man's nature than the sum total of the residuals which Morris mentions. See references for Chapter 11.

of life and that in his development he became a most extraordinary member of the primate group. A large part of Man's uniqueness centers on his capacity to abstract and to utilize symbols particularly on a verbal level, as substitutes for concrete things in nature. Anatomically, the enlarged human cortex, especially the frontal associative areas, and the skeletal modifications permitting an erect gait distinguish Man biologically from other animals and from the ape with whom he shares many anatomical characteristics. Man's lack of anatomical specialization and his late maturation predispose him to utilize sources extrinsic to his body for adaptation, among these are verbal and written traditions, a material culture, and a complex social organizational structure. This is in contrast to the genetically rooted instinctual type of adaptations which are characteristic of the rest of the animal world. Ethologists may in time throw more light on certain aspects of human behavior not fully explained by current theories in the behavioral sciences.

This chapter began with an attempt to place Man within his phylogenetic position in the animal's world. Anatomical and physiological comparisons were made with other Primates, especially the Pongidae. Proceeding from this anatomical base, some psychological, sociological, and philosophical considerations were examined. Whereas this approach yields some insight into Man's uniqueness, it was found that it did not suffice to satisfactorily answer the question, What is human about humans?

REFERENCES

ANON: *National Geographic School Bulletin.* Nov. 9, 1964.

ARDREY, R.: *The Territorial Imperative.* New York, Atheneum, 1966.

BATES, M.: *Man in Nature.* Englewood Cliffs, Prentice-Hall, 1961.

BLISS, E. L. (Ed.): *Roots of Behavior.* New York, Harper, 1962.

BRELAND, K., AND BRELAND, M.: *Animal Behavior.* New York, Macmillan, 1966.

CANDLAND, D., AND CAMPBELL, J.: *Exploring Behavior.* Greenwich, Fawcett, 1961.

CARTHY, J. D., AND EBLING, F. J., JR. (Eds.): *The Natural History of Aggression.* New York, Academic, 1964.

COLEMAN, J. C.: *Abnormal Psychology and Modern Life.* Chicago, Scott, 1964.

DART, R. A., AND CRAIG, D.: *Adventures with the Missing Link.* New York, Harper, 1959.

DE VORE, I.: A comparison of the ecology and behavior of monkeys and apes. In Washburn, S. L. (Ed.): *Classification and Human Evolution.* Chicago, Aldine, 1963.

GEERTZ, C.: The transition to humanity. In Tax, S. (Ed.): *Horizons of Anthropology.* Chicago, Aldine, 1964.

Goma, baby girl gorilla: Basel, Switzerland. *Look, 24:*121-124, Oct. 11, 1960.

GREENFIELD, N. S., AND LEWIS, W. C. (Eds.): *Psychoanalysis and Current Biological Thought.* Madison, U. of Wis, 1965.

HAYES, K. J., AND HAYES, C.: Language: a home-raised chimpanzee. In McKinney, F. (Ed.): *Psychology in Action.* New York, Macmillan, 1967.

HEDIGER, H.: *Studies of the Psychology and Behavior of Captive Animals in Zoos and Circuses.* London, Butterworth, 1955.

KELLOGG, W. N., AND KELLOGG, L.: *The Ape and the Child.* New York, McGraw, 1933.

KLOPFER, P. H., AND HAILMAN, J. P.: *An Introduction to Animal Behavior.* Englewood Cliffs, Prentice-Hall, 1967.

LA BARRE, W.: *The Human Animal.* Chicago, U. of Chicago, 1954.

LANG, E. M.: Jambo, first gorilla raised by its mother in captivity. *National Geographic, 125:*446-453, March 1964.

LEAKEY, L. S. B.: Exploring 1,750,000 years into man's past. *National Geographic, 120:*564-592, Oct. 1961.

LEAKEY, L. S. B.: East African fossil hominoidea and the classification within this super-family. In Washburn, S. L. (Ed.): *Classification and Human Evolution.* Chicago, Aldine, 1963.

LEUBA, C.: *Natural Man.* Garden City, Doubleday, 1954.

LEVITT, E. E.: *The Psychology of Anxiety.* Indianapolis, Bobbs, 1967.

LORENZ, K.: *On Aggression.* New York, Harcourt, 1963.

LORENZ, K.: *Evolution and Modification of Behavior.* Chicago, U. of Chicago, 1965.

MENAKER, E., AND MENAKER, W.: *Ego in Evolution.* New York, Grove, 1965.

OPLER, M. K. (Ed.): *Culture and Mental Health.* New York, Macmillan, 1959.

PATTERSON, B.: A new locality for early Pleistocene fossils in northwestern Kenya. *Nature, 212:*5062, Nov. 5, 1966.

PATTERSON, B., AND HOWELLS, W. W.: A hominid humeral fragment from the early Pleistocene of northwestern Kenya. Unpublished manuscript, 1967.

RENSCH, B.: *Homo Sapiens. Von Tier zum Halbgott.* Gottingen, Vanden-hoeck and Ruprecht, 1959.

SCHWIDETSKY, I.: *Das Menschenbild der Biologie.* Stuttgart, Gustav Fischer Verlag, 1959.

SIMONS, E. L.: Early relatives of man. *Sci Amer, 211*:50-62, July 1964.

SKINNER, B. F.: *Science and Human Behavior.* New York, Free Press, 1953.

STRAUS, W. L., JR.: The riddle of man's ancestry. *Quart Rev Biol, 24*:200-223, Sept. 1949.

TITIEV, M.: *The Science of Man.* New York, Holt, 1963.

WASHBURN, S. L.: Behavior and human evaluation. In Washburn, S. L. (Ed.): *Classification and Human Evolution.* Chicago, Aldine, 1963.

WATTS, A. W.: *The Way of Zen.* New York, New Am. Lib., 1957.

WATTS, A. W.: *Psychotherapy East and West.* New York, New Am. Lib., 1963.

Chapter 3

CRITERIA OF REALITY

"Truth is the whole Universe realizing itself in one aspect."
F. H. BRADLEY, *Essays on Truth and Reality*
"What is and what is not relevant evidence is, of course, a matter of opinion."
B. KEMPLER, *Contemporary Psychology*

THESE DAYS WE ARE apt to analyze, catalog, and diagnose individuals in many different ways—as adaptive, nonadaptive, goal-oriented, poorly or well motivated, normal, neurotic, and characterological or as belonging to one or another cultural adaptation, socioeconomic or ethnic group, and so on. However, seemingly, we frequently ignore in our evaluations something deeper which transcends all of these anthropological, sociological, and psychological labels. This omission involves concepts of "evidence" and "truth," that is, what kinds of criteria of reality a person is willing to accept as his own. Here I am not referring to "reality awareness" in the psychological or pragmatic sense as when a person has "realistic ambitions" in life or when a psychotic, has "broken with reality." Instead, my meaning of reality, is a philosophical one as old as philosophy itself. Often in academic philosophy, "reality" is treated as representing one school of thought or another, or as typical of a given historical period rather than something which requires self-exploration on the part of the student. That kind of academic consideration of reality will not help a student realize that "What is real?" is a cogent personal question, one which demands a personal self-exploratory answer.

VALUES AND THE BEHAVIORAL SCIENCES

Philosophical considerations of what is real lead to the

51

question of what is "valuable" and this, in turn, to a reflection of what is "good." The notion of something being "good" or "bad" in science, has been recognized as dangerous since "goodness" is a value judgment rather than a scientific interpretation. The whole idea of measuring something on a scale of values in which goodness is at one end of a continuum and badness at the other reminds us unpleasantly of those past centuries when morality was thrust upon us without our consent, creating a climate where objective scientific inquiry could not take place. Therefore, it is not surprising that Jarvie (1964), in his examination of whether we can legitimately refer to some societies and cultural adaptations as "better" or "worse" than others, finds such considerations engender forceful opposition. Cultural anthropologists have learned that we are prone to judge other cultures with bias when we apply our own norms of behavior to them.

Yet, an increasing number of scientists are wondering whether or not science is capable of existing in a completely value-free environment devoid of philosophical implications. Margenau, a professor of physics, (with Smith, 1963) writes, ". . .something philosophically noteworthy slips through the net of scientific determination." Although most behavioral and social scientists may wish to remain free of entanglement with values, the question increasingly is being asked, Can this be done?

The idea that science is nonemotional and that, therefore, can lead us by objectivity toward "ultimate truth" is a popular notion. Sanford (1965), in *Psychology, A Scientific Study of Man,* describes it this way:

> Scientific observation is, ideally, observation without evaluation. Science aspires to **objectivity.** The scientist, as such, tries to look at the world as if he had no emotion, no biases, no prejudices. He tries, while at work, to see the world as if it had no goodness or evil, no beauty or ugliness, no joy or sadness. He wants to see objectively, neutrally, what is there.

Later Sanford emphasizes this view by adding "objectivity, as opposed to evaluation is characteristic of the scientific approach to behavior." He sees "evaluation" as "subjective" and he terms it *an enemy of science.*

Opposing this view, Barron (1965) writes,

> The word *Subjective* has frequently been used as a kind of
> dirty word, a diatribe, a "red herring," if you will, to imply a lack
> of scientificity or objectivity. Yet, ironically enough, it is only
> through man's experiencing of the world that he was able to become
> scientific. I propose, therefore, that the natural state of man is
> totally subjective and that his objectivity is an inevitable con-
> sequence of his ability to subjectively experience truth . . . contrary
> to popular and some professional notions, it would be erroneous to
> believe that intellect is necessarily more rational than feelings.[1]

Meredith (1966), a psychologist who began his career in
physics and mathematics, makes the following comments on the
neutrality of science, "The great heresy of science has been its
adoption of impersonal language. For every observation involves
a private world, and science is based on observation." He views
"the pattern of science" as "dominated by the values of the
scientists" and adds, "Too long it (science) masqueraded as
the impersonal voice of Nature, another God issuing commandments. . . . Scientists must restore their own atrophied feelings."

Nevertheless, there is much to be said in favor of rigorous
scientific methods. There, certainly, would be an advantage in
neutrality while investigating human behavior. Perhaps the
problem is not one of what should be but rather of what is and
what can be. Simpson (1966), a zoologist, does not believe
that scientists are capable of avoiding personal commitments
within their scientific activities. He explains,

> Some of those who believe that science is or should be ethically
> neutral have fallen squarely into the naturalistic fallacy by their very
> efforts to avoid it. Insisting that they only describe and not prescribe,
> they deny that any consideration of right or wrong applies to their
> subject matter. Yet, in the social sciences, above all, what is
> described often does have an ethical aspect. From that point of
> view the "objective" scientist runs into some danger of condoning
> what is wrong or rejecting what is right. Or, at least, his attempted
> withholding of judgment may in itself amount to an ethical stand.

---

[1] Note that in these quotations Sanford writes **objectivity** in bold type and
Barron capitalizes and italicizes *Subjective*. Each author places special emphasis
on that word which represents his own personal orientation.

Van den Haag (1959) writes,

> . . . there is one consideration to which not enough attention has
> been paid, and which might lead some to the view that the study
> of social behavior cannot be quite neutral morally. (This is that)
> . . . what is being observed, is not neutral . . . Social scientists have
> accorded but fitful recognition to this fact, perhaps because they
> have vested interest in recognizing it whenever the anticipated effect
> of their activity are beneficial and ignoring it otherwise. . . .

Since subjectivity may always be present in any investigation,
we must identify it as accurately as we can when engaged in
scientific work. Perhaps the best way to recognize the nature of
subjectivity is to view it as constituting a "frame of reference."
Objectivity, also, is a frame of reference but of a different type.

FRAMES OF REFERENCE

Every scientist, no matter how objective he attempts to be,
has a frame of reference within which he operates. He uses
definitions for describing the phenomena which he observes. In
this sense, "something philosophically noteworthy" is present in
every scientific investigation, or any human act, since the
selection of one frame of reference or one definition in preference
to another is, ultimately, a philosophical choice.

The frames of reference which a person adopts are structured
by his criteria of reality, and their selection represents one of
the most fundamental of all human considerations. It may be
that the selection is not, in most cases, one of free choice. For
example, the biological endowments and limitations of a species
constitute a field within which frames of reference evolve. Environmental factors also evolve frames of reference which are
superimposed upon biological ones.

In spite of all differences, people who disagree on any issue
might better understand each other's point of view, if they were
aware of their own individual frames of reference. Erikson
(1964) provides us with an example:

> In northern California I knew an old Shaman woman who
> laughed merrily at my conception of mental disease, and then
> sincerely—to the point of ceremonial tears—told me of her way of
> "sucking" the pains out of her patients. She was convinced of her

ability to cure and to understand as I was of mine. While occupying extreme opposites in the history of American psychiatry, we felt like colleagues. . . . The old Shaman woman and I disagreed about the locus of the emotional sickness, what it "was" and what specific methods would cure it. Yet . . . I knew she dealt with the same forces, and with the same kinds of convictions as I did in my professional nook.

Different theories of the origin, nature, and ultimate fate of the universe exist side by side in the physical sciences such as astronomy and physics. Differences in the physical sciences stem largely from varying concepts of what is acceptable evidence. In contrast to behavioral sciences, in the physical sciences differences in methods and results can more easily be translated into comprehensible universal symbols. This makes communication less ambiguous.

Disagreement between scholars often stems from the fact that without being aware of it, they may be talking about different things. Handy (1964) puts it this way:

At least in part the disagreement between Scriven and White (two disagreeing scientists) may result from their different general orientations. White is interested in discovering regularities in human behavior. . . . Scriven, as is more typical of philosophers, is extremely concerned about logic of scientific inquiry. . . .

Unless scholars are aware that their frames of reference may not coincide, they cannot be as tolerant toward each other as Erikson, the professor of modern psychiatry, and the ancient Indian Shaman who cured mental illness by sucking out the "evil" with her lips.

Hard-Nosed and Soft-Nosed Scientists

In psychology, so-called soft-nosed scientists have devoted much effort to clinical evaluation. They use projective techniques such as the Rorschach inkblot test and find that these methods help them in arriving at diagnostic evaluations of mental patients. On the other hand, a representative of the "hard-nosed" group (Eysenck, 1950) describes the Rorschach as "all speculation and surmise." Hard-nosed psychologists prefer statistical techniques from which objective data can be abstracted. Analogous differences exist in other behavioral sciences (Willey and Phillips, 1958). Scientists who fail to recognize that their difference in outlook may involve criteria of reality cannot expect to resolve their disagreements.

Acceptance of evidence hinges on a personal formulation of what is and what is not "real." Disputes regarding "correct answers" are as futile as a dispute between two persons over correct time when the watch of one is set on eastern standard time and the watch of the other on eastern daylight savings time. Were one mathematician to use base 10 and another base 7 in a mathematical computation, both would admit that each could be "right" within his own computational framework. But some behavioral and social scientists are not as ready to concede a similar point. They have difficulty in admitting that within any given conceptionalization of validity, any construct consistent with this conceptionalization may be reasonable. They fail to understand that one cannot compare results obtained on one philosophical dimension with results on a different one, nor dispute about the soundness of reasoning in such cases.

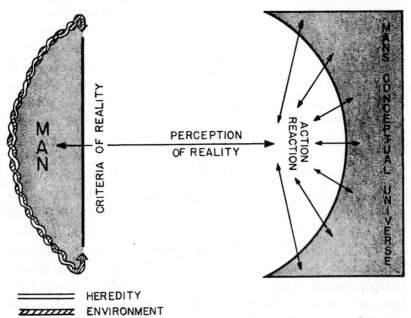

FIGURE 4.   Perception of Reality.

Differences in the use of philosophical frameworks can no more be argued than can the question of tastes, and in regard to the latter the Romans said long ago, *de gustibus non disputantum est.*

FACTORS STRUCTURING REALITY

In a nondisciplinary manner, let us examine a list of factors which may influence the kinds of criteria of reality which human beings are likely to adopt. All of the following may contribute to the adoption of specific frames of references:

1. membership in the human species,
2. membership in a specific culture (including membership both in a national and community group),
3. membership in a social or economic class,
4. membership in an ethnic or racial group,
5. educational level and vocational achievement,
6. membership in a group having a particular political orientation,
7. membership in a group having a specific religious faith,
8. living in a given time era; each time era has its unique socio-historical technological identity. (It has been said, "We are a product of our age."),
9. membership in a given family group, the vicissitudes of which we are likely to share,
10. possession of a unique constitutional makeup which includes our total inherited characteristics, our natural endowments and defects, our genetic biological predispositions,
11. our individual life experiences which consist of an interrelated composite of all of the foregoing factors within the environments to which we are exposed. These environments can be conceived of as constantly bombarding us with stimuli both from within and outside of our bodies.

The factors listed do not have equal weight for each individual, and the weight of any one of them upon the formation of a world outlook differs. For example, in some situations, membership in a particular ethnic group may have no appreciable significance when the group in question is accepted without prejudice by the majority. On the other hand, membership in an ethnic group may have a potent influence when this group is subject to majority prejudices or pressures, or when it controls the majority. Political affiliation in one country may be of relatively little importance whereas in another country it may be crucial. It is not enough to know what specific factors exist. We must pursue the matter further and analyze each situation to see what influences, singly and collectively, are significant in any given case.

VARYING VIEWS OF PERSONALITY AND SELF

The search for "self" is a never ending quest. In a sociological context there are three "selves": the self view which the person holds of himself, the self he believes others see in him, and the self which others really see in him. None of these three views of "self" need be consistent, although maintaining inconsistency between selves utilizes much psychic energy. The concept of the three "selves" illustrates one kind of frame of reference.

Freud's contributions on the nature of the unconscious mind suggest that we may not really know significant aspects of ourselves. We may be absorbed with the need to resolve conflicts between our unconscious drives and our learned habits of right and wrong, which Freud referred to as our *superego*. "Ego defenses" are used to resolve conflicts and their employment causes us to assume a variety of roles.

Another psychological frame of reference is the Pavlovian one, in which conditioning is seen as the central factor influencing behavior. This view, popular in the Soviet Union, has been expanded and modified in the United States of America by Skinner (1938, 1953, 1956) and others.

Adler's ideas of compensation and the Jungean concepts of archetypes and "collective unconscious" represent deviations from Freudian emphasis on sexuality. Among recent attempts to find a framework into which the human personality could fit are the Neo-Freudian typified by Horney (1939); Behavioristic, Wolpe (1958); Ego-Analytical, Rapaport (1959); Gestalt, Perls

(1951); Sullivan (1953); Rank (1945); Existential, May *et al.* (1958); Experimental, Whitaker and Malone (1953).

Student Self-Evaluations

In order to demonstrate how difficult it is to produce a meaningful self-evaluation without any reference point, a number of sample self-evaluations are presented below. Students in hominology were asked to evaluate themselves but were not given any method to use. The students were asked to include any philosophical orientations that would have a bearing on their self-evaluations. The following excerpts are samples of this exercise:

A. I feel that I have been adequately endowed with intelligence and that I have been graced with a very satisfactory environment upon which that basic intelligence could return knowledge. . . . I have learned from experience that little can be counted on from those around us and that it is important not to be too easily influenced by the actions of others but to set our behavior and follow through. But to maintain psychological well-being we should not only look for help from others but try to give help.

B. I expect from myself a democratic approach in the area of human relations. This means that I want to avoid the feeling that I am always right and that I have all the answers. I expect to judge people by their individual merit rather than by their physical appearance or group membership. This is hard for me since I have certain prejudices. I like to consider each person I am talking with as the most important person in the world at that time. From my community and nation, I expect to be whatever is my potential to become without discrimination, even against women. But this may be too much to expect. I hope for peace in the world, but again, I am not so optimistic about this wish.

C. I think that I should involve myself in life—especially mankind. I am beginning to believe more and more that life itself is all that counts. I think that my main purpose is to develop my capacities as fully as I can. This way my own life will become more meaningful. I expect others to accept me as I am or as I will become. . . . I expect my community to provide me with the necessary facilities so that I may function as a person more efficiently. I expect that I should add to these facilities in my own way in order to return the favor. I expect from the nation all of the rights and privileges guaranteed by our constitution and I expect the right to challenge any interpretation of this document. I am obliged to accept the burden of the duties and responsibilities associated with supporting such guarantees. . . . From the world I expect unlimited sources of knowledge, old and new so that I may partake of it to the extent that I am capable. I should return everything to it that I can.

D. A professor once told a class I attended that everyone must have a philosophy of life. Ever since that day I have tried to find my philosophy of life. I knew I had one but the problem was to recognize it and to be able to verbalize it—and this is still the problem today. . . .

E. To start with I have never really thought about what my personal philosophy of life is. But the more I think about it, the more confused I become. Why? This is something I don't know, and I wish I did. I guess, in a way, I am still searching for it. I do know that I want to improve myself in every way to become a better and more mature person. In this way I will be able to step up on the social ladder and demand the respect of my peers and society. In return I will be able to respect others and the society for what they are. We live in a sort of give-and-take world. If someone should offend me I hope that I will have the courage not to strike back but instead to help the person solve his problems. . . .

F. Self-evaluation is not either an easy thing to do or a hard thing to do, but it is something that we do not do. For most of our life is circumscribed from birth to death and there are not enough of us that attempt to break out of this routine. Personally, I like to think that I am born free and that I am free to make my own choices and associations throughout my lifetime within the conventional bounds of society. I do not believe that I am a nonconformist except to the degree that I believe it is up to each individual to make the most of himself. I have little use for the person who claims that he is not a better or more educated person because of race, religion, economic opportunity, or cultural environment.[2]

We notice in these evaluations that there appears to be a display of emotion, good intentions, and admitted "confusion," especially when it comes to expressing a "philosophy of life." However, it can be seen from this experiment that students did not utilize a meaningful framework to aid them in the task of self-evaluation. Most used only one or two aspects of life instead of presenting a comprehensive self-image.

------

[2] After completing Chapter 11, the student should return to these self-descriptions A—F and evaluate them regarding their content of developmental levels and kinds of moral values.

KNOWLEDGE AND VALUE

Fictional accounts, comic books, and mythological descriptions of plants or animals do not increase our factual knowledge since we do not accept these sources as valid criteria of reality. Just as knowledge stems from that which we believe is real, so value is derived from that which we accept as knowledge. If a primitive aborigine who has lived without any contact with civilization were to find a shortwave transistor radio, he might not consider the "box" as having any value. His judgment of value would result from his lack of knowledge of the radio's potential to provide music and entertainment. Were someone to inform him that the radio could provide entertainment without demonstrating it, the aborigine would still place no value on the "box" if he did not believe that this was the truth. Value depends on knowledge which, in turn, depends on a belief that the thing under consideration is true and therefore an acceptable aspect of reality.

Concepts Shape Attitudes

Rune's *Dictionary of Philosophy* (1960) gives several different meaning for the word, *concept*. However, in common usage, *concept* may be defined as a term that applies to any formulated and widely accepted idea of what a thing should be. The word *should* implies a value judgment. Concepts are predicated on values. Our concepts of the role of government, or of ethical behavior, or of a good method of scientific investigation are all based on a formulation of values in the areas in question. Concepts shape attitudes toward specific life areas in our environment. Attitudes are predispositions to actions. In psychology, anthropology, and sociology, manifestations of attitudes and the consequences of their expression are studied. Prejudices, hostility, role playing, anxiety, acculteration or nonacculteration— all are manifestations of attitudes. In hominology we endeavor to trace these to their philosophical roots.

Some Basic Steps to Action

Summarizing what was previously stated, we may visualize

a chain of relationships that lead to action:

1. *criteria of reality*: that which genuinely *exists*, that which is true;
2. *sources of knowledge*: stemming from what we accept as *real* and true;
3. *hierarchy of values*: drawn from our idiosyncratic *knowledge* of that which is important and significant;
4. *formation of concepts*: based on an *evaluation* of that which is known;
5. *adoption of attitudes*: derived from our *conceptual* framework;
6. *personality characteristics*: tendencies, proclivities, symptoms—manifestations of the kinds of *attitudes* we have adopted;
7. *actions*: means of expressing *personality* characteristics;
8. *reactions*: responses (incorporating the foregoing 7 items) to events and stimuli occurring in our internal and external environments;
9. *interactions*: resulting from an exchange of actions and *reactions*;
10. *rapport* and *empathy*: sympathetic identification between people stemming from *interactions*.

CRITERIA OF REALITY

Terms currently used in the study of philosophy have been adopted in this chapter where possible, so that the student can explore further by referring to the literature of philosophy. In philosophy, however, some of the terms used here have several meanings, depending on the writers who used them. In hominology I have attempted to assign only one meaning to the following categories and in doing so, I have given them an emphasis which may not, in every case, be parallel to their use in philosophy. Seven basic assumptions are presented and these will later be referred to as Criteria of Reality.

Authoritarianism

The real sources of knowledge and truth are found within

the writings and sayings of any person in whom we have faith or whom we believe to be speaking the truth. This could include parents, teachers, political or religious leaders, but it also could exclude all or some of these. A child, a roommate, a fellow prisoner in a penitentiary — *anyone* — whose opinions we accept, falls into the category of Authoritarianism for us in a specific situation but may not in another situation. Signs, symbols and traditions may represent people indirectly and, therefore, could be sources of Authoritarianism for us if we accept them and permit them to structure our concepts of reality. The Criteria of Reality are ways that we receive messages from other people and the world around us.

Advantages

Facts and ideas adopted by us from Authoritarian sources are immediately available and applicable. Facts are accepted wholly and uncritically (otherwise different criteria play a role). This uncritical acceptance simplifies the problem of ascertaining reality and enables Authoritarianism to lead directly to action. That is why in time of crises and uncertainty we are apt to turn to Authoritarianism for immediate reality apperception. Also, identifying with an authority becomes a source of strength and enables us to overcome feelings of inferiority.

Disadvantages

There could be no progress, no evolution of thought, no innovations or forward movement of knowledge if everyone would accept criteria of authority in every instance. Another problem inherent in Authoritarianism is the question of *which* of several possibly conflicting sources of authority the believer should accept. Strife and wars have been engendered by followers adhering to different ideologies promulgated by contending authorities. This kind of strife is usually particularly bitter and irresoluble since there can be no appeal to reason. Nevertheless, it is often easier to make the transition from acceptance of one kind of an authority to acceptance of a conflicting one than it is to substitute a criterion of reason or intuition for an authoritarian criterion.

Intuitionism

Intuition, or inner feeling, provides a direct apprehension of truth without reasoning, sense perception, or the existence of any external evidence. When religious feelings are involved, this form of reality is sometimes called mysticism. But this criterion is not confined to religious revelations. Any person may have a deep inner feeling about something which convinces him that it is true, just, right, or real, independent of what he has been told by persons in authority, by what is available to his senses, or by what has been indicated by his experiences. Thus a person may attend a court session and, in spite of the evidence which shows the defendant guilty, he may feel that "deep in my heart, I still believe him to be innocent." We place in this category that which is referred to as "women's intuition" based on no factual data, except perhaps subliminal clues which may be unconsciously organized to produce "intuitive" feeling.

Advantages

As is the case in Authoritarianism, the truth, when revealed from inner sources requires no verification for acceptance. It is, therefore, quickly apperceived and constantly ready for application. A certain amount of inner independence is implied by Intuitionism and there may be a concomitant of creativeness and imaginativeness. Intuitionism may be a basis for intrinsic motivation in contrast to Authoritarianism which provides extrinsic motivation.

Disadvantages

There can be no appeal to reason in Intuitionism. Apperception of what is real and true, when derived from independent inner sources (possibly, but not necessarily, with aid of subliminal clues) has been likened to a mental mutation. Since intuition is independent of observation, it cannot be verified by observation but must rely on faith for its validity. Subjectivism such as this is impervious to criticism and is not easily amenable to modification.

Rationalism

Rationalism is related to Intuitionism but differs in that *reason* rather than emotional apperception of reality is implied. Also, experience of the senses is consciously used in that it forms the source of transmission of information. The *human mind* alone, however, gives this sensory information meaning and significance. Reason is capable of grasping truths and deriving other truths from them by rational procedures and logical demonstrations. Reasons discerns universal laws, the existence of which may not be accessible to sensory experience alone. In one way, Rationalism may be viewed as a combination of Empiricism and Intuitionism, but this view is not entirely correct since intuition stems from the "heart," so to speak, and reason from the "head." Rationalists place their faith on human intellectual capacity to discover, deductively, the true nature of the world. Things are considered as being real when they are intellectually perceived as such. Sensory perception is viewed as a means of transmitting information and considered to be fallible until these sensory impressions have undergone the corrective and integrative process which occurs in the mind. For example, if there were a sound which occurred outside of the human range of hearing, the Rationalist would say that, in reality, there was no sound, since the concept, *"sound,"* becomes real only when it is heard and mentally interpreted as sound. In contrast, Authoritarianism would accept the word of a person in authority who stated that sound existed. An Empiricist would consider sound to be that which has the scientifically defined characteristics of sound whether or not any human being were present to hear it or whether or not anyone in authority declared sound existed.

Advantages

Rationalism places maximum emphasis on the capacity of the human mind to ascertain reality and, therefore, adjustments can be made and opinion can be changed when this is dictated by reason. In view of the fact that the Rationalist recognizes that sensory impressions are ambiguous, he is apt to admit error and to adjust his thinking accordingly using what he may term *common sense*. He tends to be an intellectualist and prizes the human intellect as the only sensible criterion of acceptable knowledge.

Disadvantages

The Rationalist may be prone to the error of "wishful thinking," that is, to find subjective "proof" for something that he wishes were actually true. His research effort, unbeknown to him, may be motivated by an attempt to reinforce an intellectually conceived idea.[3]

Empiricism

That which is true and real and capable of contributing knowledge is manifested through the kind of experience that can be objectively validated. Knowledge is derived from the *senses* and *experience* which, by use of quantifications, serves to arrange sense data into categories which make them intelligible and prediction possible. By using measurement and controlled experiments, the senses and the extension of the senses (i.e. scientific instruments, such as a microscope, a computor, chemical analysis) provide the mind with the only reliable raw material available to human beings. We are empiricistic when we say "seeing is believing" and when we demand a demonstration in order to judge from observation whether or not a phenomenon conforms to claims that have been made about it. In certain situations, most people feel that the truth must be seen to be believed and demand empirical evidence. If a new kind of spot remover has been advertised as "superior," we are apt to reserve judgment until we have tried it out on the coat on which we have spilled ink. Empiricists might repeat the process using different kinds of ink under various conditions. And then they might describe the effectiveness of the spot remover in

------

[3] Students who have been exposed to psychology frequently confuse the Freudian ego-defense, *rationalization*, with the philosophic term, *rationalism*. Hominology students must make a clear distinction between them. Rationalization means unconsciously making excuses for failures, whereas rationalism pertains to a reliance on reason for the establishment of truth.

quantitative terms which others could use in repeating the experiment themselves.

I once asked my students in hominology whether they would believe me if I were to state that I could leap a distance of twenty feet. No hands were raised. I feigned surprise that my students would doubt the word of a professor and protested their lack of faith. In this instance, Authoritarianism did not suffice. I then asked the students what I would have to do to convince them of my ability to make good my claim and they replied, "do it!" "Alright," I said, "assume now that I leaped twenty feet three times right in front of your eyes and that the distance jumped was verified by a tape measure, how many would then believe that I had really accomplished this feat?" Half of the class hesitatingly raised their hands. These were Empiricists. I asked the others why they would not believe their eyes. Some said that they would first have to make certain that there was nothing wrong with the tape measure. These, too, were Empiricists of a more rigorous type. Others said even if they were convinced that the measurements were correct, they still would not believe that I had performed the feat even if I had actually demonstrated it several times. They insisted that if they really had witnessed my twenty foot leap, they would, in fact, be "seeing things" (i.e. witnessing a hallucination) since the idea that I could jump that far did not seem reasonable. Therefore, in spite of the demonstration and my authoritarian position, they would refuse to believe that I could be capable of such an accomplishment since it just did not make "sense" that this was possible. These were, perhaps, the Rationalists, a small minority, in this instance.

Advantages

First and foremost, Empiricism has been historically successful. We are living in an era of empiricistic accomplishments. Empiricism has ushered into our century the scientific method which relies upon observation, experience, testability, verification, and predictability. Empiricism promotes impartiality and objectivity. By a reliance on Empiricism we are least inclined to give a personal direction to research and most likely to avoid unwarranted assumptions. By means of empirical inductive methods of inquiry, scientists have developed a common body of knowledge that is subject to public verification.

Disadvantages

Exclusive reliance on Empiricism tends to separate values and considerations of human good from results either obtained or to be pursued. In the social and behavioral sciences, critics of pure Empiricism claim that it tends to make these sciences descriptive rather than discursive and, consequently, sterile. Under such circumstances, problems may become separated from methods and methods from goals leaving a discontinuity within the investigated situation. Because of its insistence on verification by observation, emphasis may be given to that which is peripheral rather than that which may be central in a given human problem. Attempts to avoid subjectivism may cause Empiricists to fail in coming to grips with essential issues confronting society out of fear that subjectivism may enter into such considerations. They may tend to ignore phenomena which they cannot explain fully by empirical methods.[4]

Inaccessibility of Reality

A lack of action may be thought of as a form of negative action. Likewise, the conviction that genuine reality is inaccessible to human beings because of human limitations, in a negative way, reflects a concept of reality and, therefore, must be included in these criteria. Those who maintain that we really are not capable of knowing the true nature of the world around us, nevertheless, may believe that it is worth our while to act *as if* certain things were true since to do so serves a useful purpose. Under Inaccessibility of Reality, we are actually combining several different philosophical ideas which, however, are similar in respect to the belief that man lacks the capacity to ascertain real knowledge. Within this framework,

---

[4] Recent Empiricists, while maintaining the experimental approach, tend to give a large role to theoretical, mathematical, and conceptual structure as contrasted to simple observation. They mention the tentative, hypothetical, and self-correction character of science.

subjectivism maintains that objects do not exist independently of our consciousness of them. Since the real world exists only in our mind, it would then be constantly subject to distortions. From a different point of view, that which is real is believed by some to exist outside of the range of our sense organs and our power of comprehension. In either case, the practical situation justifies our acting *as if* those things, which further our causes or are beneficial to society, are true and real.

Inaccessibility under this heading pertains to reality as a major concept. It should not be confused with Empiricists' views of the "fictional" aspect of absolute truth, which can be only theoretically described when working inductively with quantitative data. Empiricists never claim that absolute truths are available to anyone. But from a practical point of view, they are convinced that a statistical estimate represents a legitimate concept of truth when it allows for quantitative variations statistically defined and circumscribed.

Advantages

The notion that reality is inaccessible relieves us of the responsibility to search for it and enables us to focus our attention instead on those matters that help us achieve desirable goals. In one sense, it greatly simplifies philosophy and also may contribute to a greater freedom of action since reality is no longer an issue which must be resolved.

Disadvantages

Inaccessibility of Reality leaves us without any anchorage and there is always the question of whether or not the search for reality is being evaded by the denial of its accessibility.

Pragmatism

In its emphasis on that form of action which works out most advantageously, Pragmatism is similar to the *as if* philosophy of the foregoing criterion. However, there is a significant difference in that the Pragmatist believes that reality is accessible and can be manifested by the practical effectiveness of an idea. An idea is thought of as real (and good) if it works beneficially.

Pragmatists may differ in how they interpret practical results of actions. Some view them in terms of their utility, others in terms of human satisfactions. Many Pragmatists would agree with Peirce (1957) that "an idea is not true because it is satisfactory — but it is satisfactory because it is true." There is a fundamental difference between the former and the latter.[5] In general, Pragmatists will test their ideas by the criterion of whether or not they are practical and useful. Most, though not all, Pragmatists will define *useful* as that which contributes to human welfare. Pragmatists have been labelled, *situationists* and *utilitarians,* because they consider reality and truth to be inextricably tied to consequences and results.

Advantages

Pragmatism, in the sense that many use it, would lead to constructive action with a minimum of "culture lag" or stultification due to tradition.

Disadvantages

Pragmatists have been accused of advocating practical expediency and of permitting the end to justify the means.

At times students have had difficulty in differentiating Empiricism from Pragmatism since both criteria seem to be predicated on "successful outcome." Pragmatism implies utilization of personal values in ascertaining what really works best. The Empiricist, on the other hand, requires verifiable evidence and statistical support, considering "real" only that which can be demonstrated by established scientific methods. He avoids entanglements with personal or moral values in his orientation. Instead, he seeks to discover laws and relationships. He is aware of the fact that a lack of neutrality could distort his perception. Pragmatism emphasizes purpose in contrast to Empiricism's emphasis on methodology. The lack of clear-cut differentiation in all of these criteria should be recognized. Pragmatist and Rationalist, both, may utilize empirical methods but do not

---

[5] Peirce distinguished his Pragmatism from the Pragmatism of Schiller, William James, Papini, and others.

depend on sensory verification as a primary source of truth but only as supportive. A goal-oriented Pragmatist may utilize empirical methods as means to an end. To the extent that any individual accepts empirical methods as capable of revealing "truth," they are Empiricists in addition to being Rationalists, or Pragmatists, etc. Later the student's own philosophical commitments in the various criteria will be explored.

Verbal Structuralism

I present this as a separate category since it appears that many persons derive their ideas of reality through their interpretation of the structure of language and speech. Usually, these people are unaware of their use of this source of reality. One kind of truth is manifested through ideas that are expressed consistently with each other. Thus, dogs are animals that bark and have four legs is a true statement since it is consistent with the definition of *dogs.*"

Slogans influence people who clearly see that the statements are obviously correct. Consider the basis of reality in the following advertisement: "Our mouth-watering X brand cookies taste so good! Yummee! They are made by a bakery that knows how to make good cookies. Our bakery is located at 123 Main Street. Come to our shop and give yourself a treat. Your family will love that oh-so good flavor!" Essentially this advertisement says no more than that something which is "mouth-watering" is tasty and this we know by definition to be true. With extensions and modifications, this type of logic inherent in language can cover much ground.

However, this verbal logic represents truth without meaning. An alien idea could be unobtrusively introduced into the verbal equations and gain an aura of truth by associations or implication. Note the fallacy in the following: All husbands are men. Men have strong tempers. Therefore, all husbands have strong tempers. Verbal Structuralism makes the first statement true, but the second statement represents a corruption since strong temper is not part of the essential definition of all men. The conclusion is, therefore, false. This kind of fallacy is not detected by some people and since Verbal Structuralism lends itself to fallacies of this type, this method of revealing "truth" is used by propagandists, advertisers, politicians, or others who wish to manipulate public opinion.

Verbal Structuralism also includes the concept of numerical structuralism in which statistics are applied that can be meaningless and misleading. Graphic structuralism is another aspect that could generally be included within this framework. In each case, truth is derived from equivalency such as when $2+2=4$. In each case, also, these structures can be misleadingly applied as, for example, when a geographical location is described as having a mean annual temperature of a "comfortable 70 degrees." Seventy degrees is, indeed, a comfortable temperature but in this particular case the thermometer typically swings from a usual 110 degrees in summer to below 32 degrees usually in the winter.

This misuse of Verbal Structuralism may be diagrammed as follows:

$$\left. \begin{array}{c} X_{4+y} = X_{5+y} \\ X_1 = X_2 = X_3 = X_4 = X_5 \end{array} \right\} \begin{array}{l} \text{extent of} \\ \text{distortion} \end{array}$$

X_1 represents a statement.

X_2 represents another statement having an identical meaning.

X_3 represents another statement with a meaning identical to the foregoing.

X_4 represents a statement with an identical meaning to X_3.

X_{4+y} represents a statement having a meaning seemingly identical to the others except that an additional element is introduced which changes the meaning slightly.

X_5 represents a statement with identical meaning to X_4.

X_{5+y} represents a statement with identical meaning to X_{4+y}.

X_4 and X_{4+y} appear to be identical but are not. In this case, y represents a subtle artifact which is slipped into the content of the X_4 in camouflaged form.

X_5 and X_{5+y} appear to be identically equated with X_1, X_2, X_3, and X_4 but actually X_{5+y} has led the reader into a new direction and this is a fact of which he may be unaware. This illustrates how truth in Verbal Structuralism can be distorted.

Advantages

Since Verbal Structuralism represents one kind of semantic truth, readily verifiable by definition, it leads to very little argumentation and easily elicits general agreement.

Disadvantages

Verbal Structuralism is devoid of meaning, but is often used as a substitute for genuine thought and exploited by those who use rhetoric and subtle distortion to force their views upon their listeners. Many of us are prone to succumb to this kind of persuasion when a hypnotic quality is used in its presentation.

DISCUSSION OF THE CRITERIA

The Criteria of Reality are subject to the same flaws as other attempts to compartmentalize aspects of human behavior. Traits, types, categories—even if identified by sophisticated factor analytic or electronic computorized methods are difficult to isolate in a "pure" or strictly independent form. In viewing a person's Criteria of Reality we may find that an empirical orientation may have been prompted by an underlying Authoritarianism in which the person in question is following the dictates of his former university professor. Instead of being a devoted Empiricist, he is actually a disguised Authoritarianist in that his Empiricism is secondary to his respect for the authority of the professor who told him to use empirical methods.

When communication difficulties stemming from Criteria of Reality conflicts are fully comprehended, it is often easy to effect compromises by deciding which person is the most deeply entrenched within his framework. Deciding this is not as difficult as it seems. A little reflection may often reveal who is the logical person to make the "sacrifice" of voluntarily entering another's framework for the sake of harmony and "togetherness." An injection of value judgments leading to self-righteousness in regard to one's adoption of one or another Criterion of Reality can, of course, hamper resolution of framework conflicts. Difficulties also occur if a person yields with a feeling of martyrdom. On the other hand, when there is love, awareness, and sincerity, the person who is least deeply committed, in a given case, may knowingly enter the other's framework as a tourist who is willing to live temporarily in another country but is not ready to take out citizenship.

It is possible to be quite diverse in the adoption of the criteria. Thus, we may hold our religious views primarily through Authoritarianism, our scientific outlook largely through Empiricism, our political ideas through Rationalism, and we may handle our own family affairs by utilizing pragmatic guidelines. Even within the same life areas, we usually combine several different criteria into a totality. In solving scientific problems, we might be partially empirical, somewhat rational, a little intuitive, and also, possibly, to an extent unknown to us, a prey to Verbal Structuralism.[6]

OTHER WAYS OF LOOKING AT REALITY

There are many other approaches to problems of reality. Space does not permit even a partial discussion of other possibilities. For example, Herrick (1956) in *The Evolution of Human Nature* poses the question, What is Real? and treats the matter somewhat differently than I did. However, in agreement with the point of view presented in hominology, he affirms that in the study of human behavior "we do need a practical epistomology—an understanding of the theory and practice of knowing." Altizer, Beardslee, and Young (1962) use still another approach in their book, *Truth, Myth, and Symbol,* The various contributors see truth as a "process," a "location of emphasis," and an "opinion" or "judgment." The idea of reality as representing a process is further explained by Huxley (1957), "We have at last discovered that the reality with which we have to deal is a hierarchy of patterned processes."

The conceptions outlined here are suffciently inclusive to lead us to hominological self-evaluation. In the following

------

[6] A somewhat similar approach to the search for reality to mine is presented in *The Encapsulated Man,* J. R. Royce, An Insight Book, D. Van Nostrand, Princeton, 1964. Professor Royce and I developed our approaches independently and it may be of interest to note the similarities and differences in the two psycho-philosophical procedural methods.

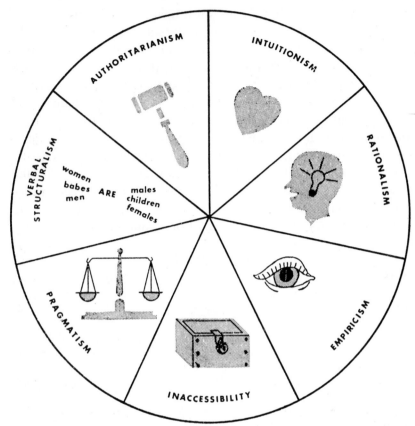

FIGURE 5.   Criteria of Reality.

chapter, the Criteria of Reality enumerated will be matched with specific Life Areas.

In Figure 5, there are seven criteria described in this chapter placed into a circle to indicate that they represent foci within a totality. The symbols used emphasize the nature of each focus.

SUMMARY

We are living in an age of evaluation. Simple descriptions as good, bad, large, small, no longer suffice for today's complicated world. The behavioral and social sciences have devised scales, categories, and type-groups which are intended to classify human beings. Some of the behavioral sciences have gone to great lengths, refining again and again their techniques of placing persons in a variety of different pigeonholes. In the scramble to categorize people, a fundamental classification is usually overlooked. This is the one that deals with how a person regards that which he accepts as real, that which he interprets as true, that which he acknowledges as valuable. Samples of students self-evaluations reveal that it is difficult to make these meaningful without guidelines. In hominology, the Criteria of Reality which human beings employ are explored. Seven such criteria were described as follows: Authoritarianism (believing), Intuitionism (feeling), Rationalism (reason), Empiricism (observation), Inaccessibility of Reality (human limitations), Pragmatism (utility), Verbal Structuralism (conditioning).

REFERENCES

ALTIZER, T. J. J.; BEARDSLEE, W. A., AND YOUNG, J. H. (Eds.): *Truth, Myth. and Symbol.* Englewood Cliffs, Prentice-Hall, 1962.

BARRON, J.: The voices of man. Voices. *The Art and Science of Psychotherapy, 1*:1, Fall 1965.

ERIKSON, E. H.: *Insight and Responsibility.* New York, Norton, 1964.

EYSENCK, H. J.: Function and training of the clinical psychologist. *J Ment Sci, 96*:710-725, 1950.

HANDY, R.: *Methodology of the Behavioral Sciences.* Springfield, Thomas, 1964.

HERRICK, C. J.: *The Evolution of Human Nature.* Austin, U. of Tex., 1956.

HORNEY, K.: *New Ways in Psychoanalysis.* New York, Norton, 1939.

HUXLEY. J.: *Knowledge, Morality, and Destiny.* New York, New Am. Lib., 1957.

KATZ, D.: The functional approach to the study of attitudes. *Public Opinion Quarterly, 24*, Summer 1960.

JARVIE, I. C.: *The Revolution in Anthropology.* New York, Humanities, 1964.

MARGENAU, H., AND SMITH, J. E.: Philosophy of physical science in the twentieth century. In Metraux, G. S., and Crouzet, F. (Eds.): *The Evolution of Science.* New York, New Am. Lib., 1963.

MAY, R.; ANGLE, E., AND ELLENBERGER, H. F. (Eds.): *Existence: A New Dimension in Psychiatry and Psychology.* New York, Basic Books, 1958.

MEREDITH, P.: *Instruments of Communication.* London, Pergamon, 1966.

PEIRCE, C. S.: *Essays in the Philosophy of Science.* New York, Liberal Arts, 1957.

PERLS, F. S., et al.: *Gestalt Therapy: Excitement and Growth in the Human Personality.* New York, Messner, 1951.

RAPAPORT, D.: The structure of psychoanalytic theory: a systematizing attempt. In Koch, S. (Ed.): *A Study of Science*. New York, McGraw, 1959, vol. 3.

RANK, O.: *Will Therapy and Truth and Reality*. New York, Knopf, 1945.

RUNES, D. D.: *Dictionary of Philosophy*. 15th ed., New York, Philosophical Lib., 1960.

SANFORD, F. H. (Ed.): *Psychology, A Scientific Study of Man*. Belmont, Wadsworth, 1965.

SIMPSON, G. G.: Naturalistic ethics and the social sciences. *Amer Psychol*, 21:27-36, Jan. 1966.

SKINNER, B. F.: *The Behavior of Organisms: An Experimental Analysis*. New York, Appleton, 1938.

SKINNER, B. F.: *Science and Human Behavior*. New York, Macmillan, 1953.

SKINNER, B. F.: A case history of the scientific method. *Amer Psychol*, 11:221-233, 1956.

SULLIVAN, H. S.: *The Interpersonal Theory of Psychiatry*. New York, Norton, 1953.

VAN DEN HAAG, E.: Man as an object of science. *Science, 129*:243-247, Jan. 30, 1959.

WILLEY, G. R., AND PHILLIPS, P.: *Methods and Theory in American Archeology*. Chicago, U. of Chicago, 1958.

WHITAKER, C. A., AND MALONE, T. P.: *Roots of Psychotherapy*. New York, McGraw, 1953.

WOLPE, J.: *Psychotherapy by Reciprocal Inhibition*. Stanford, Stanford U. P., 1958.

Chapter 4

CONSIDERATIONS IN SELF-EVALUATION

"You may have all the degrees in the world, but if you do not
know yourself, you are a most stupid person."

J. KRISHNAMURTI,
Indian philosopher and author

SELF-EVALUATIONS ARE best considered as educated guesses
which attempt to gain new perspectives and additional understanding. The results of self-evaluations are not factual. Recognition that one never before may have attempted to search for
a self-concept often represents a first constructive step in the
direction of self-appraisal. We must agree with Skinner's (1953)
succinct statement "One of the most striking facts about self-
knowledge is that it may be lacking."

This sentiment is echoed by Menninger (1951) who asks,

> But how much do people actually know about themselves?
> Usually they have some idea about their physical anatomy—the way
> their body is made and the way the parts operate. But when it
> comes to the how and why of their feelings, actions, thoughts, and
> beliefs, they rather vaguely attribute these to their "personality"
> and let it go at that.

G. G. Simpson (1966) points out that our factual knowledge is
increasing and he mentions the "knowledge explosion." But
he finds that a large number of unrelated facts does not add
up to a coherent and meaningful image of Man or of self.

One of the problems of self-evaluation stems from the fact
that the self-concept represents a relationship between self and
someone or something beyond self. The word, *image,* as used
in self-image, is well chosen since our self-concepts are largely
mirrored reflections of the outside world. The circularity of
self-knowing is illustrated by the fact that these concepts of

78

the outside world are, in turn, reflections of self-views projected outward. Most of us would agree that even in this day of increased knowledge and improved techniques of human assessment, true self-understanding is achieved by very few people.

There are many ways in which the problem of self-evaluation could be approached. Among these are introspection, comparing self with others, obtaining other people's opinion of self, listing personal assets and liabilities, getting insight into personality dynamics by using the results of psychological tests, or by case studies, psychiatric interviews, and so on.

Within the past few years, a series of new techniques involving group interaction have been developed which are also helpful in gaining self-understanding, among these are group therapy, psychodrama, and sociometry. They are finding increased application in mental hygiene centers, industry, and in institutional settings. The use of self-rating scales has become popular in the last decade. Since this chapter will introduce considerations that are later used in a self-rating scale, we shall review some of the types of scales which are in current use today.

Self-Insight Scales are those in which the subject is asked to evaluate his understanding of his motives. The amount of insight a person possesses is measured by the degree of "realism" he demonstrates in making excuses for failures.

Self-Rating Scales require the person to rate specific personality characteristics he possesses such as irritability, practicality, punctuality, cooperativeness, ambitiousness, nervousness, submissiveness, or impulsiveness. The Tennessee Self-Concept Scale (Fitts, 1965) demonstrates the questionnaire or inventory approach to self-evaluation. The subject is asked to respond to such statements as the following: "I am neither too fat nor too thin;" "I am just nice as I should be;" "I change my mind a lot;" "I find it hard to talk with strangers." In *Individual in Society,* Kretch *et al.* (1962) offer a scale adapted from an earlier study by Nunnally, in which two hundred subjects rated themselves against a concept "neurotic man" and "old man" on the following characteristics presented as a continuum: bad-good; dirty-clean; insincere-sincere; foolish-wise; sad-happy; tense-relaxed; weak-strong; worthless-valuable; passive-active; dangerous-safe; etc. It is interesting to note that in 14 out of 17 traits, the test subjects rated themselves as superior to both "neurotic man" and "old man."

Some investigators have abtained discrepancy scores by requiring test subjects to make double or triple ratings. In contrast to the flattering picture which often emerges when subjects rate themselves against "lesser" groups, the reverse occurrs when an "ideal" self is contrasted with the "real" self. An interesting example of this is seen in MacKinnon's (1963) study of architects. These subjects were asked to select descriptions of themselves as they presently were and as they wished they actually were. Adjectives with a 30 per cent or larger discrepancy between the real self and the wished-for self included the following: charming, good-looking, confident, courageous, strong, and mature. The real selves and the ideal selves came closest in regard to these adjectives: masculine, adventurous, optimistic, sympathetic, and affectionate.

DIFFERENT DISCIPLINES OFFER DIFFERENT VIEWS OF "SELF"

Psychology has made a contribution to self-evaluation by proposing traits and refining these by factor analysis. The mental health sciences have developed insight concepts and psychoanalysis as a means of achieving self-understanding. In this process, the role of the unconscious mind is emphasized. Sociology has contributed the concept of "the social self," (Cooley, 1961). Mead (1961), an anthropologist, explores the topic in *Internalized Others and the Self* by drawing upon the development of self-concepts among children and primitive peoples. Erikson (1964), a psychiatrist, discusses conflicts in the self-concepts of modern man, calling these "the uprootedness in our time."

Clinical psychologists evaluate their test subjects by using a variety of objective and projective techniques. The objective measures usually consist of questions or statements and are sometimes referred to as *actuarial methods*. In such inventories, the test subject often is required to reply to questions that must be answered by "no" "yes" or "don't know." Paper and pencil inventories, despite objections (Butcher and Tellegen, 1966), are popular because they yield convenient personality profiles and scores which can easily be statistically treated and analyzed.

Projective tests are believed to probe into the personality without being as direct and obvious as personality inventories. Some psychologists feel that projective techniques are not capable of demonstrating sufficient statistical validity whereas others who have used projective tests successfully are of the opinion that modern statistics are not yet sufficiently mature to handle such complex phenomena as the validity of projective tests.

In personality evaluation utilizing projective tests, materials such as inkblots of various shapes and colors, drawings, photographs, and a variety of structured and unstructured objects are used. All these require a standardized administration and a prescribed method of scoring and evaluation. The test materials are believed to elicit projections of feelings which may not be readily admitted by the subject in an interview. Kahn and Giffen (1960) suggest that there may be another force which accounts for the effectiveness of projection—"patient push"—the inner pressure on the part of the test subject to express his feelings.

In *Tests in Print,* Buros (1961) lists 2126 tests and techniques designed to elicit information regarding some aspect of human behavior, aptitude, or knowledge. This huge number represents only those tests available in the English language. In one form or another, the average American will be formally evaluated by dozens if not hundreds of tests and inventories in the course of a lifetime. The question is, Does all this effort lead to a significant increase in self-understanding?

Any answer must take into account the fact that there are several different kinds of self-knowledge. For example, there is vocational self-knowledge derived from vocational and educatonal aptitude tests, job descriptions, and from on-the-job observation. Some writers believe job effectiveness cannot be taken out of context of the total person and insist that self-evaluation cannot be departmentalized. For example, R. H. Simpson (1966) in *Teacher Self-evaluation* writes,

> . . . the understanding of self is possibly the most crucial of all understandings. . . . The behavior of a teacher like that of everyone else is a function of his concept of self. Success in this area can be improved by examining and re-examining certain important issues the teacher may appropriately raise with himself.

Simpson procedes to mention issues wherein self-evaluation should take place. Among these are the following questions:

> Do I perceive my success as being closely tied up with the success of others? More specifically, do I see my professional success as being largely determined by the success of pupils with whom I work?
>
> Do I perceive of myself as a person who not only tolerates diversity of point of view and procedure but even welcomes it?
>
> Do I see myself as a person able to discuss my own personal and emotional difficulties? Do I accept and even seek criticism as a part of my personal and professional development?
>
> Does the personality I have developed encourage a love of learning?

Helpful as answers to such questions are, in such attempts a person's basic values are touched upon incidentally and only indirectly. In a recent *Yearbook* of the Association for Supervison and Curriculum Development (Combs, 1962), the following viewpoint is expressed:

> Conceptions of self are not cold hard facts. They are deep personal meanings, beliefs, values, attitudes, and feelings about one's self. These are not the traditional curricula of the schools. Indeed, in many places there exists a feeling that these are spineless matters. If, however, the nature and development of the self are as important as our invited authors imply, we shall have to do far more with meanings and values than we have heretofore.

A LIFE AREA FRAMEWORK

Self-evaluation incorporating meanings and values requires a framework within which one can assess relationships and interactions. Hominology utilizes the Criteria of Reality referred to in the previous chapter as its framework for self-evaluation. However, in self-evaluation, those criteria cannot stand by themselves. The different kinds of truths with which these criteria are concerned must be applied to the essential Life Areas within which a person functions; these are Religion, Ethics, Material Goods, Science, Arts, Government, Other People, and Self.

The Interaction Complex

Human life represents an intricate interaction complex which may be viewed as having four critical points: Genetic Endowment, Criteria of Reality, Life Areas, and Learning. These are related to each other developmentally by steps comprising a circular periphery around an inner core of needs (see Fig. 6).

There is continual interaction between all elements of the

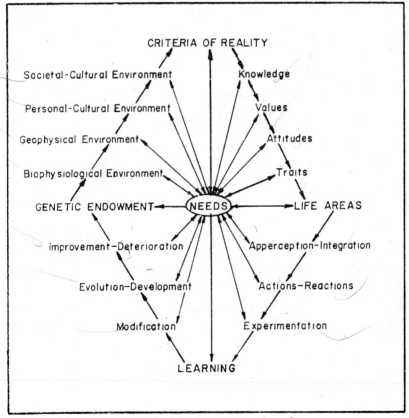

FIGURE 6.   The Interaction Complex.

continuum. After conception, the fetus enters a Biophysiological Environment and at birth, a second one—the Geophysical Environment—is superimposed upon the first. The Biophysiological consists of the biological aspects of life while the Geophysical one deals with the earth's natural phenomena. The infant's immediate family provides his Personal-Cultural Environment, which is evolved as he discovers and accepts the world of culture and people. This environment is superimposed upon the other two. The Societal-Cultural Environment represents the larger outside world to which an individual is exposed when he leaves home. Genetic Endowment mediated through these four environments creates the Criteria of Reality which a person adopts. In Figure 6, we note that knowledge stems from acceptance of Reality Criteria, and most values are derived from sources of knowledge, attitudes are rooted in values, traits reflect attitudes and all are directed at the Life Areas which comprise the apperceptive world.

When values, attitudes, and traits are imposed upon the Life Areas, an integration of stimuli within these areas takes place. This integration involves glandular, neurophysiological and cognitive processes which combine to prepare the individual for action. The feedback provided by reactions tends to encourage experimentation in order to maximize desirable and minimize undesirable effects. The reward-punishment aspect of the reactions represents a primary impetus of learning and adaptation.

Learning utilizes life experience as a perceptual control for giving modification its direction. Learning is a restructuring of precepts leading to modification. Modification causes social and cultural change (Evolution—Development in Fig. 6). On a biological level, modification occurs by a different route through gene mutations. Biological and cultural evolution may represent improvement or deterioration for the species or a cultural group. The definition of *improvement* rests on subjective judgment but we might call improvement that which leads to better adaptation, i.e., that which furthers the welfare of the group or species.

Biological modifications are reflected directly in the genetic endowment of the next generation. Cultural modification bypasses Genetic Endowment but continues along the same path shown in Figure 6 manifesting itself as the Personal-Cultural Environment which the neonate enters upon birth.

Life never returns to any point it has traveled in the past. But as Figure 6 suggests, there is a circularity which is spiral in nature. Everything that occurs in the present, influences the future. It is within the Life Areas that changes eventually are manifested as mankind evolves through time. In hominology, it is postulated that it is within the Life Areas that self-evaluation takes place.

Description of Life Areas

Religion

Where should religious ideas come from? "From God and

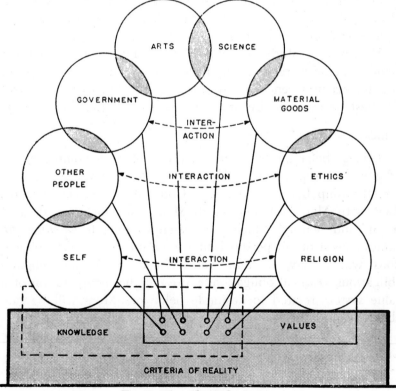

FIGURE 7. The Life Areas.

the Bible," most people in the Judeo-Christian world would reply. "As interpreted by the Church," others might add. Some would deny these premises. Religion may be accepted on the basis of Authoritarianism, Pragmatism, or Rationalism as described by Huxley (1958). Obviously, there are many different ways men may look at religion.

Religion is defined (Webster, 1963) as "1) The service and worship of God or the supernatural; commitment or devotion to a religious faith or observance; 2) a personal set or institutionalized system of religious attitudes, beliefs, and practices."[1]

There seems to be a strong tendency within the nature of Man to develop some form of religion or a religous substitute. These substitutes which we may call *religious equivalents* can be observed in every atheistic society. Because religion is based on faith and is a controversial subject, scientists have, as a rule, ignored its existence. They have adopted the attitude that religion and science do not mix.

However, a study of total Man is not complete without taking religion or religious equivalents into account. The nature of religious preferences or an absence of religious involvement can best be explored by probing a person's Criteria of Reality.

Ethics

Ethical behavior is often conceived of as a component of religion but represents a different emphasis. Religion fosters a relationship between Man and God whereas ethics concerns itself with Man's relationship to Man. This includes ideas of "right" and "wrong" which psychoanalysts refer to as *superego*. Ethics consist of our personal interpretation of our moral obligations which may, or may not, coincide with our religious obligations. Ethical obligations represent the incorporation of a value system related to desirable behavior. More will be said about this in later chapters.

Ethical values may represent components from any of the Criteria of Reality. Though ethical values are culturally trans-

---

[1] Only partial dictionary definitions have been used as applicable to the text.

mitted, they may be personality interpreted, adopted, or rejected. When an individual's ethics and those of his society are in conflict, it may result in serious disruptions of his personal well-being. It is also possible to have a gap between what is ethically professed and what is, in fact, ethically practiced.[2]

Ethics is defined (Webster, 1963) as "1) The discipline dealing with what is good and bad, moral duty and obligation; 2) a set of moral principles or values, the principles of conduct governing an individual or a group."

The utilization of material goods such as personal possessions, wealth, and power and prestige derived from ownership are subject to ethical considerations.

Material Goods

Material goods are those possessions which are either man-made or man-owned and which have a real or a symbolic value within the society in which they exist. In varying cultures and at different times these could include slaves, land, money, cattle, houses, jewelry, wives, objects of art, and everything else which could be placed under the general heading of wealth. This includes wealth as it is conceived of in a modern society, i.e. financial income which can be utilized to purchase material goods. In a manufacturing economy, wealth has three components: utility, power, and prestige. The concept of Material Goods includes services rendered which are paid for by money or its equivalent as well as rank or position which the possession of material goods create.

The utility of an object may be judged by the extent to which that object frees one from effort which would have to be expended in order to accomplish goals or satisfy needs. It is a characteristic of utility that it enables one to accomplish one's purpose faster and with less effort. A jet aircraft will take a traveler from place to place and so will walking. However,

---

[2] Ethics is viewed as one of the most important considerations within hominology. At this preparatory stage of the study it is best if the student uses the term as he presently understands it. Later, after reading Chapter 12 he may, or may not, wish to modify his concept of ethics and moral values. NOTE: Ethics, moral values, and morality are used synonymously in this text.

the aircraft will do this with fantastically increased speed and in greater comfort and, therefore, it represents an aspect of wealth. An automobile enables us to do more traveling, a tractor to do more plowing, a vacuum cleaner to do more effective housework. Theoretically, the utility of an object enables people to have more free time, greater freedom of choice, and new kinds of goals. However, on a practical level, this is not always true. The new goals may require a proportionate investment of time, effort, and a narrower concentration of thought.

The culturally induced need for specific types of achievement may serve to limit freedom of action. Luxuries have a tendency to be viewed as necessities by a following generation. This applies to television sets, refrigerators, and TV dinners, as it does to the wheel, pottery, and the bow and arrow.

In summary, material goods enable us to do more things, do them faster, frees us from preoccupation with biological needs, and substitutes a focus on psychological needs.

Science

Webster's Dictionary (1963) defines science as

1 a: possession of knowledge as distinguished from ignorance, or misunderstanding; b: knowledge attained through study and practice; 2 a: a department of systematized knowledge as an object of study, b: something that might be studied or learned like systematized knowledge, c: one of the natural sciences; 3: knowledge covering general truths or the operation of general laws especially as obtained and tested through the scientific method; 4: a system or method based or purporting to be based upon scientific principles.

For our purpose, the term, *science*, encompasses the concepts of phenomena studied in the physical and biological world. It includes the techniques and methodology employed in this study and represents that part of our apperceptive universe in which the scientific method is used for perceiving and exploiting natural laws. Chapter 6 describes the scientific method.

Snow (1964) points out two motives for science:

The scientific process has two motives: one is to understand the natural world, the other to control it. Either of these motives may be dominant in any individual scientist; fields of science may draw their original impulses from one another. Cosmogony for example—the study and the origin and nature of the cosmos—is a pretty pure example of the first class. Medicine is the type of specimen of the second.

Snow describes the practical problems of applied science and those of the "pure sciences" which attempt to understand rather than to change the universe. He points out that one usually leads to the other.

The concept "science" is difficult because it is constantly changing. Bronowski (1967), in *The Second Scientific Revolution,* describes a new view of science which is unfamiliar to many of today's behavioral scientists.

Consumer products produced by the use of the scientific method are outside of the realm of Science as used here, if these are viewed within a possession-value context. When an object created by science assumes monetary or status value, it becomes part of the content area of Material Goods. Science retains the methodology of its creation not the object itself.

Arts

The concept of the Life Area, Arts, stems from the definition by Webster (1963), "the conscious use of skill, taste, and creative imagination in the production of aesthetic objects; *also*: works so produced." Arts may be conceived of as man-made beauty. It is the nature of this beauty which is, to a certain extent, controversial and subject to a variety of Criteria of Reality.

The techniques used in creating artistic works are dependent on scientific technology—the paint brust, the pen, the development of language, the means of cutting and inscribing stone. Art does not flourish among peoples with empty stomachs and the acquisition of food requires a technology which is the product of scientific effort.

We shall confine our concept of Art to the five main areas of aesthetics—the written word in prose or poetry, the graphic arts as seen in paintings and drawings, the plastic arts as three dimensional designs, the arts of sound as in music, and the art of action such as the dance and theatre arts.

The utility of art is not considered in this context. It is known that art, among primitive people, in many instances, served as religious expression. When art is conceived of as a means to an end or as having utilitarian value, it is not classified within the Life Area, Arts. Utilitarian objects of art or artistic endeavors having monetary or status value should be considered within the category of Material Goods.

Both arts and science obtain their impetus and reach fulfilment when the political climate, created by the government in which the scientist and artist live, is favorable to their development. The Life Area, Government, is our next consideration.

Government

The dictionary definition of *government* serves our need for a description of what is involved in this Life Area. Webster (1963) defines it as follows:

> . . . the act or process of governing; specifically, authoritative direction and control . . . the office, authority, or function of governing . . . the continuous exercise of authority over and the performance of functions for a political unit . . . the ministration of policy decisions, the organization, machinery or agency through which a political unit exercises authority, performs, functions . . . usually classified according to the distribution of power within it . . . the complex of political institutions, laws, and customs through which the function of government is carried out . . . the body of persons that constitutes the governing authority . . . a political unit or organization. . . .

The Life Area, Government, includes considerations such as What should the foundations of proper and fair government be? and How should laws be made and who should make them?

There is an inevitable overlap between laws and "right conduct" as perceived of in Ethics. It should be remembered that the Life Areas are not discrete entities but interdependent and overlapping parts of one indivisible global Life Area. Nevertheless, by using focal points, it is possible to differentiate between them and to utilize the parts for our purpose of self-analysis. The focus of ethics is usually on the individual and on what is "right." The focus of government is on a group and on what is effective as well as what is "right."

We cannot conceive of government without the concept of people being governed. Without people there would be no function for government and no policy for it to pursue. The

Life Area which follows Government is therefore, *Other People.*

Other People

Actions and reactions towards other people are outgrowths of a self-concept. One of the key factors in a relationship to other people is the degree of self-investment which one is capable of having in others. If one sees oneself as part of "you" and "they," an all important identification has taken place. This may be positive—one recognizes in others that which is self-acceptable—or it may be negative—one projects onto others that which is unacceptable within oneself. A surfeit of negative identification leads to poor interpersonal relationships.

Interpersonal relationship has been described as the crux of mental health and the key to the inner meaning of Life. The context in which we shall view Other People represents a generalization of our personal opinion of the role that other people play in our lives. For this purpose we must view "other people" as "humanity" instead of thinking only of specific individuals.

It may help in generalizing "other people" to let them represent individuals with whom one will interact in the future. How would "other people" be conceived of if one had only a minimal amount of information about them?

The concept, "other people," leads obviously to Self. Individuals are "others" only because they exist outside of what is conceived of as Self.

Self

Webster (1963) defines *self* as "an individual's typical or temporary character or behavior; a person in his normal. . . condition. . .the union of elements. . .that constitute the individuality and identity of a person."

So much has been written about the self, self-concept, and merging of self with environment, that we must delineate our ideas of what we mean. For our purpose, Self refers to that part of us that is known and recognized as existing or being. More specifically, it answers the question, What are the criteria we utilize when we form opinions about our self-worth and our self-role? We must be aware that in one sense all of the Life Areas represent a reflection of self and, inversely, the self mirrors our apperception of these same Life Areas. The interdependency between self and environment is so complex that disentanglement is difficult and may not be valid. For our purpose, it may be helpful to ask, What feelings, emotions, and associations come to mind when one thinks of oneself as a person? What are the possible sources (within the Criteria of Reality) of these feelings, emotions, and associations?

Questions and Answers

As part of the program of the Second Institute in Human Understanding (Southern Colorado State College, 1967), paricipants studied the Criteria of Reality and the Life Areas. The following are some of the questions raised and their answers:

Q. How does education fit into the concept of the Life Areas?

A. Education is the process of becoming knowledgeable and competent in coping with the Life Areas.

Q. Where do social classes, socioeconomic groupings, fit in?

A. They are a function of Material Goods, Government, Ethics, and Other People.

Q. How would the economy of a nation be classified?

A. The economy is a function of Material Goods, Government, and Ethics.

Q. How would something like "philosophy" be classified within the framework of the Criteria of Reality and Life Areas?

A. Philosophy in the context of this study centers on the selection of the Criteria of Reality.

Q. What about emotions, anger, feelings, happiness, etc. within this general scheme?

A. We do not attempt to account for everything important by Reality Criteria—Life Areas pairing. However, positive emotions such as happiness, love, etc. accompany a compatibility between adopted Criteria of Reality and conceptions within the Life Areas. Negative emotions are aroused when a person is unable to find his adopted values within the Life Areas available to him.

SUMMARY

A variety of ways in which self-knowledge may be sought were reviewed. Among these were the use of Self-Insight Scales, Self-Rating Scales, Projective Tests, and Self-Evaluations. The following Life Areas were described as symbolic territories wherein human self-appraisal may take place: Religion, Ethics, Materials Goods, Science, Arts, Government, Other People, and Self. The interrelationship between these Life Areas was described in detail.

REFERENCES

BRONOWSKI, J.: The second scientific revolution. In Ware, C. F.; Romein, J. M., and Panikkar, S. K. M.: *History of Mankind.* London, G. Allen and Unwin, 1967, vol. 6.

BUROS, O. K.: *Tests in Print.* Highland Park, Gryphon, 1961.

BUTCHER, J. N., AND TELLEGEN, A.: Objections to MMPI items. *J Consult Psychol, 30:*527-534, Dec. 1966.

COMBS, A. W.: A perceptual view of the adequate personality. In *Perceiving Behaving, Becoming, A New Focus For Education. Yearbook 1962.* Washington, Association for Supervision and Curriculum Development, National Education Association, 1962.

COOLEY, C. H.: The social self. In Parsons, T.; Shilis, E.; Naegele, K. D., and Pitts, J. R. (Eds.): *Theories of Society.* New York, Macmillan, 1961, vol. 2.

DIGGORY, J. C.: *Self-Evaluation: Concepts and Studies.* New York, Wiley, 1966.

DiRENZO, G. J.: *Concepts, Theory, and Explanation in the Behavioral Sciences.* New York, Random, 1966.

ERIKSON, E. H.: *Insight and Responsibility.* New York, Norton, 1964.

FITTS, W. H.: *Tennessee (Department of Mental Health) Self Concept Scale.* Nashville, Counselor Recordings and Tests, 1965.

HUXLEY, J.: *Religion Without Revelation.* New York, New Am. Lib., 1958.

KAHN, T. C., AND GIFFEN, M. B.: *Psychological Techniques in Diagnosis and Evaluation.* New York, Pergamon, 1960.

KRETCH, D.; CRUTCHFIELD, R. S., AND BALLACHEY, E. L.: *Individual in Society.* New York, McGraw, 1962.

MacKINNON, D. W.: Creativity and images of the self. In White, W. R. (Ed.): *The Study of Lives (Essays on Personality in Honor of Henry A. Murray).* New York, Atherton, 1963.

MEAD, G. H.: Internalized others and the self. In Parsons, T.; Shils, E.; Naegeles, K. D., and Pitts, J. R. (Eds.): *Theories of Society.* New York, Macmillan, 1961, vol. 2.

MENNINGER, W. C.: *Self-understanding, a First Step to Understanding*

Children. Chicago, Better Living Booklet, Science Research Associates, 1951.

SIMPSON, G. G.: Naturalistic ethics and the social sciences. *Amer Psychol, 21*:27-36, Jan. 1966.

SIMPSON, R. H.: *Teacher Self-evaluation*. New York, Macmillan, 1966.

SKINNER, B. F.: *Science and Human Behavior*. New York, Macmillan, 1953.

SNOW, C. P.: *The Two Cultures: And A Second Look*. New York, Cambridge U. P., 1964.

WEBSTER, N.: *Seventh New Collegiate Dictionary*. Springfield, Merriam, 1963.

Chapter 5

PSYCHO-SOCIO-PHILOSOPHICAL FRAMEWORKS

"Our moral and political thinking lacks any sort of conceptual framework of its own. Even in fields which we dignify with scientific sounding names—sociology, social psychology, social dynamics—there is no conceptual basis . . . to implement deeper analysis. . . ."

S. K. LANGER,
Philosophy in a New Key

HAVING EXPLORED THE Criteria of Reality and the Life Areas, we are now ready to construct a *hominologram* in order to graphically represent the relationship of these variables. This relationship is hypothetical and has no statistical validity. Considerations of how to objectify hominolograms are discussed later in this chapter.

HOW TO CONSTRUCT A HOMINOLOGRAM

A hominologram may be either a histogram or a line graph. A line graph indicates continuity of a distribution whereas a histogram tends to emphasize distinction between intervals. Construction of the hominologram is facilitated by using paper which has ruled lines. Two coordinate axes are drawn at right angles to each other in order to relate Criteria of Reality to Life Areas. Under each one of the Life Areas, in rough estimates of per cent, the subjective evaluation of the extent of the use of the several Criteria of Reality is plotted.

Life Areas	Criteria of Reality
Religion	Authoritarianism
Ethics	Intuitionism

Material Goods	Rationalism
Science	Empiricism
Arts	Inaccessibility of Reality
Government	Pragmatism
Other People	Verbal Structuralism
Self	

In Figure 8, Hominologram I.a. represents the extent Authoritarianism is used in the Life Areas of an individual *as he, himself, sees it.*

The person who drew Hominologram I.a. indicated that authoritarian figures (parents, ministers, teachers, books, etc.) influenced approximately 75 per cent of his religious ideas, 40 per cent ethical concepts, about 50 per cent of his attitudes

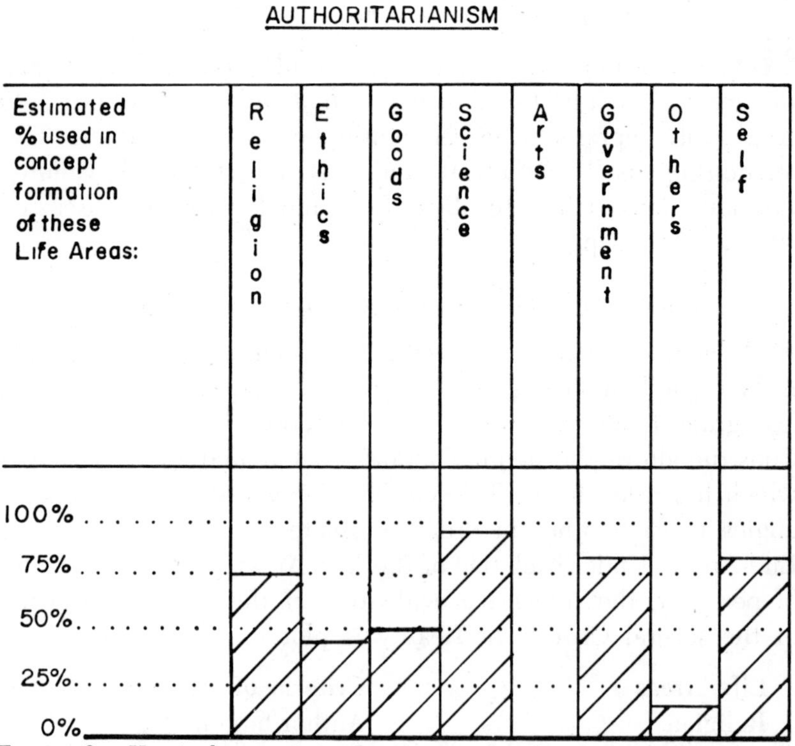

AUTHORITARIANISM

FIGURE 8.   Hominologram I.a. The Estimated Role of Authoritarianism in the Life Areas.

toward material goods, 90 per cent of his concepts on science, and played no role in his evaluation of the arts. Authoritarian sources (his family tradition in this instance) determined approximately 80 per cent of his views on government but had a negligible influence on his acceptance of other people. About 80 per cent of his impression of self came from feedback from his peer group, which, in his case, formed still another source of authority.

The same person who rated himself on Authoritarianism continued the self-rating with Intuitionism. Twenty-five per cent of his religion was attributed to this criterion. Since he had judged 75 per cent of his religion as based on Authoritarianism, which adds up to 100 per cent, he could not logically go beyond this point. Therefore, all of the other Criteria would normally have been rated as 0 per cent in the derivation of his religious views. Ethics totaled approximately 65 per cent. (About 40 per cent from Authoritarianism plus 25 per cent from In-

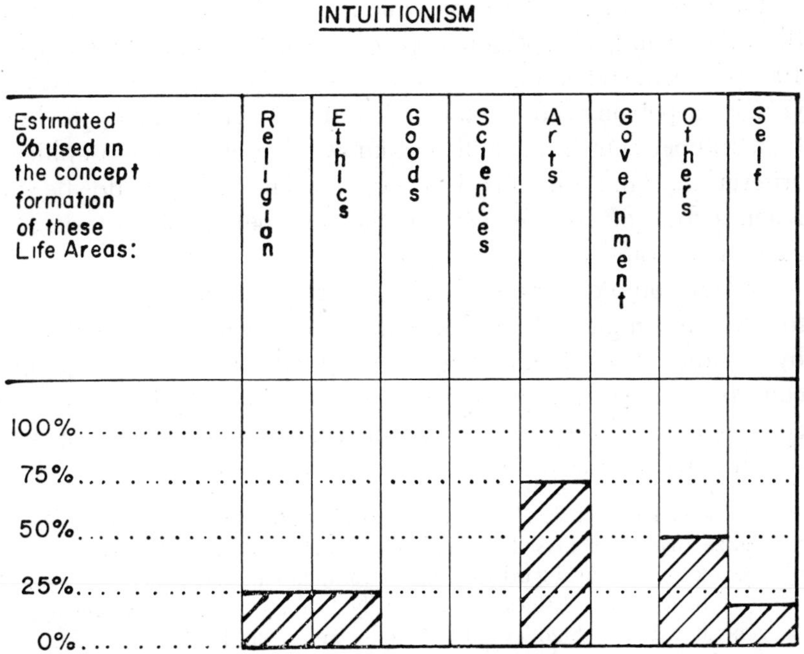

INTUITIONISM

Estimated % used in the concept formation of these Life Areas:	Religion	Ethics	Goods	Sciences	Arts	Government	Others	Self
100%								
75%								
50%								
25%								
0%								

FIGURE 9.   Hominologram I.b.

tuitionism.) Therefore, 35 per cent of his ethical views are
rooted in the Criteria not yet investigated. We do not know
how the 35 per cent are distributed unless we plot all of the
Criteria. Intuitionism plays no role on his outlook on science,
material goods, or government. As far as the arts are concerned,
he was strongly motivated by his own inner feelings as indicated
by the score of 75 per cent in Intuitionism.

Using the method illustrated in Hominologram I.a. and I.b.
one can match all of the Criteria of Reality with all of the Life
Areas. For the purpose of simplification, Inaccessibility of Reality
has been omitted leaving six Criteria which are easier to manipulate than seven. These six are considered as representing a
totality. A person who has more than 100 per cent tallied in
the use of Criteria in any one of the Life Areas is inconsistent
in his adoption of Criteria values. For example, if he states
that he has adopted 75 per cent of his religious convictions
from Authoritarianism and 60 per cent from Intuitionism, he
is admitting that one or both of these values is partially spurious—
to the extent of 35 per cent which exceeds 100 per cent. On
the other hand, the person may consciously decide to go over
100 per cent reflecting an awareness of inconsistency. Conversely, a person whose total reality investments add up to less
than 100 per cent has insufficient knowledge of the philosophical
criteria that underlie his Life Areas. The aim should be to
reach a total of 100 per cent in the distribution of Criteria for
each of the Life Areas.

When completed, the format for the hominologram should
follow the sample (Hominologram I.c.) which was contributed
by a student of hominology. He rated himself against his
concept of "the average student in his class." He followed the
construction of the hominologram with a written description
which is partially reprinted here:

> By looking where I placed Religion within Authoritarianism, I
> realize that I see myself as accepting much less authority than the
> average student in regard to religious formulations and beliefs.
> I believe that Ethics are culturally learned and that people in
> general will rate high in Authoritarianism in this Life Area. I feel
> that I will be somewhat lower in Authoritarianism and proportionately

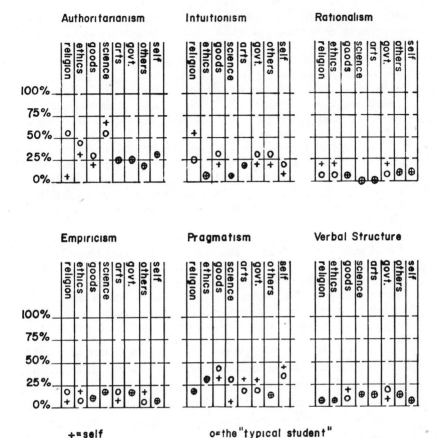

+=self   o=the "typical student"

FIGURE 10.   Hominologram I.c.   A Student Taking A Course in Hominology.

higher in Rationalism and Empiricism in matters relating to conscience.

I think that most people use Pragmatism in evaluating Material Goods but a sizeable number also use Authoritarian values. Some "impulse buyers," I would place under Intuitionism. My ideas of possession of worldly things differs somewhat from the average. Sometimes, I am a lazy thinker in regard to purchases, not because I consider newspaper and magazine advertisements sources as authority but because following these represents the path of least resistance. That is why I may be higher in Verbal Structuralism than the average student who is willing to take the time to try to obtain good value from the things he purchases.

Probably I am somewhat above average in accepting authority in scientific matters and less pragmatic than my fellow students.

Again, I realize that this may be a tendency to select the path of least resistance in matters in which I am not as involved as I am in Religion and Ethics.

I consider myself average in my acceptance of the Arts but, perhaps, I have not thought sufficiently about what my artistic tastes really are since the total does not add up to 100 per cent in this area. I marked myself somewhat more pragmatic than others because I am apt to think that a painting is the right size for the wall and accept it on this utilitarian basis.

In regard to Government, I accept authoritarian values to the same extent as the average student. I am less apt to trust intuition than others when voting for candidates. I think I am more inclined to ask, Has this candidate produced desired results? I am somewhat less prone to Verbal Structuralism when it comes to Government than others are.

My concept of Other People conforms to the norms, except that I tend to be less emotional. I feel that I obtain my self-image from the same sources which others employ. Again, the one exception is that I try to be slightly less intuitive than the average student. To a proportionately greater degree, I tend to judge myself on the basis of how my actions actually work out in terms of success or failure, using pragmatic standards as the basis for this judgment.

Hominologram I.d. was plotted by a married female student who returned to complete her college education after raising a family. Her evaluation illustrates the disadvantage of using the term *average*. She mentions that in her concept of average "one extreme. . .will be balanced by a few at the other end of the continuum." It is better to use the word, *mode*, since it represents the score obtained by the majority of persons within a given distribution. Correctly used, *average* refers to the sum of all the scores divided by the number of scores. Behavioral scientists usually refer to this measure as the *arithmetic mean*. The characteristics of the mean can be judged more accurately if it is accompanied by a *standard deviation* or a range of the scores obtained.

The students preparing Hominolograms I.a. and I.b. were not requested to limit their percentages to 100 per cent. Subsequent experience has shown that it is better to ask students to try to keep within the 100 per cent limit.

The written "Self-Evaluation" which accompanies Hominologram I.d. mentions "changes" that have taken place in the student's life throughout the years. Many students who have drawn hominolograms believe that their values would change with growth and experience. The following report by the student who drew Hominologram I.d. illustrates the self-searching which can accompany this kind of self-evaluation:

> As I began to fill out the hominologram, I was surprised to find myself, in comparison to the 'self' of a few years ago, greatly changed, not so much in actual behavior as in the less easily described aspect of my orientation to the world.
>
> Undoubtedly, with the passing years and increase of knowledge, change is inevitable; in my case the necessity for change was given

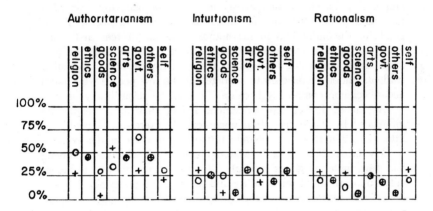

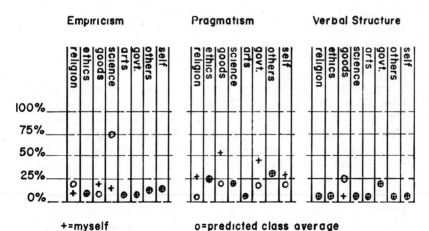

+=myself   o=predicted class average

FIGURE 11.   Hominologram I.d.   A Forty-year-old Married Female Student.

impetus by a period of personal crisis which forced me to enlarge my sheltered role of homemaker for a family of seven to a larger encompassing role of job-holder and student. The widening of horizons, in itself, was sufficient to effect changes in my Criteria of Reality. As my base of knowledge shifted, my base of values shifted also.

In almost every area in which we were asked to evaluate ourselves—in my views toward, Religion, Ethics, Material Goods, Science, Arts, Government, Other People, and even toward myself— I found that I was mentally listing changes.

In the case of Religion, the change has been a shift from Intuitionism to Authoritarianism and Pragmatism. Authoritarian acceptance must prevail to a certain extent in religion as there can be no empirical proof, but I find myself incapable of believing that what is judged to be good for the church as a whole can necessarily be good for the individual in his unique situation. I feel that I am close to the average except that, perhaps, most would not give Pragmatism any value in religion; I placed myself below the other students under Empiricism to average out the few people who might negate religion completely because it cannot be scientifically proven.

As far as Ethics are concerned, I feel that most people are influenced by Authority—often unconsciously exercised. I could see little deviation from the average rating of the class in this respect.

My orientation towards Material Goods has changed. Having had few material goods in early life caused me to put a higher value upon them. I felt security and prestige in possessing. I found it difficult to throw anything away because 'some day' I might find a use for it. Now I am more pragmatic in my attitude toward worldly goods. If I need something, I buy the best I can afford on the basis that it will serve my needs longer and more efficiently. I have long ago found that Material Goods yield little in the way of genuine security or prestige. I feel that I am now more able to resist Verbal Structuralism and I rate myself below the average of the class in this category.

In Science I rated myself higher under Authoritarianism and lower under Empiricism than the norm as I am inclined to take the word of a respected authority without feeling the need to prove a point for myself; the average person in the class, having grown up in a generation that emphasizes science above all else, is probably more inclined toward the empiristic view; therefore, I ranked them higher under this heading than I did myself.

Under Arts, I seemed to have some difficulty in evaluating myself; formerly I ascribed almost wholly to the authoritarian value of arts. This I still do to a certain extent. Now modern art appeals to me by the way it makes me feel, through color, motion, and general impact.

My attitude towards Government has changed. Because I can see its direct affect on my life and my family, I take a more active role and tend to make judgments from knowledge of facts rather than voting by party. With the large number of elected officials and policies there are to be voted upon in a single election, it is impossible to inform oneself adequately on each one of the candidates and in this case, party affiliation or backing by a prominent authority is the deciding factor. I ranked myself lower in Authoritarianism because the average person in the class is younger, less interested in government, and more inclined to vote on issues by party. This is usually the one that their own parents belong to so that their vote is seen as based on authority. I fail to see how anyone can keep from being influenced to some extent by biases slanted toward their favorite party and gave myself and the average person about 25 per cent under Verbal Structuralism.

The way one feels towards Other People is greatly influenced by parents, expectations of society or church, Authoritarianism; how one feels and thinks, Intuitionism and Rationalism; and by Pragmatism, "does it work?" Since the average person in our class is in Behavioral Science, presumably with a high interest in helping people and making the world a better place in which to live, I ranked my score and the average score about 30 per cent under Pragmatism.

OTHER TYPES OF HOMINOLOGRAMS

Interesting hominolograms have been produced by two different people interacting—such as a social worker and his client, a psychiatrist and his patient. In plotting his hominologram, one subject indicated how he imagined another person's profile would compare with his. A married student in a hominology class asked his wife to draw a hominologram also. An interesting discussion of the comparison of the two hominolograms ensued.

When members of one group plot the Reality Criteria they imagine are used by another group with a different background, they may achieve valuable insights. An experiment of this type was conducted at the Colorado State Pre-Parole Center by twenty-one parole officers who were participating in a refresher course. The parole officers were asked to plot their own Reality Criteria and, also, those they thought would represent their group's averages. On the same hominologram they were requested to profile the Criteria of the typical parolee as they envisioned him. Hominologram I.e. illustrates,

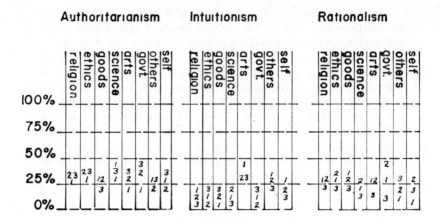

I=self   2="typical parole officer"   3="typical parolee"

FIGURE 12.   Hominologram I.e.   Parole Officer's Multiple Evaluation.

1. the calculated mean of the parole officers' individual self-rating;

2. the calculated mean of the ratings the parole officers believed would represent their group as a whole, i.e., the expected group averages;

3. the calculated mean of the rating which the parole officers believed would represent the evaluations of the typical parolee.[1]

[1] The standard deviations obtained are not shown.

There are many inferences which may be drawn from the hominologram of the parole officers. In several cases, the mean profile of the parole officers and mean profile of the "parolees" were closer to each other than either was to the mean of the individual profiles. In general, it was assumed that parolees use less Rationalism, less Empiricism, more Intuition (except in the Arts), and somewhat more Authoritarianism than the parole officers. There were exceptions and it might be interesting to consider the dynamics that play a role in the results obtained.

Hominolograms of Differences

Space does not permit the inclusions of other thought-provoking hominolograms which have been produced by well-defined groups. Catholic sisters in a convent in Colorado contributed hominolograms which revealed that most of the individual sisters had a somewhat different expectation of their own group than turned out to be the case.

Hominolographic comparisons between a small group of "hard-nosed" scientists and a group of scientists with predominantly "soft-nosed" ideas brought into focus the central point of their controversy. The "hard-nosed" scientists placed Science almost 100 per cent into the Criterion of Empiricism. The "soft-nosed" scientists, on the other hand, were found to have reality investments in Rationalism, Authoritarianism, and Intuitionism. Under these circumstances argument on "methods" between these scientists is fruitless since methodology cannot be independent of Criteria of Reality. Without being aware of it, participants in "hard-nosed" and "soft-nosed" methodological disputes are usually contending over their personal definition of the nature of truth.

It is sometimes revealing to draw a hominologram of the two or three key Reality Criteria that are crucial in a given case. A typical issue is taken from an article appearing in a city newspapaer. The following is a condensed version of the article:

AGNOSTICS IN SEMINARS RAISE AGONIZING QUESTION

Should a man be ordained to the ministry if he rejects or is agnostic about some of the basic tenets of the historic Christian faith? That may strike you as a far-fetched hypothetical question but it's a real and agonizing one for the deans and professors at many Protestant seminaries.

Some candidates shrug off the question on the grounds that doctrines are unimportant. What really matters some say, is for the church to get dynamic leadership that can make the most of its potential for social service.

Without impugning the sincerity of these arguments, one might wonder what theologians would say about a medical school that awarded an M.D. degree to a student who doubts the existence of germs.

The reader will be aware that the two groups subscribe to different Criteria of Reality. The Life Area, Religion, would be placed high in Authoritarianism by the believers and low in Pragmatism and Rationalism. The reverse would be true of the agnostics; their religious reality would stem from Pragmatism and Rationalism instead of largely from Authoritarianism. Unless these two groups understand their differences of Criteria, there can be no resolution of the conflict. The fundamental issue in such disputes is, Is there more than one kind of truth?

Medicine and Theology Not Analogous

Instead of probing this issue on the basis of Criteria of Reality, an analogy between theology and medicine was offered in the article.

Modern medicine's "reality" is anchored in Empiricism. Theology's "reality" may stem from Authoritarianism (for believers) and from Pragmatism or Rationalism (for agnostics). Therefore an analogy between medicine and theology is invalid. The validity of the germ theory can be proven since the existence of germs can be empirically demonstrated. At one time in history, medicine was also based on faith and lore. Only this type of "medicine" is validly analogous to theology.

This does not tell us where "ultimate truth" may actually be found. This question, like so many others, depends on the Criteria of Reality which are employed by the person searching for "truth." This view does not make truth relativistic but, rather, individualistic. It is helpful to be aware of the fact that a person seldom selects his Criterion of Reality freely. Choice of Criteria is influenced by many factors (see Chapter 3).

A Situationist and a Traditionalist

Although I could have used illustrations outside of religion, it happened that a good illustration was noted in another newspaper which again evolves a religious matter: "Minister Advocates Change in Ten Commandments!" This was followed by the explanation below:

Reverend John H. Williams,[2] a minister and professor of ethics at the Theological School, says he would amend the biblical Ten Commandments to read this way: "Thou shalt not covet, ordinarily." Thou shalt not kill, ordinarily." "Thou shalt not commit adultery, ordinarily." "In other words," Williams says, "for me there are no rules—none at all." Williams is considered a leading exponent of "situational ethics," which he says, "declares that anything and everything is right or wrong according to the situation—what is wrong in some cases would be right in others." Williams explained in an interview that a situationist looks only at individuals, concrete cases, not at abstract principles. "I look at situations one at a time," he said. "A situationist would discard all absolutes except the one absolute—always to act with loving concern," he said. "Oh, I know, the word, 'love' is a swampy one, a semantic confusion."

"Put it this way, then: a situationist is prepared in any concrete case to suspend, ignore, or violate any principle if by doing so he can effect more good than by following it. What is good? Good is first and foremost the good of people. Christians call it love, meaning well-being of people. The good is what works. Apart from the helping or hurting of people, ethical judgment or evaluations are meaningless." Situation ethics has been criticized, especially by those who uphold certain absolute moral laws. An American Jesuit, retorted that "It is not in Christian tradition to present love as the exclusive motive for moral action."

Williams added, "Situation ethics is criticized for saying everything is relative. But we say, this is the twentieth century. The scientifically sophisticated world view is relativistic. You are going to be left out in the cold if you think the moral sciences are somehow an exception to this rule and this influence." Williams in turn, challenges persons he calls 'legalists'—people who like to wallow or cower in the security of the law. "They want to maintain absolutes

---

[2] The names of the individuals and school are fictitious.

of good and evil, but they are not going to get away with it," he said.

The Traditionalist's View

In the same issue of the newspaper there was an article written by another minister, Rev. Langley who is known for his traditional religious views. His article was captioned: "Truth Can Survive Tyranny and Evil." The following is a condensed version of his orientation:

> God's truth cannot be destroyed. One of the sons of the biblical Josiah, Jehoiakim, who thoroughly disbelieved all the things in which his father put trust, tried in his brief reign to undo all the benefits his father's loyalty had built up and to destroy the Jehovah worship which he despised. But the durability of the word of God is almost as amazing as its inspired contents. One little royal nobody who believed he could stop the progress of truth stepped across the pathway and was run over by this enduring vehicle of truth—the gospel.
>
> Because we dislike a truth or find it inconvenient is no reason why we should destroy it. Something needs to be changed, and more often than not that thing is our hearts and minds which have harbored mistaken, or perhaps evil notions.

Reconstruction of Rev. Williams and Rev. Langley

Let us assume that after interviewing Rev. Langley and Rev. Williams, their individual hominolograms were drawn. If one of their hominolograms were superimposed upon the other (see Hominologram I.f.), unexpected results would be found which might not come to light by merely having the two men discuss their different points of view.

Hostility engendered by the emphasis on differences usually creates a *psycho-sociological distance* which would make it unlikely for them to discover their unsuspected similarities. Among these are their tastes in the arts and an almost identical voting record. Hominologram I.f. indicated that Rev. Langley's views on wordly possessions are much more pragmatic than those of Rev. Williams. Subsequent questions showed that Rev. Langley tries out everything before making purchases or investments and tends to go strictly by what works best in terms of utilitarian values of material goods. On the other hand, Rev. Williams,

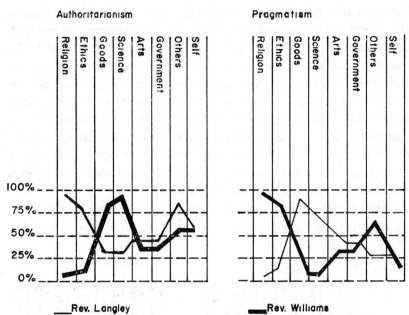

FIGURE 13. Hominologram I.f. Rev. Langley and Rev. Williams.

when making purchases, takes the advice of someone he considers to be an authority. Regarding wordly goods, Rev. Langley is an astute Situationist and Rev. Williams, a confirmed Authoritarianist.

The hominolograms reveal that Rev. Williams' faith in science is as authoritarian as Rev. Langley's acceptance of the gospel. It seems that science represents to Williams what the scriptures represent to Langley.

We note that an individual who gained national prominence as a "situationalist" is so only in a limited way and in a specific area. In some respects he is more authoritarian than a well-known fundamentalist. The similarity between these two men is obscured by the emphasis that they and society place upon their differences.

Hominolograms Portraying "Ways of Life"

Ideas, societies, "ways of life" of peoples may be represented by hominolograms. Often essential differences such as those between countries where the people may vote freely or cannot do so may be better understood by the hominolographic method. Hominologram I.g. represents a hypothetical construct of Communism and non-Communism[3] and demonstrates that the basic differences existing between them stem from selection of different Criteria of Reality. Once this is perceived, it is clear why arguments regarding "who is right" lead to frustrations in communication. People who understand the role that the nature of "truth" plays in an issue may be able to *agree to disagree* amicably. The ability to discuss controversial issues at this level should be one of the aims of education.

For example the first thing to do before participating in an argument is to ask oneself, Is the difference of opinion due

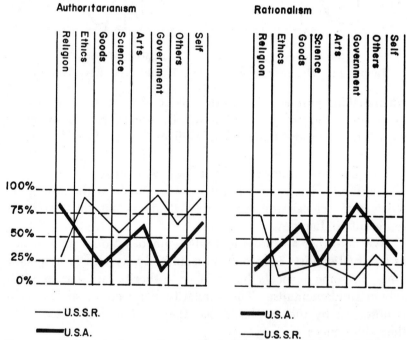

FIGURE 14.   Hominologram I.g. A Comparison of the Theoretical Orientations of the U.S.S.R. and the U.S.A.

_____

[3] Compare the theoretical hominologram of the non-Communist to the political self-view of the student in hominology (Hominologram I.c) and the political views of Rev. Langley and Williams (Hominologram I.f.).

to the adoption of different frameworks? Only when it has been established that both parties in a dispute have the same framework, can there by any question of "right" or "wrong." Actually, a better way of saying "right" or "wrong" is to determine consistency within a mutually accepted framework. Let us take an example from everyday life. If a husband and wife argue over whether one of them is wearing the "right" clothes or not, it should be determined whether a pragmatic, authoritarian, or empirical basis is used for determining "right." Many husbands wear clothes primarily for pragmatic comfort-oriented reasons. Their wives may choose their own clothes according to authoritarian norms (fashions) or by empirically tested rules of color harmony. The argument in such cases should not be on what clothes to wear but what framework to adopt. Many domestic arguments could be avoided if this were understood. The student should carry a "mental" hominologram around with him. It may save him many futile disputes.

The following personality variables have been associated with the various Criteria of Reality:

Authoritarianism: respectful, conforming, dogmatic, rigid, fatalistic, moralistic, fanatical.

Intuitionism: spiritual, emotional, labile, hysterical, manic or depressive, imaginative, artistic, creative, emotionally responsive (or over-responsive), impulsive.

Rationalism: intellectual, contemplative, self-confident, reasonable, tolerant, logical. Also, overconfident, snobbish, inaccurate, nonconforming, careless.

Empiricism: hardworking, meticulous, persistent, obsessive-compulsive, intolerant of deviation, inflexible, self-righteous.

Inaccessibility of Reality: skeptical, compromising, pliant, tolerant, imaginative, changeable, unstable.

Pragmatism: progressive, dynamic, flexible, liberal, unconventional, radical, rebellious.

Verbal Structuralism: naïve, shallow, dull, trusting, gullible, uncritical, suggestible, dependent.

These characteristics are theoretical and there is no validity involved. One student developed what he called a "Reverse Hominologram" in which he substituted the positions of the

Life Areas for the Criteria of Reality and vice versa. He then used the above-mentioned personality characteristics to make a self-profile. The lively discussion that followed indicated that his method certainly can stimulate an interesting discussion.

OBJECTIFYING HOMINOLOGRAMS

As it stands, the hominologram represents a procedure with no factual support. It serves to stimulate subjective self-exploration. To make hominolograms statistically meaningful, overlapping of the concepts would have to be recognized and statistically described. This would require standardized techniques of eliciting the information and in weighting the Criteria of Reality. The weights would have to be empirically derived from a variety of norm groups. Standardized multidimensional methods of observation might have to be developed and validity, cross-validity, test-retest, and interscorer reliability would have to be established.

Obiously, this is a considerable task and may not be possible with the type of data with which we are dealing when constructing a hominologram. Nevertheless, it is believed that, provided the limitations are recognized, the effort involved in constructing a hominologram is worthwhile if it widens the student's horizon and deepens his motivation for further self-exploration.

SUMMARY

A hominologram is a visual representation, in the form of a histogram or a line graph, of six Criteria of Reality applied to eight phenomenological Life Areas. Hominolograms are subjective and their value stems from a personal interpretation of the philosophical apperception taking place within an individual's psycho-social world. Hominolograms offer a visual frame of reference for personal exploration of the bases of one's values and the roots of one's beliefs.

The recognition that others may have a different set of values and subscribe to a different kind of "truth" may facilitate communication and create the tolerance for diversity of opinions which education attempts to encourage.

REFERENCES

BILODEAU, E. A.: Statistical versus intuitive confidence. *Amer J Psychol,* 65:271-277, 1952.

COOMBS, C. H.: Theory and methods of social measurement. In Festinger, L., and Katz, D. (Eds.): *Research Methods in the Behavioral Sciences.* New York, Holt, 1953, pp. 471-535.

DEVONS, E., AND GLUCKMAN, M.: Modes and consequences of limiting a field study. In Gluckman, M. (Ed.): *Closed Systems and Open Minds.* Chicago, Aldine, 1964, pp. 158-261.

DIRENZO, G. J. (Ed.): *Concepts, Theory, and Explanation in the Behavioral Sciences.* New York, Random, 1966.

FINCH, J. R.: Scientific models and their application in psychiatric models. *Arch Gen Psychiat, 15:1-6, July 1966.

FISHBEIN, M. (Ed.): *Readings in Attitude Change.* New York, Wiley, 1967.

GREENE, L. S. (Ed.): Conservatism, liberalism, and national issues. *Ann Amer Acad Political Soc Sci,* 344, Nov. 1962.

JAMES, B. J.: Social-psychological dimensions of Ojibwa acculteration. *Amer Anthropologist,* 63:721-746, Aug. 1964.

KEETON, M.: *Values Men Live By.* New York, Abingdon, 1960.

KUHN, M. H.: Factors in personality: socio-cultural determinants as seen through the Amish. In Hsu, F. L. K. (Ed.): *Aspects of Culture and Personality.* New York, Ablelard-Schuman, 1954, pp. 43-65.

LITTLE, I. M. D.: Social choice and individual values. *J Political Economics,* 60:422-432, 1952.

LOWE, C. M.: Value orientations—as ethical dilemma. In Nunokawa, W. D. (Ed.): *Human Values and Abnormal Behavior.* Chicago, Scott, 1965, pp. 2-9.

MILLER, M. H.: On building bridges. In Greenfield, N. S., and Lewis, W. C. (Eds.): *Psychoanalysis and Current Biological Thought.* Madison, U. of Wis., 1965, pp. 3-9.

MILLENSON, J. R.: *Principles of Behavioral Analysis.* New York, Macmillan, 1967.

PALMER, S.: *Understanding Other People.* Greenwich, Fawcett, 1964.

RAPOPORT, A.: What is a viable system? *ETC Rev Gen Semantics, 23:533-534, Dec. 1966.

SCHROEDER, W. W.: Lay expectations of the ministerial role. *J Sci Study Religion, II:217-227, Spring 1963.

SCHWEITZER, A.: *The Philosophy of Civilization.* New York, Macmillan, 1960, pp. 221-270.

SHONTZ, F. C.: *Research Methods in Personality.* New York, Appleton, 1965.

(See the book review by Marlowe, D. in *Contemporary Psychology,* 12:258-260, May 1967.)

STOODLEY, B. H. (Ed.): *Society and Self.* New York, Free Press, 1962.

WELKOWITZ, J.; COHEN, J., AND ORTMEYER, D.: Value system similarity-investigation of patient-therapist dyads, *J Consult Psychol,* 31:48-55, Feb. 1967.

WHITEHEAD, N. A.: *A Philosopher Looks at Science.* New York, Philosophical Lib., 1965.

SECTION TWO
INFORMATION FOR HOMINOLOGY

Chapter 6

METHODS IN THE HUMAN SCIENCES

"An approach to anything is no better than its methods."
F. S. C. NORTHROP

S CIENCE MAY BE divided into two large segments: physical science and biological science (also called "Life Science"). The sciences which deal primarily with human beings represent divisions within biological science and are known as social and behavioral sciences. For ease of communication and because they cannot be dichotomized into separate entities, the social and behavioral sciences shall be referred to simply as *human sciences*. This chapter, then, concerns itself with the diverse methods by means of which Man's nature may be studied and their classification within the human sciences.[1]

Students of the human sciences should first understand the role of objectivity within scientific investigation. In empirical science, the methods, themselves, are never neutral. Neutrality is something in the mind of the investigator and has little to do with methodology. Any method may be used in a neutral or non-neutral manner. Neutrality deals with how facts are selected, and methods are concerned with how facts are identified.

Precision in communication is aided if a distinction is made between method, technique, procedure, system, process, and modes of inquiry. *Method* is a general term and represents either an abstraction or a concrete procedure having orderly, logical, and effective arrangement. It connotes regularity or formality. *System* is a fully developed and carefully formulated

---

[1] Underlying the entire concept of methods in hominology is the question of how the student accepts and interprets reality. Therefore, in studying Chapter 6 he should keep in mind the Criteria of Reality which he identified as his own in Chapter 5.

method. *Procedure* is the preferred term when the stress is on the routine course to be followed. *Technique* deals with the technical manner in which details are treated and is also used as a means of accomplishing a desired aim. *Process* represents a gradual change along expected lines. It refers to a series of actions or operations leading to a particular result. *Mode*[2] is sometimes used interchangeably with method, but erroneously so, since it seldom implies an orderly or logical arrangement. Instead it denotes an order or course pursued as the result of custom, tradition, or personal preference.

There are several different approaches to the study of Man. The scientific method is used when physical measurement and observations can be made. Intuitive methods are used by some when it is impossible or considered undesirable to use physical measurements. Each of the approaches is discussed here.

THE SCIENTIFIC METHOD

Different disciplines have various ways of applying the scientific method and different persons prefer their own names for component parts of the method. There is no fast rule of where a methodological sequence begins. Both the beginning and the end of a sequence may depend on the nature of the problem being studied. Sequences in applying the scientific methods may end at different points depending upon the extent to which our knowledge is limited. For example, in some problems it is possible to formulate a theory whereas in other problems we cannot go beyond the point of expressing a hypothesis. The scientific search for knowledge often is analogous to a spiral which may begin with observation of phenomena, proceed through a phase of systematizing data, then continue with observation of phenomena on a higher level of organization. The following outline may help clarify the series of steps that are usually included in the scientific method.

I. Observation and the gathering of data: The collection of data or gathering of facts requires observation. The observation must be repeatable since one-time events which cannot be

---

[2] Mode in statistics has a different meaning. As a measure of central tendency it represents the largest number of scores in a distribution of scores.

observed again are outside of the domain of the scientific method.

II. Analysis of data and definition of the problem: Evaluation and analysis of data leads to the definition of the problem. A problem is often defined by asking a question about the observations that have been made.

III. Formulation of a hypothesis: A *hypothesis* is an "educated guess" which attempts to answer the question that has been asked in the definition of the problem. The history of science reveals that some very diverse characteristics have played a role in the formulation of a hypotheses, i.e. experience, genius, intuition, insight, accidents, and coincidences. However, a hypothesis is not valid unless it can be tested.

IV. Experimentation: The validity of a hypothesis is established by experimentation and by statistical analysis. Experimentation must be controlled. On the basis of the experimentation, the hypothesis is either rejected or accepted. The result of the experiment is called evidence. If the hypothesis is rejected, we must go back to an earlier point in the method, but if the hypothesis is accepted, we may proceed to the next step.

V. Theory formation: A theory is more than a tested hypothesis; it is an attempt to explain the interrelationship between the observed facts. Theories do not imply absolute truths but indicate a high degree of probability. If additional data are gathered that do not fit a theory, it may be modified or rejected. Theories have predictive value and may be used to anticipate the collection of additional data. Many persons believe that the aim of science is to develop theories and use them to discover more facts.

VI. Laws or principles: A theory which continues to show interrelationships between an accumulating body of facts and is generally accepted by the scientific community becomes a law or principle. Testing over a long time is usually required for a theory to become a law or principle. Often a concept is called a theory by some people and a law by others.

The scientific method does not make moral decisions and value judgments nor does it have at its disposal the means to discuss these meaningfully. Therefore, all the disciplines whose content is predicated on the scientific method alone are incapable of studying total Man since such a study of Man certainly must include consideration of his moral values. Hominology attempts to study Man's moral nature and discuss it meaningfully, using the scientific method where it is applicable and nonscientific speculation where the scientific method cannot apply. Speculations must be clearly labelled what they are and an attempt should be made to identify the sources and biases.

The student of hominology must understand the scientific method and recognize its advantages and limitations. This will help him to differentiate between evidence and personal opinion. It will assist him in being aware of when he is or is not using the scientific method in his search for Man's total nature. A discussion of the implications of the scientific method follows.

Observation and the Gathering of Data

The large approaches to making observations and gathering data in the human sciences are often represented by five methodological categories within which the gathering and processing of information takes place. Although there may be variation, a typical list includes historical methods, survey methods, case methods, statistical methods, and experimental methods. Four of these are described by Koenig (1957). He defines these in the following manner within the social and behavioral sciences:

> The *historical method* calls for study of events, processes, and institutions of past civilizations for the purpose of finding the origin or antecedents of contemporary social life and thus understanding its nature and workings.
> The *comparative method* involves comparison of various kinds of groups or peoples in order to disclose differences as well as similarities. . . . The method may be used in the study of existing groups or of past groups. . . .
> The *statistical method* is used to measure social phenomena mathematically in order to disclose relationships and thus arrive at generalizations regarding their nature, occurrence, and meaning . . . the sampling and control techniques are a very important part of this method.
> The *case study method* may be employed in studying a condition, group, community, institution, or individual. Underlying it is the contention that any case being studied is representative of many, if

not all, similar cases, hence will make generalization possible. The method involves investigation and an analysis of all factors entering into the case and an examination from as many points of view as possible.

There is logic in such classification, but some of the rationale that contributes to this logic is derived from a disciplinary orientation rather than from the inherent structure of method. Historical methods are related not only because they deal with phenomena in the past but also because they are associated with specific disciplinary fields such as history, anthropology, and the humanities, while experimental methods have been primarily associated with psychology and physiology.

The traditional manner of classifying research methods does not permit discrete separation upon which effective classification must depend. If matter which has been classified cannot remain stabilized within the category to which it has been assigned, a revision of the system seems justified. According to Koenig's description, the historical method incorporates past events, but when events occurring in the past are compared with each other, it is called the comparative method. Research using case study methods also falls within the scope of the statistical method if case study generalizations are treated by statistical techniques. One cannot circumvent the onus of overlapping by using the term *combined methods* in such cases for then the very idea of classification is nullified.

Under such circumstances, a method often has a variety of different meanings. Good *et al.* (1941) are among those who deplore the difficulty of classifying methods:

The overlapping of research techniques may be shown by . . . an example drawn from the testing field . . . if . . . testing is for the purpose of ascertaining children's capacity in relation to other children or a norm, the procedure is normative-survey rather than experimental. The testing done to equate groups of children for experimental purposes . . . may be considered survey character, but fits into the larger purpose or pattern of the experiment and properly may be regarded as a definite part of the experimental investigation. To use a different illustration, if an intelligence test is administered year by year to a group of children who have lived under normal and uniform conditions during the time involved, with maturation as the single variable operating, the resulting curve of mental growth is the product of an experimental procedure. A study of the accompanying age norms and of the factors operating to produce such growth takes on genetic and casual characteristics. (Under these circumstances it becomes part of the genetic method instead of the experimental method.)

These authors assign psychometric testing to normative-survey methods.[3] Later, however, they remark,

> Of course, viewed in a broad way, it is possible to think of the administration of any standard (psychological or achievement) test as an experimental procedure. . . . The experimental factor may be thought of as the instruction which the pupil undergoes between testing periods, the effect of which is measured.

Therefore, psychometric testing equally qualifies for inclusion under experimental methods.

Schema of classifying methods often fail to distinguish between methods for gathering data and those for analyzing data. Categories such as "statistical methods" or "case study methods" refer both to methods of collecting information and methods of interpreting it. Yet collecting and analysis of data are separate functions serving different purposes. One of the reasons for this confusion is that, traditionally, methods have been grouped by similarity of content.

It seems logical to categorize methods of inquiry by the kinds of data or information with which they deal. However, in practice, this has not always worked out well and has lead to considerable overlapping. An alternate way of classifying data is suggested in this chapter. It ties classification to the kind of confrontation the investigator has with the data. By avoiding terms such as *experimental* or *historical* and, instead substituting the "direct" or "indirect" contact with the source of information, it has been found that the various methods used in the human sciences fall into groups with less overlap.

In this way of grouping methods, the focus of classification is removed from the data itself and placed upon the scientist who does the investigating. Questions asked in classifying methods include the following: 1) Did the investigator come

---

[3] The authors define *normative-survey* as methods that use specialized procedures such as questionnaires, tests, and checklists.

TABLE VI

CLASSIFICATION OF METHODS BY HOW THE INVESTIGATOR
CONFRONTS DATA

A. *Unmanipulated Data Sources*
  1. Direct confrontation by investigator
     a. Interviews
     b. Surveys
     c. Samples
     d. Descriptive observation
     e. Participant observation
     f. Field studies
     g. Psychoanalytic methods
     h. Case histories
     i. Natural "experimentation"
     j. Documentation from original sources

  2. Indirect confrontation in which persons or instruments are intermediary
     a. Psychometric methods
     b. Computorized methods
     c. Structured paper and pencil methods
     d. Bibliographic methods
     e. Chemical and geological methods
     f. Physiological methods
     g. Art comparative methods
     h. Literature comparative methods
     i. Second-hand documentary methods
     j. Methods based on reports of others

B. *Through Manipulation of Data-Producing Sources* (Direct or Indirect Confrontation)
  1. Experimental Methods
     a. Controlled experimentation
     b. Models
     c. Controlled situational evaluations
  2. Nonexperimental Methods
     a. Psychodrama
     b. Play-diagnostic methods
     c. Controlled situational evaluations
     d. Sociometric methods
     e. Hypnoanalysis
     f. Drug interviews

into *direct contact* with the original source of information as occurs when a psychiatrist interviews a patient? 2) Did the investigator obtain his information *indirectly* as occurs when a social worker interviews the patient's neighbor who can supply some behavioral facts about him or when a psychologist uses a personality test to ascertain the patient's diagnosis? 3) Was an artificial situation created as in psychodrama where the patient acts out his problems in a contrived setting enabling a group of participants to obtain insight into his behavior? In this case it might be said that the source of data (the patient) was *manipulated* (given a specific role to act out) by the investigator in order that a certain kind of information could be elicited.

Another way of illustrating the three ways of obtaining information is to use light as an example of a source of data. In this case let us imagine that we are studying the light emanating from a star. Direct confrontation of the data source is illustrated by viewing the light with one's eyes. Indirect confrontation of the source of the data occurs when one views the light through a telescope. The third method is illustrated by using a prism and breaking up the light (manipulating the data source) into component parts. This makes it possible to obtain information which would not be available by using the previous two methods.

Methods in which the investigator directly confronts un-manipulated sources of information represent the oldest form of gathering information. Under uncomplicated conditions, the methods within this classification require less preparation and equipment than the other methods. In actual practice, however, this does not always prove true. Preparation for a field trip in a primitive area, for example, or the necessary preliminaries to the selection of representative samples of a large city population will, obviously, take considerable amounts of careful planning and preparation.

It may seem strange to find that conducting natural experiments and making surveys are classified under the same heading. Berelson and Steiner (1964) assign the natural experiment to experimental design methods and group it with laboratory and other experiments. Their logic for this stems from their definition of natural experiments:

> Frequently the major elements of an experiment occur or are produced in the natural habitat of the behavior under study. Such experimentation avoids many of the problems of the laboratory situation, e.g. oversimplification and artificiality. In the natural experiment the subjects ordinarily do not know that they are under investigation and hence do not modify their behavior as a result of being watched. On the other hand, natural experimentation is usually less precise, because pertinent events are less fully under the experimenter's control.

The same authors described a survey as

> The investigator . . . collects some measures on the appropriate characteristics of the population being studied (number of television sets or children in the household; how the members feel about Russia or religion; what they know about India or space; and so on).

From this it appears that the key difference between natural experiment and survey is that in one case the subjects know they are being observed and in the other case they do not. The behavior of owning a television set, opinions on Russia, India, space, etc. would not be modified by a survey. In other words, awareness by the subjects appears to be the only basis for the difference in classification between natural experiments and surveys. Yet, subject awareness is not defined as playing any role in discriminating between experimental and survey methods as defined by these same authors.

By using classifications based on the investigator's actions rather than the subject's, one can place natural experiments together with surveys, without violating the definitions upon which the system of classification hinges. Following is a description of representative methods used within each of the three methods of classifying data.

Direct Confrontation of Unmanipulated Sources

Interviews are person-to-person discussions designed to gather information. They usually involve face-to-face meeting (sometimes telephone) between an investigator and one or more persons. The investigator's purpose may be to gather information which will help him to make generalizations that apply to a larger population than the sample group interviewed. *Focused interviews* attempt to concentrate information within a narrow field. *Informal interviews* may be relatively unstructured permitting much latitude in the kinds of information elicited.

Surveys are studies of large or widely scattered groups or conditions. *Sample surveys* involve a fraction of a total population from which inferences can be drawn. Interviews are often used as means for conducting surveys.

Samples use small portions of a human, animal or plant population. These portions are considered as containing identical elements found in a much larger group or population.

Descriptive observation takes place when events or people are studied and information about them is recorded as it occurs. The data obtained is usually employed as auxiliary to other methods or as a basis for later study.

Participant observation is a form of a descriptive observation except that the observer strives to become a member of a group being studied in order to obtain first-hand experience of the characteristics of the group. It is used in anthropology and sociology.

Field studies are conducted in the area or habitat where the behavior studied is taking place or where the source of the desired information is located. The lack of a contrived environment avoids the artificiality of the laboratory situation but may do so at the expense of better control and diminished opportunity for observation. Such studies are used in sociology, anthropology, economics, political science, psychology, and social psychiatry.

Psychoanalytic methods represent a means of furnishing a patient with insight through a period of free associations which enable him to re-experience past traumatic events that were central to his adjustment difficulty. This method is primarily used by psychoanalysts and psychotherapists.

Case histories in medicine and social work are intensive studies usually conducted by personal interview, in which a trained worker obtains a history of the individual preliminary to diagnosis and treatment. Social workers, physicians, psychiatrists, and clinical psychologists are trained in taking case histories. *Case study methods* may be used in studying a condition within a group or a community. Cultural anthropology, medicine, psychology, and sociology utilize this approach.

Natural "experiments" take place after a change has occurred in a previously stable situation such as a flood, earthquake, or a disruptive social or cultural event. The investigator, himself, does not manipulate the situation. An example of a natural experiment is a study of the effect of introducing items from one culture to another, such as guns where previously only the bow and arrow were known. Studies of this sort take place in sociology, anthropology, social psychiatry, psychology.

Documentation from original sources is differentiated from documentation from secondary sources where an intermediary person or persons describe the original document or event. The information the investigator receives secondhand falls into the category described as indirect confrontation of sources of data. A will, birth certificate, or diary are documents of an original nature. A Spanish priest's description of the religious practices of the Aztecs represents indirect documentation. The priest in this case, acts as an intermediary between investigator and the original information. Library or bibliographical methods may fall into either category depending on whether the information comes from direct or indirect sources.

DISCUSSION. Tape recordings of interviews, photographs of persons or places, drawings, maps, or written records may be considered direct confrontation in some cases but not in others. If the photograph is studied for gaining understanding of the technique of photography used or for evidence of photographic excellence, the investigator is confronting the source of his data directly. If a photograph depicts a ritual dance, the observer studying the dance is confronting his data indirectly since the picture cannot duplicate the original scene. A tape recording of a primitive song represents direct confrontation if the song is the sole object of the study and if it came unchanged from the original source. The point is that the investigator would have heard the identical sounds had he been there in person.

Whenever *identity* exists as between a telephone interview and a face-to-face interview (assuming there is no significant voice distortion), direct confrontation has taken place. Obtaining an impression by using a psychological test represents indirect confrontation since it is assumed the identical information the test yielded could not have been obtained by an interview. If the psychologist's impression is gained from a combination of test results and observation of the test-subjects' reactions to the test, he is using two methods, indirect (assessment of the personality by test responses) and direct (assessment of the personality by observation of behavior).

If in a study of wild birds that would fly away when approached, the observer must use binoculars in order to see details, the confrontation is indirect since the binoculars enable him to do something *different* than would have been possible by direct confrontation. On the other hand, if the observer watches tame pigeons with binoculars which bring these birds no closer than he could have seen them by walking up to them, he is using direct confrontation since the binoculars offer him the identical data he would have been able to obtain by direct observations.

Instruments used for convenience only or for the purpose of saving time (which do not reveal anything beyond what could have been as clearly observed without their use) are considered to be within the category of direct confrontation of data. In order to be classified as indirect confrontation, the instrument intervening between the observer and the source of the data must offer something more, or something different than that which could have been obtained by the use of direct contact with the sources of data.

Indirect Confrontation in Which Persons, Instruments, or Devices Are Intermediary

Psychometric methods consist of objective and projective tests. Objective tests are paper-and-pencil methods which require the test subject to answer specific questions designed to measure aptitudes, interests, or personality. The Minnesota Multiphasic Personality Inventory is an example of an objective test. Projective tests such as the Rorschach inkblot method are designed to investigate personality. A psychologist's individual interpretation of the responses plays a role in the evaluation of projective techniques. The fundamental idea in this kind of testing is that the test subject is expected to project outwardly covert inner feelings. These methods are used primarily in clinical psychology, and increasingly in cross-cultural studies.

Computorized methods utilize the electronic computor to identify desired data and extract them from a source of data storage. Computorized methods may fall into several different categories depending on how they are used.

Structured paper-and-pencil methods includes *questionnaires* which are often components of psychological tests, sociological surveys, and opinion polls. They are used in developing sociograms and in political science, economics, and business administration. *Inventories* and *checklists* are modifications of questionnaires. *Scales* are devices used to rate characteristics such as performance, by a graded series of steps. *Schedules* are forms or outlines (such as a checklist), on which a research worker may record his observations. Whether or not a method in which a schedule is used is classified within the direct or indirect category depends on whether the schedule is viewed as incidental to the investigator or whether the investigator is considered incidental to the schedule. Schedules which are self-administrating, information-gathering devices where the investigator role is essentially that of distributor and collector, fall within the indirect confrontation category. On the other hand, methods in which a schedule or a checklist is used merely as a rough outline around which an interview is structured, are classified as direct confrontation.

When devices are merely adjunctive and serve primarily to facilitate direct contact, their use does not make the method of confronting data sources indirect. Only when the device is essential to the unique quality of the method, i.e. if the very nature of the method depends on it, can the method be conceived of as falling within the indirect category of confrontation of data sources.

Bibliographical methods common in the humanities are not used extensively within the human sciences. They consist of library research where information is gleaned from books and manuscripts. In many respects they are identical to what I have called documentation.

Chemical and geological methods include the fossil dating technique such as fluorine, carbon-14, potassium-argon, etc., or utilizing geological information for dating archeological sites, such as used in archeology, human paleontology, and prehistory.

Physiological methods include physical examinations in which calibrated equipment is used. Any information gained by the use of devices such as the sphygmomanometer, thermometer, anthropometer, etc. fall within this category and these are frequently used in medicine, biology, psychology, sociology, and physical anthropology.

Art comparative methods utilize the graphic and plastic arts to gain information on a variety of subjects. An analysis of art may give insight into many aspects of a culture; i.e. religion, social class systems, methods of food production, etc. Drawings and paintings are studied to identify emotions and maladjustments of mental patients. Dances and adornment are sources of information about the beliefs of primitive peoples. Anthropology uses art in the study of cultures, whereas psychology concerns itself with drawings as a means of determining personality variables.

Literature comparative methods represent a trend in which

literature is utilized for illustrating conditions existing in actual life. The implication is that through a study of literature, interpretation of actual events are facilitated and given depth and perspective. Such comparisons may serve to offer easily accessible insights into human nature and are often used in cross-disciplinary studies. Rabkin (1966) in *Psychopathology and Literature* illustrates this approach.

Secondhand documentary methods involve the examination of written reports by witnesses, letters, and official descriptions by authorities. It is sometimes used in anthropology and elsewhere in the human sciences when there is a review of the literature.

Methods using reports by other persons are used in law enforcement and in many other activities. The witness represents the variable intervening between the source of the data and the person seeking to use the data.

Manipulation of the Data-Producing Sources by the Investigator

In the previous classification the methods used extracted information either directly or indirectly from phenomena as these occurred within nature or within their indigenous environmental setting. The environment from which the information was drawn was not disturbed. To do so would affect the information sought. This category, however, utilizes the very thing that the previous methods avoid. The investigator manipulates the data source—animal, man, social, or physiological condition—in order to study the ensuing variation produced by the change. Without such manipulation, the data would not be accessible to the investigator.

EXPERIMENTAL METHODS. Controlled experiments require manipulation of a variable by the investigator and stable conditions for observation, recording, and measuring. Within the human sciences, the classical experiment consists of matching two groups of people which have been equated, introducing a variable, and measuring the difference in behavior or physiological function which can be ascribed to the introduced variable. The latter is usually referred to as the *independent variable*. The response elicited is sometimes called the *response variable* or *dependent variable* and represents the event which the scientist is investigating. Classical experiments are used in many of the human sciences where research is conducted.

Controlled experiments with animals or persons use measurement to ascertain the condition of the animals before the introduction of a new variable. The condition after the variable has been introduced may then represent the experimental situation. Measured differences before and after give the experimental results. Scientists are careful to avoid selective factors (extraneous variables) which would distort the results obtained. For example, in an experiment to measure the effect of a drug, an extraneous factor such as the deprivation of sleep or food could be partially responsible for behavioral changes which might be erroneously ascribed to the effect of the drug. This type of experiment is used in medicine, genetics, psychology, pharmacology, physiology, biology, and physical anthropology.

Models are "environments" or "situations" constructed by the investigator. Within the human sciences, they facilitate exploration of physiological and behavioral patterns by serving as simpler forms from which analogies may be drawn. In cybernetics, the electronic digital computor with its feedback potential is used as a model of the human nervous system. Model situations in sociology create opportunities for understanding more complex analogous conditions. In anthropology, models are used by students and museums as replicas of objects of culture. Theoretical models and hypothetical constructs of behavior, personality, methods of learning, and modes of reacting in psychology may consist of diagrams of three-dimensional projections in which statistical or computorized factors serve as the framework of the model.

Controlled situational evaluations are obtained by observing a patient placed in a particular situation such as in a special ward, in occupational or recreational therapy, or perhaps in a new environment outside of the hospital. The method is also used in industry when an employer places a worker in a new job situation to observe changes in his attitude or productivity. The manipulation, in this instance, is not altogether different from the controlled experiment. In both cases an individual is placed in a situation where the results of his behavior may be evaluated and contrasted with a previous known standard.

NONEXPERIMENTAL METHODS. Psychodrama is used for gathering a specific type of information. The setting is artificially manipulated by the investigator. The roles played by the participants are products of the imagination. The situation is structured to obtain information useful to the participants or the therapist in resolving personality conflicts. Five other nonexperimental methods are listed in Table VI.

Analysis of Data and Definition of Problem

After data have been gathered and information obtained, evaluation and analysis can take place. We shall review some of the methods available for this purpose.

Methods of statistical analysis have greatly augmented the investigator's knowledge of the nature of the factors with which he is dealing. Within the human sciences, statistical analysis is often concerned with the probability of an event occurring. Statistical methods of comparing variables yield information about the significance of occurrences in mathematical terms. If, for example, one finds a larger number of arrests of delinquent boys in the slums than in the suburbs, by using statistics it is possible to tell to what extent this difference is due to chance or to sampling error. Another kind of statistics may be applied to analyze such groups to determine whether or not the slums or suburbs represent a significant variable. *Descriptive statistics* help reduce data to manageable proportions by using such computing measures as percentages, means, standard deviations, and correlation coefficients. *Inductive statistics* are used to infer generalized properties on the basis of known sample results. Inductive statistics are based on probability theory, a branch of mathematics, and serve as a rational basis for inductive reasoning. Induction and deduction are discussed later in the chapter.

Structural analysis consists of examining the framework of the entity under observation. If enough data have been gathered to describe the leadership within a group, structural analysis of the material could reveal information such as the lines of communications, the nature of the social structure, and the hierarchy of authority or power within the group. Sometimes structure is most easily disclosed by a graphic treatment of the data.

Sequence analysis requires the knowledge of a series by means of which similar events, objects, or situations may be compared. For example, seriation, a method of analysis in anthropology, is used to determine a sequence of change by comparison of a series of cultural material or historical events.

Pattern analysis is similar to sequence analysis except that the pattern sought is not sequential. Meaning is inferred when the data fall into a pattern which can be related to an already known pattern or to an idea. Computorization greatly aids the process of pattern analysis by clustering coded material into units which lend themselves to interpretation by the investigator.

Content analysis is similar to structural analysis except that the total gathered data are searched for all ingredients from which meaning may be derived independent of any framework.

Intuitive analysis takes place when the investigator obtains insights or finds relationships without being aware of how the new understanding became known to him. There may have been subliminal clues or relationships seen by an internal synthesis not subject to present-day scientific formulation.

Hypothesis, Theory, Law

After data have been analyzed and a meaningful pattern of relationships has emerged, hypothesis or theory formation represents the next step in data processing. Theories and laws have been described earlier in this chapter. We shall now go into greater detail.

Theory and *hypothesis* are often interchanged in general use. Both denote an inference from data and both are used to explain abstract principles that lie behind observed phenomena. However, *hypothesis* implies tentativeness and well-founded conjecture which may reasonably account for phenomena. A *hypothesis* may serve as a point of departure for scientific discussion or as a tentative guide for further investigation. On the other hand, *theory* presupposes much more supporting evidence than *hypothesis* and it implies a much wider range of application and greater likelihood of truth. Darwin's explanation of the origin of species is regarded by some as a *hypothesis* but is more often designated as the "theory of evolution." The term, *law,* in science emphasizes certainty or proof and, therefore, applies to an invariable relationship or order. When so-called laws are disproved or altered by additional evidence, the term should be changed to *theory.* For example, what has long been known as Newton's law of gravitation has been revised as a result of Einstein's discoveries and is now designated as "Newton's mathematical theory of universal gravitation."

The construction of theories and the formulation of hypotheses draw upon the scientist's power of organization and creativity. Controversy in the human sciences often centers on what is, and what is not, acceptable theory formation.

Theoretical constructs may come into being through two approaches, *inductive* and *deductive.* Empirically pure science favors the inductive approach since it gathers particulars of observed events first, then organizes them into generalities, and only later formulates hypotheses which are amenable to being tested. The test usually involves prediction which must be confirmed. If exceptions occur, they must be explained by the same rigorous methods as were used to establish the original hypothesis or theory.

To be scientifically acceptable, a theory must have the following characteristics: agreement with the observed facts; nonconflictive with laws which have been empirically demonstrated as true; communicable to others working in the field; and, finally, verifiable. A theory cannot be verified unless it can be experimentally tested.

In inductive theory, conclusions must sum up but not go beyond the observed facts. Obviously, in any practical situation, the scientist must make inferences from observation of a partial class or category of phenomena. Therefore, conclusions which are inductive in this sense are only probabilities, not certainties. Accuracy in induction depends on 1) the difficulties in obtaining representative samples; 2) the amount of homogeneity or variation of the phenomena being investigated; and 3) the precautions taken in selecting the evidence.

Instead of going from the particular to the general, as in inductive theory, deductive theory proceeds from a given premise and attempts to predict or explain particulars which follow logically. Thus deduction moves from the general to the concrete. A deductive theory cannot be conceived of as probable but must be viewed as a certainty if the original premise is correct and all inferences are logical. The vulnerability of deductive theory lies in the difficulty of accepting with certitude the premise which is the starting point of the deduction. A second problem stems from the necessity of accepting as completely sound the logic of each inference which hinges on the previous inference. Classical deduction has been modified among modern theorists but the basic approach remains as described.

Illustration of Inductive Reasoning[4]

ZZXYXYZYYZZZYXZZZY

1. *Observation*: In the above line there are X's, Y's, and Z's in different amounts, and there are no other letters.

2. *Measurement*: Z occurs 9 times; Y occurs 6 times; X occurs 3 times.

3. *Organization*: The reader who reads the line of capital letters will read Z three times as often as X, and Y twice as often as X. This conforms exactly with the number of times the writer of the line (if it is typewritten) pressed the Z, Y, and X keys.

4. *Prediction*: If the writer acts under exactly the identical conditions in the future utilizing the three letters A, B, and C, the distribution of these letters will be 9, 6, 3.

5. *Testing*: The identical situation under which the line of X's, Y's, and Z's was typed is recreated experimentally. Only one change is introduced: A, B, and C are substituted for X, Y, and Z.

6. *Confirmation*: The new line is examined and it is seen that there are 9 C's, 6 B's, and 3 A's.

7. *Generalization*: Any three letters written under the

---

[4] 1. Represents Gathering Data; 2. and 3. Analyzing Data; 4. Formulating a Hypothesis; 5. and 6. Verification.

identical field or laboratory condition in which the typing took place will be produced in the following proportions: 9:6:3.

Illustration of Deductive Reasoning

1. *The Given Premise*: N, T, and V are objects made out of the same material. N is larger than T; T is larger than V. Size and weight are positively correlated.

2. *The Deduction*: N is larger than V.

3. *Extension of Deduction*: N is heavier than V.

4. *Prediction*: If N is placed in one of the pans of Mr. Jones' accurately calibrated weighing scale and V in the other pan, the pan holding V will rise.

5. *Testing*: Testing takes place to insure that no extraneous selective factors were introduced into the demonstrated situation.

6. *Confirmation*: If the premise is true and the theory is not confirmed, it will be either because of errors of logic or mistakes in creating the testing conditions. The premise, accepted as true, cannot logically be questioned. In modern application of deduction, however, the entire process is reviewed when confirmation does not result and modifications are made which may involve the original premise.

7. *Conclusion*: In the future, Mr. Jones' scale will always be imbalanced in the predicted direction under the circumstances described. Similarly, Mr. Smith's scale will show the same imbalance under identical conditions. If their scales are identical, the angles of deflection of the pointers on Mr. Jones' and Mr. Smith's scales will correspond.

Dichotomies and Personality

The use of a deductive versus an inductive approach depends on the circumstances of the investigation, on the nature of the problem, and also on the personality of the scientist.

There are other dichotomies which are important in the human sciences. DiRenzo (1966) refers to *nominal definitions* which are rational only and *real definitions* which are empirical as perhaps the oldest dichotomy of definitions. He believes, "The distinction between these two types of concepts becomes critically significant in the matter of developing a theory."

Osborn (1965) compares the "judicial" and "creative" mind and states, "our thinking mind is mainly twofold: (1) *a judicial mind* which analyzes, compares, and chooses; (2) *a creative mind* which visualizes, foresees, and generates ideas. Judgment can help keep imagination on the track, and imagination can help enlighten judgment."

Tyler (1965) mentions two types of investigators, "the *analyzers* who concentrate on details and tend to see separate parts; and the *synthesizers* who observe the field as an integrated whole but may miss some of its details." Tyler describes *objective* and *subjective perceivers* and indicates that their differences may be related to personality characteristics. Quoting a research study, she writes about investigators "with obsessional tendencies . . . showed objective pattern . . . whereas (investigators) suffering from anxiety were more likely to show the subjective pattern." This raises the question, To what extent is what we consider acceptable in methodology a characteristic of our emotional makeup and to what extent is it a decision of our cognitive judgment?

The effectiveness of any methodology applied to human behavior depends upon the manner in which the data are gathered and on the underlying motivations and attitudes of all the participants. It is well to be aware of the fact that the experimental setting and the feeling tone between the experimenter and the human subjects are as important to successful research as the particular methodology selected.

COMPUTORIZED METHODS

After World War II when electronic feedback mechanisms were introduced to machines, a new technology came into being whose distinguishing features were the utilization of automatic control devices called *servomechanisms*. This type of system exerts control of its own operations by means of electronic circuits which send back continuous (or intermittent) signals that automatically calculate errors and correct them. Killingsworth (1962) describes the advantages of servomechanisms as follows:

Because the manipulative ability of the human is sluggish, servomechanisms are excellent replacement in control operations which call for precision and fast reaction time. Also, because the human is limited in the number of devices he can control simultaneously, servomechanisms can readily accomplish control in situations where the number of elements to be controlled are too numerous for a human operator to cope with.

Cybernetics is a word coined by Wiener (1950) derived from the Greek meaning "the art of a pilot or steersman." In its simplest form, cybernetics is the study of messages. Wiener's thesis is that the operations performed by living individuals and the operations of some of the newer communication machines "are precisely parallel." Both have sensory receptors, a special apparatus for collecting information and classifying it into a new form available for further stages of performance. Finally, in both, performed action can be corrected and reported back to a central regulatory apparatus. Wiener uses cybernetics as a means of exploring the relationship of man to machine, and of both to society. By understanding "communication" in its total sense (and this includes the feedback principle), Wiener feels a deeper appreciation of Man's nature may be achieved, and a more rational future may be planned for society.

Computer simulation may be achieved through giving the machine instructions by using tapes or prepunched cards. This is called *programming*. This process is described by Hovland (1963):

> Simulated thought, a new and promising technique, is currently being used by a wide range of behavioral scientists—psychologists, sociologists, linguists, and political scientists—to simulate thought processes, interpersonal interactions, the learning of language, and the structure of complex organization patterns.

Storage of information by machine methods is achieved by using input coding which permits an enormous amount of space reduction in the storage and filing of facts, data, and ideas.

Selection of information is quickly accomplished by the electronic digital computor which can draw any combination or series of combinations of component parts from stored information. Portions of information may be related to other portions selectively and their relationship expressed in ratios, percentages, fractions, or any desired mathematical terms.

Clustering by computors provides scientists with an automatic means of objective theory formation. The only kind of subjectivity which can emerge in such a process is that which has been programmed into it at the beginning. Computors may be equipped with certain safeguards which can assist in minimizing the input of subjective information.

Process control by digital computors is currently used in manufacturing. The fear some persons express of automated regulation of human life by the electronic digital computors stems from the possibility of applying process control to human beings. Like many other things, automation may be utilized either to aid mankind or to exploit it.

Whereas the computor can calculate, synthesize, and process data, it cannot feel emotions nor act independently without prior programming. The electronic computor is an aid to the human brain not a replacement for it. Should the mechanical brain of the computor ever make final decisions regarding the disposition of human beings, men will become automatons and machines will be their masters. Men, by creating the machines that rule them, would then have succeeded in enslaving themselves. Human brain and machine reach their highest level of value to society when each assists the other in the task of solving problems with the responsibility of final decision-making firmly kept in hand by Man.

INTUITIVE METHODS

Intuitive methods are in a class by themselves but also fall within the category of conceptual ideas having methodological implications.

Purely intuitive or occult methods are not accepted by science. Nonetheless, they are of interest to some scientists who feel that they should be investigated further to see whether a scientific basis can be discovered and, also, because their existence represents an aspect of human nature. Individuals and groups believing in the validity of any of the following methods are utilizing Criteria of Reality other than Empiricism. If Empiricism is accepted as one's own Criterion of Reality and this framework is applied to intuitive methods, one must arrive at the conclusion that these methods are unacceptable. On the other hand, if another framework for validity is used, a different conception of truth emerges. All methods are "correct" if they are consistent within their own framework.

1. *Revelation* implies knowledge derived from a supernatural source through a personal method of receiving information. The method is neither confirmable nor demonstrable. In many instances it is accepted as valid for the apperception of religious truths.

2. *Dreams* have been subjected to much scientific investigation such as their relationship to eye movement during sleep. Electroencephalography and brain implantations in animals have also been used in dream studies. Symbolic dream interpretations play a role in psychoanalysis. However, here we refer to occult methods in which dreams are used as intuitive communications by nonscientifically oriented individuals, as in "the truth was revealed to him in a dream."

3. *Hallucinations* are sensory phenomena that are private to the individual experiencing them. They represent classical symptoms of a variety of psychoses. Hallucinatory experiences have been used by some primitive peoples as a means of foreseeing the future. When induced by drugs, some claim hallucinations reveal supernatural insights.

4. *Parapsychology* (Extra Sensory Perception) has four aspects: *clairvoyance,* the perception of an object without the use of any of the known senses; *precognition,* the capacity of mentally seeing a future event; *telepathy,* the perceiver's ability to learn what the sender is thinking without use of known sense organs; *psychokinesis,* a person's ability to influence physical objects or events by thinking or concentration. Murphy (1958) and Hansel (1966) have reviewed parapsychology and have divergent opinions on the subject. In general, ESP as a phenomenon is not accepted by science because it cannot be measured by scientific criteria at the present time.

5. *Contemplation* requires concentration on spiritual matters until there is a state of mystical awareness in which new insights are obtained and truths perceived.

6. *Divination* is a method for foreseeing future events or

discovering hidden knowledge by unusual insights, supernatural powers, or intuitive perception.

7. *Ritual* is an established form of ceremony or observance. By participation in a ritual, it is believed the future may be affected in an occult manner outside of the empirical laws of cause-and-effect.

8. *Magic* refers to the methods used in primitive religions to invoke supernatural powers and subject them to human control. By means of imitative magic, priests or members of a tribe act out or designate by dances, ritual, or works of art that in which they desire assistance from supernatural powers.

9. *Prayer* is a means by which religious persons seek to change present and future events through appeal to a diety. Some who do not believe that prayer can affect external changes still feel that prayer may be a source of emotional support and hope. Members of most religious faiths believe that prayer can transcend physical nature and achieve supernatural results. They believe that important forces exist in the world that are beyond empirical validation and that these emanate from God or gods described in their oral or written tradition.

10. *Teleology* embodies the idea that plan or design are part of nature, that natural processes are goal-oriented, and that evolution has a "purpose" to achieve. Teleology conceives of natural and universal forces as directional in contrast with a mechanical view of the universe where such forces are seen as governed by statistical laws of chance. Teleology explains the present in terms of the future, in contrast to mechanisms which explain the present in terms of the past. Teleology has been put to methodological use to explore human nature by Nogar (1966) and Teilhard de Chardin (1961). The concept of teleology is unacceptable to pure empiricists who believe that it originates in intuition and that it is undemonstrable.

The Role of Intuitionism

Intuitionism may have a variety of meanings depending on how the term is used. In general, there are two kinds of intuition—the mystical idea of revelation which is believed to surpass the power of the intellect in establishing truth and the mathematical idea of an axiom or a self-evident proposition universally accepted as true, such as "two parallel lines will never meet."

Within recent years there has been a reappraisal of the nature of mathematical, physical, and geometric truths. With the advent of relativism, many axioms which represented absolutes were modified and displaced. Aristotelian and Newtonian axioms once considered unassailable have given way to the new scheme of things as visualized in Einstein's era. The day may come when Einstein's concepts will be modified by still newer ideas. The difference between axioms and revelations should be clear. Although axioms represent absolute truths of the moment, they may be displaced by newer concepts. Intuition, however, is considered to be such a pure and undiluted aspect of truth by the believer that its validity can never be questioned.

CROSSCURRENTS IN SCIENCE

Any exposition of methods such as the one in this chapter, is likely to leave the reader with the impression that science represents an orderly harmony. In one sense this is true but in another this picture is false. It is essential to be aware of the conflicting currents and cross-currents of opinion that exist today in the area of scientific methodology. Science is full of controversy as it both rejects and encourages new ideas. It is the function of science to seek innovations leading to discovery of new knowledge while adhering to the scientific tradition of maintaining the authenticity of evidence.

SUMMARY

The scientific method was described and it was pointed out that hominology must include explorations of phenomena outside of the scope of science as well as those with which the scientific method can deal. Values, moral judgment, and ethics must be discussed within the framework of Man's total nature. A new system of classifying methods within the human sciences was introduced. This system is predicated on the kind of confrontation the investigator has with the sources of data: direct, indirect, or by the manipulation of the environment as when an artificial situation is created by the investigator in order to elicit certain kinds of data. Like the old system of classification, the new one has advantages and disadvantages but permits a more discrete separation of methods minimizing overlap. Methods used in automation, intuitive methods, and inductive and deductive theoretical formulations were described. Differences between hypothesis, theories, laws, and principles were discussed.

REFERENCES

BERELSON, B., AND STEINER, G. A.: *Human Behavior.* New York, Harcourt, 1964.

BROOM, L., AND SELZNICK, P.: *Sociology.* New York, Harper, 1963.

DiRENZO, G. J.: Toward explanation in the behavioral sciences. In DiRenzo, G. J. (Ed.): *Concept, Theory, and Explanation in the Behavioral Sciences.* New York, Random, 1966.

GOOD, C. V.; BARR, A. S., AND SCATES, D. E.: *The Methodology of Educational Research.* New York, Appleton, 1941.

HANSEL, C. E. M.: *ESP; A Scientific Evaluation.* New York, Scribner, 1966.

HOVLAND, C. I.: Computer simulation in the behavioral sciences. In Berelson, B. (Ed.): *The Behavioral Sciences Today.* New York, Harper, 1963.

KILLINGSWORTH, C. C.: Industrial relations and automation. *Ann Amer Acad Political Soc Sci,* March 1962, vol. 340.

KOENIG, S.: *Sociology, An Introduction to the Science of Society.* New York, Barnes & Noble, 1957.

MURPHY, G.: Trends in the study of extrasensory perception. *Amer Psychol, 13*:69-76, Jan. 1958.

NOGAR, R. J.: *The Wisdom of Evolution.* New York, New Am. Lib., 1966.

OSBORN, A. F.: *Applied Imagination.* rev. ed. New York, Scribner, 1965.

RABKIN, L. Y. (Ed.): *Psychopathology and Literature.* San Francisco, Chandler, 1966.

TEILHARD DE CHARDIN, P.: *The Phenomenon of Man.* New York, Harper, 1961.

TYLER, L. E.: *The Psychology of Human Differences.* New York, Appleton, Meredith, 1965.

WIENER, N.: *The Human Use of Human Beings.* Cambridge, Houghton, 1950.

Chapter 7

HISTORICAL PERSPECTIVES IN
HUMAN EVOLUTION

"A firemist and a planet
A crystal and a cell
A jelly-fish and a saurian
And caves where cave-men dwell;
Then a sense of law and beauty,
And a face turned from the clod
Some call it Evolution
And others call it God . . ."

QUOTED BY J. W. N. SULLIVAN,
Limitations of Science

IN THE PREVIOUS CHAPTER, some of the methods used in the human sciences were classified and described. These methods have contributed to the scientific progress which typifies our age. At the same time, they have led to the fragmentation of knowledge mentioned in the first chapter. Hominology is concerned with how fragmentation may be minimized for students in human sciences who search for a comprehensive picture of Man.

Let us turn once more to the problem with which hominology was designed to cope. This problem is summarized by J. Huxley (1957):

> Specialization has led to the accumulation of vast quantities of new knowledge; but also to the paradoxical result that much of that knowledge cut itself off from any central common pool and from cross-fertilizing contacts with other currents of thought. Some branches of science have shown tendencies towards isolationism and autarkic self-sufficiency strangely similar to those shown by various nation-states in their economic and cultural affairs. This has had its counterpart in education, notably in the compartmentalization of subjects of study at our universities. Wherever and however manifested, these tendencies act so as to sterilize great volumes of

144

knowledge and to impede the growth of a common tradition and a common basis for human action.

FRAGMENTATION VERSUS COMPREHENSIVE VIEW

Why does compartmentalization, which Huxley finds "sterilizing," persist when its disadvantages are recognized? Is it because existing methods and techniques acceptable to science do not lend themselves easily to the task of formulating an integrated view of Man? By demanding that scientists reveal a picture of total Man, are we asking them to step outside of their own Criteria of Reality? To be complete, such a picture must include considerations of values, goals, faith, goodness, evil, determinism, and freedom. Can we blame scientists for not wishing to mix scientific methods with speculations not amenable to scientific inquiry?

Fathers Teilhard de Chardin (1961) and Nogar (1966) are among those contemporary scientists who have tried such a combination. These priest-scientists have attempted to relate organic evolution to the tenets of Christianity. In doing so, they have actually involved themselves with one of religion's traditional roles. Most religions offer accounts of mankind's genesis, and many correlate events occurring at that time with contemporary Man's nature and his present struggles.

A fundamental question in a scientific study of total Man is this, In spite of the limitations of its methodology, does science, nevertheless, have the potential resources for coping with human nature in a comprehensive and unfragmented manner? Is science capable of treating such a topic as total Man without mixing Criteria of Reality? Past experience has shown that scrambling physical with metaphysical concepts satisfies no one. Must science, then, leave total Man to religion and concern itself exclusively with parts and particles?

No matter how we may answer this question, it seems that the search for a meaningful picture of Man within science will be pursued. Whereas science considers values, ethics, faith, and human purpose as largely outside of its empirical realm, it has yet to offer scientific proof that this inevitably need be so. Many have been disturbed by the thought that to be empirically pure one must split Man into halves with one part beckoning the scientist, the other, bearing signs: No Trespassing! Bronowski (1965) comments,

> Is it true that concepts of science and those of ethics and values belong to different worlds? Is the world of *what is* subject to test, and the world of *what ought to be* subject to no test? I do not believe so.

Shapley (1964), an astronomer, asks,

> Have we now come to the end of the journey, or are there other steps ahead? In view of the rapid growth of scientific techniques and the continual exercise of the logical imagination, it would not be wise to suggest that we shall *never* find need for further adjustment of the concept of man's place in the universe— that we shall never discover a reason for an orienting adjustment which transcends both the physical and biological orientation. . . .

Perhaps, the redefining of terms may make it possible for science to accept concepts now considered outside of its periphery. Sinnott (1955) suggests, "By defining the concept of purpose in these terms (mechanical regulation) . . . one can make it biologically respectable again and relieve it from the stigma of 'final' causation and mysticism." He quotes Herbert J. Muller (1954), "purpose . . . need not be puzzled over as a strange divine something. . . . It is simply implicit in the fact of organization and it is to be studied. . . ." And Burr (1962) a professor of anatomy comments on the dilemma the human sciences face as follows:

> It should be obvious that this whole question stems from the fact that we have not come to grips with the nature of man or the meaning of existence . . . It behooves us to ask if there is not some way out of the dilemma, some way by which we can find some universals, some factors, operating in . . . London, New York, Peking. Science has discovered many such universals—gravitation, electricity, chemical formulae and reactions, the laws of movement of the heavily bodies. Using them, man has been able to predict the coming of an eclipse, the result of mixing certain chemicals, the trajectory of a missile and of its ultimate fate in space. If Science, aided by technology, can do this, might it not be that the application of the methods of science to the study of mankind would yield equally valid and useful consequences? To do this we must, perforce, start with Man.

The comprehensive treatment of Man requires an exploration

of Man's biological beginnings and his changing bio-social development throughout time. These can then be related to his present individual and group behavior. The horizontal picture of men living today and their forms of culture reveals much useful information. But an examination of the present alone cannot yield relevant perspectives. For this, the vertical (longitudinal) view is required. The case history of the human species gives the study of contemporary human problems the vertical guidelines which the past provides. In its simplest form the relationship between the past, present, and future is illustrated in Figure 15.

The line AB represents time; DC, change. However, time and change do not correspond exactly. Each moves at its own pace. They do exist in such a manner that time serves as a frame of reference for change and vice versa. Change depends on many factors, including time. A study of total Man requires the exploration of the entire area ABCD. The theory of organic evolution provides convenient framework for an exploration of the past.

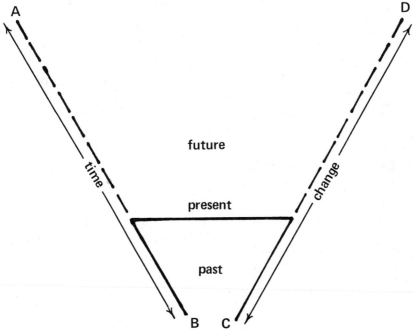

FIGURE 15.   Time-Change Perspectives.

EVOLUTION THEORY

The concept of evolution is not a product of modern thought.[1] Early Indian and Greek philosophers speculated on the evolvement of life from lower to higher forms. Thales, who lived in the sixth century B.C., hypothesized that there is one single elementary cosmic matter that accounts for all things within nature and speculated that this was water. He followed this with the theory that all life had a marine origin. Aristotle spoke of life in terms of development and so did the Greek philosophers who belonged to the early Atomistic School. However, the notion of natural selection as a basis for evolution did not occur till the nineteenth century. The eighteenth century—Age of Enlightenment—provided the necessary receptive climate for ideas on human behavior and produced such writers on these topics as Diderot, Voltaire, Rousseau, Hume, Thomas Paine, Lessing, and Kant. These men foreshadowed Charles Darwin and Herbert Spencer one century later.

Darwin and Spencer

Darwin, one of the co-discoverers of the natural selection theory (with Alfred Russel Wallace), published his monumental *Origin of Species* in 1859. Knowing the temper of the times, Darwin wrote his publisher, "If after looking over part of the MS you do not think it likely to have a remunerative sale, I completely and explicitly free you from your offer."

As could have been expected, the book met with a storm of both praise and abuse. This situation was renewed when twelve years later, Darwin published the *Descent of Man* (1871). To Darwin, "survival of the fittest" through physical struggle was the most important aspect of selection. For this reason, he saw doom for social systems that tried to eliminate struggle. Darwin viewed the morality existing in the society of his time as a

---

[1] As used within hominology, the theory of evolution offers a framework which the student may feel entirely free to adopt or reject. Presented in this way, the study of evolution represents no threat to those whose Criteria of Reality differ, i.e. the people who for one reason or another cannot accept this theory. Even for these, however, it is worth studying since it has had historical influences that have helped shape modern thinking.

development of early social human instincts. However, he did not claim that instincts were necessarily the only basis for morality.

The writings of Herbert Spencer, a self-taught biological philosopher, embraced much of the scientific knowledge of the day and he wielded a tremendous influence in his time (1820-1903).

The starting point of Spencer's deductive system was the conservation of energy or "persistence of force" as he called it. His final conclusion was that the human species would evolve into a harmonious and stable society "of the greatest perfection and the most complete happiness." Combining biology and physics, he defined evolution as an integration of matter and a concomitant dissipation of motion, "during which matter passes from indefinite, incoherent homogeneity to definite, coherent, heterogeneity." Adaptation was seen as the process which brought an ordered universe into being. The process was "cyclic" in which evolution was followed by dissolution and integration by disintegration. But this could not go on forever. Eventually a state of equilibrium would be reached. In an organism this would be death while in society the end of the process would represent homeostasis.

The wide scope of this prolific writer is reflected in the titles of his written works. Among these are the following: *First Principles* (1864); *Synthetic Philosophy* (1892); *Biology* (1864-1867); *Psychology* (1870-1872); *Sociology* (1877-1896); *Ethics* (1892-1893); *The Study of Sociology* (1873).

The basis of Spencer's ethics was that "every man is free to do what he wills, provided he infringes not the equal freedom of every other man" and this theme represented the ultra-individualism for which he became known. He noted that present Man's nature still reflected the vestiges of early predatory life but he believed that if the natural processes were not interfered with, an acme of human perfection would evolve. This could not occur, however, if the state inhibited the natural processes which tend to eliminate the weak and the unsuccessful.

Since Spencer equated adaptation with ethical progress, nonadaptation was seen as the root of all evil. Spencer viewed the state as an agency of nonadaptation. The state helped to keep the unfit alive. But if adaptation were to lead to ultimate perfection, then those who were unfit must not be perpetuated. His view was, "The whole effort of nature is to get rid of such, to clear the world of them, and make room for the better." Since he felt that the state should not interfere with private initiative, Spencer opposed state banking, state supported education, state charity for the poor, state support and regulation of housing, and even tariffs and government postal services.

Spencer did not oppose voluntary charity. He wrote also on the injustice of private land ownership and on the rights of women and children. But the rights he defended most vigorously were the "right to ignore the state" and the right to an unopposed individualism.

This championing of free enterprise made him the prophet of the businessmen who wielded power in the industrial revolution and its aftermath. He became the spokesman of the laissez-faire tradition at a time when rapid industrial expansion was accompanied by an unrestricted exploitation.

It was not Darwin but Spencer who supplied the phrase "survival of the fittest" and he developed from this concept a morality which lent a philosophical sanction to the commercial and industrial methods of his time. In this he did not remain unchallenged. Henry George, a contemporary, wrote, "Mr. Spencer is like one who might insist that each should swim for himself in crossing a river, ignoring the fact that some had been artificially provided with corks and others artificially loaded with lead." Spencer insisted that this "loading" was one of natural endowment and that interference with its free expression would encourage the deterioration of the human species.

Some sociologists do not credit Spencer with any significant achievements. Others acknowledge that he has made contributions which include his concept of functional analysis. Kardiner and Preble (1963) review Spencer's work as follows:

> Spencer . . . was not satisfied with merely collecting and classifying data on primitive peoples; he wanted to make some sense out of the evidence, to discover what it was about the particular arrangement of institutions in a society that kept the society in equilibrium

. . . He was willing to go off the 'beaten track' . . . to discover what mattered to people in their daily lives. . . .

Above all, Spencer believed that human behavior, as expressed in social structure and process, is susceptible of scientific inquiry . . . He over-simplified the complexities of human life, and his conclusions have failed to stand the test of time. He erred on the side of optimism, but that failure seems preferable to the cynicism of much of modern anthropology with respect to the possibility of establishing a science of man.

Since Spencer examined Man through the entire spectrum of the human knowledge available to him in his time, he may be considered as having worked along hominological lines—not so much because of what he was able to accomplish but because of what he attempted to do.

Nietzche

Friedrich Nietzche, the German philosopher, predicted the creation of a ruler class of superior men. He rejected Christian virtues which he viewed as antithetical to the natural law of "tooth and claw" from which his concept of ethics was drawn. Nietzche saw virtue in the use of ruthless brute strength. Compassion, softness, meekness—the "Semitic" values were described as degrading to the human race and represented a "trap" into which Man had fallen.

Whereas Nietzche's views are rejected by most ethical philosophers, May, *et al* (1958) and some existentialists interpret him differently and these credit him as being among "those visionaries who accurately foresaw (the) growing spilt between truth and reality in Western Culture" and "who endeavored to call Western man back from the delusion that reality can be comprehended in an abstracted, detached way." Some of Nietzche's writings described how blocked instinctual powers are turned inward and transformed into self-hatred, resentment, and aggression. Freud acknowledged Nietzche as one of the men who had discovered some of the important insights into human nature which later culminated in the concept of psychoanalysis.

Sumner and Keller

In the United States, William Graham Sumner represented

the group which some called *Social Darwinists*. These attempted to apply evolutionary theories to society. Influenced by the writings of Malthus (1798) and Spencer, Sumner decided not to devote his life to theology as he had planned but instead studied sociology to become a reformer of the "survival of the fittest" school. The struggle for existence became his yardstick for measuring the legitimacy of social and legislative action. His disciple, Albert Galloway Keller,[2] edited Sumner's *Folkways* 1906) and published Sumner's *Science of Society* (1927) after the latter's death.

The concept of human society as a mirror image of organic evolution led to a reaction in which an entirely different emphasis was given to the development of social theories. This reaction deepened as evolution was used to justify racism, poverty, and all manner of exploitation. A number of social philosophers adhering to the evolutionary model arrived at conclusions that were quite unlike those of Spencer and Nietzche, among these were Fiske and Kropotkin.

Fiske and Kropotkin

John Fiske and Pyotr (Peter) Alexeyevich Kropotkin were both born in 1842; one in the United States, the other in Russia. Fiske was a historian and philosopher who attempted to reconcile moral values with evolution and human biological processes. Most of his writings were dominated by the search for a unifying principle which could be applied to the course of human life from origin to final destiny. He interpreted Darwin's theory of evolution philosophically and came to the conclusion that it "shows us distinctly for the first time how creation and the perfecting of Man is the goal toward which Nature's work has all the while been trending."

His *Outline of Cosmic Philosophy* (1874) elaborates the thesis that survival required not only competition but also per-

---

[2] Keller headed the Department in which I majored at Yale. I can easily recall his florid face, benign features, solid frame, abundant white hair, booming voice, and dynamic personality. His courses were popular because he spoke with conviction, sincerity, and humor on a topic—the human society—in which students have a natural interest.

sistent social cooperation within animal species, including Man. This difference in emphasis led him to conclusions which were direct opposites of those held by Spencer. Fiske explained that Man's moral nature stems from human helplessness at birth and from the prolonged human infancy (*The Meaning of Infancy,* 1909). It is this, Fiske argues, that makes Man different from all other mammals and provides the possibility for humans to acquire a sense of devotion and sacrifice which the care of the human neonate demands. The relatively short period of human gestation permits the human infant to be socially pliable at birth in contrast with the newborn in the rest of the animal world. The longer periods of socialization on the part of the nurturing adults has led Man from family life to clan, and finally, to a civilized society. The recognition of the important role of Man's prolonged infancy represents Fiske's primary contribution to evolutionary moral theory.

Kropotkin, the Russian revolutionist, is known to the world as a leading philosopher of anarchism. He came from a princely family but abandoned first a military career and then one as a geographer. His anarchistic views were not sympathetic to Marxist political philosophy and his life included exile and prison. Kropotkin's *Mutual Aid* (1902) emphasized cooperation as a major factor in evolution and supported this thesis with observations of mutual aid among species of rodents, birds, and deer of the Siberian tundras. Using his wide reading and erudition, he documented his work from an impressive range of literature. His interpretation of evolution led him to very different conclusions than those reached by the social "tooth-and-claw" thinkers. He explained his views in *Mutual Aid* as follows:

> . . . competition is not the rule either in the animal world or in mankind. It is limited among animals to exceptional periods, and natural selection finds better fields for its activity. Better conditions are created by elimination of competition by means of mutual aid and mutual support . . . competition is always injurious to the species, and you have plenty of resources to avoid it . . . (avoiding competition) is the surest means for giving to each the greatest safety, the best guarantee of existence . . . that is the tendency of nature . . . that is what nature teaches us.

From Drummond to Bellamy

Henry Drummond, a Scottish preacher, considered the struggle for life as it took place in evolution to be only the first factor which was followed by a second one on a higher level termed "the struggle for life of others." In his *Natural Law in the Spiritual World* (1883), he offered a teleological interpretation of evolution in which moral behavior was rooted within nature. Mindful of the implication which many saw in Darwin's *Descent of Man*, Drummond delivered a series of lectures (Lowell Lectures, Harvard University, 1894) entitled *The Ascent of Man* in which he attempted to portray evolution as having benign social goals.

A British writer, Benjamin Kidd, expresses similar objectives in his *Social Evolution* (1894). Lester Ward, an American sociologist, developed a theory of planned progress (*Dynamic Sociology,* 1883) which he called *telesis.* He maintained that through education and intellect, Man would master his destiny and direct social evolution.

When, at last, theology became reconciled to Darwin's theory of evolution, it drew from it conclusions which were intended to strengthen the Christian universal view. Walter Rauschenbusch (1912) wrote,

> Translate the evolutionary theories into religious faith and you have the doctrine of the Kingdom of God. This combination with scientific evolutionary thought has freed the kingdom ideal of its catastrophic setting and its background of demonism, and so adapted it to the climate of the modern world.

Both the altruistic and competitive interpretations of evolution developed against a background dominated by two British writers, Thomas Robert Malthus (1766-1834), an economist, and Jeremy Bentham (1748-1832), a philosopher. Malthus, to whom Darwin acknowledged indebtedness, contended that poverty is unavoidable because population increases by a geometric ratio and the means of subsistence by an arithmetic ratio. He saw "moral restraint," war, famine, and disease as the only preventative checks on the growth of human population and his predictions of the future of the human race were correspondingly gloomy. Bentham, the founder of *utilitarianism*, took the position that the goal of social ethics is to achieve the greatest good for the greatest number. Spencer who lived in Bentham's era did not dispute this goal but did not agree with Bentham's theory that the purpose of political institutions and laws should serve the requirements of social ethics.

With Edward Bellamy's contention that the economic system caused many unfit, instead of those most fit, to succeed, the cycle of survival concepts completed its full turn. Bellamy was an American novelist and his influential novel, *Looking Backward 2000-1887* (1889), describes a socialistic utopia. The hero of his book awakes in the year 2000 A.D. to discover that human nature had not changed but that social institutions had undergone a radical transformation. Bellamy started a social political movement predicated on the "principle that the Brotherhood of Humanity is one of the eternal truths that govern the world's progress on lines which distinguish human nature from brute force."

His strong expressions against the social value of competition did not remain unchallenged nor were they accepted as the final word either in his time or later. One of Bellamy's contemporary critics wrote, "I must deem any man very shallow . . . who fails to discern in competition the force to which it is mainly due that mankind have risen from stage to stage in intellectual, moral, and physical power" (Walker, 1876).

BIOLOGY AND SOCIETY

The impact of Darwinism on theories of society was examined by Richard Hofstadter (1955) in *Social Darwinism in American Thought*. After discussing the theoretical justifications of social trends which followed in the wake of Darwin's writings, Hofstadter concludes that most humanists now believe

> that biological ideas as the 'survival of the fittest' whatever their doubtful value in natural science, are utterly useless in attempting to understand society; that the life of man in society, while it is incidentally a biological fact, has characteristics that are not reducible to biology and must be explained in the distinctive terms of a cultural analysis; that the physical well-being of men is the result of

their social organization and not vice-versa; that social improvement is a product of advances in technology and social organization, not of breeding or selective elimination; that judgments as to the value of competition between men or enterprises must be based upon social and not allegedly biological consequences; and finally, that there is nothing in nature or a naturalistic philosophy of life to make impossible the acceptance of moral sanctions that can be employed for the common good.

Earlier in England, T. H. Huxley (1894), a defender of evolution as biological process, reacted to Spencerian doctrines and denied that evolution or cosmic law is capable of providing any basis for human ethics or social theory. He agreed with Spencer that biological evolution represents a brutal struggle for survival but claimed that social development could not be rooted in it. He maintained that biological and sociological evolution are two entirely distinct and separate processes and that no relationship whatsoever existed between them.

The analogy between the struggle for existence and social dynamics as conceived by the social Darwinists suffered from a number of false assumptions. Below are some of the errors inherent in doctrines predicated on the existence of a one-to-one relationship between organic evolution and the evolution of human social values:

1. Whether evolution is seen as a "merciless struggle" or as "group cooperation," the organic development of life is placed into a misleading narrow focus. Regardless of whether one attributes conflict, competition, harmony, or solidarity to it, such interpretation represent an oversimplification of the many complex factors which are involved. In both views, the implication exists that if two processes, such as biological evolution and human evolution, are developmentally related, they must exist within the same dimensional level. It ignores the possibility of *transcendence* which we shall discuss later.

2. All inflexible theories rigidly formulated around the existing knowledge of one epoch which allow no room for modification are usually discarded when additional knowledge becomes available. This happened when Lamarkian concepts of the inheritance of environmental modifications were challenged by three new ideas which together undermined the basic premise

that characteristics acquired during one's lifetime can be genetically passed on to the following generation. Among the new discoveries were the Mendelian laws of heredity, Weismann's doctrine of noninheritability of acquired characteristics, and DeVries' theory of "sports" or mutations.

3. Teleological views conceive of evolution as a process heading into a predetermined direction, implying that nature has a purpose or goal which, if correctly interpreted, can explain the route that social development will, or ought to, follow. All that is necessary is to correctly assess the nature of the "universal goal" and one then has the answer to questions about future development. Teleology may also supply information on what is "right" or ethical. If nature has a purpose, obviously, those concepts which are in harmony with this purpose are the correct ones.

The matter of teleology is an exceedingly troublesome one. Teleological implications creep into situations in which the word, *ought* is employed. The teleological dilemma is evident in the question, Ought we to say ought? There are some who, without any hesitation, would reply in the affirmative but one would usually find that their Criterion of Reality, in this instance, is an authoritarian one. Those within the empirical fold are likely rule out the implication of "ought" in natural phenomena. Since purpose in nature has neither been proven nor disproven, the matter of teleology remains controversial. However, a review of contemporary scientific writings suggests that the position of some scientists to teleological arguments is not as inflexible as it was a number of years ago. Churchman (1966) in *Science* writes,

> The scientific interpretation of "purpose" and "choice" probably do not satisfy the basic psychological wish of man to be a free agent, but modern teleology has certainly cleared the air enough so that the classical issue of freedom versus determinism can be redefined in a significant manner.

Nevertheless, to postulate evolution or any cosmic process as having a "purpose" places the burden of proof upon the holder of this point of view. Simpson (1951) considers it a basic weakness to try to find out "what evolution has been up to, or even what evolution seems to *want* and then to assume that promotion of this is ethically right." He equates this with "placing evolution in the position occupied by God or by His revelation in intuitive ethics." He states that this is "an evasion of responsibility" for he sees that finding a predetermined "purpose" obviates the necessity of making a choice.

It is not for this reason, however, that teleology is methodologically rejected by most scientists. Science cannot accept that which cannot be proven and still remain *science* as it is presently defined. Many believe that to change the definition of science is one way to weaken and possibly destroy it.

In spite of the danger of making false assumptions and engaging in "wishful thinking" as Keller called it, the necessity to search for a meaningful relationship between Man's biological evolutionary past and his contemporary social, cultural, and ethical present remains. If it exists, the understanding of such a relationship is necessary for those who view mankind as being engaged in a continual process of *becoming.* This awareness of becoming has a correlary: we cannot possibly be expected, as yet, to have *arrived.*

In the early turn of this century, evolution was the pliable tool that could "prove" anything which suited the need and ideas of a given reformer regarding Man's moral nature. When the topic was finally played out, social scientists were inclined to shy away from the temptation of renewing the exploration of a relationship between organic evolution and ethics.

But people began to ask whether one could avoid the question of a possible interrelationship between the nonorganic and organic worlds and human society. This coupled with the need for an unfragmented picture of Man, helped reopen the issue of the role and place of evolution in Man's current struggle to find and understand himself. Sinnott (1955) observes, "Philosopher and biologist both should learn to widen their horizons."

SUMMARY

A comprehensive treatment of Man requires an exploration of Man's biological beginnings. Organic evolution provides a framework within which such a study may take place. After publication of Darwin's *Origin of Species*, a group of writers attempted to relate Man's social evolution to organic evolution and they were called Social Darwinists. The works and ideas of these writers were reviewed and their influence on subsequent sociological theory examined. It was pointed out that one cannot validly postulate theories on human behavior using an interpretation derived from natural selection as it operates in evolutionary theory. Three false assumptions were described. Because of the errors made in the past by those who used biological interpretation naïvely, contemporary behavioral scientists are inclined to avoid considering organic evolution as a possible source for understanding human behavior. The question of whether or not there are interrelationships between the non-organic, organic worlds, and human society remains largely unanswered.

REFERENCES

BELLAMY, E.: *Looking Backward 2000-1887*. Boston, Houghton, 1889.

BRONOWSKI, J.: *Science and Human Values*. New York, Harper, 1965.

BURR, H. S.: *The Nature of Man and the Meaning of Existence*. Springfield, Thomas, 1962.

CHURCHMAN, C. W.: *Perception and deception*. Science, 153:3740, Sept. 2, 1966.

DARWIN, C.: *Descent of Man*. London, J. Murray, 1871.

DARWIN, C.: *The Origin of Species*. London, J. Murray, 1859. (Reprinted, New York, New Am. Lib., 1958.)

DRUMMOND, H.: *Natural Law in the Spiritual World*. New York, Pott, Young, and Company, 1883.

DRUMMOND, H.: *The Ascent of Man*. New York, A. L. Burt, 1894.

FISKE, J.: *Outline of Cosmic Philosophy*. Boston, Houghton, 1874, 2 vols.

FISKE, J.: *The Meaning of Infancy*. Boston, Houghton, 1909.

HOFSTADTER, R.: *Social Darwinism in American Thought*. Boston, Beacon, 1955.

HUXLEY, J.: *Evolution in Action*. New York, New Am. Lib., 1957.

HUXLEY, T. H.: *Evolution and Ethics and Other Essays*. New York, Humbolt, 1894.

KARDINER, A., AND PREBLE, E.: *They Studied Man*. New York, New Am. Lib., 1963.

KIDD, B.: *Social Evolution*. New York, Macmillan, 1894.

KROPOTKIN, P.: *Mutual Aid*. London, Heinemann Imported Bks., 1902.

MALTHUS, T. R.: *An Essay on the Principle of Population*. London, 1798.

MAY, R.; ANGEL, E., AND ELLENBERGER, H. F. (Eds.): *Existence, A New*

Dimension in Psychiatry and Psychology. New York, Basic Books, 1958.

MULLER, H. J.: *The Uses of the Past.* New York, New Am. Lib., 1954.

NOGAR, R. J.: *The Wisdom of Evolution.* New York, New Am. Lib., 1966.

RAUSCHEBUSCH, W.: *Christianizing the Social Order.* New York, Macmillan, 1912.

SHAPLEY, H.: The fourth adjustment. In Rapport, S., and Wright, H.: *Science: Method and Meaning.* New York, Washington Square, 1964.

SIMPSON, G. G.: *The Meaning of Evolution.* New York, New Am. Lib., 1951.

SINNOTT, E. W.: *The Biology of the Spirit.* New York, Viking, 1955.

SPENCER, H.: *Biology.* New York, Appleton, 1864-1867, 2 vols.

SPENCER, H.: *Ethics.* New York, Appleton, 1892-1893, 2 vols.

SPENCER, H.: *First Principles.* New York, Appleton, 1864. (Reprinted New York, De Witt Revolving Fund, 1958.)

SPENCER, H.: *Psychology.* New York, Appleton, 1870-1872, 2 vols.

SPENCER, H.: *Sociology.* New York, Appleton, 1877-1896, 3 vols.

SPENCER, H.: *Synthetic Philosophy.* New York, Appleton, 1892.

SPENCER, H.: *The Study of Sociology.* New York, Appleton, 1873, 8 vols. (Reprinted Ann Arbor, U. of Mich., 1961.)

SUMNER, W. G.: *Folkways.* Boston, Ginn, 1906. (Reprinted New York, New Am. Lib., 1960.)

SUMNER, W. G.: *Science of Society.* New Haven, Yale U. P., 1927, 4 vols.

TEILHARD DE CHARDIN, P.: *The Phenomenon of Man.* New York, Harper, 1961.

WALKER, F. A.: *The Wages Question.* New York, Henry Holt, 1876.

WARD, L.: *Dynamic Sociology.* New York, Appleton, 1883, 2 vols.

Chapter 8

CONTEMPORARY SEARCHERS FOR
MAN'S BASIC NATURE

"Man, the scientist and technologist, has outstriped man, the moral and natural philosopher. Discoveries aggregate, with speed and pretentiousness, without much evidence that the moral philosophers and theologians can evaluate them as part of the meaning and purpose of man, or that the natural philosophers can integrate them in the unity of Nature."

GUY S. METRAUX,
Secretary-General, International
Commission for a History of the
Scientific and Cultural Development
of Mankind

OLSON, E. C. (1966) has used the label, the *Searchers,* for the contemporary writers who are exploring the nature of Man within the larger framework of natural history and cosmology. In their treatment of Man, these authors examine not only human evolution but the evolution of all life. The theory of evolution with which they deal with has undergone a number of modifications since the days of Darwin. Olson summarizes these changes as follows: "physical struggle is now considered a minor part of selection. Any shift in the genotype operates as a factor in adaptation. No element of physical struggle is necessarily involved." Gould, writing in *Natural Science* (Dec. 1975), views the recent concept of genetic variability occurring in both stable and unstable environments as "a threat to Darwinism." He refers to a school of "neutralism" which is not in accord with Darwin's views on natural selection in evolution.

Borrowing a term from Emerson, Olson (1966) describes the ecological state which evolution achieves as *dynamic homeostasis* in which there is a "balance adjustment of organisms to each

161

other and to their physical environment." Olson speculates teleologically, "If there is a goal of dynamic balanced adaptation, then many aspects of 'good' and 'bad' can be defined as they contribute to, or detract from, attainment of that end."

CONTEMPORARY HOMINOLOGICAL WORKS

The list of contemporary "searchers" (in the sense that Olson used this term) is relatively small. He has no difficulty in describing their work in a few pages. In the following pages, his list has been augmented by the addition of other authors who use the hominological approach in investigating the past, present, and future within the context of total Man. These writers differ in their Criteria of Reality, nationality, religious outlook, methodology, and in their final conclusions, but all of them explore the present and future within the broad boundaries of organic evolution. These authors go beyond the consideration of our species, *Homo sapiens*, and trace their way back to the advent of *Homo*, the genus, *Man*. Most of them go back much further than this to the very beginning of the universe, the formation of the earth, and the evolvement of life on earth. In every case, their treatment of the subject is nondisciplinary and they avoid compartmentalization by emphasizing developmental continuity using a cosmic frame of reference. All the books referred to are the works of individual men, not the collective effort of a group of specialists. A group effort in which each member writes on a topic of his personal interest and competency cannot produce the level of integration which an individual writer is capable of achieving. Furthermore, all of the writers in our list have gone beyond their own specific disciplinary field and have become generalists in their study of Man.

1. *Human Destiny*, Lecomte du Noüy (1949). This book, by a biologist, begins with a table showing the ages of life on earth extending back 1200 million years. In his introduction the author writes,

> The rapid development of the material side of civilization had aroused the interest of men and kept them in a kind of breathless expectation of the next day's miracle. Little time was left for the solving of the true problems: the human problems. Men were

hypnotized by the incredible brilliant display of new inventions following one another almost without interruption from 1880 on, and were like children who are so fascinated by their first view of a three-ring circus that they even forgot to eat and drink.

Du Noüy develops a *telefinal hypothesis* to explain how moral ideas may be derived from an assimilation of scientific phenomena and how there may be a dissociation between "body" and "spirit." According to his view, "this dissociation is no longer considered an act of faith, but as a scientific fact . . ." He summarizes the longitudinal process as follows:

> First of all we observe the reality of five fundamental, undeniable facts: The beginning of life, represented by extremely simple organized beings; the evolution of life towards more and more complex forms; the actual results of this long process, namely man and the human brain; the birth of thought and of independent development of these ideas in different parts of the terrestial globe.

Not many biologists give du Noüy's "facts" unqualified endorsement. His implication that evolution is an unswerving lineal process does not tally with modern concepts that evolution can be, and has been, retrogressive at times and that it is sometimes impossible to state just what phenomenon is truly an "advance" towards complexity. Complexity is not only a mere matter of greater accumulation of cells and structures but can manifest itself in different ways and on different dimensions. Evolution has, at times, moved from complexity to simplicity. Some scientist would question the implication in the statement, "the spontaneous and independent development of spiritual ideas in different parts of the globe." The whole problem of separating parallelism from diffusion enters into play when separate origins are claimed as evidence.

Looking at the present and the future, du Noüy sees evolution developing

> . . . on a different plane, a plane no longer physical but psychological, as every improvement, every new *structural* complication of the brain manifests itself, on our scale of observation, by *psychological* phenomena. Any psychological evolution is expressed mainly by the improvement of abstract, moral, and spiritual ideas. It follows from this that anything which opposes this evolution in the moral and spiritual realm, "which tends to bring about a regression toward

the animal to place man under the dictature of the body . . .
represents . . . Evil."

2. *The Meaning of Evolution,* George G. Simpson (1951).
Olson calls this book by a paleontologist "one of the most complete syntheses of evolutionary ethics." Simpson approaches the matter of human moral values from an empirical base. Olson (1966) states,

> In this account the author has made a searching study of the significance of evolution with reference to ethics. His is primarily an ethics of personal knowledge and responsibility. Like most students who have proceeded primarily from an empirical basis, he has considered ethics only as they are suitable to the state of evolution as it exists. Ethics for man must be based on what he is and how he came to be. Such a code is not absolute, but is, like man, a subject of evolution.

As did du Noüy, Simpson presents a geological time scale going back to the Precambrian era which he describes as "beginning unknown; on the order of 3000 million years." Simpson starts with a chapter entitled "The Course of Evolution," in which he writes,

> The meaning of human life and the destiny of man cannot be separated from the meaning and destiny of life in general. 'What is man?' is a special case of 'What is life?' The extent to which we can hope to understand ourselves and to plan our future depends in some measure on our ability to read the riddles of the past.

In the chapter, "The Search for Ethics," Simpson finds that man is a moral animal. Simpson concludes in the epilogue of his book,

> It is another unique quality of man that he, for the first time in the history of life, has increasing power to choose his course and to influence his own future evolution. The possibility of choice can be shown to exist. This makes rational the hope that the choice may sometimes lead to what is good and right for man. Responsibility for defining and for seeking that end belongs to all of us.

There are fatalists and determinists who would not agree with Simpson's thesis that there is a freedom of choice. Most of the writers mentioned in this chapter involve themselves with the difficult problem of determinism versus freedom. Simpson stresses that we must not search for an à priori meaning within evolution to explain Man. He sees Man as a new kind of an animal—an ethical one whose moral values must be developed within a new framework of Man's own construction, one which is consistant with, but not necessarily derived from, organic evolution.

The question that can be raised in regard to Simpson's thesis that Man has developed his own framework of ethics is, What criteria will Man use to ascertain whether or not his choice of an ethical framework is valid, beneficial, reasonable, or universal? Simpson's concept leaves one undefended against any attack on any given moral framework one has accepted. In order to justify a moral value such as the Golden Rule, for example, Simpson would have to find still a larger ethical framework into which this one could appropriately fit. Those who claim that all ethics are man-made end up just where they started. That is, they must find *the* framework which Man used to make his framework. Religion can answer the question easily. In Chapter 9 we shall attempt to explore a framework having a scientific orientation. Naturalistic and religious frameworks may be accepted concurrently.

3. *Evolution in Action* and *Knowledge, Morality, and Destiny*, Julian Huxley (1957, 1960). Huxley is a biological philosopher who has written extensively on the subject of human nature and evolutionary trends. The earlier book serves as an introduction to the second. In *Evolution in Action*, Huxley explains that evolution is the joint product of "biology, pure physics, chemistry, cosmogony, geology, history, social science, archeology, prehistory, psychology, and anthropology." Therefore the outlook of a generalist is required in the study of evolution in its totality and in its relationship to Man. When evolution is studied in this manner, Huxley finds that we are able to grasp that the "universe is a process in time, and to get a glimpse of our true relationship with it." He notes that

> All phenomena have an historical aspect. From the condensation of nebulae to the development of the infant in the womb, from the formation of the earth as a planet to the making of a political decision, they are all processes in time; and they are all interrelated

as partial processes within the single universal process of reality. All reality, in fact *is* evolution, in the perfectly proper sense that it is a one-way process in time; unitary; continuous; irreversible; self-transforming; and generating variety and novelty during its transformations.

Huxley suggests "It may be desirable to coin a new term" to describe this "comprehensive process" inherent in evolution when focused on Man. By examining natural selection, biological improvement, development of mental activity, biological progress, and the human phase, he searches for an answer to the question, How Man became Man? in *Knowledge, Morality, and Destiny*, Huxley begins with the thesis of *transhumanism* in which he attempts to give a redefinition of progress. He begins this chapter with the following statement:

> As a result of a thousand million years of evolution, the universe is becoming conscious of itself, able to understand something of its past history and its possible future. This cosmic self-awareness is being realized in one tiny fragment of the universe—in a few of us human beings. Perhaps it has been realized elsewhere too, through the evolution of conscious living creatures on the planets of other stars. But on this planet, it has never happened before.

In the final chapter, "Evolutionary Humanism," Huxley sounds a note of warning to those who might confuse what he considers legitimate hypothesizing with dogmatic proselyting. He argues that

> Hypotheses are valuable and necessary instruments of the human mind. They have the dual task of adding to and organizing its knowledge. But they become dangerous when they are erected into absolute affirmations or dogmas and pernicious when they claim immunity from constant testing against fact.

4. *The Phenomenon of Man*, Pierre Teilhard de Chardin (1961). Father Teilhard, a Jesuit priest and paleontologist, attempts to show an interrelationship between organic evolution and the tenets of Christianity. Differing from Simpson and Huxley and agreeing with du Noüy, he believes that teleology is necessary in order to explain the evolution of life meaningfully. Huxley wrote the introduction to this work which differs radically from his own approach to the identical problem of finding

meaning within nature. In the introduction Huxley writes, "As I discovered when I first met Père Teilhard in Paris in 1946, he and I were on the same quest, and had been pursuing parallel roads ever since we were young men in our twenties."

In the preface, Teilhard emphasizes his scientific intent. He points out,

> If this book is to be properly understood, it must be read not as a work on metaphysics, still less as a sort of theological essay, but purely and simply as a scientific treatise. This book deals with man *solely* as a phenomenon; but it also deals with the *whole* phenomenon of man.

Later in the foreword he adds

> This work may be summed up as an attempt *to see* and *to show* what happens to man, and what conclusions are forced upon us, when he is placed fairly and squarely within the framework of phenomenon and appearance.

The book has been called difficult to understand and follow. Using a biological analogy, Teilhard sees Christ as a "mutation" within spiritual evolution offering mankind a new direction for the expression of love and sacrifice. One reviewer of *The Phenomenon of Man* writes,

> He has effected a threefold synthesis—of material and physical world with the world of mind and spirit; of the past with the future; and of variety with unity, the many with the one . . . In its scope and vision, the book reminds us of Bergson's *Creative Evolution*.[1]

Like the other hominological authors, Teilhard considers the origin of the universe and the beginning of matter within the general context of the study of total Man. He adds a new argument for taking the longitudinal approach: "To push anything back into the past is equivalent to reducing it to its simplest

---

[1] Henri Bergson, a French philosopher, was born the year Darwin published the *Origin of Species*. Before his time, nature had been seen as uniform with a fixed pattern repeating itself mechanically. Living at a time when the meaning of evolution was under active discussion in Europe, he saw it as a "flux" in which something new was being produced all the time. He was a persuasive intuitist critical of the exclusive and dominant role which empiricism was occupying in his time. He expressed the deep and persistent conviction that freedom is real, not an illusion, and that one could probe validly though intuitively, into the meaning of time and the creative possibilities of life.

elements." The implication is that the past can serve as a model of the present. Situations and conditions existing in the past throw light on continuing trends within nature that are currently too complex to be perceived clearly.

Teilhard distinguishes between the ontogenetic evolution of the individual and the phylogenetic evolution of the species and comes to the following conclusion:

> . . . if above the hominisation . . . in each individual, there is . . . another hominisation, a. collective one of the whole species, then it is quite natural to (expect) the three same psycho-biological properties (continuing onward in time) that originally produced the . . . (power of) reflection (within) . . . the individual. The three properties are: a) the power of invention; b) the capacity for attraction and repulsion; c) irreversibility.

The following is the final paragraph of Huxley's evaluation of this work.

> We, mankind, contain the possibilities of the earth's immense future, and can realize more and more of them on condition that we increase our knowledge and our love. That, it seems to me, is the distillation of *The Phenomenon of Man.*

5. *Nature and Man's Fate,* Garrett Hardin (1961). Hardin started his career as a microbiologist but shifted his focus to the analytical evaluation of basic biological concepts. In the prologue of his book, Professor Hardin gives the reader an idea of why his interests turned from microscopic to the cosmic considerations:

> The lecture was over. I tried to explain heredity to a general audience in one hour's time, a task that requires about forty hours in a college course. I asked for questions—and got them.
> "You say that X-rays and atomic radiations cause mutations, and that almost all mutations are bad?"
> "Yes."
> "But isn't it true that all evolutionary progress has been made possible by new mutations?"
> I could see it coming—but I answered simply, "Yes."
> "Don't those two statements contradict each other?"
> So: he had seen the binding point. Now what was I to do? I knew there was no real contradiction—but could I convince others with less than twenty-hour lecture? That was plainly out of the

question, so I tried to resolve the apparent paradox in a few words. But I don't think the questioner was satisfied. I hope he wasn't.

His question had uncovered a point that has only recently become clear: that the truth or falsity of the theory of evolution is now seen to be a matter of the most practical political importance.

Using his biological orientation, Hardin explores the relationship of variables that are not usually associated together: "Genes and Personal Decisions"; "Darwinism, Deity and Process." Writing in a popular style, he speculates on new dimensions and directions in evolution. He considers the role of the "inner directed" and "outer directed" man[2] within the context of waste. As he sees it, "Just as biological evolution has been made immensely more luxuriant and productive through mechanisms that prevent complete efficiency . . . so social evolution progressed most rapidly under circumstance that insured a considerable measure of waste." Hardin obtains historical perspectives by reviewing patterns within organic evolution and evaluating their significance to human progress.

6. *African Genesis* and *The Territorial Imperative*, Robert Ardrey (1963, 1966). Ardrey describes himself as a layman, but in a genuine sense this is not true since he has done an immense amount of informal research and study. He is a successful playwright and screen writer. With this background some scientists may consider his entrance into the complex field of philosophical-bio-anthropology as an intrusion. It is interesting that Ardrey, in *The Territorial Imperative*, explores the nature of just this kind of a reaction in humans—the staking out of territories and defending them against intruders. Ardrey demonstrates that the instinct of territorialism is almost universal within the animal world and uses elaborate documentation to support his premise that this instinct exists also in Man. He examines the consequences of territoriality in contemporary national and international affairs.

In preparation for *African Genesis*, Ardrey spent many years traveling to interview paleontologists, anatomists, and anthropologists on three continents. Both of his books are written in the dramatic manner of a playwright. It seems that sometimes he

---

[2] These concepts are taken from *The Lonely Crowd*, Riesman, *et al.* (1953).

succumbs to the drama of the topic to such an extent that the reader is left wondering whether fact or fiction is being described. Ardrey attempts to make his appeal to the public at large instead of to scientists. In this he was eminently successful since both of his volumes became best sellers. In spite of these faults, Ardrey's books present some challenging ideas which are worthy of serious consideration by scientists.

Loren Eisely, who himself took a longitudinal view of Man in his *The Immense Journey* (1946), reviewed *African Genesis*:

> This quarrel about innate nature of man began outside the gates of Eden, was continued by Darwin and Wallace, and now looms menacingly across the threshold of the United Nations. Mr. Ardrey has peered into our inner human darkness with wisdom gained from new discoveries of natural history. Whether we dissent from his view or not, we will turn the pages of his book conscious that we are in the presence of an informed and forthright mind.

Ardrey's *African Genesis* presents a two-page illustrated phylogenetic chart. The first page is captioned "The Last Five Hundred Million Years, The Emergence of Complex Life"; the second, "The Last One Million Years, The Emergence of Man." Ardrey examines the thesis that Man is descended from forebearers who were essentially killers of their own species, and in this they differed from the rest of the animal world. He claims the existence of such instincts as the struggle for dominance and territoriality and describes them as more influential in shaping human nature than sex and other "drives." In his characteristic vivid style, he asks the question,

> What things do we know about man? How much have the natural sciences brought to us, so far, in the course of a silent, unfinished revolution? What has been added to our comprehension of ourselves that can support us in our staggering, lighten our burden in our carrying, add to our hopes, subtract from our anxieties, and direct us through hazard and fog and predicament? Or should the natural sciences have stayed in bed?

Ardrey's own answers are repudiated by most scientists and his assumptions are considered naive, derived from incomplete observations and faulty generalizations. Instincts, territoriality, and aggressive tendencies in humans are generally unacceptable ideas in sociology and anthropology today. But since ideas do change and Ardrey's theories are controversial and thought-provoking, they are included. Additionally, see pages 309-314, 333-335, and 368-369 for different views on this subject.

New discoveries in natural science, according to Ardrey, offer us glimpses of Man's true nature. His hypothesis is that Man cannot master his innate brutality (which, in his view, was essential in creating *Homo sapiens*) by denying it. Instead Man's nature must be circumvented by finding socially constructive substitutes for it. Man's tendency to prey on Man, which is now a residual of an earlier adjustment, threatens Man's total destruction.

In *The Territorial Imperative*, Ardrey modifies some of his earlier ideas and finds morality in Man linked to the sense of territoriality. He also introduces the formula $A = E + h$. Amity among men and animals corresponds, and is proportionate to, the amount of Enmity (and/or natural) hazard that a species or a group finds in its immediate environment. The Enmity of one group towards another produces Amity within both groups and thus not love but hatred and danger is the binding organizational force in nature and in Man according to this view. This does not exclude love as a force, but love must be seen in its correct perspective. Ardrey concludes this theme with an examination of the reasons for wars in the light of territorialism and the human capacity to sublimate instinctual needs.

7. *The Death of Adam* and *Darwin and the Modern World View*, John C. Greene (1959, 1963). Greene, a professor of history, is included among Olson's "searchers." He faces the problem of how the "Adam that is within each man" handles the problem of personal ethics. Greene takes the longitudinal view and makes comparisons between the biblical version of human development and the one which natural history provides. His second book is an extension of the ideas proposed in the first one. It consists of only four chapters: "Darwin and the Bible"; "Darwin and Natural Theology"; "Darwin and Social Science"; and the "Conclusion." It is Greene's contention that if Darwin were to return today and view the present state of the social sciences, he would find it lacking in the insights that evolutionary perspectives could provide:

In the Social Sciences Darwin would encounter the greatest change of all. He would find evolutionary problems largely neglected and his own theory of social progress through natural selection in great disfavor. In the current emphasis on man's uniqueness as a culture-transmitting animal Darwin might sense a tendency to return to the pre-evolutionary idea of an absolute distinction between man and animals.

8. *The Wisdom of Evolution,* Raymond J. Nogar (1966). Father Nogar is a member of the Dominican Order and also a college professor. Whereas Father Teilhard was prohibited from teaching evolutionary theories in France by his religious superiors, Nogar's book has the Church's official stamp of approval: *Nihil obstat Censores Duputati.* It is not that Father Nogar's book differs essentially from that of Father Teilhard in what it covers. The explanation is that the Catholic Church has changed its stand on what it finds acceptable. It now approves of the instruction of evolution provided it is taught as a theory which permits the idea of God's creation to enter the picture somewhere along the evolutionary ladder. Most religions now make a similar concession.

In his chapter, "In Search of an Elusive Fact," Nogar explores prehistory. Noting the change in the concept of evolution since Darwin's time he states,

> To say that the dust of the storm caused by evolution has settled and the intellectual atmosphere surrounding the idea is genial again is one thing. But to say that there are no serious questions about evolution is disputed and, according to most contemporary biologists, Mr. Webster would have to revamp his definition of the term to include the thinking of the scientific majority today.

What, then, is an acceptable modern view of evolution? Scientists participating in the Darwin Centennial Celebration in Chicago in 1959 agreed to the following which Nogar also endorses:

> Evolution is definable in general terms as a one way irreversible process in time, which during its course generates novelty, diversity, and higher levels of organization. It operates in all sectors of the phenomenal universe but has been most fully described and analyzed in the biological sector.[3]

------

[3] Sol Tax, Ed. (1960).

Nogar presents a time scale which begins with the creation of the universe estimated to be at between 13 and 20 billion years before the present. The origin of the earth is placed at 4.5 billion years ago. Nogar has a number of tables designed to clarify cellular organization, the structure of organisms, functional characteristics of plants and animals. He defines four kinds of evolution—biological, cultural, physiochemical, and cosmological.

Nogar observes that Man is the only creature who questions his own origin, and through studying evolutionary laws, this questioning leads Man to the conclusion that there is a "Guide" in the universe.[4] Utilizing italics to give the statement emphasis, Nogar explains that *"evolutionary prehistory does not in any way weaken the force of the traditional argument for the existence of God."* This is an important point to emphasize since many people still fear that a study of the theory of evolution will undermine their religious faith. As Nogar, a theologian, sees it, such a study can also strengthen faith.

9. *Life: Its Nature, Origin, and Development,* A. I. Oparin (1964). Oparin is a Russian naturalist and a professor who holds an active membership in the Academy of Sciences of the Union of Soviet Socialist Republics.

As others who belong to the group of authors listed, Oparin is concerned with origins. He finds that

> . . . an understanding of the nature of life is impossible without a knowledge of the history of its origins. Usually, however, the nature and origin of life have been regarded, and are now regarded, as being two separate problems.

He reviews what is presently known of the formation of the earth's crust and of organic and nonorganic substances and postulates a chemical evolution which antedates the evolution of life and made it possible. His book provides information and theories which compare living with nonliving properties.

> There are some particular properties, found in all living things . . . First there is the ability to absorb substances selectively from

---

[4] Compare this view with Durkheim's (1961) observations: "Animals know only one world, the one which they perceive by experience, internal as well as external. Men alone have the capacity for perceiving the ideal, of adding something to the real."

the surrounding medium and to excrete the products of metabolism back into that medium. Then there is the power of growth, multiplication, self-reproduction, dispersal in space and, finally, the responsive reaction of organisms to external influences which is so characteristic of everything living, its irritability.

Oparin's explorations lead him to the dialectic materialist view and within this orientation he searches for the thread that ties past to present and future. He finds a clue in the structure of living things:

> . . . the clearly defined interaction between living bodies and the world around them, and also the adaption or purposiveness of structure which is so characteristic of all living objects without exception and . . . runs like a red thread through the whole development of life, right from its origins to the present day.
>
> The paths followed by life in its further evolution are also incomprehensible on the basis of physical and chemical laws alone for, out of the extremely wide field of possibilities open to it under these laws, life has only pursued strictly selective directions which were dictated by an historically determined necessity.

Oparin notes that evolutionary "development of matter is going on faster and faster, as if it were following a steeply ascending curve." He compares the change that slowly occurred as inorganic matter developed into living cells with a similar kind of a change that took place when biological evolution in Man developed into a "social form of the movement." He concludes with the statement that "the main highway of human progress does not now lie through biological development" but through improvement of life by "progress in the social form of the movement of matter."

10. *A Million Years of Man*, Richard Carrington (1964). This author is a British zoologist, anthropologist, and a geographer. He presents a chart of Quaternary time in which he lists geological divisions, archeological divisions, main cultures, and human and subhuman types. This chart represents one million years. Another chart describes evolutionary events and goes back to the Jurassic period which he places at 180 million years before the present. Carrington explores the races of Man and discusses the nature of early civilization throughout the world in much greater detail than most of the other books in

this group. His final two chapters are entitled "Man, Evolution and the Cosmos" and "Human Destiny and the Individual."

In agreement with the others, Carrington recognizes the need to see Man within the context of larger universal considerations:

> In the last chapter of a book we arrive at the stocktaking. At best we must sum up the major features of what has gone before and consider our own individual predicament in the modern world. Our theme has been man, and, throughout the study of this vast subject we have established, I think, that the nature of man can be understood only by relating him so far as our limited vision will allow to his context in space and time. It is impossible to understand the human phenomenon except by considering it as an aspect of the universe as a whole.

His view of Man's potential is an optimistic one. Through understanding of ourselves and translating this knowledge into actions, he believes that our species may "become fully conscious of its evolutionary destiny and its special role in the universal scene."

11. *Life's Long Journey*, Kenneth Walker (1961). This small book of approximately two hundred pages by a British surgeon and scientist attempts to cover the area in which hominology is concerned from a generalist's point of view. Walker sees the problem as "The existence of so many specialists and the lack of any correlation of their finding has long been causing anxiety to the scientists themselves and many of them have drawn attention to the unsatisfactory state of affairs."

Walker quotes one of his scientific colleagues as suggesting that the concept of organic evolution represents an example of integration which went far beyond any one disciplinary specialty. Similarly, "the best way of remedying the difficulties caused by the ever increasing fragmentation of knowledge is for less strictly specialized scientists to undertake the work of synthesis and integration."

The generalist is likened to the observer of a painting who stands back and looks at the picture as a whole in order to comprehend the artist's meaning, in constrast to the specialist who stands close to grasp the technique of workmanship employed. However, Walker sees disadvantages to the total view which the generalist employs:

> The non-specialist who undertakes this important task of synthesis starts with both advantages and disadvantages, but the former outweigh the latter . . . He will be less highly conditioned than is the pure specialist and consequently will enjoy a greater measure of freedom. Another of his advantages will be that he is much less likely to be concerned with his own professional reputation, for as a non-expert working on an unfamiliar subject he will be granted a license by his colleagues which a recognized authority on the subject would not be given. It is true that the non-specialist who writes about subjects outside of his domain, as the author of this book is doing at the present moment, runs the risk of being dubbed a busybody and a dilettante, but what do such professional pinpricks as these matter to anybody anxious to arrive at the truth?

12. *Sense and Symbols,* Paul R. Miller (1967). This is another book by a physician, an American neuropsychiatrist, which also attempts to treat Man in a cross-sectional, broad spectrum manner. The title of the book is somewhat misleading in terms of what the author attempts to do. Because of the fact that the hominological approach is still new as a recognized systematics, it may be of interest to compare the twelve chapter headings that each of these last two authors use to develop the generalist's theme of total Man. The following are the headings of their various chapters:

	WALKER	MILLER
Chapter 1.	The Limitation of Science	Basic Scientific Concepts of Human Behavior
Chapter 2.	The Conditioning of the Mind	A Theoretical Framework for Studying Human Behavior
Chapter 3.	What is Life?	Biological Needs
Chapter 4.	Mind and Body	Affect
Chapter 5.	Evolution	Autochthonous Processes
Chapter 6.	Other Factors in Evolution	Psychophysiological Integration
Chapter 7.	Dramatic Moments in Life's Journey	Developing Capacities (from Foetal to Adolescence)
Chapter 8.	Homo Faber	Roles of Parents and Children
Chapter 9.	The Goal of Evolution	Reality Concepts
Chapter 10.	Man's Political Future	Thinking
Chapter 11.	The Scientist's View of Man's Future	Conflict Resolution
Chapter 12.	Where will the Long Journey End?	Self-Concepts

These two authors, one a surgeon and the other a psychiatrist, both come to a conclusion which many physicians also reach in the course of their medical practice, namely that in illness the *entire* man must be treated, not just the diseased organ or the troubled mind. Hominology was originally designed as a program for psychiatric residents in order to give young doctors the broad human outlook which places illness and health within wider perspectives.

Miller views the need to understand Man this way:

> Whoever involves himself in the study or the care of human beings has the responsibility of knowing the basic facts and theories of human behavior. Even though the systematic study of human behavior is still in its early stages, it has advanced to the point that it can be very useful. This study is addressed to all students of human behavior who recognize that scientific fact and theory will contribute to their professional understanding and practice.

But as Walker recognizes, the moment one turns to the study of human behavior one is confronted with a formidable obstacle:

> Everything within Nature forms a part of a great and harmonious whole which man's mind looks at and breaks down into a number of serviceable pieces. But unfortunately the disparity in the sizes of the fragments is so great that we are unable to fit them together again.

Both Walker and Miller have used the nonspecialist's approach in their effort to cope with this obstacle.

Diverse Opinions and Role-Training

The foregoing represent a cross-section but not an all-inclusive list of contemporary works that appear to follow a hominological approach. The authors are a diverse group and this should be expected, since there is no background which precludes searching for answers to the "Big Question" as Nogar put it or the "Problem of Problems" using Simpson's phrase. Who *really* are the searchers? Among the foregoing list of authors we find scientists and laymen, professors and physicians, Frenchmen, Englishmen, Americans, and a Russian. But also among the genuine searchers are the young men and women who are attending colleges and universities throughout the world. In a very real sense, we humans are all searchers. In a world of ever increasing complexity and ever accelerating technological advancement many of us, however, do not know what we are looking for.

As one reviews what these men have written, one may wonder what would have happened if the priests, Chardin and Nogar, had found that an analysis of organic evolution led inescapably to the validity of atheism while Huxley (an agnostic) and Oparin (a Communist) both discovered that evolution pointed unequivocally to the existence of God. It would be an interesting experiment to have authors assume different orientations than their own and then observe how this would affect their final conclusions.

Whereas it is unlikely that we could persuade the real authors to engage in this kind of role playing, several students in an advanced hominology class engaged in such an experiment after they had studied and discussed the different opinions and theories which the authors in this chapter presented.

Three Ways of Dealing with Knowledge of Man

In what area of scholarship are the twelve authors in our group identified? We might find that within the human sciences there are three separate ways of dealing with knowledge.

1. *Disciplinary involvement*: The emphasis is on the discovery of new data about human beings and on fitting these into a scheme of knowledge which is organized around specific disciplines. Integration of data centers in behavioral or social science areas, fields of knowledge, and disciplinary domains.

2. *Teaching involvement*: The primary commitment is in the communication of facts, knowledge and skills in the social and behavioral sciences (gained from sources in items 1. or 3.) to those who are less informed in order to stimulate motivation, interest, and discussion of related topics.

3. *Hominological involvement*: The emphasis is not on producing new data but on a synthesis of already existing data into a comprehensive, nondisciplinary interpretation of human nature. Thus, the hominological involvement entails integration

and organization first, and through this, discovery, instead of discovery first followed by organization and interpretation as in item 1.

Any scientist may combine the above mentioned involvements but each emphasis represents a distinct type of activity serving its own unique function.

SUMMARY

Twelve contemporary writers were selected as representing a cross-section of a modern hominological view of Man. They differed in method and in their final conclusions but all of them used a comprehensive, multidimensional, nondisciplinary approach which takes into consideration the longitudinal development of Man and utilizes it to understand the present and to probe the future. All of them consider human values and morality within the greater framework of the entire history and prehistory of Man. All are works of synthesis and interpretation rather than productions of new material or original data. The content of these works were briefly described and some typical quotations were offered to illustrate the various points of view expressed.

REFERENCES

ARDREY, R.: *African Genesis.* New York, Dell, 1963.
ARDREY, R.: *The Territorial Imperative.* New York, Atheneum, 1966.
CARRINGTON, R.: *A Million Years of Man.* New York, New Am. Lib., 1964.
DU NOÜY, L.: *Human Destiny.* New York, New Am. Lib., 1949.
DURKHEIM, E.: *The Elementary Forms of the Religious Life.* New York, Crowell-Collier, 1961.
EISELY, L.: *The Immense Journey.* New York, Random, 1946.
GREENE, J. C.: *Darwin and the Modern World View, Rockwell Lectures, Rice University.* New York, New Am. Lib., 1963.
GREENE, J. C.: *The Death of Adam.* Ames, Iowa State, 1959.
HARDIN, G.: *Nature and Man's Fate.* New York, New Am. Lib., 1961.
HUXLEY, J.: *Evolution in Action.* New York, New Am. Lib., 1957.
HUXLEY, J.: *Knowledge, Morality,* and *Destiny.* New York, New Am. Lib., 1960.
MILLER, P. R.: *Sense and Symbol.* New York, Harper, 1967.
NOGAR, R. J.: *The Wisdom of Evolution.* New York, New Am. Lib., 1966.
OLSON, E. C.: *The Evolution of Life.* New York, New Am. Lib., 1966.

OPARIN, A. I.: *Life: Its Nature, Origin, and Development.* Translated by A. Synge, New York, Academic, 1964.

RIESMAN, D.; GLAZER, N., AND DENNEY, R.: *The Lonely Crowd.* Garden City, Doubleday, 1953.

SIMPSON, G. G.: *The Meaning of Evolution.* New York, New Am. Lib., 1951.

TAX, S. (Ed.): *Evolution After Darwin.* Chicago, U. of Chicago, 1960, vol. III.

TEILHARD DE CHARDIN, P.: *The Phenomenon of Man.* New York, Harper, 1961.

WALKER, K.: *Life's Long Journey.* New York, Nelson, 1961.

ADDITIONAL READING

ARDREY, R.: *Social Contract,* New York, Dell, 1974.

HUXLEY, J.: *Tomorrow and Tomorrow and Tomorrow.* New York, Harper and Row, 1972.

MORGAN, E.: *The Descent of Woman.* New York, Bantam, 1973.

RIDENOUR, F. (Ed.): *Who Says?* Glendale, Regal, 1971.

RIEGLE, D. D.: *Creation or Evolution?* Grand Rapids, Zondervan, 1972.

SIMPSON, G. G. (Ed.): *The Meaning of Evolution,* Revised, New Haven, Yale U.P., 1967.

TEILHARD DE CHARDIN, P.: *Christianity and Evolution.* New York, Harcourt-Brace, 1974.

VON DANIKEN, E.: *Chariots of the Gods.* New York, Bantam, 1974.

Chapter 9

UNIVERSE, LIFE, AND MAN THROUGHOUT GEOLOGICAL TIME

"A thousand years in Thy sight are but as yesterday when it is past."

PSALM 90:4

"Time will explain it all."

EURIPIDES

"Those who cannot remember the past are condemned to repeat it."

GEORGE SANTAYANA

"Time goes, you say? Ah no! Alas, Time stays, *we* go."

HENRY AUSTIN DOBSON, *The Paradox of Time*

ALTHOUGH ORGANIC EVOLUTION draws upon many disciplines for its sources of information, it may be taught with a primary emphasis in any of the following: historical geology, paleontology, biology, zoology, or anthropology. It may also be studied within a broad spectrum approach such as hominology. The danger of errors, unsupported assumptions, and unwarranted speculations increases as the emphasis shifts from the physical to biological and then to the human sciences. This danger is greatest when an attempt is made to integrate organic evolution within the bio-socio-philosophical context of hominology. The reasons for this increased likelihood of succumbing to fallacies stems from the complexity of the relationships involved, the presence of new factors demanding explanations, and the increased tendency of unintentionally mixing Criteria of Reality while formulating hypotheses.

Before examining the historical development of life, we may ask how does evolution fit into the larger study of total Man? Evolution is useful in offering

1. time perspectives with which to view Man as emerging and evolving;

2. a source of developmental trends and patterns with which to view contemporary human problems;

3. a vehicle for relating Man's past, present, and future.

When using evolution in the foregoing manner, unwarranted speculations may be more easily avoided if they are recognized as sharing one or more of the following characteristics:

1. They are predicated on mixed Criteria of Reality without either an awareness nor an explanation of this by the person speculating.

2. They are not derived from factual sources. (Intuitive speculations are not "unwarranted" if they are clearly designated as not adopting an empirical framework.)

3. They fail to utilize logical inferences and would lead to contradictory, absurd, or mutually exclusive propositions if they were fully developed.

4. They are not pertinent to the matter under consideration.

What, then, are acceptable speculations? First, of course, they do not have the characteristics of unwarranted speculations but the answer also involves the distinction which Brown (1963) makes between *idealizations* and *unobservables.*

IDEALIZATIONS AND UNOBSERVABLES

Idealizations are imaginary concepts about situations which could not possibly exist under any circumstances. Brown offers the following examples of such impossible but useful ideas: perfect vacuums, volumeless molecules, perfect gases. Idealizations are related to Inaccessibility of Reality Criteria and like these demand an *as if* approach. The difference is that while Inaccessibility of Reality Criteria conceive of certain truths as unaccessible because of human limitations, idealizations are conditions that Man is capable of apperceiving but which nature is incapable of producing. In this case nature's limitations—not Man's—prompts the *as if* attitude. Idealizations help explain natural phenomena and, therefore, they are an aid to conceptual thinking.

Unobservables represent beginning-and-end points of continua. Brown calls them "extreme types" which, in contrast to idealizations, have possible existences within a conceptual system. In the human sciences, idealizations are rarely used since social and behavioral scientists tend to make classifications rather than formulate behavioral laws. Both classification and laws explain human phenomena but each does this in a different manner.

Since idealizations are seldom used in the human sciences, White (1949, 1966) faced difficulty when he first introduced his concept of *culturology*. DiRenzo (1966) describes White's view as follows, "Cultural phenomena can be explained as cultural phenomena only when treated *as if* they had a life of their own, quite apart from organisms—just as a physicist must treat a falling body as if there were no atmospheric friction."

Opponents of White's culturology insist that there cannot be any real concept of culture without people and that human behavior cannot be viewed as a thing-in-itself without the human beings who use and produce it. White, however, argues that the real nature of culture cannot be understood until we examine it in a manner which excludes people in an "extra-somatic context" to use White's own phrase.[1]

Unobservables are easier to define. All we need do is think of the two ends of a continuum in any distribution of variables within a theoretical universal population. In distributions such as human weight, height, and endurance, there are extremes such as the smallest and the tallest, the heaviest and the lightest. In most cases these extremes are only theoretical reference points but contrary to idealizations, it is assumed that they actually exist. Boundaries of distributions are defined by these extreme cases even if they are unavailable and unobservable to the investigator.

Specialists in the various human sciences appear committed

---

[1] White claims that by his invention of culturology he has returned the subject of culture to anthropology removing the "threat" that "psychologists and psychologizing sociologists" would view it as within "their field." What he has actually done, however, is to place it unwittingly out of reach of both psychologists and anthropologists (as these specialists currently define themselves) and into the realm of philosophy where abstract and intangible ideas on mankind, normally originate. That is one reason why many anthropologists have found culturology difficult to deal with.

to classification and tend to shun idealizations which, when placed within a human context, become philosophical constructs. An integrated study of Man, however, requires idealized formulations since it deals with values, human goals, and Man's future.

When this is recognized, it will be seen that integration within the human sciences requires more than an exchange of ideas between scientists. Nevertheless, Hsu (1954) writes,

> Some practical difficulties inherent in an integration may be overcome by long sessions—perhaps three month summer periods to be aided by foundations or other independent sources of funds—involving highly informed, congenial, and relaxed personalities from numerous disciplines.

Hsu continues to say that he foresees difficulties in interdisciplinary integration because "scientists do not propose to be subjected to a dictatorship, even of the majority," that scientists may fear that a "bureaucracy will be required to achieve and maintain an integrated approach," and that scientists imagine that integration will lead to "the abolition of specialities."

Hsu, however, fails to see the real difficulty which is that diverse scientists lack a pertinent philosophical framework within which to jointly view total Man. Unfortunately, all the exchange of factual information cannot produce such a framework no matter how congenial the atmosphere may be. It should be noted that each of the authors developing a hominological approach to Man in Chapter 7 found it necessary to concomitantly develop a philosophical framework before he was able to speculate about the totality of Man's nature.

Allport (1955) in *Becoming* comments on the dilemma in which human scientists find themselves when attempting to integrate a variety of spheres of interest. First, he mentioned that "our principle problem is to relate the earlier stages with the latter."[2]

Then he states "that the cultural approach yields valuable facts one cannot possibly deny, for culture is indeed a major condition of becoming. Yet personal integration is always the more basic fact." He starts the last paragraph in his book with

----

[2] He refers to ontogenetic stages. Hominology extends this view to phylogenetic stages.

"But since psychology is a non-normative science, it is unable by itself to provide the stencil of values by which to assess becoming."

The situation which Allport describes applies with equal validity to the other human sciences. They are all non-normative in that they cannot produce absolutes nor handle idealizations effectively.

Good *et al.* (1941) consider the matter of frequency studies (i.e. statistical classifications) as they are used in the behavioral and social sciences. "Such studies are the mainstay of these sciences and they constitute the basis of much of their methodology." The authors, however, find that

> Frequency studies need a large amount of interpretation if they are to be put to practical use with profit. Perhaps their full contribution . . . must await the more complete development of a procedure for properly finding a frame of reference which utilizes other criteria besides frequency (and) which gives due consideration to integrating principles, balance, and orientation . . . the technique has not yet developed a philosophy which will properly interpret its findings.

Bergson (1911), writing on how evolution should be perceived, offers an explanation of the differences between partial and total views of Man:

> The real whole might well be, we conceive, an indivisible continuity. The systems we cut out within it would, properly speaking, not then be *parts* at all; they would be *partial views* of the whole. And with these partial views put end to end, you will not make a beginning of the reconstruction of the whole any more than by multiplying photographs of an object in a thousand different aspects, you will produce the object itself.

Why Conclusions Differ

Whereas the authors described in Chapter 8 agree in general on what should be observed and interpreted in a study of total Man, their conclusions differ in many important respects. How may we account for the different points of view? It is likely that students of hominology will differ among themselves for the same reasons. The variation in opinions and conclusions may be explained by one or more of the following:

1. differences in structuring reality (see Chapter 3);
2. different selection of Criteria of Reality (see Chapter 3);
3. differences in how data are integrated (stemming from items 1 and 2);
4. differences in methods used to interpret data (see Chapter 6).

In view of these differences, how can consensus on the subject of total Man be achieved? Societies which utilize authoritarian criteria in all, or nearly all, of the Life Areas make consensus their goal, while within those permitting freedom of expression and encouraging exposure to a variety of points of view, consensus on Man's nature need not be achieved. In such societies, gaining an understanding of why differences occur is the desirable objective.

Differences in ideas of how phenomena should be interpreted need not preclude agreement on what should be examined in a study of total Man. Long ago Protagoras said, "Man is the measure of all things," and within a hominological context this is reversed to read, "All things are the measure of Man." That is, everything of which Man perceives reflects his own nature and must be included in the study that represents his entire totality.

How does one "measure all things" relating to Man's apperception of his universe? Obviously such a task is impossible. And to the extent that we are unable to consider and weigh all factors relating to Man's apperceptive universe, any study of total Man is incomplete. Since "all things" cannot be measured or investigated, a partial failure is a foregone conclusion. Precepts as vague as "everything human" require structure and sequence before they can be made intelligible. Where should sequence begin? Back as far as Man's imagination can take him, seems to be the verdict of some of those who have struggled with this problem before.

MAN AND TIME

Time is the thread that runs interminably through past, present, and future, gives these their definition, and ties them sequentially together. Time is also a factor of the individual who experiences it. A consideration of time enters into every branch of knowledge from philosophy to physics, and bacteriology to social work. It is a key ingredient in all evolutions and it plays a role in everything that is termed, *developmental.* In another sense, time is an aspect of every scale of measurement that has ever been devised.

How may *time* be defined? There is no inclusive definition. Much depends on whether the position taken is a physical one, a philosophical one, or a psychological one. In the past, Man has thought of time as an endless process. In religion, time may be considered something circumscribed within God's plan. In the era of Einsteinian physics, time is seen as relative. Another definition of time describes it as the arrangement of things and events in an irreversible order within an absolute, infinite, one-dimensional continuum. But Einsteinian concepts have turned "absolute" to "relative," and transformed "infinite" into "finite." As a physical reality, "absolute time" is meaningless since it cannot be measured.

Only the lapse of time between events happening in space is measurable. This lapse is related to the speed of light in a vacuum—186,283 miles per second. If an observer found himself in an astronomical system having a speed which approaches that of light, time as defined by geophysics would come close to a standstill.[3] More correctly, time, as experienced by any observer, is proportionate to the speed of the given astronomical system in which he lives.

The concept, "time," evolved by the observation of recurrent natural events such as the length of day and night, the revolutions of the moon around the earth, the earth around the sun, the beat of the heart, the cycles of menstruation, the ebb and flow of tides, and the seasons of the year. The rotation and revolutions of the earth provide two very important measures—the year and day. Methods of keeping track of time among nonliterate peoples vary, but several of the higher civilizations have worked out calendrical systems that are very similar. They also made calculations of the periods of rotation of the planets and the

---

[3] Assuming that another time framework is used by an observer living within a different astronomical system.

moon. By the seventh century, the Maya, who lived in Meso-America, had computed the period between two successive new moons as averaging 29.53020 days, which is amazingly close to the actual 29.53059! For Man, time, represents a tool which helps him organize phenomena, gives him a framework for relating events, and offers him a basis for social structure.

Measures of Time

The standard reference of time measurement is a *second*. A second is defined as approximately 1/31,557,000 of a year. The problem with this definition is that if the year varies, so will the second and all its multiples. Another measure that could be used in defining a second is the number of cycles of vibration of the cesium atom. Using this standard, a second represents exactly 9,192,631,770 cycles of vibration. The two standards can be used to check each other since one is astronomic while the other atomic. Both operate independently on different principles.

However, there are many other ways in which time may be measured. The study of tree rings, *dendrochronology*, is used to date individual archeological sites in the arid American South-west where wood is easily preserved. Water-living organisms respond to seasonal variations and freshwater clams sometimes show annual growth rings that resemble tree rings. The effect of seasonal changes and recurrent variations in wet and dry seasons are reflected in erosion and deposition of sediment. Glacial deposits, results of ice action, the deposits of sediments, and the saltiness of the ocean are among the methods used by geologists to establish the elapse of time.

Methods of ascertaining age also include a system of dating based on radioactivity. The disintegration of radioactive atoms takes place at a constant rate which is not influenced by ordinary conditions on earth and so provides a means of dating organic substances. Describing this method Stokes (1966) writes,

> Analysis of thousands of specimens has given the following "time table of creation": earth solidified about 4.5 billion years ago; first extensive rock masses formed about 3.5 billion years ago; fossil records begin 2 billion years ago; abundant fossil record commences with the beginning of the Cambrian Period about 0.6 billion years

ago. The age of most meteorites for which radiometric dating is possible is also about 4.5 billion years. Widely divergent age estimates for the universe range between a low of 6 billion and a high of 20 billion.

If we accept the expansion-contraction theory of the universe, time has no cosmic meaning since there is no beginning or end to be determined. According to this theory, matter which was once compacted has been flying outward at tremendous velocities for about ten billion years but will slow down, contract and then expand again. Contraction and expansion are endlessly repeated. Such continuity provides no reference point for time to "start." In contrast, the explosion theory of the origin of the universe gives time a definite, but as yet unknown, beginning.

Not only in the realm of Einsteinian physics but also in the psychology and physiology of living organisms, time is relative. Time varies within subjective experience. It may run "quickly" or "slowly" depending on an animal's psychological or physiological state. Hibernation, sleep, unconsciousness, pain, pleasure, glandular secretions, state of health, and the extent of the conscious awareness of time are among the factors that add to, or subtract from, the subjective length of a measured hour. Therefore, when one asks, What is a long time? the question is meaningless since, in order to make sense, time must be associated with familiar events in life. Such an association gives meaning to both time and the events in question.

Kinds of Time

Some different kinds of time include the following:

1. Astronomical time expressed in light-years. This measure converts interstellar distances to units of terrestial time multiplied by the speed of light. Thus, a light-second equals the speed of light per second in a vacuum. On this scale, a light-year represents 5,878,000,000,000 miles. The vastness of the universe may be appreciated when we realize that the nearest star (excluding the sun) is 4.3 light-years away; Sirius, the brightest star is 8.7 light-years off; and the distance to other stars is measured in hundreds, thousands, and even millions of light-years.

2. Atomic time is determined by cycles of vibration of molecular particles.

3. Sideral time is measured by the revolution of the earth around the sun using the fixed stars as a reference point. It differs slightly from solar time.

4. Solar time is based on the earth's rotation around the sun. Since solar days are unequal in length, modern time reckoning is based on the mean solar day as computed by the Royal Observatory, Greenwich, England, whose longitude is accepted by international agreement as 0.

5. Psychological time is determined subjectively and represents an individual's impression of the length of an interval between events. It may or may not conform to chronological time which is divided into regular periods so that dates can be assigned to events and transactions.

6. Physiological time depends on the physiological state of the organism. For example, an animal may be "physiologically old" due to glandular or nutritional factors while still chronologically young.

7. Geological time is based on five main eras and their subdivisions. The eras are Archeozoic, Proterozoic, Paleozoic, Mesozoic, and Cenozoic. Each era marks a different stage in life development involving structural changes.

8. The concept, "philosophical time," illustrates some of the controversies which the idea of time has evoked among philosophers. Parmenides, in ancient Greece, maintained that time, change, and becoming were irrational illusions. On the other hand, Heraclitus asserted that there was no permanence and that time-created change characterized everything without exception. The crux of the question was, Does time move or does it stand still? According to Newton, time was independent of events, but Leibnitz viewed time as determined by events and maintained that the succession of events gave time apperceptive meaning.

Existential time embraces a philosophical concept that all past and future converges on the present moment of existence. By the same token, it is the moment that is being experienced by an individual—the here and the now—that makes all time, past and present, significant. Barrett (1963) explaining the role of time within Existential philosophy writes,

Among all the animals, man stands in a unique relation to time because he stands open to a future in which the present conditions of his life can be transformed. Standing open to his future, he orders his present and connects it with his past. Hence our lives become meaningful to the degree that we bind together tomorrow, today, and yesterday in an active whole. Time is thus the fundamental condition of our existence; without time there would be no human meaning.

Existential time is not an abstract quantative concept but rather an experience that must be viewed in terms of present realities and challenges. Time is, therefore, seen as a creative force rather than one which has made Man a victim of clocks, calendars, and timetables. Barrett continues,

> But time, real time, is never the abstract "once upon a time" of the fairy story; it is always time here and now, urgent and pressing upon us. We are temporal beings not because we reckon with abstract mathematical time sequences, but because we experience time in the historical pressure of our generation with its challenging and fateful tasks.

9. Religious time may be based on concepts of how God utilized time as described in revelations dealing with the creation of the universe and the earth. Some religions, myths, and fables do not mention time as a major consideration in their descriptive literature or oral tradition. Others consider time important and use the position of the stars, moon, and sun to determine the occurrence of religious events.

10. Future time is a controversial concept since something which has not yet occurred can only be inferred. The future can only be conceived of as an image or a composite of images reflecting past events. Certain philosophical positions deny that "future time" exists. For example, Morgenstern (1960) equates future time with "opportunity" and he explains that

> We have identified time with action; it follows then that what has not yet entered into action cannot belong to time. The future does not belong to time. Time extends from whatever beginnings we may choose to refer to up to now. Time is determined. But it does not extend beyond the now, and this must remain undetermined. Reality at this point comes to an end . . . Beyond the now stretches endlessly the realm of all unreality, of chance and doubt and will. And it is this which we name the future. Instead of being a division of time the future is time's antithesis.

The concept of "future time" represents an idealization—an imaginary condition which in spite of its "unreality" serves a useful purpose. Future time is a construct which has a rational basis that exists within the human mind.

Future Time and Personal Problems

In order to relate the concept of future time to personal life, hominology students were asked to think of five problems that they faced this very day. A problem was defined as any event or condition existing at the present moment causing the student to feel anger, sadness, irritation, disgust, or other forms of disagreeable emotion. After the five problems were selected, the students indicated by a check on the chart whether the problem disturbed them "very much," "much," "somewhat," or "very little" (Table VII). They were not asked to reveal the nature of their problems. They then estimated how long these problems will continue to disturb them in the future: tomorrow, one week from today, one month from today, one year from now, five years hence, fifteen years from today, thirty years in the future, or all of their lives.

The time perspectives chart—"My Five Problems"—has been found to yield no consistent pattern in a small pilot study that was conducted. Its value consists primarily of stimulating an exchange of views regarding the intensity of certain types of problems shared by different students. Different judgments

TABLE VII
MY FIVE PROBLEMS
A hominology student's time perspectives of his five personal problems

Estimate Time Problem Will Last:	Problem One	Problem Two	Problem Three	Problem Four	Problem Five
All of Life			X		
30 Years					
15 Years		X			
5 Years	X				
1 Year					
1 Month					
1 Week				X	
1 Day					X

Today these problems anger, disturb, sadden, or frighten me:

	Problem One	Problem Two	Problem Three	Problem Four	Problem Five
Very Much	X				X
Much			X		
A Little		X			
Very Little				X	

regarding the intensity and duration of problems which students experienced produced a stimulating exchange of ideas.

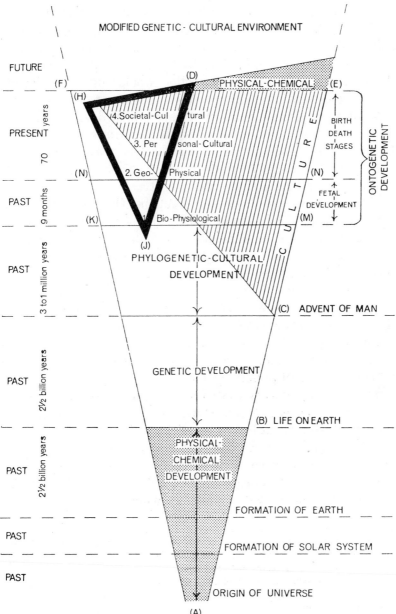

FIGURE 16. A Concept of Total Man.

Man's Journey Through Time

The sequential events that structure Man's journey through time are presented in an evolutionary context in Figure 16.

The continuum having at one end the Origin Of Universe, and at the other end Man's future Genetic-Cultural Environment[4] is represented by diagonal lines which do not meet at the bottom (A) because intersection would suggest a definite beginning or starting point in time—a "beginning of beginnings." But *cosmogony,* the branch of science which develops theories on the origin of the universe, does not allow for such an answer. Only religion is able to give an absolute fixed beginning—a "First Cause" through revelation—and this is acceptable to those utilizing authoritarian Criteria of Reality.[5]

Science offers two theories of creation. The first is known as the *evolutionary hypothesis* which states that about ten to thirteen billion years ago the universe contained a tightly packed mass of matter which was shattered by a cataclysmic explosion that hurled radiant energy into space and created the present chemical elements. Elements came into being through the combination of neutrons, protons, and electrons. The conditions for this kind of a combination were favorable for only a short time during the explosion. Thereafter, matter and energy sped outward for many millions of years. During this time, matter was broken up and dispersed by radiant energy as fast as it was formed. Finally, gravity caused matter to differentiate itself into primordial gaseous galaxies. However, the expansion caused by the initial explosion still goes on at the present time.

The other hypothesis does not envision a specific initiating event in time or space. This is called *steady-state hypothesis.* It postulates neither a beginning nor end because matter is being continuously replenished in one place while it is being destroyed

---

[4] It should be noted that conception is already culturally tinged although this is not shown on the diagram. Cultural factors, such as exogamy, endogamy, monogamy, fashions of sexual beauty, sexual taboos, and marital customs, play a role in the selection of mates and, consequently, in genotypology.

[5] A person believing in evolution need not reject religious accounts of creation but may accept these as beliefs occurring within the authoritarian Criterion of Reality.

in another. Originally, matter appeared as extremely rarefied hydrogen gas which was activated and compressed by radiation. When a sufficient mass of gas susceptible to the influence of gravitation had been accumulated, matter contracted and rotation began. A galaxy had its inception as a rotating mass of gas without stars or light. But as this mass continued to rotate, it developed eddies and clouds of unequal density. Within the denser areas, gravitation caused additional condensation until bodies were produced which broke away from the center of the cloud because of the force of rotation. These dense bodies developed into stars.

According to the steady-state hypothesis, the heavier elements in the universe were created continuously and therefore there is no need to conceive of an initial cataclysm. Conditions existing in certain stars called *red giants* cause heat and pressure to build up heavy elements such as lead and bismuth from elemental hydrogen. Heavier elements can also be created during the sudden explosion of other stars called *nova* or *supernova*. Such explosions occur when hydrogen has diminished to the point where the star commences to shrink. This causes an accelerated rate of rotation until finally the star's mass is showered into space, mixing with elemental hydrogen and becoming available for the construction of new galaxies and stars.

Recent modifications of the steady-state hypothesis have been necessary because of the discovery of quasars[6]—objects that appear to travel at speeds much faster than anything previously observed in the universe. One estimate is that some quasars are moving away from the direction of the earth at 80 per cent of the speed of light. Their enormous energy is a puzzle to astronomers who estimate that the light of one quasar (represented by a few fuzzy lines on a photographic plate taken by the 200-inch telescope at Mount Palomar) must have started its journey soon after the inception of the universe.

This observation raises the following questions: Is the universe in a continual state of flux, expanding for billions of years, then contracting to a dense ball of matter, then expanding again?

------

[6] The term is a contraction of quasi-stellar radio source.

It is possible that only parts of the universe are pulsating, including our corner, while other parts remain unchanged? Was there really a huge explosion involving all matter—and will there be another one? Perhaps the very questions are definitive of the nature of Man and one of his striking differences from other forms of animal life. We repeat once more what Nogar (1966) points out, "Man is the only animal that questions his own origins."

SOLAR SYSTEM AND EARTH

Let us return to the earth and the solar system, whose mysteries seem to be more nearly within our grasp. Our earth is one of nine major planets which revolve around the sun, each in its orbit. Thirty-one natural moons or satellites revolve about these planets. Mercury, Venus, and Pluto have no moons. The other planets have from one to twelve. Additionally, there are thousands of asteroids, scores of comets, and untold millions of meteors within our solar system. The sun, which has been worshipped by so many different peoples in ancient time, is the central star of our solar system and makes up over 99 per cent of its total mass (weight).

It was the genius of Nicholas Copernicus, the Polish astronomer, who for the first time in history envisioned a method for determining the relative distances of the earth and the planets from the sun. In a famous treatise, *De revolutionibus orbium coelestium* (1543), he upset the prevailing medieval concept of the earth as the center of the universe[7] by describing the earth as revolving around the sun. This founder of modern astronomy was a gifted man in many areas such as medicine, art, mathematics, and politics. Possibly he was also an astute psychologist since he dedicated the book describing his revolutionary solar theory to Paul III, the reigning Pope, whose protection he claimed for his speculations and to whom he commended his solar and

---

[7] The Greek philosophers also suggested the heliocentric theory in which the earth circled the sun but it was not adopted until the Ptolemaic geocentric view proved incapable of explaining observed motions of heavenly bodies. Einstein's principle of relativity makes the Copernican theory a consideration of convenience rather something which can be proven as true.

lunar tables as a contribution to the problem of reforming the calendar.

Composition of the Earth

The core of the earth begins 1,800 miles beneath the surface and continues another 2,160 miles to the center of the earth. It is divided into inner and outer portions, and it appears that the inner is solid whereas the outer is liquid. Over the core is the earth's mantle which makes up about 68 per cent of the total earth and may be the original source of both core and mantle. The outermost shell of the solid earth is called crust. The term was coined at a time when it was believed that the interior of the earth was entirely molten. The crust varies in thickness and composition as indicated by the irregular topography and by the diversity of the geological material which forms the earth's surface.

Molecular Evolution Preceded Organic Evolution

Inorganic evolution which preceded organic evolution began with a glowing state of the earth approximately four to five billions of years ago.[8] A glowing liquid period was followed by a glowing skin phase. Later an ocean phase appeared in the *Azoic* era, about three billion years ago. In this period of oceans without life, the first rains fell over hot and intensely salty seas. During this time, up to the *Eozoic* era, progressive changes in molecular and submolecular structure of inorganic material were taking place. Oparin (1964) writes,

> No doubt, during the thousands of millions of years which elapsed before the formation of the Earth and the origin of life on it, the hydrocarbons on its surface underwent many . . . possible reactions. They could not remain unchanging for a long time but had to enter into chemical reactions both between themselves and with the other substances around them, forming a variety of complicated organic compounds quite unlike those of the inorganic world. This fact gave them a very special position in regard to the origin of life.

The importance of carbon lies in its capacity to build up molecular rings and chains of almost endless variety. In this

---

[8] Estimates of the age of the earth vary and are constantly revised.

way extremely large and complex molecules were formed such as the nucleoproteins which are the basic substance of all life.

The most important proteins in the living cell are found combined with simpler compounds called nucleic acids because they were first recognized in the cell's nucleus. Among these is DNA (deoxyribose nucleic acid), a substance which is sometimes referred to as carrying the genetic code which enables reproduction of inherited traits to take place.

However, the matter is not that simple. It is known that a specific enzyme is required to bring about the "reproduction" of DNA. And then, the process can only reproduce a part of itself. To reproduce itself, an organism, no matter how simple, requires derivatives of other acids (such as ribose nucleic acid—RNA) and protein synthesizing mechanisms. Reproduction is the result of a "team effort" of the constituent parts of a unit sometimes called *system.* No single ingredient, acting alone, is capable of reproducing itself even in the simplest form of life such as a virus. Since a virus is not a system, it does not reproduce in nonliving media but instead insinuates itself into a living system which serves as its host. The virus DNA enters into a compatible kind of cell and utilizes the host's DNA system to reproduce itself at the expense of the host's raw material.

These considerations are important in terms of the hypotheses that are designed to account for the origin of life. One of them holds that the first living thing must have something like the photosynthetic green plants of today. This point of view is expressed in a report by Meinschein (1965). He writes,

> Molecular precursors of life were presumably formed by irradiation of primordial atmosphere . . . It is believed that biochemical evolution over a long period gave rise to photosynthesizing plants, and that oxygen released by plants during carbon fixation transformed the primordial atmosphere, producing marked changes in the quantity and quality of solar radiation that was received and retained by earth.

As others have done, Meinschein places the beginning of life further back in time:

> Until ten years ago it was widely believed that life on earth originated near the beginning of the Cambrian period, approximately 550 million years ago. (Now there is new information) . . . about

the varied forms of fossils in . . . two billion year old chert, proving that complex, highly distinctive organisms existed long before the Cambrian period.

Another hypothesis states that the first organisms must have resembled viruses. But since most viruses must be surrounded by a living cell in order to reproduce, the question is, Where would these cells come from?

Hardin (1961) examines this situation and offers the following explanation:

> The difficulty, formidable as it appears at first sight, proves not to be insurmountable. It has its origin, it would seem, partly in the structure of common speech. In the world of today there is organic matter only because it is constantly resynthesized by living organisms. Organic matter is not stable in our world: "It decays," we say, Yet . . . this is not true . . . "It is decayed"—by bacteria, molds, and other microbes. In other words, on the surface of the earth before there was any life, should any organic material have been synthesized, *it could have persisted.*

HOW DID LIFE BEGIN?

If among the variety of molecules in the Azoic period even one molecule were produced which might have continued to replicate itself, it could have started the chain of living things that reach down to our time. However, no one can say with any certainty that life as we now know it began this way.

Laboratory success in artificially creating a semblance of life will not guarantee that life actually started out in the same manner approximately three billion years ago. Fox (1960) observed the pertinency of the question, How did life begin?

> The scientific question of the mechanisms of life's beginning is a more sophisticated version of the personal question, Where did I come from? This question, appropriately phrased, is one which man has generally asked himself and which man individually asks from childhood. If we accept the proposition that the impetus of the scientist is curiosity, virtually all thinking men are to a point scientists because of their special curiosity about this problem.

From the beginning of the universe (A) on Figure 16 to the formation of life on earth (B), development was centered on molecular and physical action. With the beginning of life, the developmental focus became genetic. Genes and chromosomes now represented the developmental force in evolution. With the advent of Man (C), culture replaced genetics as the key factor in subsequent human development.

We reach the inception of the ontogenetic level when conception takes place. Our first environment is a bio-physiological one which exists *in utero*. Man's four environments are

1. bio-physiological
2. geo-physical
3. personal-cultural
4. societal-cultural

The Bio-Physiological Environment is largely an internal and an instinctual one. Its external function is to receive stimuli which it integrates internally. It reacts to these stimuli setting the stage physiologically for a secondary reaction towards the outside world. Internal stimuli dominate this environment. At birth, the infant is absorbed in it. Hunger pangs, ingestion of milk, warmth, pain, tactile stimulation, excretion, and pleasant and unpleasant sensations are the focus of the infants attention.

After birth, the four environments continue to exist concurrently, merging and interacting with one another. Ontogenetic exposure to them, however, follows a chronological order. First, the Bio-Physiological Environment mediates sensation. As the child gradually becomes aware of his surroundings, he responds to stimuli differentially depending on whether they bring him pleasure or pain. Upon grasping the concept that there are places and things in the external world, the infant discovers his Geo-Physical Environment.

This environment consists of space, time, temperature, and the shape, feel, and structure of the physical world all around him. He explores it early in life as he touches things, feeling them as rough, smooth, sharp, or round; listens to sounds that are not yet symbolic for him; sees the world of light and dark and color; feels warmth and cold; and gradually learns that all these have an existence outside of his own body.

As soon as he has become aware that things and sensory impressions differ from the world of people and social interactions, he has discovered the Personal-Cultural Environment.

The child recognizes his mother's voice and responds to her touch before this discovery takes place. It is out of this special relationship between child and mother that the Personal-Cultural Environment evolves to embrace later all the members of the immediate household. In the process of adapting to this new environment, he absorbs the family's values, norms, habits, customs, speech, and modes of adjustment. If they fail to be satisfying to him, he may react negatively toward them, attempt to construct his own culture or search for one outside of his family circle. In one way or another, however, he responds to the influences within his home, integrates them in a manner consistent with the two previously mentioned environments, and derives from these his own individual personality.

Every group develops unique cultural characteristics derived from the interaction of the individuals who comprise it. Therefore, a new cultural environment must be faced when a person leaves his family to live elsewhere.[9] Exposure to this new environment is usually a gradual process, beginning with early playmates, visits, school, or kindergarten. The set of attitudes which an individual forms towards this larger environment outside of the family also develops gradually.

Societal-Cultural Environments vary in content and structure with time, place, and historical development. Many different kinds of Societal-Cultural Environments may coexist within one political boundary. When this occurs, an individual may identify primarily with one of these, or he may react to a composite of several of them. The kind and amount of interaction between two kinds of cultural environments may vary from family to family.

Some family units may actively resist the cultural influences of the larger society of which they are geographically a part. In such cases, only a limited amount of acculturation will take place. Since there is a tendency to adjust to and identify with a

---

[9] "Cultural" as used here is not interchangeable with "social." It consists of more than an interaction of people. It includes everything that the person's group has produced and everything that they use, their hierachy of values as well as their material possessions. Thus culture represents everything that is man-constructed in the widest sense. Another way to define culture is to say what it is not. It is not instincts, natural forces, or raw, unmodified genetic endowments.

dominant social group, an incompatibility between environments (3) and (4) creates tension in persons unwilling or unable to acculturate. These tensions may be handled in two ways—they may be internalized or externalized. If internalized, they will cause dissatisfaction with self; if externalized, they may create hostility towards both the Societal-Cultural and the Personal-Cultural Environments. In the rest of this chapter, the term *development* is used in preference to "evolution" except when referring to organic evolution as envisaged by Darwin.

The following phylogenetic developments have contributed to the emergence of the human individual and are conceived of as telescoping into each other; they are sequentially inter-dependent in that none of them could have come into being without the existence of the preceding ones:

1. Physical-Chemical Development involving thermo-dynamics, atoms, molecules, and space;

2. Biological development in which single cellular structures formed aggregates that proliferated and differentiated into many kinds of plant and animal life including early Primates;

3. Anatomical modifications including a visually oriented brain leading to Hominoidea;

4. Development of bipedalism, vocalization, and symbolization characteristic of Hominidae;

5. The era of cultural development and emergence of *Homo sapiens;*

6. Ontogenetic Development[10] which begins with embryonic life and continues through birth to death of an individual member of the human species;

7. Modified Phylogenetic-Cultural Development which results from changes brought about by the actions of an individual during his life-span. We shall call these *ontogenetic residuals* which represent the personal contributions an individual leaves the species after his death. Modification is the essence of all development and the ontogenetic residuals form the basis for modifications of Man's future environment. These modifications are of two types: genetic and cultural. Genetically as parents, we contribute to a redistribution of genes within the gene pool

---

[10] Some view the later stages of life as ontogenetic decline but we may still include this within the concept of "development."

of future generations. Our children's genetic constitution is partially determined by whom we select as a mate. Additionally, we contribute towards the cultural endowment of the future. Upon our death, the kind and extent of the contribution we have made depends largely on the kind of life we have lived.

Within these developmental areas there are the following *reference points*:

I. Physical-Chemical Development to nucleic acids (10 billion (?)-3 billion years B.P.[11])
    A. Beginning of the universe and our solar system
    B. The formation of the earth
    C. The development of nucleic acids and protein molecules
II. Biological development to early Primates (3 billion-55 million B.P.)
    A. Evolvement of life on earth
    B. Development and proliferation of life throughout geological time
    C. Advent of first Primates during the Paleocene
III. Development of Primate line to Hominoidea (55 million-26 million B.P.)
    A. Enlargement of brain emphasizing visual areas
    B. Development of flexible fingers and opposable thumb
    C. Advancement in vocalization and socialization
IV. Development from Hominoidea to *Homo* (26 million-2 million B.P.)
    A. Divergence of Pongid and Hominid lines
    B. Upright gait and omnivorous diet
    C. Development of cortical brain areas permitting symbolization
V. Cultural development to *Homo sapiens* (2 million-10,000 B.P.)
    A. Evolution of brain to permit formation of speech
    B. Development of sophisticated stone and bone tool industry

---

[11] B.P. stands for Before the Present Time. Dates are only approximations. Assigning dates to remote events in the geological past depends on which of several theories one accepts. In hominology, dates are assigned to events in the remote past primarily to offer students time-perspectives within which to consider human development.

      C. Increase in complexity of social organization and kinship concepts

VI. Human development to the present time (10,000 B.P.- 20th Century)

      A. Invention of agriculture and domestication of animals

      B. Progressive increase in mining and use of metals

      C. Development of atomic sources of energy

It should be noted that these reference points are arbitrarily selected and that with equal validity an entirely different set of events could have been chosen in their place. The accomplishment of the genus, *Homo,* cannot effectively be reduced to six items. Therefore, a more detailed chronology of events incorporating the periods (V) and (VI) will be given later.

At the inception of the human line, biological modification and cultural development are difficult to separate. It is not possible to give a fixed chronology for the occurrence of cultural events since advancement progressed in different sequences and at different rates in various parts of the world. There is also the question of cultural diffusion and cultural parallelism to consider when we speak of the nature of cultural progress. Diffusion occurs when cultural ideas are carried from one group to another; parallelism implies an independent cultural development within two groups that are not in contact. Another difficulty is that the further back we go in time, the less material exists from which we can obtain precise facts.

Neither cultural changes nor anatomical evolutionary modifications occurred at any regular intervals or at any given rate. Environmental pressures were usually the determining factor influencing the speed and the direction in which such changes took place. Environmental pressure is meaningfully associated with survival. It is the force which permits or prohibits a species from giving birth to and maintaining alive its next generation. The struggle for food, avoidance of enemy, the maintenance of warmth are all subsidiary to this biological achievement of successful reproduction.[12]

------

[12] Overpopulation would not be considered as "successful reproduction" since the latter implies maintaining a desirable ratio between population, food supply, and living space.

Culture in the past, as in the present, aids the process of survival by assuring a stable food supply and providing surpluses with which to maintain the species in times of shortages. Culture, in the form of an oral or written tradition, also represents a means of accumulating knowledge of the physical world, appreciation of beauty, and techniques with which to conquer men, animals, and disease-causing organisms.

Reference points are necessary to establish critical periods as these develop through time. Such delineation of critical periods make it possible for evolution to be associated and compared with other types of processes with which the student is familiar. Sequential arrangement of events permits analysis to take place. Scott (1962) observes, "The concepts of critical periods is a highly important one for human . . . welfare . . . The discovery of critical periods immediately focuses attention on the developmental processes which cause them."

When we are dealing with human behavior, a study of critical periods within development offers perspectives which are not otherwise available. Critical periods are steps which are necessary to the conception of development or evolution. A recent news item (Anon, 1967) states, "After years of ignoring evolution as a force in human behavior, psychologists and psychiatrists have been gripped by the idea that some human actions and feelings may be understood in an evolutionary context." Neither the evolution of culture nor organic evolution consists of a simple progression of events within time. Instead the process of development is a complicated one and consists of elements that do not always seem to be chronologically synchronized.

When psychologists and psychiatrists turn to evolution to seek understanding, they are apt to be disappointed by the difficulty they face in using evolutionary facts for forming readily applied laws of behavior. Steward (1966) comments on the modern trend to search cultural evolution for processes and causes that may have implication for contemporary society. He observes,

> The concept of cultural evolution, dominant a century ago in anthropology, faded to insignificance early in the present century but has been revived in the last decade or two. Today, however, the

important connotation of cultural evolution is a scientific interest in cultural causality—in the factors and processes that operate in cultural change—rather than a continuation of the 19th century heritage. The recent scientific orientation, in fact, began as a sharp departure from early 20th century historical particularism and cultural relativism, which denied the possibility of ascertaining causes.

The Development of Culture

Cultural evolution does not consist of continuous homogeneous entities but of separate Life Areas (see Chapter 4) having individual developmental histories which are not always chronologically related to each other. For example, ethics and science are both aspects of culture. However, there have been civilizations which are highly developed in one and not the other. Nor does history indicate that an inverse relationship between any two aspects of culture exists. Instead, it seems that the Life Areas represent entities which, though not entirely independent of each other, require different kinds of social conditions for their development.

Under the circumstances, the following list of cultural events does not necessarily represent an accurate chronology but is merely a series of significant steps in cultural evolution,[13] leading from the past to contemporary time, which will serve as a basis for discussion.

1. Adaptations to the climatic changes of the Pleistocene.
2. Gathering food and carrying it in arms.
3. Adaptation of bones and sticks for weapons.
4. Adaptation to an omnivorous diet.
5. Crude chipping of pebble stones for tools.
6. Inception of hunting techniques and, possibly, cannibalism.
7. Discovery and control of fire.
8. Use of natural products for shelter and clothing.
9. Beginning of an oral tradition.

------

[13] A chart of cultural stages by Washburn (1961) shows the development of industries, hunting, extension and control of environment, arts, and beliefs, and relates these to various types of hominids.

10. Further development of communal responsibility.
11. More complex social organization including greater division of labor between sexes.
12. Greater skill in use of bones, stones, and wood as weapons and tools.
13. Intensification of social organization for hunting, raiding, and protection.
14. Burying of dead accompanied by simple ritual.
15. Formation of clans and systems of kinship.
16. Further development of language and symbolic art forms.
17. Incorporation of myths and legends into an oral tradition.
18. Sophisticated use of bone, wood, and stone and first use of metal for weapons, tools, and decoration.
19. Beginning of agriculture and the Neolithic Revolution.
20. The use of the wheel and increased water transportation.
21. Domestication of animals for food.
22. Beginning of urbanization and a written tradition.
23. Increased communication utilizing pictographs, hieroglyphics, and written symbols.
24. Advanced forms of art and philosophy.
25. The development of God-Man centered religions.
26. Further development of a sense of obligation tied to land and national affiliation.
27. Mining and use of progressively harder metals.
28. Invention of the printing press.
29. Invention of microscope and telescope and subsequent changes in Man's view of his place in nature.
30. The invention and use of the steam engine.
31. Industrial revolution and its consequences.
32. Use of electricity in communication.
33. Advancement of medicine, the control of disease, and beginning of the population explosion.
34. Understanding of conditioning and Man's unconscious processes.
35. Einsteinian physics and the splitting of the atom.
36. Computorization and automation in research and industry.
37. Man's venture into space.

38. Advanced concepts of Man's world-wide social responsibility.

The foregoing list starts with adaptations to the Pleistocene climate and then continues with gathering food and carrying it in arms. This period is envisioned as existing before hunting. Gathering food, as such, is not necessarily a cultural activity. However, when in the early Miocene, a species approximating *Ramapithecus*[14] carried food that otherwise might have had to be abandoned (with arms that were shorter than those of related species), this could be considered as a rudimentary cultural act since it was not primarily instinctual.

Whether or not the adoption of an omnivorous diet can be considered within this context is debatable. There is evidence, however, that such a change did take place and it may well have required adaptations which could fall within a broad definition of culture. Using animal flesh for food suggests first scavenging, then hunting. Hunting, in turn, requires social organization and an associated communication system. Also, stones now had to be sharpened to cut into skin and flesh.

The advent of the changing climatic conditions during the Pleistocene coupled with hominid dispersal, implies new adaptations which may have involved the use of animal skins for cover and shelter. After fire from lightning or volcanic origins was maintained and its control learned, Man had made a sensational step forward. Undoubtedly the manipulation of fire and its maintenance intensified social organization and also provided protection and new techniques in hunting and food preparation. These activities led to a further development of communal responsibility and also probably to an oral tradition related to fire maintenance.

The burial of the dead suggests the existence of some form of concepts of a metaphysical existence.

The Neolithic Revolution

Family groups developed into clans and tribes, which in turn,

---

[14] The authors who place *Ramapithecus* as ancestoral to the Hominidae are Simons (1963), Simons and Pilbeam (1967), Campbell (1966).

required systems of formal relationship between members of the community. Cro-Magnon Man had both art and language. No evidence of his language remains but he has left samples of his incredibly life-like paintings on the walls of caves such as Altamira in Spain and Lascaux in France. He was still a hunter and his painting had religious significance related to hunting, but he was able to accumulate enough food to permit the leisure required for works of art. There is also evidence of a limited commerce at this time (about 25,000 to 15,000 B.P.).

With the end of glaciation began the so-called Neolithic Revolution when food gathering and hunting traditions gradually gave way to food producing technologies which included farming and domestication of animals. From here on, dramatic changes occurred in cultural development. The Neolithic Revolution which permitted the accumulation of surplus food made specialization possible for some who could turn their attention to art, government, religion, warfare, or invention. This, in turn, caused an acceleration of cultural evolution. This acceleration was further spurred on by the beginnings of urbanization.

Many preliterate people saw in spirits, which they envisioned as inhabiting the animate and inanimate world, dangerous and often spiteful beings who had to be bribed or propitiated to continue their work of causing the world to proceed normally. Some spirits were viewed with fear, some with amusement, and others required constant appeasement. Some had to be outwitted to prevent their making mischief and doing harm. Myths and legends also depict benign deities who helped mankind.

However, the concept of a universal, loving God who serves all of mankind without discrimination is of later origin. Such a concept foreshadowed the idea of brotherhood among men giving universal peace a rationale and sanction it did not have before. At first, the concept of such a God was held only by small minorities or, perhaps, a few individuals. It was probably preceded by the use of hieroglyphics and pictographs as means of communication. These marked the beginning of a written tradition which spurred knowledge and science to new heights.

The use of metals paved the way for the development of

complex machinery and also sophisticated armaments. The printing press, invented separately in several places, was first used in ancient Korea. In the western world, the invention is associated with Johann Gutenberg and it permitted a great increase in the diffusion of written traditions. The steam engine and the Industrial Revolution inaugurated modern technology and spurred a wide distribution of manufactured goods. It was accompanied by considerable exploitation of labor and resulted in a great increase in urban populations. Electricity as a source of illumination and as a means for sending messages ushered into being an "energy revolution."

On a different dimension, an evolution of concepts led mankind from 1) an earth-centered world to one in which the earth is a planet within one of several million solar systems; 2) a Man-centered to a life-centered earth; 3) a view of self as totally conscious to a recognition of an unconscious psyche capable of harboring dynamic forces.

Control of disease brought with it overpopulation—a phenomenon with which Man has had only limited historical experience. By saving many more of the human newborn, medicine has disturbed Man's natural ecology and has discovered that restoring this balance by means of birth control poses many complex problems.

It is characteristic of Man's uneven development that he has gained mastery over space and distance before being able to deal effectively with his own population trends and control of the atom before he has learned how to handle his own emotions.

Ontogenetic Development

The species consist of individuals and individuals together comprise the species. Contemporary time represented by the area KFEM in Figure 16, Page 193 is the period in evolution when our species and the present living generation coexist. Ontogenetic Development consists of two phases. The embryonic phase begins with the production of the sperm and ovum by the parents. It terminates at birth. The birth-death phase is represented by eight developmental stages which will be described later. The Modified Genetic-Cultural Environment represents one way to view Man's future.

Good reasons exist for treating embryological development separately from the development which takes place after birth since a whole new set of influences are brought to bear upon the neonate upon emerging from the uterus. Among humans, culture and learning play a decisive role and effect every aspect of post partem ontogenetic development. At one time it was thought that human embryonic development was not subject to cultural influences but now it is believed that culture may affect embryonic development to some extent through the mother's exposure to cultural environmental factors. This shift has occurred as a result of a new awareness of the dependency between fetal development and the mother's physiological condition. The mother's physiology may be adversely affected by inadequate diet, poor health, toxins, hormonal imbalance, or radiation hazards. Radiation hazards and toxins can affect embryonic tissue directly.

Theory of Recapitulation

The theory of recapitulation (Baer, 1837; Haeckel, 1879[15]) maintains that embryos of animals repeat some of the developmental stages of their ancient ancestors. Biologists observed that the structural characteristics of embryos—as they pass from stage to stage—resembled the structures of animals lower on the scale of evolution. Recapitulation may aid classification when adult structures leave biologists in doubt of the existing relationship between species.

The human embryo passes through developmental stages beginning with a single cell—the fertilized ovum. Mitosis takes place to produce new cells, and aggregations of cells lead to specialization. In the process of growth, the human embryo

----

[15] Baer postulated a recapitulation of the young of a species, while Haeckel proposed that adult forms were involved. Haeckel was among many writers of his time who attempted· to apply the doctrine of evolution to philosophy and religion. His studies led him to a chemical and mechanical explanation of life with an emphasis on the capacity of living organisms for locomotion. Baer's theory has been described in English by de Beer (1958).

develops a yolk sac within the first week, a vestigial occurring in the embryonic development of all vertebrates. Fishlike gill slits appear at the end of the first month. At one point in embryonic development the hands are weblike and resemble paddles. Later, a tail develops which is occasionally carried into postnatal life to be surgically excised by the physician. Moody (1962) writes,

> We have noted that all animals above single-celled protozoa are similar in the early stages of development, and that in general there is a direct relationship between similarity of adult structure and the proportion of embryonic development which is similar in different animals. Thus, dissimilar animals are found to follow like paths of development for a time and then to diverge, each going its own way. The more dissimilar the animals, the shorter the period of embryonic development they have in common. Why do dissimilar animals share any similarity of embryonic development at all? The most reasonable explanations seems to be inheritance from common ancestry.

The following twelve stages of human embryonic development are presented to indicate key periods leading from *reduction division,* in which the number of chromosomes of the sperm and ovum divide in half, to the birth of the human infant approximately nine months later.

Embryonic Phase (9 months)

1. Production of sperm and ovum by parents (meiosis).
2. Insemination of female.
3. Fertilization of ovum by sperm.
4. Period of cleavage of embryo (first week).
5. Period of two-layered embryo (second week).
6. Period of three-layered embryo (third week).
7. All organs systems of individual recognizable (4th week).
8. The five basic brain vesicles differentiated (5th week).
9. Testes and ovaries distinguishable (8th week).
10. Face looks "human" (sixteenth week).
11. Dramatic change in circulary system to permit lung breathing in preparation for birth (9th month).

The theory of recapitulation has been extended to explain the various stages of childhood. Some think that the grasping instinct of the infant is related to earlier primate ancestry and crawling is similarly associated with the prebipedal evolution. Hall (1904) and his predecessors suggested that cultural as well as phylogenetic stages are reflected in the development of an individual. *Cultural recapitulation* was thought to explain different play patterns of children. Hall wrote,

> I regard play as the motor habits and spirit of the past of the race, persisting in the present, as rudimentary functions sometimes of and always akin to rudimentary organs. The best index and guide to the stated activities of adults in past ages is found in the instinctive, untaught, and non-imitative plays of children . . . Thus we rehearse the activities of our ancestors, back we know not how far, and repeat their life work in summative . . . ways.

Hall's idea stimulated considerable research but was finally abandoned in favor of other explanations such as the freudian concept of ego development.

Freud searched for the cause of neurotic symptoms and this led him to the patient's earliest childhood. Here he identified stages of "infantile sexuality" which are perhaps less subject to misunderstanding if they are viewed as foci of sensory stimulation. At birth, the infant's focus is on oral activities related to sucking. A tactile focus also exists so that the child obtains stimulation and reassurance from stroking, hugging, and fondling—activities which correspond to the mother's need. By the sixth month, biting is a prominent feature of the infant's oral activities. The oral stage, like all others, leaves residuals which are carried forward into adulthood and which are stronger if the need is not adequately satisfied.

During the second year, sensation is focused in toilet training. For the first time, in many cultures, the child must now learn self-control and receives acceptance on the basis of his conforming to social demands. Some believe that the kind of toilet training a child receives may have a lasting effect on his adult personality. As he outgrows the anal stage, the boy's focus is on his relationship with his mother, while a girl may have a corresponding focus on her relationship with her father. This is known as the Oedipal stage (Electra for the girl), and it can best be explained by viewing it as a step which helps the child to abandon infantile auto-eroticism or self-love, in preparation for a later heterosexual relationship with a member of the opposite sex. The parent's role during the Oedipal stage serves as a bridge between self and outside world in this process.

With the advent of puberty, a *period of latency* begins in which boys prefer the company of boys and girls prefer to be with girls. This has been described as the "lull before the storm"—the storm being adolescence. In our culture the period of adolescence is greatly prolonged and often dependency on parents or society is drawn out to last until young adulthood and beyond.[16]

The following stages compose Man's birth-death phase. They are consecutive periods of personal-social adjustment associated with physiological growth and decline.

TABLE VIIA

Ontogenetic Stages	Ages in Years	Some Emphases and Concomitants
1. Birth	—	Emergence of potential
2. Infancy	1-2	Psycho-physiological needs and sensory exploration of the environment
3. Childhood	3-9	Acculteration and play exploration
4. Puberty	10-14	Psycho-sexual maturation and (males) dominance exploration; (females) sexual-maternal-cultural exploration
5. Youth	15-20	Group identifications and (males) search for symbolized hunting experiences; (females) search for symbolized maternal experiences
6. Adulthood	21-35	Vocational, parental, and marital adjustment; (males) consolidation of dominance status
7. Middle Age	36-65	Security; (males) defense of and relinquishment of physical-dominance status; (females) defense of and relinquishment of youth-bio-sexual status (menopause)
8. Age	66-85	Psycho-physiological needs and a reorientation from future to past
9. Death	—	Cessation of potential

A DIAGRAMMED VIEW OF EVOLUTION

Figure 16 on Page 193 includes some of the major developmental steps which have been discussed in this chapter. The distances shown are not proportionate to geological time. The straight lines in the diagram should be irregular, especially in regard to cultural development in which there were many static

---

[16] Other psychological theorists viewed developmental stages in a somewhat different manner: Adler (1914), Jung (1953), Horney (1950), Fromm (1947), and Sullivan (1953).

and accelerated periods. However, the diagram was designed to represent relationships rather than processes and straight lines help to make relationships more easily apparent.

Everything that has occurred since the Origin of the Universe has played a role—even if only a very minor one—in forging contemporary Man and the environment in which he finds himself. This total environment has been described as *Umwelt* and consists of the four environments, mentioned earlier, acting together to form environmental totality. The area, JHD, multiplied by approximately three billion, represents the world's current population. This is the here and the now of our own generation living in the same fraction of a second of geological time. Culture and Man began at point (C). With time, cultural influence grew until it dominated more and more of Man's life.

The word, *culture*, is used differently by various writers. It is used here as meaning everything tangible or intangible, which Man has produced. Another way it might be defined is that culture represents Man's "interference" with nature. Whereas culture has only a minimum influence on fetal life, at the moment of birth the neonate emerges into a culture saturated environment. The techniques of the midwife, nurse, or physician delivering the baby are aspects of culture. So is the regimen of the hosiptal or the home in which the infant finds himself upon birth. The physician's forceps, the slap to assist the start of respiration, and the drops forced into his yet unopened eyes all serve the newborn baby as an introduction to the man-made world of culture in which he is destined to live.

It should be noted, however, that *cultural intrusion* (shaded area in Figure 16) into ontogenetic life starts gradually because of the infant's limitations and is never complete. Physiological responses, needs, and the biological imperatives are genetic factors which culture may modify but cannot nullify. With growth, culture increasingly modifies and prescribes acceptable modes of expression for genetically rooted needs.

There comes a time, however, in advanced age when cortical inhibitory and integrative ability lessens due to irreversible brain tissue damage often hastened by arteriosclerosis. Then, the trend towards increased cultural receptivity is reversed and a decline in cultural absorption begins. There are considerable individual variations in symptoms, advent, and extent of senility but as death approaches, internal physiological factors carry increasing amounts of weight in structuring the apperceptive responses to life. Upon death, as it was before birth, culture ceases to exist as far as the individual is concerned. His body "returns" to an organic physical-chemical state and we are reminded of the phrase from the Old Testament, For dust thou art, and unto dust shalt thou return.

On a different dimensional level, an individual's ontogenetic residuals after death modify and maintain the environment into which the future generations will be born. By his activities in life, his influence persists after his death in one form or another as long as the human species continues to exist. In this sense death certainly cannot be viewed as termination (see Fig. 16 area above line FE).

The following are considerations in the Modified Genetic-Cultural Development of which future Man's oral and written tradition and his genetic endowment will be composed.

Modified Genetic-Cultural Environment (The Future)

1. Modifications of the gene pool (through offsprings)
2. Modifications of culture and cultural norms (through a personal contribution towards change)
3. Religious—metaphysical considerations (questions of life after death, spiritual aspects)
4. Mankind's future development (the impact of ontogenetic influences on phylogeny and future cultural direction)

LIFE AFTER DEATH

Most religions have metaphysical explanations of a life after death. Speculations of what happens to the human personality, mind, spirit, or soul after the body ceases to live may go back to the very beginning of mankind.

Actual evidence of the burial of the dead can be traced to the Neanderthal Man. At Wadi-el-mugharet in Palestine, bodies of Neanderthaloid inhabitants with their flint weapons beside them were found laid in trenches cut in the cave floors. Skeletal remains of a Neanderthal child were discovered in a shallow slab-lined ditch in Teshik-Tash, in Transcaspian Russia. Horns of mountain goats with points stuck in the ground encircled the grave. At La Ferrassie in the Dordogne, France, Neanderthal adults were buried in a cave under a covering of stones. Near them, a child's skeleton had been placed in a small trench and by the child's grave, bones and cinders were found suggestive of cooked offerings or the remains of a funeral feast. These events occurred well over fifty thousand years before the birth of Christ.

The Western world uses the beginning of the Christian era for dating the years. Much has happened to the world and to Man since those ancient days of Roman hegemony. Siddhartha Gautama, better known by his title, Buddha, the enlightened one, and Confucius, the Chinese teacher of ethics, lived a scarce five hundred years before this time. Six hundred years after the birth of Christ, the prophet, Mohammad, had visions which were collected and recorded in the sacred book of Islam, the Koran.

In considering these dates in the light of Man's total time on earth, we recognize that as we approach modern times, human progress has accelerated at an astonishing rate.[17]

An Analogy of Man's Progress in Time

The time relationships that are involved in the advent of Man may be illustrated by the following analogy: New York's tallest skyscraper, the Empire State Building, is 1,250 feet high. Let us assume that its length represents the entire time life has existed on our planet. By this measure, the time that has elapsed since the birth of the great religious leaders and the present moment amounts to the thickness of two pages of this book. Using this same scale, ten pages would easily take us back to the beginning of *Homo sapiens*. Three books such as this one would represent the total time since the genus, *Homo,* has existed on earth. It would take several Empire State Buildings

---

[17] However, much depends on our definition of "progress." Some may maintain while others deny that progress as defined by Western standards has proceeded along narrow and circumspect lines.

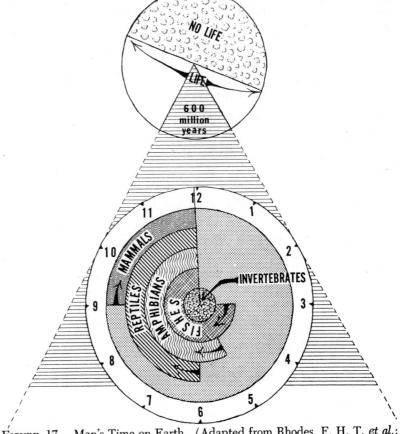

FIGURE 17.   Man's Time on Earth. (Adapted from Rhodes, F. H. T. *et al.*:
Fossils. New York, Golden Press, 1962.)

placed end to end to take us back in time to the origin of our
solar system and the universe.

In Figure 17, the first circle represents the earth of approximately five billion years ago. Life has existed about half of that
time. The small segment includes 600 million years—the period
of abundant fossils. These 600 million years are represented by
the large circle, below the smaller one. The numbers one through
twelve have been superimposed on this circle to represent the
dial of an imaginary clock which instead of a single hour has
fifty million years between each number. Invertebrates existed
throughout the entire period. The appearance of fishes, am-

phibians, reptiles, and mammals have been indicated on the face of this "clock." A single line shows Man's time on earth in relation to other animals. Transposing this dial back to a real clock, one might say that Man entered the scene one minute before midnight.

SUMMARY

Hominology's concern with evolution was discussed. The role of speculations within the human sciences was examined and unwarranted speculations were defined. The differences between idealizations and unobservables were described and it was pointed out that idealizations are difficult for the scientist to apply within the human sciences. It was suggested that a total treatment of Man may require idealizations since these clarify values, goals, and concepts of the future. A number of reasons were offered explaining the role of organic evolution within a hominological context. The possibility of reaching unwarranted conclusions in making analogies from organic evolution was described.

In a discussion of time perspectives, various kinds of time were defined. Developmental steps ranging from the origin of the universe to the present were sequentially listed within a time context. Key points and critical periods dealing with the phylogeny, culture, and ontogeny of Man were listed.

REFERENCES

ADLER, A.: Der Aggressionstrieb im Leben und in der Neurose. In Adler, A., and Furtmüller, C. (Eds.): *Heilen und Bilden; ärtzlich-pädagogische Arbeiten des Vereins für Individual psychologie.* Munich, Reinhardt, 1914.

ALLPORT, G. W.: *Becoming.* New Haven, Yale U. P., 1955.

ANON: On ethology. *Sci News,* 91:20, May 20, 1967.

BAER, K. E. VON: Über die Entwickelungsgeschichte der Thiere. Königsberg, Theil, Gebrüder Bornträger, 1837.

BARRETT, W.: What is existentialism? In Thruelson, R., and Kobler, J. (Eds.): *Adventures of the Mind.* New York, Random, 1963.

BERGSON, H.: *Creative Evolution.* Translated by A. Mitchell, New York, Henry Holt, 1911. (Reprinted, New York, Random, 1944.)

BROWN, R.: *Explanation in the Social Science.* Chicago, Aldine, 1963.

CAMPBELL, B. G.: *Human Evolution.* Chicago, Aldine, 1966.

COPERNICUS, N.: De revolutionibus orbium coelstium. Nuremburg, 1534. In Shores, L. (Ed.): *Collier's Encyclopedia*. New York, Crowell-Collier, 1962, vol. 7.

DE BEER, G. R.: *Embryos and Ancestors*, 3rd ed., Oxford, Oxford U. P., 1958.

DiRENZO, G. J. (Ed.): *Concepts, Theory, and Explanation in the Behavioral Sciences*. New York, Random, 1966.

FOX, S. W.: How did life begin? *Science, 132*:200-208, July 15, 1960.

FROMM, E.: *Man For Himself: An Inquiry into the Psychology of Ethics*. New York, Holt, 1947.

GOOD, C. V.; BARR, A. S., AND SCATES, D. E.: *The Methodology of Educational Research*. New York, Appleton, 1941.

HAECKEL, E. H.: *Evolution of Man: Popular Exposition of Human Ontogeny and Phylogeny*. New York, Appleton, 1879, 2 vols.

HALL, G. S.: *Adolescence: Its Psychology and Its Relations to Physiology, Anthropology, Sociology, Sex, Crime, Religion, and Education*. New York, Appleton, 1904, 2 vols.

HARDIN, G.: *Nature and Man's Fate*. New York, New Am. Lib., 1961.

HORNEY, K.: *Neurosis and Human Growth*. New York, Norton, 1950.

HSU, F. L. K. (Ed.): *Aspects of Culture and Personality*. New York, Abelard-Schuman, 1954.

JUNG, C. G.: *Collected Works*. New York, Pantheon, 1953.

MEINSCHEIN, W. G.: Soudan formation: organic extracts of early precambrian rocks. *Science, 150*:601-605, Oct. 29, 1965.

MOODY, P. A.: *Introduction to Evolution*. 2nd ed., New York, Harper, 1962.

MORGENSTERN, I.: *The Dimentional Structure of Time*. New York, Philosophical Lib., 1960.

NOGAR, R. J.: *The Wisdom of Evolution*. New York, New Am. Lib., 1966.

OPARIN, A. I.: *Life: Its Nature, Origin, and Development*. Translated by A. Synge, New York, Academic, 1964.

SCOTT, J. P.: Critical periods in behavioral development. *Science, 138*:3544, Nov. 30, 1962.

SIMONS, E. L.: Early relatives of man. *Sci Amer, 211*:50-62, July, 1964.

SIMONS, E. L., AND PILBEAM, D. B.: A preliminary revision of the Dryopithecinae (Pongidae, Anthropoidea), In Genóves, S. T. (Ed.); Brooks, T. S. (Assoc. Ed.), and Lasker, G. W. (Assoc. Ed.): *Yearbook of Physical Anthropology, 1965*. México, Published for the American Association of Physical Anthropology, Instituto de Investigaciones Históricas, Universidad Nacional Autónomas de México, 1967, vol. 13.

SIMPSON, G. G.: The meaning of taxonomic statements. In Washburn, S. L. (Ed.): *Classification and Human Evolution*. Chicago, Aldine, 1963.

STEWARD, J. H.: Toward understanding cultural evolution. *Science, 153*:729-730, Aug. 12, 1966.

STOKES, W. L.: *Essentials of Earth History*, 2nd ed., Englewood Cliffs, Prentice-Hall, 1966.

SULLIVAN, H. S.: *The Interpersonal Theory of Personality.* New York, Norton, 1953.
WASHBURN, S. L. (Ed.): *Social Life of Early Man.* Chicago, Aldine, 1961.
WHITE, L. A.: Definitions and conceptions of culture. In DiRenzo, G. J. (Ed.): *Concepts, Theory, and Explanation in the Behavioral Sciences.* New York, Random, 1966.
WHITE, L. A.: *The Science of Culture.* New York, Grove, 1949.

Chapter 10

THE QUESTION OF MAN'S ORIGINS

"The image of Man is rich and complex beyond expression. It is a curious paradox that although this very richness is a result of symbolic character, symbols and language are incapable of expressing it to the full. There is always something in the image of man, even of the most intelligent and sophisticated person 'beyond what words can utter.'"

KENNETH BOULDING, *The Image*

"Man's identification rests, at least in part, not only on what kind of a creature he was in skeletal terms, but on what he did with a piece of flint and a spark of fire . . . One wonders why and how man evolved at all."

HAL BORLAND, *The Enduring Pattern*

W HO WERE MAN'S ancestors? When did the human deviation occur in the Primate evolutionary line which led to *Homo sapiens?* For several reasons, this is not an easy question to answer. Not all human paleontologists are in unanimous agreement as to the hominid classification of the early fossils which show humanlike characteristics. Hominization was a gradual process which consisted of mutational changes leading to bipedalism and associated modifications including the large convoluted human brain. One cannot pinpoint a definite beginning to the human line without first defining what characteristics should be included within the hominid designation. This leaves room for a considerable difference of opinion.

The number of fossils available for establishing hominid descent are sparse, and this has prompted the use of "educated

---

[1] The new interest in Man's common ancestor represents an emerging universal trend towards human brotherhood. For this reason this relatively recent interest (reflected even in the comic strips) is of great significance. It is a manifestation associated with our new involvement in Development Level Seven (see Chapter 11).

guesses." For example, Black, a Canadian professor of anatomy, established the existence of *Sinanthropus pekinensis*—Chinese man of Peking (*Homo erectus pekinensis*)—on the basis of a single humanlike molar tooth. Two years later, the evidence for the species was strengthened by the discovery of a well-preserved, fossilized skull. Still later, additional *Sinanthropus* fossil remains found in a cave in Chou-kou-tien confirmed Black's guess completely. Leakey's *Homo habilis* consists of parts of a pair of parietal bones, partial mandible, one isolated tooth, a clavical, and some foot bones. All phalanges are missing. Yet from these remains, it can be established that the foot was hominid and that, in many ways, it resembled that of modern man (Day, 1965).

GEOCHRONOLOGY	YEARS BEFORE PRESENT	TOOL TYPES	HOMINID FORMS
	10,000		
		Blade Tools	
UPPER PLEISTOCENE	70,000		*Homo sapiens*
		Flake Tools	
_ _ _ _ _ _ _ _ _ _	100,000		
	200,000		
MIDDLE PLEISTOCENE			
	400,000	Biface and Flake Tools	*Homo erectus*
_ _ _ _ _ _ _ _ _	500,000		
LOWER PLEISTOCENE	1,000,000		
		Pebble Tools	*Australopithecines*
_ _ _ _ _ _ _ _ _	3,000,000		
	5,000,000		
PLIOCENE			
			Ramapithecus
	12,000,000		

FIGURE 18. One Interpretation of Mankind Evolving Through Time (Not Drawn To Scale).

FOSSIL FORMS

Lucy

Perhaps now recognizable origins of the human line can be traced further back than was thought possible. Recent discoveries in Ethiopia by Don Johanson suggest that Man may be far older than previously thought, necessitating the re-evaluation of established theories of the origins and age of mankind's ancestors. Johanson made a remarkable discovery called Lucy, a 3 million year old fossil. Forty percent of the complete skeleton was recovered permitting anthropologists to infer that this was a 3½ foot, 20 year old female hominid who walked upright on two legs. Her exact place in Man's line is still being evaluated.

Heidelberg Man

Physical anthropologists and paleontologists are capable of an almost uncanny ingenuity in developing a theoretical picture of a complete animal from isolated fragments such as those described. However, limitations are reached when an attempt is made to reconstruct the fleshy parts of the animal since these leave no fossil traces. However, bony promontories and ridges yield clues as to type of musculature that was attached to bone, and this, in turn, suggests the weight and extent of the flesh which covered the parts involved.

Sometimes, only one body part is found in isolation. One October day, in 1907, workmen at a sandpit near the village of Mauer, six miles southeast of Heidelberg, uncovered a large human-looking fossilized lower jaw judged to be about a half a million years old. Many people have since looked for additional fragments of this Heidelberg Man (*Homo erectus heidelbergensis*) in vain. The Heidelberg mandible remains the isolated specimen of a *Pithecanthropus*[2] which lived in Europe before the second glaciation.

------

[2] Howell (1960), in a reappraisal of the Heidelberg material, suggests that it may be an example of the early Neanderthalers.

When only a few isolated fragments of former hominids are available for study, the question may be asked, To what extent are the characteristics of these specimens typical of the species as a whole? If, in a million years, someone were to discover a femur belonging to a contemporary African pigmy and if this were the only specimen of *Homo sapiens* available at that time, generalized conclusions about the height of our present species would probably be in error. It is conceivable that we might make the same kind of a mistake when, with only a very few samples, we attempt to envision anatomical characteristics of a long extinct species. Therefore, when approximating a total skull or skeleton from limited fossil material, allowances must be made for reasonable variations.

Oreopithecus

The history of the scientific search for Man's ancestors consists of events so unlikely and incredible that they may be said to surpass fiction. It is not surprising, therefore, that accounts of human evolution have become popular reading. There are many books available which do justice to the fascinating story of the search for Man's ancestors, among these are *In Search of Adam,* Wendt (1963); *Adam's Ancestors,* Leakey (1960); *Adventures with the Missing Link,* Dart and Craig (1959); *Man: His First Million Years,* Montagu (1958); *A Million Years of Man,* Carrington (1964); and *Early Man,* Howell (1965).

The search for Man's beginnings takes us back millions of years, into the Miocene. The following proto-apes have been identified from available fossil materials: *Pliopithecus,* which may have been ancestral to the chimpanzee or gorilla; *Dryopithecus,* first of the fossil great apes, whose remains have been unearthed throughout Europe, India, and China; and *Oreopithecus,* which serves as an excellent example of the difficulty in deciding whether a given fossil is or is not a precursor of the human line.

The remains of *Oreopithecus bambolii,* geologically dated as approximately ten- to twelve-million-years-old, were found in Tuscany, Italy. At first, some paleontologists considered the fossil to be a cercopithecoid monkey, while others saw it as an early anthropoid ape. Later, some paleontologists viewed it as a link between monkey and ape.

In 1954, Professor Johannes Hürzeler, of Basel, Switzerland, challenged these classifications and claimed that *Oreopithecus* was a hominid and a member of the evolutionary line which led to Man. Hürzeler himself recovered the remains of several specimens from a lignite mine at Baccinello, Italy. During a visit to Hürzeler's laboratory in Basel, I viewed these specimens still encased in their lignite matrix and learned of the risks which he had taken in order to rescue every possible fragment of these remarkable fossils before the lignite mine in which they were found was demolished.

Hürzeler's designation of *Oreopithecus* was not unanimously accepted. Straus (1963) presents an analysis of the various claims that have been made in regard to the classifications of these fossils. His final conclusion is that *Oreopithecus* is a hominid as Hürzeler has maintained.

Ramapithecus

For many years *Ramapithecus* was considered the earliest manlike Primate. Its incisors, canines and premolars were smaller than those of the Miocene *Dryopithecines* and present day apes. Today there are some paleontologists who suggest that *Ramapithecus* may have been a female *Dryopithicus*. Partial upright gait has been inferred by Pilbeam and Simons (1967) as well as others who have studied existing fragments.

, A gap of nine million years separates *Ramapithecus* from *Australopithecus*—a genus now generally agreed to be hominid. The story of the discovery of *Australopithecus africanus* is a fascinating one.

Dart's Baby

In 1924, Dart, a professor of anatomy at the University of Witwatersrand, South Africa, reported the find of a nearly perfect child's skull dated at approximately a million years old. In his book, *Adventures with the Missing Link* (1959), he describes this discovery as occurring while he was scheduled to be the best man at a wedding which was proceeding in his home. Two boxes of breccia had arrived the day of the wedding from the commercial quarries near Taungs, Rhodesia. While he delved into the contents of the boxes dressed in his tuxedo, he was oblivious to the guests in his house waiting expectantly and, for good reason, none too patiently, for him to appear to assume his role in the marriage ceremony.

Dart recalls the event:

> I wrenched the lid off the first box and my reaction was one of extreme disappointment. In the rocks I could make out traces of fossilized eggshells and turtle shells and a few fragmentary pieces of isolated bone, none of which looked to be of much interest.
>
> Impatiently I wrestled with the lid of the second box, still hopeful but half-expecting it to be a replica of its mate. At most I anticipated baboon skulls, little guessing that from this crate was to emerge a face that would look out at the world after an age-long sleep of nearly a million years.

This face, to which Professor Dart referred, was not the first thing that caught his attention upon opening the second box. By a rare coincidence, after the lid was lifted, the box revealed the fossilized cast of a very unusual brain.

> As soon as I removed the lid, a thrill of excitement shot through me. On the very top of the rock heap was what was undoubtedly an endocranial cast of mold of the interior of the skull. Had it been only the fossilized brain cast of any species of ape, it would have ranked as a great discovery, for such a thing had never been reported. But I knew at a glance that what lay in my hands was no ordinary anthropoidal ape. Here in lime-consolidated sand was the replica of a brain three times as large as that of a baboon and considerably bigger than that of any adult chimpanzee. The startling image of the convolutions and furrows of the brain and the blood vessels of the skull were plainly visible.

Professor Dart now forgot all about the wedding that was taking place only a few feet away and did not even recall later that his wife had twice remonstrated with him urging him to play host to the guests in his home. Instead, Dart asked himself, "Was there among this pile of rocks, a face to fit the brain?" He answered,

I ransacked feverishly through the boxes. My search was rewarded, for I found a large stone with a depression into which the cast fitted perfectly . . . I (worked) away with a hammer, chisels and knitting needle, in constant fear that the slightest slip of the chisel would shatter the relic within. No diamond cutter ever worked more lovingly or with such care on a priceless jewel. . . .

On the seventy-third day (of working on it) the rock parted. I could view the face from the front, although the right side was still embedded. The creature that had contained this massive brain was no giant anthropoid such as a gorilla. What emerged was a baby's face, an infant with full set of milk teeth and its first permanent molars just erupting.

I doubt if there was any parent prouder of his offspring than I was of my "Taungs baby" on that Christmas of 1924.

Dart named the specimen *Australopithecus africanus*—southern ape of Africa—and, in doing so, stated that it was probably a connecting link between ape and Man. Later, other finds of the *Australopithecus* group were unearthed. They were approximately 3½ feet tall with an average brain capacity of less than 600 cubic centimeters and identified as meat-eaters by their teeth. Other discoveries followed such as the larger, heavy-boned *Paranthropus*, a vegetarian australopithecine, who is thought to have become extinct. Is *Homo habilis* a third australopithecine form or does it belong to a distinct separate group?

Recent discoveries such as Richard Leakey's fossil, "1470," with a brain capacity of 800 cubic centimeters, and Mary Leakey's 3.75 million year old finds need further study to ascertain where they fit into the picture of Man's ancestors.

Pithecanthropus

The first remains of our own genus, *Homo*, were discovered in conglomerate deposits in the valley of the Solo River near Trinil in Central Java. The original finds included a few teeth and the top of a cranium. Later, a thighbone was found in the same geological stratum.

These remnants belonged to Java man, or *Pithecanthropus*

erectus (*Homo erectus erectus*), as he was called, when discovered by a Dutch anatomist, Eugene Dubois. The term, *Pithecanthropus*, had been coined by Haeckel earlier, before there was even a single specimen to support the existence of such a creature. Dubois was misled by the ever enthusiastic and imaginative Haeckel into thinking that an ape-man or "missing link" could be found in an area inhabited by gibbons, and he joined the Dutch Colonial Army as a surgeon to explore the Netherland East Indies, where these small anthropoid apes had their habitat.

By an extraordinary coincidence, workmen hired by Dubois uncovered a skull cap at the banks of the Solo River which neatly fitted Haeckel's conjectured missing link between man and ape. This specimen had a low cranial vault, prominent supraorbital ridges, and a cranial capacity of approximately 900 cc. This falls just about half way between the cranial capacities of anthropoid apes and modern men.

Dubois believed that the upper thighbone his workmen uncovered upstream from the original site, after removing a twelve-yard layer of soil from the river bank, belonged to the same individual as the skull cap and that these fragments could also be associated with molars found in the area. The thighbone not only indicated that the creature walked erect but also that it lacked the curvature of Neanderthal Man's thighbone, resembling more closely that of modern Man. He was confident that his discovery of *Pithecanthropus erectus* would convince the heretofore skeptical world that ape-men were not science-fiction-like figments of the imagination but living beings which actually existed before the advent of modern men.

In 1896, professors from all over the world traveled to the city of Leiden to personally inspect the box of fossils which Dubois had brought back with him from Java. After a lively discussion in which there was much disagreement, the Leiden Congress broke up without giving Dubois' discoveries an endorsement. Rudolph Virchow, the eminent German pathologist, anthropologist, and founder of cellular pathology, enumerated a host of objections to Dubois' theories about the fossil fragments. Detecting a healed growth on the thighbone, he argued that any

ancient man with this affliction would have died. But the growth
in the bone had healed and, therefore, the creature could not
have been a primitive being but must have been a modern one.

Dubois was deeply distressed by the cold reception given
his *Pithecanthropus erectus*. To vindicate his fossils, he gave
lectures at congresses in France, England, and Germany, but
the attacks on him continued and he became increasingly em-
bittered. From that time on, he angrily kept his fossil fragments
under lock and key and refused to show the materials to anyone.
Throughout the following years, he remained stubbornly deaf
to all entreaties. After the Java specimens had been locked
up for almost thirty years, two eminent anthropologists were at
last permitted to inspect the fragments. By this time, the world
was ready to accept the human status of the Java fossil. However,
Dubois was now living as a recluse and no longer showed any
interest in the controversy which his discoveries had precipitated.

Later, Von Koenigswald, a capable young paleontologist,
followed Dubois' footsteps and found a more complete skull of
Pithecanthropus erectus in the same general area. This put an
end to all disputes on the hominid position of Dubois' fossil.
Vindication, however, came too late to afford the discoverer of
the Java ape-man any sense of personal triumph.

Neanderthal Man

The discovery of the Neanderthal skull (*Homo sapiens
neanderthalensis*) received a similarly frigid reception. The
same influential Virchow who discredited Dubois challenged
Johann Fuhlrott, a natural science teacher in an area of Germany
now called Neanderthal. When the owner of a nearby quarry
showed Fuhlrott some "old bear bones" his workmen had
uncovered, it occurred to the astounded country school teacher
that the coarse, massive skull cap and thick thighbones belonged
to an early type of human being. After receiving some cautious
support on his theory of a Neanderthal Man, he presented his
views at the Anthropological Congress in Kassel. Here the skull
cap and thigh bone were described by some of the experts of
the time as belonging to "a fallen Cossack whose corpse had
putrified in Neanderthal," "the remains of a feeble-minded idiot,"

"an old Dutchman," and "a member of the Celtic race." The final blow to the schoolmaster's hopes came when the eminent Virchow declared with finality, "It cannot be safely assumed that mankind lived as early as the mammoth. There is no justification for the statement that the human race in prehistoric times was more primitive than it is at present."

Virchow explained that the Neanderthal skull found by Fuhlrott had belonged to a contemporary individual whose anatomy had been changed by disease. The eminent scientist spoke convincingly and applause broke out after he had finished. Thereafter, scholars launched bitter attacks against Fuhlrott and his supporters. When the discovery of other human fossils similar to those of Fuhlrott's Neanderthal Man finally convinced skeptics that such primitive humans had, indeed, existed, the much maligned schoolteacher who intuitively grasped the correct significance of the Neanderthal remains was no longer alive.

The Piltdown Affair

Quite a different reception was given to skeletal remains found by an English lawyer. This was the discovery of *Eoanthropus,* the "dawn man" by Charles Dawson, an energetic man, who had an interest in natural science and spent his leisure time collecting fossils of extinct reptiles. On one of his frequent trips, Dawson watched workmen in a gravel pit at Piltdown about to destroy a discolored human skull. Aghast, he scolded the men soundly and rescued the skull taking it home to add to his growing collection.

Several years later he submitted a skull and some bones he had collected to Arthur Smith Woodward, keeper of the Department of Geology at the British Museum. Woodward was delighted and assigned these specimens to an early geological era. Dawson, accompanied by Woodward, undertook further excavations at Piltdown. Together, they found another fragment of a skull and unearthed a strange, simian-looking mandible and a few unusual teeth. Later, the two Englishmen were joined by a French paleontologist who discovered more teeth that seemed to belong to the strange jaw. Surprises continued as primitive flints were found at the Piltdown site along with something which resembled a large, petrified cudgel. When the various fossilized bone fragments were put together, the ape-like jaw perfectly fitted a very human-looking skull. The skull resembled that of any modern Man and had no brow ridges or other primitive features. The discovery seemed to prove that creatures with modern, human foreheads, possessing crude, ape-like jaws, roamed the earth about 500,000 years ago. The scientific world was astounded at this amazing discovery, and Dawson became a celebrity.

Sir Arthur Keith and other anthropologists used the Piltdown Man to support the thesis that modern man is very ancient, predating Neanderthal Man and *Pithecanthropus*. The human cranium and the simian mandible were studied by scholars from all over the world, many expressing puzzlement, but only a few voiced doubt about the authenticity of the *Eoanthropus dawsoni*.[3] Woodward had appended Dawson's name to the species.

Unlike many other discoveries of human fossils, the English lawyer was honored throughout his lifetime for his epoch-making find. In 1953, forty years after his death, modern chemical tests revealed that the Piltdown Man was a fake and perhaps the greatest hoax in scientific history. Dawson had offered no deathbed confession but took with him into his grave the secret that the Piltdown finds represented a modern ape's jaw with whittled-down teeth, which had been artificially aged and shaped to fit a skull only 50,000 years old. The skull and jaw were buried so that both would be found together to give the impression that they belonged to the same individual. The bone tools had been formed with a steel knife, and the stone artifacts had been artificially stained and buried in the Piltdown gravel pit with the skull fragments. It was determined that "the molars" of *Eoanthropus* actually belonged to an ancient elephant which must have been imported by Dawson from a foreign source. The scientific world was amazed at the patient and expert craftmanship required to falsify the jaw and teeth and wondered what caused this strange deception.

---

[3] Weidenreich and Klaatch were among those who did not recognize the authenticity of the Piltdown Man.

The matter did not rest here. On November 1953, a member of the British House of Commons presented a bill to vote "no confidence" in the Trustees of the British Museum for their delay in ascertaining that the Piltdown find was a forgery. Among those "accused" (by virtue of their membership on the board of trustees) were Prime Minister Churchill, Foreign Secretary Eden, and the Archbishop of Canterbury. The ludicrous charge of neglect against these men was finally shelved but not before it caused some to ponder on how ironic it is that acknowledgment is often withheld from those making genuine discoveries while those who produce what is worthless, receive recognition which only the passage of time erases.

Steinheim and Swanscombe

At the present time, our increased knowledge of morphology and more accurate dating methods make it unlikely that past errors and episodes such as Piltdown will be repeated. Discoveries as those in Steinheim, Germany (1933) (*Homo sapiens steinheimensis*) and Swanscombe, England (1935) (dated 150,000 - 250,000 B.P.), resulted in extensive re-evaluation of earlier fossil specimens. Neanderthal Man in Europe was associated with the Mousterian culture which existed in the early part of the last glaciation (Pleistocene). The Steinheim skull was associated with earlier artifacts, fauna, and flora, indicating second or possibly early third interglacial age (Day, 1965). The relatively small cranial capacity of about 1,100 cc differentiates the Steinheim find from the later Neanderthalers and from modern Man. However, the skull resembles modern Man in its relatively high forehead, rounded occipital region, and in the total pattern of the facial area. In these respects it can be sharply differentiated from the later Neanderthalers.

The Swanscombe skull was discovered just twenty miles southwest of London by Alvan Marston, a dentist, who personally knew the lawyer Dawson. Like the Steinheim fossil, the skull is early or preclassic Neanderthal. It belonged to a young adult female. The implements found at the site included numerous hand-axes and flake tools. The morphology of these remains fitted the evolutionary picture and, this time, there was no doubt about their authenticity. Recent reinvestigation of the Swans-combe material suggests that it can be assigned to a Neanderthal intermediate group which anthropologists place in the Mindel-Riss interglacial period (see Fig. 18).

Zinjanthropus and Homo Habilis

With each new discovery, existing theories of human chron-ology may have to be changed to fit the facts which the new find reveals. This happened when Louis S. B. Leakey,[4] with the aid of his wife Mary, discovered *Zinjanthropus* and later *Homo habilis*. These discoveries are described in a *National Geographic* article (Payne, 1965) which shows pictures and a map of the mile-wide Olduvai Gorge where erosion has cut through two million years of sediment, offering us, in earth and stone, a veritable textbook of fossil history.

Dr. Payne describes the discovery of *Homo habilis*:

> Deep in the distant past—nearly two million years ago—a manlike creature roamed the shores of a now vanished lake. He killed small animals for food and fashioned tools, Dr. Leakey feels, with hands that had a grasp approaching ours. With death, his bones lay embedded in the earth until their discovery in Olduvai Gorge.
>
> The anthropologist named the new species *Homo habilis*, or "man with ability," and considers him direct ancestor of modern *Homo sapiens*—a belief fostered by study of fossil fragments, including two incomplete *habilis* jaws. (One of these) belonged to a young adult female whom the Leakeys nicknamed Cinderella. She seemed to have been short-statured, small-brained, and of light weight.
>
> Cinderella lived about 800,000 years ago, whereas the owner (of the other) . . . jaw . . . a *Homo habilis* child, preceded her by about one million years.

The broad, U-shaped inner curve of the jaws would have permitted free movement of the tongue and Dr. Leakey believes that *Homo habilis* may have, in a primitive way, been able to speak. The size, shape, and wear of the teeth suggested that *Homo habilis* was already a meat-eater. Payne continues,

> A skull of *Zinjanthropus* 1,750,000 years old came to light at Olduvai Gorge, where the Leakeys later found *Homo habilis*. The

---

[4] Leakey is British by descent, born in Kenya, and by adoption is the only white member of the local Kikuyu tribe.

much younger Zinj jaw came from a cliff near Lake Natron . . . Its sharp V shape indicates that this hominid could not move its tongue freely. Eventually, Zinjanthropus vanished, the Leakeys theorize, whereas *Homo habilis* survived to become one of the ancestors of modern man.

MAN'S ANCESTORS

The matter of exactly which early hominid was the direct ancestor of modern Man is open to question. Some anthropologists regard the classic or late Neanderthal Man as having followed a dead-end street phylogenetically, whereas the Steinheim Man, an early Neanderthal type, is seen as in the direct line of modern Man. *Australopithecus*, an earlier hominid is seen by some as ancestral to Man while others classify this fossil as a possible evolutionary dead end. Current research suggests that perhaps australopithecines roamed the earth as early as 5.5 million years ago. Whereas much is known about Man's ancestors, much remains speculative and controversial, and that, perhaps, is part of the fascination of the continuing search. Tomorrow's find in some distant gorge or riverbed may bring with it new theories and revised dates.

If Man is to be understood, he must be viewed historically and phylogenetically as well as ontogenetically. In their attempt to comprehend human nature, many contemporary behavioral scientists are not sufficiently cognizant of the influence of phylogeny in shaping Man's inner forces. Carl Jung (1875-1961) has written on the *collective unconscious* and on *archetypes*, but he failed to show where racial memories come from, how they are transmitted genetically, and what organ system controls them. Much of what Jung postulated had to be accepted intuitively, but this is not the framework which empirical science can accept. Do we now have at our disposal ethological information which can put the idea of a racial unconscious on a firmer scientific basis? This question will be explored later.

Before proceeding further, it may be well to clarify a popular misconception regarding Man's phylogenetic descent. The popular literature on human evolution usually describes Man as "descended from apes." Even in the professional literature, Man's progenitors are sometimes described as "apes." In terms such as *Pithecanthropus, Australopithecus,* and *Ramapithecus,* "pithec" is derived from the Greek word, *ape* or *monkey.* This leads to confusion since the English term *ape* and *monkey* usually refers to a contemporary species of Primates who, like Man, have undergone specialized evolutionary changes from earlier primate types.

It is just as incorrect to call prehuman and protohuman Primates "apes" as it is to call Miocene proto-apes "humans." Figure 19 shows that Man, Ape, and Old World Monkey had common ancestors in the Oligocene era. In the Miocene,[5] the anthropoidea—Man and Ape—diverged into separate evolutionary

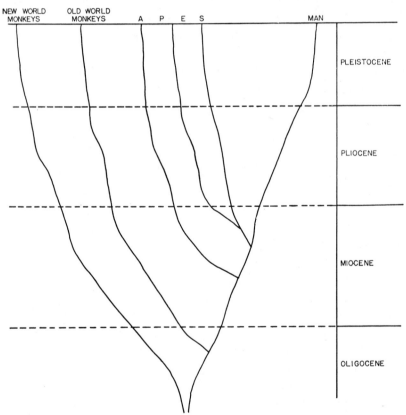

FIGURE 19. Divergent Lines of Man, Ape, and Monkey.

------

[5] A more recent divergence between man and ape has been postulated by some scientists.

lines. Creatures such as *Ramapithecus* may have been similar to modern apes in respect to hairiness, cranial capacity, and some body proportions, etc., but these similarities were matched by significant differences.

Once Man and Ape diverged, an unbridgeable chasm developed between these evolutionary lines. Although most students would not misinterpret the statement that "Man is descended from apes," it could confuse some and, therefore, such a term as *apes* should not be used to designate early hominids or protohumans.

HUMAN EMERGENCE STEMS FROM STRUGGLE

In reviewing the history of Man's emergence from more primitive primate forms, we must not forget that Man is still emerging. Even cultures that have found ecological niches and seemingly achieved homeostasis are actually changing but more slowly than others whose ecology has not been stabilized. War, colonialism, slavery, commerce, trade, exogamy, and migrations are among the "insurance policies" Man has devised to obviate national, racial, or tribal stagnation. These methods do not permit Man to live and let live but they do insure interaction leading to cultural and phylogenetic modification. Human population units lose their identities as old ones merge and new ones emerge throughout time.

Man differs from most other animals in that he has seldom permitted nature alone to supply the instigation for diversifying his gene pool. In one sense, then, armed conflicts between men have yielded major evolutionary advantages. Perhaps, for this reason, Man's dual nature is ambivalent towards war in that he both wishes to avoid it and actively seeks to precipitate it.

In a related way, men both wish to maintain discrete cultural units and desire to obliterate them. There are forces which tend towards acculturation, social accommodation, and integration; and, also, there are influences which stress separation, segregation, and maintenance of cultural identity. The cultural unit is pulled into opposing directions, and it must constantly face the dilemma of Hamlet—"to be or not to be?" History shows poignantly that culture groups and nations do not always have a free choice in the matter of whether or not to continue to exist. Man's unmitigated interference with his neighbor's *status quo* has had a measure of survival value in the long process of human emergence, but the time may come—or has already come—when the deleterious effect of interference of this kind may outweigh any possible advantages.

Protohuman culture hinged largely upon the weapon and the tool. Any improvement in methods of hunting animals and subduing human foes represented progress of a very significant type. But culture in its evolvement also took other directions. Arts, ethics, religion, philosophy, and certain aspects of science (such as "pure science") represented a new kind of a cultural advance.

Nations with weapon superiority subdued nations having superior nonweapon cultures. Rome conquered both Greece and Israel, while the Mongolian nomads subdued China. But, in another sense, the victims, in their defeat, were often able to affect a different kind of conquest—a cultural one—over the victors. Thus, Christianity, the religion originating in Israel, converted Rome as the literature of Greece had earlier re-educated the Romans. Likewise, the forces that caused mixture and cultural amalgamation were powerful in molding Man, but these forces were often violent and destructive and have left scars upon him as well as bringing him benefits.

CULTURE LAGS, CULTURE GAPS, AND HOMINOLAGS

Examples of culture lags may be found in styles of clothing, architecture, forms of address, language, food preparation, methods of transportation, certain medical practices, superstitions, and economics (such as, perhaps, the use of gold as an international monetary standard). Within every culture lag, the adaptation originally served to increase the efficiency of a function (e.g., use of gold as a standard for trade). A culture lag develops when, due to changes, the original adaptation continues even though it is no longer efficient. A negative culture lag exists when the reason for the continuation is primarily inertia or social stagnation. A positive culture lag is present when the original adaptation, though no longer useful, has gained a sentimental value, traditional status, or a new utility unrelated to its original purpose.

A social culture lag occurs when members of any minority group (ethnic, racial, national, economic) desiring to acculturate with the majority fails to do so. For example, the term *nouveaux riche* has been applied to a lower socioeconomic class which has acquired wealth but is incapable of merging with a higher socioeconomic class because of the social culture lag between the groups.

If a minority group desires to maintain its identity and resists acculturation, the term, *culture lag*, is not applicable. Instead, a *culture gap* is present which serves to socially isolate the minority group, keeping it from being assimilated. Culture gaps exist when tourists visit a country where the mores, dress, and other characteristics of the indigenous people differ from their own. If the tourists attempt to act, live, and merge inconspicuously with the native population but fail to do so, a social culture lag exists.

An entirely different kind of a "culture lag," which might be confused with those already mentioned, relates to culturally sanctioned forms of expression for biologically rooted emotional drives or tendencies. These kinds of "culture lag" will be referred to as *hominolags* because no other term is available to distinguish them. A hominolag exists when a form of cultural sanction dissipating a biological drive tends towards disorganization rather than to effective organization or survival. The original adaptation of a culture lag represents an invention having utility, whereas the original adaptation of a hominolag represents a means of displacing aggressive impulses.

Banging on a desk with one's fist is considered an acceptable substitute for an employer's impulse to strike the head of an employee. Swinging a golf club on a golf course is acceptable but thrashing the air with a stick outside the golf course might be regarded as a disturbance of the peace. Killing in wartime is considered a duty but killing in peacetime may lead to life imprisonment. If banging desks, playing golf, waging war, at one time absorbed aggressive components of drives or tendencies, but, if under changed circumstances, such activities no longer are capable of doing so, they are hominolags if they are continued.

There is another kind of hominolag. Activities designed to

absorb or redirect drives and tendencies often offer society some additional advantage as a by-product. Thus golf has become a source of additional commercial enterprise and warfare has created a host of new inventions ranging from surgery to atomic energy. When, however, an activity becomes more destructive to society than constructive, it is also called a hominolag, if it is continued.

Is Warfare a Hominolag?

In today's world, many human institutions exist which could offer displacement for some of the complex emotional needs which warfare accommodates. First, there are the pageantlike national sports such as football, baseball, and other forms of social recreation. There are also international sport rivalries, the "cold war," the war against poverty, the war against disease, the battle for men's mind, and a host of other efforts which could drain off martial emotions and redirect them into noncombatant channels.

These efforts together with political attempts have failed, as we all know. Displacement activity seems to work effectively for nonhuman species (Ardrey, 1966) but it appears that *Homo sapiens,* more than other species, has an affinity for intraspecies strife. If Nature is seen as Man's mother who has nourished him, Mars has been his father who has taught him well. For it seems that much of his progress may be attributed to the relentless needs culminating in warfare. War develops cohesiveness within a society, creates a tradition to which the members of the society can adhere, and releases the boredom of daily living. War offers Man the chance to sacrifice, to become "bigger than himself," to identify with a cause, and to give expression to a variety of tabooed emotions. It offers him a change of pace, an opportunity for excitement, a chance to prove his worth and courage. Admittedly it will be difficult to find an adequate substitute for the many services war renders. The search for such a substitute remains as one of mankinds most urgent and challenging tasks.

In a Gallup Poll survey sponsored by *Readers' Digest* (see *Readers' Digest,* June, 1968) the results of participating in the

Vietnam conflict were assessed. The survey found that a large number of soldiers felt that they had gained self-confidence and learned how to accept responsibility. Whereas few wanted to go, many, later, claimed that they were glad for the experience.

Human beings are prone to glamorize past experiences no matter how unpleasant they may have been (see p. 369). Perhaps that is why the "glory" of war rather than the horror of it is passed on from generation to generation. And that may also be why behavioral studies on the causes of war are relatively rare.

In an issue of *Science News* (Anon, December 16, 1967), war is termed a *human idiosyncrasy* and is described as follows:

> Man's curse, constant companion, and social invention—war—doesn't often come under close scrutiny. Men simply do it all the time; they don't know why, and seldom ask.
>
> Anthropologists this year asked why and amassed a bulk of evidence that goes far toward opening up two questions: What drives us to legalized (killing) and what are the consequences to ourselves and nature?

The question regarding the causes of war were raised at a symposium at the annual (1967) meeting of the American Anthropological Association in which the views of cultural, physical, and medical anthropologists were reflected:

> From the start the anthropologists drew a sharp line between aggressive behavior in animals and human wars, a parallel often used to explain warfare. "I think there is no continuity between animal aggression and what we call war," said Dr. Margaret Mead, curator of ethnology at the American Museum of Natural History. "There is much continuity between the action of a man who gets his foot trod on in a subway and comes back with a punch in the ribs, or between fighting stags and human rivals," said Dr. Mead. But war is something else. "War depends on man's capacity to symbolize."

In Chapter 2 Man was described as having the ability to easily break up a configuration. This is something other animals have difficulty in doing. The human species is a configuration which Man is typically capable of dismembering. He develops from the dismembered parts concepts which he identifies with "I" and "Thou," "we" and "they." The parts "thou" and "they" may then be acted upon as if they were not a member of the same configuration, and the "I" and the "we" can be developed into exclusive configurations to which the "others" do not belong. The article on war continues,

> Legal killing . . . arose hand-in-hand with the developing human ability to break down natural perceptions into symbols—thought, ideas, and words. Once a man could make a symbolic distinction, he was able to identify his own men as "insiders," other men as "outsiders" and therefore less than human. "The human symbolic capacity allows men to deny others their species," said Dr. Mead. The others become "legitimate prey—or predators . . ." The symbol becomes a trap.

Another anthropologist pointed out that symbols such as clan, tribe, race, state, nation, and ideology served survival by inspiring a high degree of social cooperation but they also produced an increase in frustration and aggression, and war is one of the outlets for these negative by-products of social cooperation.

A number of modern thinkers, among whom is Margaret Mead (in an address at the American Anthropological Association Meeting, Chicago, 1962) claim that for the first time, an adequate substitute for war has become available to society through the space race. Like war, space exploration is competitive, dangerous, glamorous, a source of novelty, excitement, and, most important, demands tremendous resourcefulness, ingenuity, and untold financial sacrifices. If our current competition in space actually serves such a purpose, it will represent a major adaptive revolution but one that is not without a precedent.

Potlatch

The Northwest Coast Indians of British Columbia and southeastern Alaska developed a ceremony, *potlatch*, which is a remarkable substitute for physical violence. In the long history of Man, it seems to have been one of the few really successful substitutes for armed conflict. Driver (1964) notes how the destruction of property during the potlatch developed first from an exchange of gifts.

> The potlatch of the Kwakiutl Indians . . . was probably the most ostentatious and dramatic of all and has been studied in most detail. There were altogether 658 titles or positions in all the thirteen

local subdivisions of the Kwakiutl. The translation of the names of some of these positions are: "creating trouble all around"; "giving wealth"; "throwing away property"; "about whose property people talk"; "envied"; "satiated"; "getting too great."

Driver explains that the potlatch served as a check in increasing wealth in Kwatkiutl society by providing a method of destruction of wealth and property. This elaborate destruction of property and giving away of gifts advanced the status position of a tribal chief, and it also invited a reciprocation of gifts and destruction of material goods by a rival tribal group. Thus, many of the ingredients of war were present. There was ostentatious display, rank among participants, fire and vast destruction but (except for the loss of an occasional slave) there was no loss of life. Blankets, canoes, and cold hammered native plates of copper of great symbolic value were destroyed. Driver explains that

> The destruction of a copper, by breaking it into bits and tossing them into the fire or into the sea demonstrated that a man was so wealthy he could afford to lose a fortune. A rival of a copper destroyer might feel compelled to destroy another copper of even greater value, as indeed he would have to do to surpass the first man's act of destruction.

Potlatches, like wars, were of all degrees in magnitude. One Kwakiutl potlatch involved the destruction and giving away of six slaves, fifty-four dressed elkskins, eight canoes, three coppers, two thousand silver bracelets, seven thousand brass bracelets, and thirty-three thousand beautiful handwoven blankets. Different points of view are expressed by behavioral scientists to explain potlatch but Driver notes that

> A more recent and convincing justification, however, is that it had become a substitute for physical violence. Disputes or rivalries which would have led to feuds a century or more ago were settled by potlatching in later times . . . Regardless of the cause of the change, the destruction of property is to be preferred to the loss of lives, and the outlet for aggressions provided by the potlatch made it desirable. . . .

Potlatch has been given a number of other interpretations. The excesses in the destruction of property are viewed by some as symptoms of the cultural disintegration of the people. Not only war but all cultural devices which society creates to deflect, rechannel, or absorb drives may become hominolags when they no longer serve their purpose successfully or when a device develops side-effects which are harmful to the society that adopted it. A resilient society may gradually inaugurate changes when this occurs whereas a static and inflexible one may retain a hominolag because of resistance to change.

On the beastway HANS HAEM IN NEBELSPALTER (RORSCHACH, SWITZERLAND)

FIGURE 20. A Hominolag?

Different Kinds of Changes

There are many kinds of change. Four are of special interest to students of hominology; these are 1) progressions and regressions, 2) configurational changes, 3) transformations and metamorphoses, 4) transcendences.

Progressions and regressions occur when changes are linear and continue along the same dimension in a given direction. For example, if a boy blows into a balloon it will increase in size. This increase depends on how much air he blows into the balloon. Conversely, every time the boy permits air to escape from the balloon, there is a decrease in its size.

Erosion of mountains by winds and water, the growth of an animal or plant, the filling up of a ditch with rain water are illustrations of progressive changes. The evaporation of water by heat may be called a regressive change but the difference between regression and progression is always one of personal judgment or viewpoint.

Since progressive and regressive changes are relatively simple and are common in nature, one easily falls into the error of anticipating that all changes will be of this kind.

However, there are configurational changes in which there is a new organization of the parts that constitute the whole. Let us use the same example of the boy blowing into the balloon. Having observed the balloon increase in size, a person who had never before witnessed such an event might predict that the balloon will continue to increase in size as long as someone continues to blow into it. But this does not happen. At one point in the process the balloon bursts. For a naïve observer, this is an unexpected and a dramatic change which he did not anticipate. A great deal must be known and understood about the nature of the materials before configurational changes can be predicted or understood.

Transformations and metamorphoses occur when there is a transmutation of substance such as electricity into light or when the energy of a falling tree is converted into sound. Chemical reactions often fall into this category. Metamorphosis is the series of changes in structure and function such as those that take place in the transformation of a caterpiller into a butterfly. It is much more difficult to anticipate these kinds of changes than configurational ones and progressions. It is doubtful whether even an excellent scientist who had never been able to see transformations or metamorphoses in a given case would be able to anticipate such occurrences. Once observed, however, scientists could explain them and probably predict them accurately.

The most difficult kind of changes to anticipate, predict, and understand are transcendences. It has been this lack of understanding which has confused many who have attempted to interpret organic evolution. Often students of Man's cultural and social progress have failed to take transcendental changes[7] into account.

Transcendences imply that the change that has occurred is not only one of kind or of substance but there is an implication that something—not previously existing—has been added. It suggests that there is "more" than before the change had taken place. Some may call this "more" an illusion but the result of transcendence in every case *appears* to add a nonequatable characteristic that was not previously present. The change inherent in the conversion of inorganic material into living protoplasm represents a transcendence. The appearance of culture—and that means Man himself—represents transcendence. *Total Man cannot be comprehended except as the product of a series of transcendences which, throughout time, have eventuated in a concept of ethical behavior.* Only by postulating such transcendences can sense be made out of an evolutional development which led from inorganic matter to the self-reproducing cell, from this cell to abstraction and symbolization, and from symbolization to the human conscience.

------

[7] It may be argued that all changes are progressions and that even transcendences are progressive or regressive changes of a particular devious and complicated kind. However, this claim can be substantiated only when change is studied atomistically. When changes are viewed broadly and their effect is considered, the differences between the various kinds mentioned are real and substantial.

ETHICS AND THE NATURALISTIC FALLACY

It is not surprising that from earliest times on, Man tended to relate his own emotions and feelings to the natural phenomena around him. It is typical for Man to doubt himself and to trust nature since nature appears to be infinitely wiser and more powerful. By ascribing to nature the causes of his feelings and finding within nature the reason for their being, Man endeavors to give these feelings validity and perpetuation.

Since and before Darwin, Man has looked to nature for help in legitimatizing ethical concepts (Glass *et al.*, 1959; Waddington, 1960). This has led to what some philosophers call the *naturalistic* fallacy in which ethical ideas are defined in nonethical terms. It is like trying to fill a barrel full of oranges by putting apples into it. Moore (1953) maintained that ethical values are not states of mind, and he criticized those who defined the meaning of "good" in terms of pleasure or utility.

The danger in the formulation of a natural ethical system lies in the human tendency of projecting onto nature that which represents nothing more or less than the cumulative cultural conditioning to which one has been exposed throughout one's life. Many theorists believe that concepts such as culture and ethics have an independent being which is self-evolved and is not analogous to anything within nature. The difficulty with this view is that nothing as fundamental to Man as ethics can stand alone. It is difficult to see how culture or ethics can claim a spontaneous creation totally unrelated to all that came before. Even if culture and morality represent new evolutionary directions transcending previous evolutionary trends, they are still interdependent with past developmental events and these events together with ethics must fit somewhere within the total nature of the universe. Viewing ethics and cultural values against the background from which they have been drawn may offer us additional perspectives.

Referring to ethics, morality, and culture, Waddington (1960) writes,

. . . it is possible to discern in the results of evolution some general overall direction of change which can truly be regarded as a special direction. The existence of such a direction has been asserted by many other authors, who have usually referred to it as the direction of evolutionary progress. This implies merely that a change in this direction is one which we are willing to recognize as progressive. I have, however, asserted, or at least implied, something more than this, namely that the direction is one which in some way arises as the result of the general structure of the universe. . . .

SUMMARY

The search for Man's ancestor was described by relating the experiences of early paleontologists. The discovery of *Australopithecus* and *Pithecanthropus* were among those mentioned. The Neanderthal controversy and the Piltdown hoax also were discussed. It was shown that Man is not descended from apes but from pre-men and proto-men.

Human institutions such as war, potlatch, and ethics were examined. Various kinds of changes were identified. These were progressive, configurational, metamorphic, and transcendental. Their significance to human development was described. The attempt to explain ethics and moral values by direct application of biological laws as they are seen to work in evolution was shown to lead to a "naturalistic fallacy." The danger of falling into this fallacy was mentioned. Postulating a series of transcendences offers an alternate method to account for the development of ethical values and human progress.

REFERENCES

ANON: War, a human idiosyncracy, anthropologists· conclude. *Sci News*, 92:583-584, Dec. 16, 1967.

ARDREY, R.: *The Territorial Imperative*. New York, Atheneum, 1966.

CARRINGTON, R.: *A Million Years of Man*. New York, New Am. Lib., 1964.

DART, R. A., AND CRAIG, D.: *Adventures With the Missing Link*. New York, Harper, 1959.

DAY, M.: *Guide to Fossil Man*. Cleveland, World, 1965.

DRIVER, H. E.: *Indians of North America*. Chicago, U. of Chicago, 1964.

GLASS, H. B.; TEMKIN, O., AND STRAUS, W. L., JR. (Eds.): *Forerunners of Darwin: 1745-1859*. Under the auspices of the Johns Hopkins History of Ideals Club. Baltimore, Johns Hopkins, 1959.

HOEBEL, E. A.: *Man in the Primitive World*. 2nd ed., New York, McGraw, 1958.

HOWELL, F. C.: European and northwest african middle pleistocene hominids, *Curr Anthropol, 1*: 195-232, 1960.

HOWELL, F. C.: Recent advances in human evolutionary studies. *Quart Rev Biol,* 42: 471-513, 1967.

LEAKEY, L. S. B.: *Adam's Ancestors,* New York, Harper, 1960.

LEAKEY, L. S. B., TOBIAS, P. V., AND NAPIER, J. R.: A new species of the genus *Homo* from Olduvai Gorge. *Nature,* 202: 7-9, 1964.

LEAKEY, R. E. F.: Further evidence of the Lower Pleistocene hominids from East Rudolph, North Kenya. *Nature,* 231: 241-245, 1971.

MOORE, G. E.: *Some Main Problems of Philosophy.* New York, Macmillan, 1953.

MONTAGU, A.: *Man: His First Million Years.* New York, New Am. Lib., 1958.

OXNARD, C. E.: Some African fossil footbones: a note on the interpolation of fossils into a matrix of extant species. *Amer Journ Physical Anthropol,* 37: 3-12, 1972.

PAYNE, M. M.: Family in search of prehistoric man. *National Geographic,* 127: 194-231, Feb. 1965.

PILBEAM, K. R. AND SIMONS, E. L.: Some problems of hominid classifications. In Genoves, S.T. (Ed.): *Yearbook Of Physical Anthropology,* 1965. Mexico, published for the American Association of Physical Anthropology, Instituo de Investigaciones Historicas, Universidad Nacional Autonomas de Mexico, 1967, vol. 13.

PILBEAM, D. R.: *The Ascent of Man.* New York, Macmillan, 1972.

PREUSCHOFT, H.: Body posture and locomotion in some East African Miocene Dryopithecinae. In Day, M. H. (Ed.): *Human Evolution,* published by the Symposia of the Society for the Study of Human Biology, 1973, vol. 11.

SIMONS, E. L. AND PILBEAM, D. R.: Preliminary revision of the Dryopithecinae (Ponigdae, Anthropoidea). *Folia Primatologia,* 3:81-152, 1965.

STRAUS, W. L., JR.: The classification of Oreopithecus. In Washburn, S.L.: *Classification and Human Evolution.* Chicago, Aldine, 1963.

WADDINGTON, C. H.: *The Ethical Animal.* Chicago, U. of Chicago, 1960.

WENDT, H.: *In Search of Adam.* Translated by J. Cleugh, New York, Crowell-Collier, 1963.

SECTION THREE
INTEGRATION WITHIN HOMINOLOGY

Chapter 11

MAN'S DEVELOPMENTAL LEVELS

"Granted that early security and affectional relationships are the ground of becoming . . . we are still in possession of only one part of the truth."

GORDON W. ALLPORT

"The evolutionary idea of Nature and life brings us to a profounder view."

SRI AUROBINDO,
Indian teacher and philosopher

In TRACING EVENTS back to the origin of the universe, we may find it useful to postulate eight hypothetical transcendental levels. These may be accepted on the basis of any of the Criteria of Reality, including Inaccessibility of Reality.

There is no direct relationship between these developmental levels and geological time. The levels do not represent abrupt changes. On the contrary, they are only hypothetical focal points along an evolutionary spiral. In an earlier paper, I have tried to describe these evolutionary stages (Kahn, 1965):

> . . . changes in evolutionary direction are consistent with past experience. Moving from one focal point to another would have been disastrous to the species had it occurred out of its proper sequence in the evolutionary spiral. If we wish to understand modern man, we must keep in mind that as we have moved from focus to focus, beginning with the first rudimentary forms of life to the present moment, the residuals of what we have passed through remain with us.

The following eight postulated levels represent theoretical evolutionary peaks in an overlapping developmental movement, having progressive, regressive, configurational, metamorphic, and transcendental characteristics. Each of the following levels represents the focus of a transcendence which has emerged from a previous developmental level:

1. Developmental Level One, *Potential for Existence*
2. Developmental Level Two, *Our Earth Before Life*
3. Developmental Level Three, *Emergence of Life*
4. Developmental Level Four, *Maintenance of Existence*
5. Developmental Level Five, *Survival of the Fittest*
6. Developmental Level Six, *Emphasis on Fulfillment*
7. Developmental Level Seven, *Emphasis on Dedication*
8. Developmental Level Eight, *Beyond Dedication* ?[1]

The Past: Developmental Level One, *Potential for Existence*

Everything that exists demonstrates by its being that the laws of the universe are such that its existence is possible. In fantasy, we can conceive of many different kinds of things, some of which can never actually exist because the thermodynamic universal laws do not permit it. For example, we may think of a bug as large as an elephant, but the laws of nature make it impossible for insects to become larger than a given size because of the limitations of their breathing apparatus. An insect, then, cannot become an elephant in size but it was possible for a primitive reptile to evolve into a human being, for a fish to develop into a reptile, and for an unicellular organism to develop into a fish.

What make some things possible and others impossible? The answer may be found in the nature of the universe and the numbers and kinds of electrochemical reactions and interactions that can take place among subatomic particles. Man must have been a possibility for he is here. And, before he was here, he must have had some kind of a shadowy nonexistence as a *Potential* that could be realized. This must have been something different from an elephant-sized beetle, which can never be. The most illusive kind of transcendence is something coming into being which previous to its existence had only the potential of becoming that which it presently is.

---

[1] Level Eight has also been termed *Potential for Nonexistence.* Such "Nonexistence" could take place on several different dimensional levels.

The Past: Developmental Level Two, *Our Earth Before Life*

The earth evolved through a series of transcendences initiated at the beginning of the universe (Gamow, 1967). Over a period of approximately two billion years, the earth's surface underwent changes which provided favorable conditions for the emergence of life. These changes were described in Chapter 9.

The Past: Developmental Level Three, *Emergence of Life*

The living cell issued into being an era in which nature took a radical new direction. Protoplasm developing from inorganic matter reveals that there is a transcendental potential inherent in the elemental substance of which the universe is constructed. This raises the question of where the line is drawn that divides animate from inanimate matter. Scientists are now attempting in their laboratories to recreate the events that led to life. However, many questions remain to be answered before this can take place. For example, the molecular approach to understanding the nature of life has not succeeded in revealing by experiment, the precise nature and complexity of the cell's chemistry. Microbiology is the field in which much significant research on the nature of life is taking place. Some authors in this field use terms which might cause a behavioral scientist to raise an eyebrow—*Cell Sociology*— (Kalckar 1965) for example. The advent of life on earth is a topic on which much philosophical and theological interest is focused. The developmental levels which follow represent hypothesized transcendental changes[2] which enabled evolution to take significant new directions.

The Past: Developmental Level Four, *Maintenance of Existence*

It is suggested that the initial struggle faced by living matter was to maintain itself. After coming into being, the great challenge for life was ingestion, respiration, and reproduction. Essentially, there are two ways for living matter to obtain the carbohydrates and proteins which are necessary to sustain life—manufacture them or take them from other forms of life that manufacture them. Using the sun's energy, the earliest forms

---

[2] Progressive and other kinds of changes precede and culminate into transcendental changes.

of life may have used chlorophyll to sustain themselves as plants do today. Experiments have shown that light acting on certain simple chemical compounds can produce slight traces of sugar and other organic matter without the aid of chlorophyll.

The stage represented by Level Four conceives of life as noncompetitive. The forms of life existing at this time were neither so abundant nor so advanced as to utilize each other as prey. The struggle in which living matter engaged required only a favorable environment for the production of the materials necessary for elemental existence. On Level Four, the focus is on sustaining what has been won.

The Past: Developmental Level Five, *Survival of the Fittest*

The new direction represented by Level Five emphasized *improvement*. Over the millions of years, life proliferated and won the battle for existence. The new emphasis is now on improvement. Not that previously there was an absence of adaptive improvement. Improvement, of course, took place, but it was not the primary emphasis of life in the periods which came before as it is in this one. Competition is one means nature used to create improvement in life. It is Developmental Level Five which has given evolution the "red tooth and claw" image. Improvement is dearly bought through ever-fiercer competition.

There are two kinds of competition having different derivatives and it is important that we distinguish between them. There is the competition for dominance which is intraspecies, self-limiting, and of survival value to the species. There is also interspecies competition which is not self-limiting and may lead to the extermination of one or the other species. Animals usually do not use the same part of their body for establishing dominance in intraspecies rivalry as they do in interspecies fighting. This emphasizes how basic the difference is between these two kinds of competition.

Among humans there are also two kinds of competition, one rooted in the establishment of dominance within the same group the other in the extermination of a different and dangerous group. The former may bring out the best efforts among men for their mutual good, the other is ruthless and destructive and represents a regression to Level Five among human beings.

To put it in its simplest form, in one kind of competition you want your rival to live, in the other, you want him to die.

It should be noted, however, that when one is dealing with as vast a subject as evolution one cannot easily generalize. Nevertheless, it may be pointed out that some confrontations serve to establish dominance hierachies, preserve leadership, and facilitate organizational structure, while different kinds of confrontations clearly represent life-and-death struggles (either between the same or different species) continuing until an ecological balance within nature is achieved.

The demands of adaptation were so adamant and the threat of failure so severe (extinction) that under pressure to adapt, many species overreached themselves. Not only specialization but overspecialization occurred. When environmental conditions changed, species that were overspecialized were the first to pay for their "error." Those species that maintained flexibility were capable of adjusting to changes. But those who had specialized too narrowly found that in an altered environment their former source of strength was now their liability.

In the last fifteen million of the many millions of years of struggle, one of nature's most anatomically unspecialized creatures emerged from within the order of the Primates. He walked erect and this gave him his start. His teeth were negligible as weapons; he possessed no claws, nor even great strength. His anatomy afforded him little protection against climate or fierce predators. Yet this creature lived through climatic upheavals marked by ice, floods, and searing heat. Of all Primates, he was the most adaptable and with an ever-increasing brain, he invented new nonanatomical methods of adaption—culture. He changed his diet to include more and more animal flesh as vegetable sources of food diminished. Whatever he did, he did exceedingly well and that includes being a predator.

In four hundred thousand generations, Man, during the Pleistocene, emerged by virtue of his expanding brain which stood him to greater advantage than fang, horn, claw, or fur. Some see in the human brain a form of overspecialization which could contribute to make Man a victim of his own inventiveness. However, the human brain is also capable of realizing this danger and of producing an antidote. Man may become a victim of his inventiveness only if his not-so-adaptive emotional makeup inhibits the more adaptable portions of his brain in the search for solutions to problems of human survival.

MAN NEEDS CHALLENGE

The hairless, hideless, defenseless Primate that Man was, faced the dwindling food supply and the cataclysmic climatic changes of the Pleistocene and survived. His weakness and the harshness of nature's verdict were the essential ingredients of his emerging strength. Child of adversity, he became master of all. And today, he still requires challenge to keep himself alert and healthy. The need for challenge was bred into his makeup. Contemporary Man in his new security attempts to create adversity artificially because of boredom and monotony. The lack of challenges more effectively sap human vitality than the fiercest struggle.

Man's need for excitement has phylogenetic roots. When hunting gradually gave way to agriculture during the Neolithic Revolution, Man lost one of his most precious possessions—the challenge which hunting had provided. After the food supply became more plentiful, synthetic diversions had to be invented. Perhaps only in war was Man able to recreate the old spirit of limitless challenge which had served him so well on the road to becoming Man. Many of contemporary Man's most irresoluble problems stem from the changes which the Neolithic Revolution brought. The very qualities which created flesh-eating Man out of brachiating, foraging, tree-bound, small-brained vegetarians became a liability after the Neolithic Revolution. It was not easy to discover new challenges that could substitute for the old after Man had won the battle of the survival of the fittest. After he had vanquished all competition, the tools of his victory seemed to be a liability—except when they were turned upon his fellow Man.

The Past and Present: Developmental Level Six, *Emphasis on Fulfillment*

We now reach the historical times, a mere few thousand

years ago. Again, progressing evolution developed a new focus—
modern Man. He established food-producing centers supported
by agriculture and animal domestication. In the tiniest fraction
of geological time, Man, the tool and weapon maker, with his
power of speech and his ability to use symbolic substitution,
remade much of that part of the world in which he lived. Man
developed food surpluses and this gave him leisure to discover
art, astronomy, and architecture. At the same time, the organization of land required for agriculture spawned conquerors
whose empires rose and fell and were extinguished.

Man's new focus was represented by gods, pharoahs,
emperors, and kings, whose lives embodied the dominant theme
of the epoch—*maximum fulfillment of all desires.* In previous
eras, Man, like other animals, deemed himself successful if he
could remain alive to bring into the world another surviving
generation. The new emphasis changed that definition to equate
success with the most lavish satiation of appetites and fullest
appeasement of drives. It reminds one of the fling taken by
those who have lived through a period of austerity. Man projected onto his gods and rulers this wish for limitless self-
gratification.

The vast majority of the men living during this period
could not indulge themselves in this wish but rather served
as slaves to help others live out the dominant theme of the
era. Though slaves, they could live this theme vicariously by
helping their master reach an ever greater level of appetite
and power fulfillment. In an age centered on self-gratification,
fueled by war and ambition, technology improved and gathered
momentum at an accelerated pace. Fulfillment in every human
sphere was attempted and this included, among others, the
esthetic one.

First, beauty through the arts was practiced for the glori-
fication of the kings and gods. Later, as individual Man became
more emancipated, the drive toward fulfillment continued on
the higher level of self-expression. But even in this more refined
form, fulfillment still remained the key word epitomizing the
age. We are well within the fringes of this age today. But,

in a precarious and hesitating way, we also have one foot planted within the epoch that follows fulfillment. The focus of this new era again takes a different evolutionary course. Many of the problems and inconsistencies we face today can be explained only by realizing that contemporary Man is in transition between two forces representing contradictory evolutionary directions.

The Present and the Future: Developmental Level Seven, *Emphasis on Dedication*

Risking oversimplification, one might say that the influence dominating Level Five was biological; the one controlling Level Six was cultural; and the one emerging within Level Seven is a moral one. Each is superimposed upon the other, growing out of it and proliferating from it. Man must deal with and integrate the residuals of his phylogenetic as well as those of his ontogenetic past in order to be able to live in harmony[3] with himself and his fellow man. Some behavioral scientists might assume that within his ontogeny, Man has absorbed his phylogeny and, therefore, need not consider himself subject to two different influences. But there is an advantage in the recognition that some of these influences have primarily phylogenetic roots while others have primarily environmental ones. Though these influences constantly interact and merge, the study of human behavior benefits when their separate roles are understood. Psychoanalysis attempts to do this when it assigns one function of the psyche to the id and another one to the superego. However, in postulating the superego, psychoanalysis[4] leans exclusively on conditioning, and hence, ethics becomes no more than a reflection of the behavioral norms parents or society have adopted through previous conditioning. However, ethics and *libidinal drives* are subject to evolutional, genetic mutational modification and are not immutable and changeless throughout

---

[3] I refer to a harmony which includes challenges and imbalances (see Chapter 2).

[4] This is more true of Freudian than it is of Jungian psychoanalysis. Jung was mystical and used mythology to bolster his concepts of a "racial unconscious." He lived before ethology emerged as a new behavioral science.

time, as they are sometimes conceived of. Such changes are capable of modifiying the effect of cultural conditioning.

We do not know whether it is cultural evolution alone or evolutionary changes in human genetic makeup that accounts for the dominant theme of the emerging Level Seven—dedication. Muller (1958), under the heading of *Genetic Foundation of Altruistic Values* writes,

> Under certain circumstances, including those of ground-dwelling primates, which are relatively defenseless individually, there proved to be comparative safety from predators in numbers, also other advantages, as in hunting, when it emerged, in sharing fire, and in sharing services and abilities. From then on, genetic variations leading to associations among families, and to partial extention of the affective family ties to the other members of the community, were rewarded by enhanced survival and multiplication. All this meant a step-by-small-step development of the genetic bases of social feelings and behavior—that is, of the complex sometimes comprised under the term *brotherly love.* [Italics are Muller's.]

Muller sees a "slowing down of natural selection of social traits" in larger communities typical of modern times but, under such conditions, cultural components may replace genetic ones and the trend towards social altruism may be continued. Whether or not a good case for a genetic basis for morality can be made, it is diagnostic of our time that scientists such as Muller are sufficiently concerned to search for it.

Not many would agree that Man is presently on the threshold of an age of altruism. The contrary appears to be the view held by most people. Today's youths especially feel that a lack of altruism is characteristic of our contemporary world. This disillusionment among the young[5] is matched by the self-accusation among the older generation regarding its "moral failure" in putting an end to wars and threats of wars, crime, poverty, and materialistic values.

Ignoring the fact that these conditions were not of their

---

[5] In every age of historic time, dating back to the Egyptians, the young are apt to be disillusioned with the old just as the older generations appear to be disapproving of the doings of their offsprings. There is, however, in different eras, a considerable variation in the degree of mutual antagonism between the old and new generation.

own making, the present generation of adults seems to blame itself for conjuring them into being. Such self-accusation may have therapeutic value in alleviating guilt and also may have motivational benefit in spurring people on to greater efforts, but it also has its danger, for in conveying to the younger generation feelings of unworthiness, the adults are very apt to be believed. It is not difficult to convince the younger generation that these feelings of "moral failure" are genuinely deserved. And when, in turn, the younger generation rebels against this "failure" of the adult world, it is ironic that this rebellion is viewed with bewilderment and confusion. Although the cause of this rebellion is misunderstood, it offers this older generation still one more thing to feel guilty about.

Some deny that an age of dedication is upon us or that such an age will ever exist. Others see evidence of its arrival in many spheres of contemporary human activity.

ARE NATIONS MOVING TOWARDS DEDICATION?

War is still with us and some of the possible reasons for its persistence have already been discussed, but note that the *reasons* given for waging war have changed dramatically throughout the ages. Within Level Six, ancient conquerors boasted openly about their purpose in making war. It was for looting, for capturing slaves, for power, or for annexation of territory. Two thousand years ago Rome waged war to make the world Roman. Fifty years ago the United States of America entered World War I "to make the world safe for democracy." Many now call this an "empty phrase" and say that such slogans camouflaged expansionists and selfish interests. Whether true or not, the fact that modern nations feel compelled to offer virtuous reasons for engaging in armed conflict reflects on the conscience of the times and sharply differentiates the modern war-making conscience from that of the previous era.

Some people point to the neutrality of Switzerland and Sweden as evidence that Man can exist currently without waging wars. But there may be a fallacy inherent in this reasoning. It is possible that nations who are able to remain neutral do so by experiencing the war vicariously through a nonbelligerent participation in the wars around their perimeters. In spite of a technical "neutrality," both Sweden and Switzerland were actually deeply involved financially and emotionally in World War II. They were manufacturers of weapons, centers of intrigue, bankers for the warring nations, etc. Their involvement in this sense was actually no less than that of the noncombatant citizens of the belligerent nations working in factories, banks, etc. and avidly reading the exciting news from the battle fronts. By indentifying with one or the other of the belligerent nations, these "neutral" countries were, in one sense, at war also. Perhaps, if these countries were alone in the world and did not have proxies to do their fighting for them, they would make more frequent use of the excellent weapons that they maintain in constant readiness.

After World War I, some territory was taken by the Allies but when World War II was ended, the defeated countries— Germany and Japan—were helped by one of the victors, the United States of America to the extent that they soon emerged as the most prosperous among the world's nations. Much of the credit of their achievement is due to the purposefulness of their populations, but we can hardly imagine victorious nations in medieval or ancient times taxing their own populations in order to assist the economies and feed the populations of a defeated enemy.

The governments of both the Soviet Union and the United States of America have offered altruistic motives for their involvement in the Vietnamese war and explained their motivation as a desire to assist the Vietnamese people achieve "freedom," and "dignity," and "a better life." Even if it can be shown that the "real" motives of one or both of these nations were the furthering of national interests, this does not detract from the significant fact that both the United States of America and the Union of Soviet Socialist Republics felt compelled to explain to the world that their involvement was primarily altruistic. Some see in this only "hypocrisy," but the behavioral scientist must ask why should hypocrisy (if it is hypocrisy) be necessary?

It has been said that "hypocrisy is the tribute that vice pays to virtue." A virtuous explanation clearly reveals the existence of the virtue and tacitly acknowledges that its absence is undesirable. Words often are the forerunners of acts, and virtuous explanations serve to foreshadow virtuous deeds. Verbal rationalizations sometimes indicate the direction in which an individual or a society feels obligated to move.

What has been said about dedication as the reason given for waging war is even more evident in activities such as the Peace Corps, the War on Poverty, and related activities in the United States of America and in other countries around the world.

Are We Moving Toward Dedication in Business?

In a recent article, newspaper columnist Sylvia Porter pointed out a trend which other writers have also observed:

> . . . the story which . . . clearly has not yet got through to the today's college student is that the majority of big U. S. business corporations are now becoming deeply and seriously involved in some of the most challenging socio-environmental problems facing the nation. The "new involvement" entails far more than the traditional billions dutifully contributed by business to worthy causes. It no longer consists of well-meaning speeches and seminars.
>
> For the U. S. business community now is beginning to move operations and jobs into the big city slums, to educate and train the hard-core unskilled and unemployed, to tackle such massive nation-wide problems as air and water pollution.

Noting that there are great differences from company to company and from industry to industry, the columnist mentions industry's role in slum rehabilitation, education of unemployed, assistance to those who plan to set up their own businesses, counseling, and on-the-job training for handicapped, etc. Mrs. Porter's conclusion is

> It is more than a beginning. It is clearly an identifiable trend. There was not a raised eyebrow in the room when Robert J. Weston of the Boise Cascade Corp. told a recent meeting of the Committee for Economic Development: "Corporations must look toward the establishment of dual goals in the service to shareholders and service to society."

This is a far cry from the days of the Industrial Revolution (1750-1850) and its aftermath when labor was exploited to its utmost and when men, women, and children toiled in factories from dawn to dusk at bare subsistence wages. As we all know, a vigorous labor movement forced business to move into the direction of improved work conditions. And certainly no one would claim that business is now motivated exclusively by altruism. On the other hand, no one who has made a study of modern industrial trends can deny that a new social conscience exists among a significant number of business leaders.

Dr. C. D. Jones remarked in his book, *Hominology — Psychiatry's Newest Frontier* (C. C. Thomas, 1975) that genuine dedication is most likely to occur in a voluntary, freedom-oriented social climate. The action theme of Level Seven will help such a climate to survive and prosper. That is why businessmen can help to insure the survival of capitalism by replacing the major emphasis on wealth and power by one that is oriented towards service to people. Such a change in emphasis would assist the preservation of the free enterprise system. Participation within the action theme of Level Seven requires that dedication is direct and primary rather than indirect and secondary. Albert Schweitzer touched upon this when he wrote:

> "It (the concept of genuine dedication) does not allow the scholar to live for science alone, even if he is very useful to the community in doing so. It does not permit the artist to exist only for his art, even if this gives inspiration to many. It refuses to let the businessman imagine that he fulfills all the legitimate demands in the course of his business activities. It demands from all that they should give a portion of their lives for others. He who has experienced good in life (Level Six) must feel the obligation to dedicate some of his own life to the needs of others (Level Seven)."[6]

The moral strength of nations is proportionate to the amount of Level Seven activities that take place within their borders. Jones *(ibid)* maintains that this bears a direct relationship to national survival.

Dedication in Science and Religion

Many other important areas of human activity support the

---

6 Quoted in Zarfoss, G.: Why Volunteer? *Retired Officer*, Oct. 1971.

thesis of the dawn of a new age of social responsibility. An editorial in *Science* entitled "The Moral Sense of the Scientists" (Reistrup, 1967) begins,

> The recent meeting of the American Association for the Advancement of Science provided an impressive body of evidence that many scientists *now* are indeed worried about their social responsibility. [Italics are Kahn's.]

The "now" in the quotation implies that the trend towards social responsibility of scientists is a recent one.

In religion, too, we see consistent evidence of this contemporary trend. Many religious groups have, in modern times, shifted their emphasis from ritual to a deeper involvement with people. The shift seems to be one from sectarianism to humanitarianism, from sacrifice for personal salvation to dedication for human salvation, and from a total concern with heaven to a greater concern with human suffering and social justice on earth.

CONTEMPORARY MAN'S ANXIETY

Many writers have termed our present age one of anxiety. This question of contemporary Man's anxiety should be examined within the context of the hypothetical developmental Level Seven, whose emergence we may presently be witnessing. Coleman (1964) writes,

> The seventeenth century has been called the Age of Enlightenment; the eighteenth, the Age of Reason; the nineteenth, the Age of Progress; and the twentieth, the *Age of Anxiety*. With the conquest of many physical ills which have afflicted him throughout his history, there have come) . . . a host of subtler psychological plagues— worry, value conflicts, loneliness, disillusionment. . . .

Philosophers have described today's Man as alienated from his former faith and likewise alienated from himself. He is seen as "homeless," "bureaucratized," and "a fragmentary being." Those observers of the current social scene who view Man as materialistic, callous, and indifferent to spiritual values would naturally dispute that we are currently participating in the birth of an age of dedication.

The legitimacy of opposite views on issues such as these

helps keep hominology from being a dull subject. Of course, there is no right or wrong interpretation on such issues; there are only *personal* interpretations which must await the verdict of history for their validation. Assuredly there is sufficient evidence to support the thesis that in today's world we are moving away from dedication rather than towards it. In either case, progression or regression is not a straight-line process. As always, the interpretation one makes of the world outside of oneself may partly be a projection of one's own inner pessimism or optimism. And, also, one's view may reflect ideas that happen to be popular at the time. Then, too, we would expect differences between those who look forward to see how far Man has yet to go, and those who look backward to see how far Man has already come.

A number of writers, especially in the mental health field diagnose contemporary Man's anxiety as evidence of his decline. But is it not also possible that his anxiety represents the presence of a conscience and the recognition of an obligation? Some have ascribed the presence of the anxiety to the complexity of modern society and to the bewildering number of choices and decisions we must make in today's world. But could not some of this anxiety be viewed as the by-product of our transition between two opposing forces—one which pulls us back towards self-aggrandizement and another, which pushes us forward towards a higher morality? Barrett (1962) observes,

> . . . our psychological problems cannot be solved by a regression to a past state in which they have not yet been brought into being. On the other hand, enlightened and progressive thinkers are equally blind when they fail to recognize that every major step forward by mankind entails some loss, the sacrifice of an older security, and the creation and heightening of new tensions.

There was "security" in previous levels of adaptation and the anxiety of being in transition can be relieved by yielding to regressive, primitive, backward-pulling impulses. And even as Man moves forward, these impulses may get out of hand, as they did in Nazi Germany and in all other countries where brutality is the dominant national force.

Wagar (1963) observed that, "We (contemporary Man) are the vital link between the traditional civilizations of a well remembered past and the emergent world civilization. We stand between them." The fear of the unknown towards which the adoption of new values may lead us and the concomitant fear of falling back, or of not moving on, are sufficient causes for the existence of the anxiety of our time.

After all, the essential difference between Level Six and Level Seven is that which exists between taking and giving. A difference of such a magnitude cannot be resolved without ambivalences which make anxiety inevitable. Those who see weakness in ethical behavior and who view love[7] of fellowman as a mark of human decline have a good and convincing argument if they use Level Six as their frame of reference. But there are many [Ewing (1953); van den Berg (1964); Erikson (1964); Mead (1955); Dobzhansky (1962, 1967); Montagu (1963); Waddington (1960); and Whipple (1967)] who see in the present age the development of a moral code in which there is an increased opportunity for individual freedom demanding a concomitant increase in self-sacrifice and personal responsibility.

Perhaps it will help some accept the idea that we are in the throes of such a new adaptation if it is kept in mind that our species has not emancipated itself from the level of self-gratification and, therefore, some people may be thoroughly uncomfortable in the new moral climate of the emerging age. As Gardner observed (see Kerr, 1964), "Many moderns would rather walk barefoot over hot coals than utter an outright expression of moral concern. They have to say it obliquely, mix it with skepticism or humor, or smother it with pessimism."

The important phrase in this quotation is, "They *have* to say it." Therein camouflaged (and, perhaps, unrecognized) lies the seed of Level Seven. *How* it is said and the disguise in which it appears may represent the as yet unrelinquished influences of Level Six.

---

[7] *Love* is defined here as the willingness to serve the need of another person even if this be at the expense of one's own need.

Future: Development Level Eight, *Beyond Dedication?*

Some believe that the possibilities within future developments are unlimited. Others think that they are relatively circumscribed. Most people, however, recognize that since the future is uncertain, there is inherent in it a source of potentiality. Development may take a number of alternative directions which depend on situational influences. Because Man's future is irrevocably linked to potentiality, we have completed the developmental spiral returning in Level Eight to the question of potentiality where we began in Level One.

What is potential beyond dedication? What direction would such a development take? Would it embody mystical concepts which are presently poorly understood or not yet discovered? Might it embody transcendental changes in which the individual self disappears completely to be merged with a universal self so that Man and the universe become a total and inseparable one? Would this be a loss or would it be a gain?

Can the Eastern concept, *Nirvana* (see Chapter 2), represent the final transcendence of which Man is capable—the transcendence of transcendences— the point beyond which there are no more changes possible? Is the attempt to reach Nirvana now an artificial method used to catapult oneself beyond the evolutionary developmental plateau of one's own temporal era? If loss of identity is what the future individual faces, will it be a knowing, voluntary, self-relinquishment in favor of a group or universal self? Or will "a world mind" be subject to a central power source issuing orders to a human species having the mechanical reflexes of a swarm of bees? In that case, Man's own inventions—radio, television, newspapers—will play a role analogous to a giant nervous system and individual man will respond as if he were a cell within a human social superorganism. Will Man be able to maintain his individuality, his sense of selfhood?

The choice between reflex and reflection may not be ours to make after the forces representing total centralization have gained ascendancy. Whether future Man will automatically obey computorized directives or retain the role of decision-making will depend on what happens to the concept of individual freedom. However, this statement in itself is not very helpful since it evades the hazard of prediction. The difficulty of prediction is voiced by Iklé (1967) who asks, "How can we tell a good prediction from a bad one?" He observes that "Unless we have some way of gauging the quality of predictions, all our efforts to forecast, conjecture about, or anticipate the future must remain essentially dilettante." When men predict, they tend to project *themselves* instead of anticipating events.

Kahn and Wiener (1967) have offered a framework for speculation which attempts to provide a basis for objectivity. Although their predictive illustrations are short range—the year 2000—the framework these writers have devised may be useful as a model for longer range predictions of social processes. They see the problem of prediction in the following terms:

> Scientists, engineers, and managers who deal directly with modern technology and who are also interested in broad policy issues often overestimate the likely social consequences of technological development and go to extremes of optimism or pessimism, while those more oriented to cultural heritage often bank too heavily on historical continuity and inertia. The problem, of course, is to sort out what changes from what continues and to discern what is continuous in the changes themselves.

THE NEW GENERATION'S FRUSTRATION

What is continuous in the changes themselves? If this question is directed at the hypothesized eight levels of development, further thought will have to be applied before we can answer with conviction. Progressive and transcendental changes (as well as metamorphic ones) occur side by side. There are progressive changes within transcendental ones and likewise within progressive changes a continuous series of minor transcendental ones may occur. Eventually there is an alteration of directional focus of major proportions. It is then that a new developmental level has been reached.

As we have seen, fulfillment at its lowest level was self-aggrandizement and satiation. The Roman banquets come to mind where self-induced regurgitation of food was practiced in order to permit the ingestion of still more food. Gluttony and self-indulgence, in time, gave way to the kind of self-fulfillment which is still the hallmark of our present day, i.e. the search for talent, big and small, and the feeling of obligation to give every man the right to see this talent utilized. Piano lessons, ballet instruction, art expression—how great our feelings of duty are today to our children in this repect! But dedication (though still, in one sense, a kind of "fulfillment") represents a transcendental change and brings into being a host of new kinds of obligations which we, at this juncture, do not yet understand. The modern parent tries his best to give his son and daughter maximum opportunity "to make the most of himself," i.e. express his talents. But he is not as aware that the new age which we are now entering requires that he give his children another kind of opportunity in addition to fulfillment, one that exists within a different dimensional framework. This is the opportunity to dedicate.

Stages Within Levels

Each level incorporates a variety of developmental stages representing intralevel changes in focus. For example, within the action theme of Level Six the following stages may be discerned: 1) appetites and expression of raw emotions; 2) power, glory, status, wealth; 3) self-actualization in the arts and expression of skills, capacities, artistic talents; and 4) satisfactions derived from being of service to others, participation in helping people for the purpose of satisfying only one's personal needs while doing so. This latter is called "pseudodedication" and represents a borderline between Levels Six and Seven. Genuine dedication is associated with Level Seven behavior. Within this action theme service to others is not need-based or self-oriented but represents a genuine desire to help others for the sake of doing so.

Within an age in which dedication and self-sacrifice appear as the emerging focus of the times, we offer our children nothing to sacrifice for and nothing to sacrifice with. Thereby, we are depriving them of the opportunity of being in touch with the emerging spirit of our epoch. Our indulgence towards our children may well satisfy, in a somewhat perverted way, our own need to sacrifice for a cause, but this same permissiveness represents a special form of deprivation for those whom it deprives of life's challenges. This indulgence practiced by society and the modern parent may find support from certain derivatives of Freudian psychology; however, in translating this desire "not to frustrate" our children into a way of life, we are exposing them to the greatest frustration of all—the only one history has shown Man cannot endure. This is the absence of frustration.

EVIDENCE VERSUS EXPLANATION

It is important to remember that the examples given to illustrate the foci of each of the hypothesized Levels were not intended to prove or represent *evidence* that such levels have a real existence within organic or cultural evolution. Instead, all descriptive illustrations used to identify the hypothesized Levels One to Eight were presented as *explanations* of why the classifications were made. The Levels serve the need for a classification (which will be put to practical use in the following chapter) of Man's total developmental process. The very nature of the task of such a system of classification demands an "as if" approach.

There are many other ways in which developmental stages could be viewed, and some of these would bear little relationship to the eight hypothetical Developmental Levels that have been offered in this chapter. Which particular framework the student of hominology adopts is not as important as that he adopts one which will help him think of past events as developmentally related to each other ontogenetically, historically, and phylogenetically. There are no teleological implications in viewing evolutionary development in terms of stages. Dobzhansky (1958) maintains that

> . . . evolution in general has no program and the evolution of man is no exception. No biological law can be relied on to insure that our species will continue to prosper, or indeed that it will continue to exist. However, man is the sole product of evolution who knows that he has evolved and who has continued to evolve. It is up to man to supply the program for his evolutionary development which nature has failed to provide.

The eight Levels described in this chapter have been devised to assist the student in the task of exploring such "programs" as the one to which Dobzhansky refers. Viewing human development in a nondisciplinary manner requires an approach which postulates processes within which the various disciplinary contributions may be integrated. Voget (1960) observes that

> Through process, explanation of the human event, rather than a cultural, social, geographical, or historical event turns out to be the essential problem. Realization of this fact explains why some anthropologists gradually have concluded that the concept of culture is inadequate to explain the human reality.

The human reality began with a creature like *Ramapithecus*. Very slowly in mortal eyes, and yet with the rapidity of lightening in geological time, that protohuman being became contemporary Man with all the problems and dilemmas he now faces. In historical perspectives, these problems may not be much greater than yesterday's, because we have today's tools, knowledge, and historical perspective to cope with them. We are inclined to minimize the problems of the past, magnify those of the present, and ignore those that may occur in the future.

SUMMARY

Eight hypothetical Developmental Levels representing significant transcendental changes were described. The focus of the first level was potential, then followed earth before life. Emergence of life and the struggle for existence led to an emphasis on the survival of the fittest. The age of fulfillment represents historical times but contemporary Man is in a state of transition between this stage and the era whose focus is on dedication. Modern tensions and anxieties were partly ascribed to the conflicting directional influences of this transitional period. Today's young generation was described as being vitally involved in these directional conflicts. The older generation's difficulties in relating to the younger one was, in part, accounted for by ascribing to the former a sense of guilt for being unable to provide the young people of today with the opportunity and incentive that would make dedication meaningful.

REFERENCES

BARRETT, W.: Irrational Man. Garden City, Doubleday, 1962.

COLEMAN, J. C.: Abnormal Psychology and Modern Life. Chicago, Scott, 1964.

DOBZHANSKY, T.: Changing man. Science, 155:409-414, Jan. 27, 1967.

DOBZHANSKY, T.: Evolution at work. Science, 127:1091-1098, May 9, 1958.

DOBZHANSKY, T.: Mankind Evolving. New Haven, Yale U. P., 1962.

ERIKSON, E. H.: Insight and Responsibility. New York, Norton, 1964.

EWING, A. C.: Ethics. New York, Macmillan, 1953.

GAMOW, G.: History of the universe. Science, 158:766-769, Nov. 10, 1967.

IKLÉ, F. C.: Can social predictions be evaluated? Daedalus, J Amer Acad Arts Sci, 96:733-758, Summer 1967.

KAHN, H., AND WIENER, A. J.: The next thirty-three years: a framework for speculation. Daedalus, J Amer Acad Arts Sci, 96:705-732, Summer 1967.

KAHN, T. C.: An Experimental Program for Teaching Hominology. Mimeographed for student use, Pueblo, Southern Colorado State College, 1965.

KALCKAR, H. M.: Galactose metabolism and cell "sociology." Science, 150:305-313, Oct. 15, 1965.

KERR, C.: Society and the status quo: the individual and the innovative society. Science, 144:164-165, April 10, 1964.

MEAD, M. (Ed.): Cultural Patterns and Technical Change. New York, New Am. Lib., 1955.

MONTAGU, A.: Race, Science, and Humanity. Princeton, Van Nostrand, 1963.

MULLER, H. J.: Human values in relation to evolution. Science, 127:625-633, March 21, 1958.

REISTRUP, J. V.: The moral sense of the scientists. Science, 155:271, Jan. 20, 1967.

VOGET, F. W.: Man and culture: an essay in changing anthropological interpretation. Amer Anthropologist, 62:6, Dec. 1960.

WADDINGTON, C. H.: The Ethical Animal. Chicago, U. of Chicago, 1960.

WAGAR, W.: The City of Man. Boston, Houghton, 1963.

WHIPPLE, R. O.: The view from Zorna. Main Currents in Modern Thought, 24:42-47, Nov.-Dec. 1967.

VAN DEN BERG, J. H.: The Changing Nature of Man. New York, Dell, 1964.

Chapter 12

MAN'S MORAL VALUES

"While the values of one period may be totally irrelevant to another, they persist as part of the individual's outlook on the world."

M. W. CHILDS AND D. CATER,
Ethics In A Business Society

"Speaking generally, our moral and practical attitude, at any given time, is always the resultant of two sets of forces within us, impulses pushing us one way and obstructions and inhibitions holding us back."

W. JAMES, *Varieties of Religious Experiences*

"What is Goodness and Badness . . . ? Is it most important to notice that, for the people of a time and place, their own mores are always good . . . The reason is because their standards of good and right are in their mores."

W. G. SUMMER, *Folkways*

"Until the person is able to abstract and define rationally the idea of good, and unless he can run the gauntlet of all objections, and is ready to disprove them, not by appeals to opinion, but to absolute truth, never faltering at any step of the argument unless he can do all this, you would say that he knows neither the idea of good nor any other good; he apprehends only a shadow, if anything at all, which is given by opinion and not by science; dreaming and slumbering in this life, before he is well awake here, he arrives at the world below, and has his final quietus."

PLATO
Republic, Book II

Mᵁᶜᴴ ᴴᴬˢ ᴮᴱᴱᴺ written about moral values, goodness, badness, right, wrong, virtue, and ethics. It is strange, therefore, that on this subject there remains so much puzzled doubt. In spite of sermons, lectures, and prolific writings, people continue to ask questions about the moral values which our society adopts and attempts to pass on to a less-than-enthusiastic younger generation. Why are moral standards being questioned? Why the reluctance in accepting them? Hominology, as the study of total Man, explores the nature and consequences of Man's moral values.

In searching for reasons why moral values are being questioned today, we must take into account the exposure our contemporary young people have to science which is empirical in its quest for answers. Moral values, on the other hand, are currently taught in an authoritarian manner. Science encourages doubt when there is insufficient empirical evidence. This doubt is difficult to encapsulate within only one area of human concern. Doubt tends to diffuse and to permeate into areas which in non-scientific ages were safe from questioners and unassailed by skeptics.

Teachers, parents, and leaders of our contemporary society have not been able to explain values to the younger generation. During the long process of educating the young, they have failed to inform them where moral values come from, what they consist of, and why they should be adhered to. Instead, moral values have been described as a set of rules that must be automatically adopted. Our children have been told, "if you do not believe this, you are bad!"; "If you do not do this, you lack virtue!"

Upon religion has been placed the unfair burden of justifying these rules of conduct even when they are enforced in a secular and nonreligious setting. Some blame religion for society's failure to make its rules palatable to a generation of science-oriented youngsters who have been taught to use the inquiry approach to problem solving.

One of the reasons for this failure stems from our inability to define moral values and explain their component parts and origins. Postulating various levels of development, as in the previous chapter, does not shed much light on the question of where moral values come from and what kinds and categories of moral values exist.

Admittedly, definitions dealing with the human conscience are difficult. All the more so, since there appear to be no universally accepted norms of human conduct [Benedict (1934); Mead (1963); Lisitzky (1960); Firth (1963); Opler (1959); Honigmann (1959)]. If definitions of morality differ and contradict one another, how will one know which ones should be included and which excluded in a comprehensive treatment of the subject?

It would be simple to evade coming to grips with the problem by temporizing that definitions of morality are valid only as they apply to a particular group, society, or culture. By this point of view, we are implying that we must consider moral values to be temporary and situational. But the speed of communication has made the modern world grow smaller and a search for universal elements within codes of moral behavior becomes daily more imperative.

Some may say that human conscience and moral values were promulgated by God and prescribed for Man in the Scriptures. Those who wish to confine their quest to purely religious explanations are fortunate in that they have found fully acceptable answers within their own Criteria of Reality (see Chapter 3). However, we must still deal with those persons who, instead of religious explanations, or in addition to them, desire clarifications within the framework of the behavioral sciences. Also, there are an increasing number of clergymen and theologians who are vitally interested in seeing what kind of a case behavioral science can make for itself when it attempts to handle such difficult topics as the human conscience. Some of them also believe that religious jurisdiction is limited and that society is obliged to attempt to give a rational justification for the rules which it imposes.

FOUR CATEGORIES OF ETHICAL BEHAVIOR

In an attempt to explore the different kinds of behavior which are incorporated in the concepts, "morality" or "ethics", it is convenient to examine the Scout Law which is repeated by Boy Scouts in every town and city in the country. It goes this way: "A Scout is trustworthy, loyal, helpful, friendly, courteous, kind, obedient, cheerful, thrifty, brave, clean, and reverent." It is easy to see that these attributes cannot be equated. Obviously, a sad but loyal scout is to be preferred to a cheerful and disloyal one. An unfriendly though trustworthy scout is more desirable than one who is friendly but untrustworthy.

Since there are variations in the characteristics which are considered "good," can these be classified and defined so that we can obtain a clearer view of what we mean when we refer to moral values?

The following represents an attempt to distinguish between four major categories of ethical behavior. These categories are 1) the Graces, 2) the Virtues, 3) the Duties, 4) the Dedications.

The Graces

The Graces are primarily manifested in how a person appears to others as he goes about his daily tasks. One of their purposes is to emphasize the difference between Man and animals. They may also be viewed as representing the "oil" which keeps society lubricated and helps prevent superficial antagonisms between people who must come into contact with each other.

If a person is lacking in the Graces and discloses his animal nature, he is likely to be referred to by the very name of the animal which his behavior has failed to disguise: "he eats like a pig;" "clumsy as a bull in a china closet;" or "brusque as a bear." Good manners, politeness, neatness, courtesy, and adherence to prescribed patterns of dress and speech are among the Graces with which we are most familiar. Society often maintains the Graces by means of ritualized and stereotyped behavior. Among different cultural groups, there is considerable variation in the kinds of Graces adopted. But as we go from graces to dedications, we shall find that with each category we come closer to approaching a universal norm.

The Virtues

Whereas the emphasis of the Graces is on *disguise,* the emphasis of the Virtues is on *repression*—more commonly referred to as "self-denial." A person is considered to be virtuous if he is able to repress instinctual drives and aggressive emotions including those of sex, fear, anger, pride, and greed.

Among the Virtues are chastity, courage, even-temperedness, modesty, and generosity. The Virtues are maintained by taboos in simple societies and by religion and social norms in complex societies. The Virtues assist in the orderly regulation of society and insure the stability of social processes. However, they also serve a more difficult to recognize, secondary end. They provide Man with a challenge against which he can pit himself with all his energy. Because the battle with one's inner impulses is a never ending one, the attempt to practice virtue helps life from becoming dull. The struggle against the self may displace the need for physical challenges. Since man-self conflicts tend to reduce man-man conflicts, the Virtues have gained religious sanctions and social approval.

The neurotic reaction which repressions may induce represents the other side of the coin. It appears that primitive human emotions cannot simply be repressed and forgotten. The Virtues reflected in the norms of society, in the self-concept, and in the superego make it necessary to submerge undesirable emotions, desires, and impulses into that part of the mind Freud called the unconscious. But the repressed impulses cannot lie dormant there. They exert psychic pressure which can be released only by giving the unacceptable impulses expression in an altered or disguised form. These have been called ego-defenses or compromise reactions. They may be beneficial or harmful depending on how they are utilized.

The Duties

The Duties represent expressed or implied contracts between people. The emphasis of the Duties is on *obligation*. Obligations may be inherent in one's position, membership in a group, rank, or in a given situation, as in parenthood. Within the concept, Duties, there is an intellectual component. In order to perform them, one must have the intelligence to recognize what one's duties are and the capacity to appreciate that the duties one performs represent an essential aspect of social cooperation.

Reciprocity is implicit in the duties. The assumption is if you are honest in your dealings with me, and, if in return, I am honest with you, we shall both benefit and so will society. There may be "delayed repayment" as when parents who do their duty towards their children, will be assisted by their children later when they are old. By social security for the aged, youth has been deprived of an opportunity to reciprocate and this has had a disquieting effect on both parents and children—one which is subtle and not well understood. However, a vicarious reciprocity remains in that children can "repay" their parents later by doing their duty towards their own off-spring.

As in all of the moral values, performance of Duties requires an element of struggle and self-denial. But even if the sacrifices within the Duties are considerable, even if they involve the loss of one's life, repression of instinctual needs are, at most, a secondary focus. The primary emphasis is not on repression as much as it is on the intellectual recognition of the intrinsic fairness of the requirement that each person in a group should carry his share of society's burdens by displaying characteristics called for in a code of conduct, such as honesty, dependability, and trustworthiness. Depending on the society to which an individual belongs, codes may apply to a small number of in-group persons or they may be generalized to apply to all men. Much variety exists in this, but the essential elements, co-operation and reciprocity,[1] remain, whether or not codes of conduct are narrowly or broadly applied.

The Dedications

Whereas Duties focus on obligations, the emphasis of the Dedications is on going *beyond* obligations. Within the Dedications, cooperation and reciprocity play no significant role. As a matter of fact, the very absence of reciprocity constitutes an important characteristic of this moral value. Dedication is derived from an idea or ideal rather than from loyalty to a group of people or a code of conduct. In the Duties, recognition and self-recognition (self-respect) play a central role, but in the Dedication, recognition plays no role. Those who perform Duties and those who dedicate are both responding to a self-

------

[1] The reciprocity need not be a quantitative one but may be qualitative. The reward or return may be on different dimensional levels than the contribution. Often the reward consists of nothing more than the feeling of having done one's duty, or maintained a self-image.

image but the kind of self-image which each evokes is different. Doing one's duties evokes personal pride as the basis for self-respect. Being dedicated elicits satisfactions associated with having sacrificed for someone else not for self-respect but because of a self-other identification in which other is more important than self.

Both the Virtues and the Dedications require sacrifice (as do all of the moral values) but the focus of the Virtues is on the inhibition and denial of "the flesh" with the emphasis on the sacrifice itself as a form of self-redemption. In the Dedications, the sacrifice is a secondary by-product of doing something to aid or comfort others.

Unlike Duties, Dedications are noncognitive so that a person who is intellectually incapable of doing his duties may still be capable of being dedicated. Intelligence, however, is required to make Dedications meaningful, (i.e. of value to society). Persons who are mentally ill may lose their inhibitions and thus be incapable of practicing the Virtues. They may also be unable to perform their Duties. They may, however, still be capable of dedication although in a pathological and distorted manner. Dedication represents a state of mind in which another person or persons, or even a thing or an idea, become more important to a person than he is to himself. Love is a Dedication; it cannot be a Duty, a Virtue, or a Grace.

One may adopt Duties, Virtues, and Graces because of external pressure to conform. But Dedications thus adopted would only be pseudo-Dedications. To be genuine, they must be voluntary, that is, the motivation for dedicating must come from within the person himself. But these inner sources must not consist of fear, guilt, or atonement, since then dedication would still be involuntary. Dedications stemming from guilt-derived psychic pressures are also pseudo-Dedications.

ORIGINS OF THE MORAL VALUES

The development of the moral values was a concomitant phenomenon of the transcendental changes that occurred throughout the developmental phases that are identified within hominology.

The Graces facilitated the changes occurring in Level Five

which led its development into Level Six. The era of raw competition which Level Five exemplified became "oiled" by the use of politeness and associated rituals in order that symbiotic interpersonal relationships between men could take place. These were necessary so that an emphasis on fulfillment could occur.

Just as the Graces served to soften the emphasis on competitiveness, the Virtues, with their advocacy on self-control and repression, served to counteract the emphasis on self-indulgence and fulfillment which was the developmental focus of Level Six.

The Duties are of early phylogenetic origins and may represent an outgrowth and elaboration of the developmental focus of the maintenance of life (Level Four). They may stem from the fundamental characteristic of nature to create equations such as action-reaction, stimulus-response, and the tendency towards the establishment of equilibriums. Later in the development of life, Duties may have been genetically manifested by maternal and paternal instincts which with the proliferation of populations took the direction of reflex among insects and an intellectually and emotionally reinforced "sense of responsibility" in Man.

The Dedications are the characteristic morality of Level Seven. They may eventually lead to a gradual modification of the self-concept that will ultimately eventuate in an as yet not understood Level Eight. The Dedications to be realistic or rational (i.e. to have the quality which we term *common sense*) must not be performed at the expense or by negation of the other moral values. For example, dedicating while neglecting to adhere to the Duties is likely to cancel out any resulting social benefits.

The Roles and Hierarchies of Moral Values

Although there may be considerable overlapping within any one culture and differences among several cultures, some social institutions assume proprietorship or have vested interests in certain of the moral values. Thus, the Graces are usually associated with the home, the Virtues with the church, the Duties with society, and the Dedications with the developmental level which an individual or society has attained.[2] When moral values are lacking, adjectives such as "bad mannered" are applied to the Graces; "sinful" to the Virtues; "irresponsible" to the Duties; and "selfish" to the Dedications. When moral values are present, terms such as *self-control* are associated with the Graces; *self-denial*, with the Virtues; *cooperation*, with the Duties; and *sacrifice for others*, with the Dedications.

We cannot assign ranks to the moral values such as "higher" or "lower" since the hierarchy or system of priorities which a person adopts is an aspect of his personality and cannot be delegated.

The moral values may be transmitted from one generation to another and from one person to another. All the moral values except Dedication can be inculcated by negative and positive conditioning (i.e. rewards and punishments). Dedication, however, must remain voluntary, conscious, and unconditioned. Adoption of moral values, including Dedication, may be brought about by a discussion of their nature and purpose. Such a discussion would include a definition of the various kinds of moral values and an explanation of the consequences of, and alternatives to, adopting them.

Even though the moral values are a reflection of the personality, they can be taught since the personality is amenable to modification through learning. All of the moral values may be self-discovered and self-imposed. This applies especially to the Dedications. Moral values may be transmitted through imitation when a person whom one accepts as an ego-ideal (i.e. someone greatly admired) sets the example of using them.

However, in the Dedications, more than imitation is required. There must be an element of discovery present also. No one at this time can explain the exact motivational factors that contribute to Dedication. It is possible that they may include physiological or constitutional predispositions, though it is dangerous to jump to any such conclusion without considerable supporting evidence. Many different social, cultural, and psychological factors contribute to making one person sensitive or insensitive to the needs and feelings of another person. The

---

[2] Currently there is much discussion of the role that religion should play in specific types of dedications.

developmental level of the species (as suggested in the previous chapter) may play a role in this, but we must consider what a multitudinous variety of diverse constituent parts go into the simply stated concept—"the time is ripe."

ACTS ARE NOT MORAL IN THEMSELVES

Confusion exists today regarding the morality of specific acts or actions. However, acts cannot be moral in themselves. Acts cannot be separated from intent nor from the circumstances in which the acts occur. This is not an argument in favor of situational ethics as the following illustration will show.

A person may falsify in order to serve the Graces. For example, if we have been taught to be polite, we may deny the fact that an out-of-town acquaintance is visiting us at an inconvenient time of the day. Most people would condone such a lie but would not accept one made for the purpose of shirking one's duty or gaining unfair advantage. A lie which saves another person's feelings may even be considered to be a moral necessity.

A physician may deceive a critically ill person about the death of a near relative if he believes that this news would further impair his patient's health. If the physician could not evade the question and lied to the patient, no one would question the moral values of the physician. Instead, if he told the truth and this shocked his patient into a worsened condition, the physician would be considered irresponsible. Therefore, the question of whether or not it is wrong to lie must be answered by another question—What is the purpose or intent of the lie? If acts are tied to intent, moral values need not be viewed as situational.

The same question may be asked of killing. Is it wrong to kill? Yes, under ordinary circumstances. No, in self-defense, and no, when a policeman or soldier kills in line of duty. So, at least, says society.[3]

----

[3] This does *not* indicate that the means justifies the end. It indicates that the means and the end cannot be morally separated—one is an inherent part of the other. Only when the two are seen as one can the morality involved be evaluated.

Whether ethics are situational or not depends on one's Criteria of Reality (See Chapter 3). But any act itself is an impersonal event which takes on meaning only when it is incorporated into one of the Graces, Virtues, Duties, or Dedications. Confusion stems from the attempt to view an act independently as a moral or immoral thing-in-itself. For example, it is impossible to determine the "goodness" or "badness" of slashing someone with a knife unless one knows whether it is for the purpose of robbery or surgery. Even the virtue of chastity can be considered a vice if it occurs consistently year after year on the marriage bed.

In any real sense, an act can never exist alone. It must be coupled with intent, and the two must consist as one. The result of the act must also be included in the total evaluation of the morality that is involved.

If, therefore, we teach a child that *all* lies are bad and that he must never lie, we are confusing him when he learns later that some lies are good and necessary under certain circumstances. A better way to instruct a child is to teach him the nature of the moral value that has been violated, provided the child is capable of comprehending such an explanation. For example, if a child took cookies which a mother planned to serve for dessert and denied that he took them when questioned, a parent may scold the child for "lying" and for "taking things."

But if the parent, himself, understood the meaning of the moral values, he would recognize that the fault was within the province of the Duties rather than in the act itself. Instead of emphasizing "lying" and "taking," which under some circumstances may be right or wrong, he would scold the child for not considering the needs of others and for lacking the courage to admit a mistake.

The Morality of Intent

The question of intent raises further problems. If a person *intended* to practice a moral value but failed, how can this be evaluated? Is a person moral because of his intentions alone? Another form of the same question is, Is it morally wrong to hurt someone if doing so was unintentional? A related question is, Is a person dedicated when no one has been helped by his dedication?

If intent is present, all that may be required are explanations or instructions to convert intent into a moral act. Thus, if a person hurts someone unintentionally, unknowingly, and is intelligent enough to be capable of learning, he can be instructed to redirect his efforts. If he is not intelligent enough to avoid harming society, he must be removed from the position which enables him to do this. If a person is harmful to society because of carelessness, giving him awareness or fear are alternate remedies. If someone actually intends to hurt society, insight, psychotherapy, or fear—singly, or in any combination—may have to be applied. A person who is dedicated but helps no one may be a victim of self-delusion. Whether or not a person is moral because of intentions alone is a philosophical question that must be decided on the basis of one's own Criteria of Reality (see Chapter 3).

Several Categories of Morality in One Act

A breach of morality may involve one or more categories of morality. Within Western civilization, sexual promiscuity represents a violation of the Virtues. If a married person is promiscuous, an additional factor is involved which is contractural in nature. An agreement has been violated and, therefore, the act of promiscuity then involves the Duties as well as the Virtues.

In most cultures, murder involves the entire spectrum of moral values. Not only is murder "impolite," thus violating the Graces, but represents a sin involving the Virtues, is a crime within the context of the Duties, and represents a total reversal of the objectives of the Dedications. Though different moral values may be involved in a moral violation, often the focus of the violation is within one of them. In some instances it may be more meaningful to classify acts by their foci than by the number of different moral values that are involved.

Other Characteristics of the Moral Values

In addition to cultural determinants and sacrifice or inhibition, the moral values have two other characteristics—*dimensions* and *degrees of freedom*. The dimensions depend on the scope of a person's identifications with others. More exactly, they depend on his personal definition of "others." Thus, within the Duties, an individual may confine his cooperation to members of his family and community only. Degrees of freedom pertain to the amount of free will that is involved in complying with the moral values and to what extent a moral act is voluntary.

Dedication may be considered to have still one more characteristic. This deals with the *direction*. The direction of a dedication may take the path of expression on people, ideas and ideals (i.e. abstractions), and things (elements within nature or culture which are available to apperception by the senses i.e. concretions). Thus, when evaluating the Dedications, three factors should be considered: the dimensions, directions, and the degrees of freedom. In one sense, dedication can be expressed validly only towards other people. However Dedications are valid if while directed to ideas, these incorporate concepts of people. Dedication to ideas then is an indirect dedication to people. However, a dedication to things borders on pseudo-Dedication and represents a mild form of perversion, since such dedications have usually symbolic anthropomorphic aspects. Often such dedications are neurotic in nature. They have been included within hominology to distinguish them from opportunistic pseudo-Dedications to people and ideas.

The Dimensions

The dimensions which represent the extent and intensity of a person's *identifications* with other members of his species are an important component of morality viewed within the context of total Man. But where do identifications begin and where do they end? To answer this question we must explore the major boundaries within which Man has traditionally forged his identifications. Service (1962) provides us with a description of such boundaries:

It would seem that qualitatively distinct means of integration are few in human society. They appear to be five in number, although it is possible to think of subvarieties of each: (1) familistic bonds of kinship and marriage which by their nature can integrate only the relatively simple societies that are called bands; (2) pantribal sodalities which can integrate several bandlike societies into one; (3) specialization, redistribution, and related centralization of authority which can integrate still more complex societies; (4) the state, further integrated by a bureaucracy employing legal force; (5) an industrial society (consisting of a complex network of specialized, interdependent occupations).

It is assumed that Service's last category is international in scope. It is, however, limited by the concept, "interdependent occupations." We can postulate two more categories within which identification may take place. One precedes Service's list and the other follows it. We might begin with "self" as the smallest area within which identification can exist and this

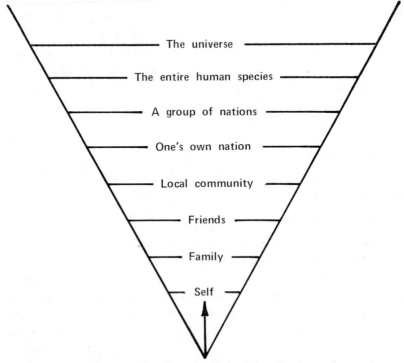

FIGURE 21.   Growth of the Identifications.

would precede "familistic bonds of kinship." In other words, it is possible for a person to be so aborted in his identification and development that he never emerges from his infantile self-centeredness and self-involvement. This kind of a person does not even identify with members of his own family. On the other end of the continuum, there are individuals who do not limit themselves to any of the boundaries which Service lists but make their identification apply to all men without any kind of restriction whatsoever (see Fig. 21).[4]

Identifications can be positive or negative as reflected in the *we-they* dichotomy. If identifications are positive, they elicit feelings of kinship and similarity. If they are negative, they provoke expressions of enmity and elicit feelings of difference. If we identify positively with someone, we see qualities in that person which we are willing to admit we share. If we identify negatively, we see within the person our qualities which we deny. This need to deny an aspect of ourself (because of cultural norms) stimulates aggression within us and that is one reason why negative identification is associated with hate.

Throughout the evolutionary process, negative identifications have had survival value for the species. Their roots lie not only within psychology but also in ethology and anthropology. Negative identifications make the intraspecies struggle for dominance possible, and they help to maintain territoriality. Benedict (1934) is among many who have observed that

> Primitive man never looked out over the world and saw "mankind" as a group and felt his common cause with his species. From the beginning he was provincial and raised the barriers high. Whether it was a question of choosing a wife or of taking a head, the first and important distinction was between his own human group and those beyond the pale.

The tendency to adopt negative identifications remains with us and represents a contemporary challenge. Benedict continues,

----

[4] There is a hierarchy in these "means of integration" which Service lists. Supplemented by the two I have supplied, they may be applied to the Development Levels described in Chapter 11 as follows: identification with self only, Level Four; identification with familistic bonds, Level Five; identification with tribes, nations, and societies, Level Six; identification with all men, Level Seven.

> So modern man, differentiating (mankind) into Chosen People
> and dangerous aliens . . . has the justification of a vast historical
> continuity behind his attitude . . . We are not likely to clear our-
> selves easily of so fundamental a human trait, but we can at least
> recognize its history and its hydra manifestations.

Some anthropologists would deny the implications in Benedict's observations. They would insist that primitive Man was
as generous to his fellowmen as his particular situation permitted.
Obviously, the situational opportunities for anything resembling
universal brotherhood were limited in his day. Since the concept
of *all* men being brothers and owing each other equal consideration is a relatively new one in human history, we need not
be surprised by the fact that contemporary Man must struggle
intensely in order to understand and apply concepts of universal
brotherhood.

The Degrees of Freedom

All societies, modern, ancient, simple, complex, primitive, or
civilized have one common element in that some measure of
cooperation between individuals always has taken place. But
there are a variety of degrees of freedom involved in cooperation.
The extent to which cooperation is voluntary or involuntary
depends on many complex factors.

Ethical and moral values in Man have been developed from
characteristics inherent in cooperation. Cooperation is also
typical of nonhuman social animals at many phylogenetic levels.
However, such a development of ideas gives rise to many problems as Bates (1961) observed when studying cooperation among
insects:

> The ants and other social insects, with their partners, guests,
> hangers-on and parasites, represent a problem . . . closely analogous
> to man with his partners, guests, hangers-on and parasites . . . (There
> is) the difficulty of drawing sharp distinctions between associations
> for mutual benefit of one partner without harm to the other; and for
> the benefit of one partner to the detriment of the other. Establish-
> ing the benefit or detriment is not always easy—since it often
> depends on your guess or my guess as to whether a certain number
> of fleas are good for the dog or not.

Obviously, there are different kinds and levels of cooperation.

By employing the word *cooperation* in a somewhat loose (and, perhaps. not entirely correct) manner, four hierarchical categories will be identified.

First, there is genetic cooperation which is programmed into an organism by the mechanisms of heredity—the genes and chromosomes. This kind of cooperation, typical of some insects, is involuntary and automatic.

The second kind of cooperation is also involuntary but not genetic and not automatic. It is the cooperation which a slave or a prisoner offers his master out of fear of reprisal or punishment.

A third type of cooperation stems from an exchange of services or values. It is usually voluntary and based on a mutual agreement in which there is an exchange of benefits between two or more people.

The fourth kind of cooperation is entirely voluntary and stems from a feeling of responsibility and a wish to be of service in matters that are important to society whether or not there are any benefits accruing to the cooperating person.

AN ANALOGY. The various levels of cooperation may be clarified further by the following analogy. Let us imagine that we lead a hungry, young boy into a candy shop, leave him there alone, but first tie him securely to a chair. Upon returning several hours later, it would be foolish to praise the boy for not having stolen candy. Obviously, since he was securely tied down, he was incapable of stealing. He can feel no pride nor sense of accomplishment in his "honesty," since he could not help but be honest under the circumstances. The first kind of cooperation is genetic and is analogous to being strapped to a chair since this eliminates any struggle with one's conscience.

The second kind of cooperation stems from fear. If we place the boy alone in the candy shop, untied, but threaten him with punishment if he takes any candy, he still will not deserve credit for not stealing. As before, he would have no basis for any feelings of achievement.

The third level of cooperation relates to mutual gain. This time when we invite the boy into the candy shop, we inform him that we are hiring him to guard the shop and that he will be paid for watching it. The boy needs the money he will earn to purchase a new bicycle tire. He resists the temptation to steal candy because he recognizes the fairness of the mutual arrangement. He may fear that if any candy is missing he will not be reimbursed. Also, he may be afraid that if he breaks his word, he will never be trusted again. To the extent that the boy values his word and keeps his contract because he feels that his honor is at stake, he is practicing an important form of morality. It involves the recognition of fairness and the obligation of being truthful. Society would disintegrate if men could not trust each other to fulfill their contracts. Such trust (sometimes reinforced by threats) represents social accommodation, and it insures the continuation of the social structure.

Finally, we come to the highest form of cooperation. We now imagine the boy volunteering to guard the candy shop after hearing that the owner has been called home because of an accident.[5] Since the boy is very hungry and loves candy, he is torn between desire to taste the shop's delicacies and recognition that the candies are the owner's means of livelihood. The boy identifies with the owner by putting himself in his place and realizes that the loss of candy might cause a hardship. He is also aware that there is a principle involved in not stealing since society could not endure if such a practice were condoned. He realizes that if he did take some candy, the owner might not notice it, or if it were noticed, nothing would be said about it because of his gratitude.

When the owner returns, he will call the boy "good"! The boy will realize that he *has* been good and that being good has meaning and entails sacrifice and struggle. This gives him a feeling of inner strength which can only be attained by victory over temptation.

Cooperation represents a process within the moral value of the Duties provided there is an element of freedom of choice involved. The first two reasons for not stealing do not represent moral values since zero degrees of freedom were present. As degrees of freedom approach one hundred per cent, acts within

---

[5] If he volunteered without expecting any gain from this act it would fall within the realm of the Dedications instead of Duties.

the Duties are termed *Commitments*. These differ from Dedications in that reciprocity, status, pride, or an enhanced self-image is involved. As one moves from the Graces to the Dedications an ever-increasing amount of freedom of choice is required for an act to maintain its moral qualities. Moral behavior may be enforced by fear but such behavior would have survival rather than moral value.

IS MAN BASICALLY RUTHLESS?

Any review of Man's phylogenetic past will reveal that early Man was not "born in innocence" in terms of the ethical standards which contemporary Man has adopted.[6] The biblical version of the expulsion from the Garden of Eden is mirrored in Man's early phylogenetic history with a startling clarity as authors such as Calder (1962), Campbell (1966), and Morris (1967) have noted. By all existing evidence, Man was not only a slayer of his own kind but a persistent cannibal, using first one reason, then another, to justify this practice [Dart and Craig (1959); Leakey (1960); Washburn (1961); Hawkes and Woolley (1963)].[7]

If one wishes to indulge in somewhat fanciful speculation, one might say that Man distinguished himself early in his existence by discarding the genetic "command" to which all other higher mammals adhered, Thou shalt not eat of thine own kind!

The fruit of the "family tree"—the animal's own species—was seemingly "forbidden' by a biological inhibition. Man transgressed and ate this forbidden fruit (his fellowman) and seemingly it gave him wisdom, but it also gave him fear. In hunting the cleverest animal alive, he accelerated the struggle which led to improvement. He developed superior weapons for attack and defense, and, with his new ingenuity learned from killing his own kind, he fashioned better and more deadly weapons than if he had only hunted creatures less intelligent than himself. This fratricide brought with it more than sophisticated weapons. The same brain that developed these weapons could look upon the creature that had been killed with pity and feel guilt. For this,

---

[6] With a few exceptions here and there. See Hogg, G.: *Cannibalism and Human Sacrifice*. New York, Citadel Press, 1966.

[7] Man is actually omnivorous rather than carnivorous.

he had to find atonement or rationalizations. When killing his fellowman no longer served his own needs, in many areas Man continued the practice of cannibalism, maintaining that he would gain mystical strength by devouring the organs of his slain victim.

Since cannibalism had helped him grow mighty, Man attributed a lust for human blood to his gods who were mightier than he. In the course of history, millions were put to death to appease the hunger of divinities which man invented to match his own image.

Broderick (1964) is one of many who write on this subject:

> In the Batak country of Sumatra there are places where cannibalism flourished until the turn of the century—and maybe later. The slain enemy was eaten and the taste of the human flesh . . . was not only pleasing but by eating his flesh one ingested the virtue and valour of a dead warrior . . .
>
> There is evidence for violent death in hominid skulls from the most remote times. The skull of *Pithecanthropus modjokertensis* had its hind part smashed by a terrific blow. All the skulls of *Pithecanthropus pekinensis* had their basal region hacked away and a hominid femur was split lengthwise, presumably to extract the marrow. Solo Man was a head-hunter and cannibal; in all the skulls except two, the region of the *foramen magnum* is completely smashed. Modern head-hunters also hack away at the *foramen magnum* . . . At Krapina were the charred bones of certainly forty neanderthaloid men, women, and little children who may have been eaten. . . .

This trait, which is so utterly repudiated by modern civilization and would be considered one of the greatest depravities were it to occur in our society today, nevertheless, appears to have been "a distinguishing feature wherein hominids differ from anthropoids" according to Broderick. Blanc (1961) after reviewing the evidence of cannibalism observes,

> We may therefore state that the only available objective evidence of an ideology in the pithecanthropian race points definitely to an extremely early birth of a tradition that was to survive major evolutionary events undergone by mankind, through Neanderthal stages, and that persist in the ethnography of present "Homo sapiens." . . .

Blanc theorizes on what channels of expression this cannibalistic "tradition" takes in modern times:

> In the Dionysiac mysteries of ancient Greece, a goat used to be

eaten symbolyzing Dionysus. Ritual symbolic theophagy had obviously its origin in former ritual effective cannibalism. The original *Einstellung* was the same, and the mental functionings involved were identical: the urgent need (a typical human psychological feature) of establishing a relation with the unknown and a mystic link between life and death. Only gradual sublimation of the practice once it had become symbolic, rendered obsolete the continuity of the tradition through the ages. [Italics and parentheses are Blanc's.]

Blanc concludes with these thoughts:

. . . some primitive mental folds that characterize the human mind had their inception in the very early stages of human development, have persisted through the ages (and through the conspicuous changes in the cultural and somatic features of mankind and its racial differentiation), and are undefeatable surviving even in highly "civilized" cultures. [Parentheses and quotation marks are Blanc's.]

Carrying the thesis that we must somehow sublimate a cannibalistic wish and anxiety somewhat further leads us to the roles which modern religions have adopted to absorb this "mental fold" and render it harmless.

Concepts of Morality Without "Evil" are Meaningless

Hitler's near successful massacre of the European Jews can only be conceived of as his equating the Jews with cannibals and drawing upon Man's latent fear of being cannibalistically consumed. Calder (1962) observes, "There is also economic 'cannibalism.'" Instead of sublimating this fear which religions assist us in doing, Hitler proclaimed the Jews "economic cannibals" and thus was able to invoke one of Man's deepest anxieties. He provided the rationale and the "justification" for cannibalizing the Jews themselves. In view of the fact that such unacceptable and unrecognized forces may have been at work in this and similar types of human tragedies, it is not surprising that moral philosophers were devoid of explanations and could merely shake their heads at seeing a civilized nation "stoop so low."

Writing of Man's orality within an ontogenetic context, Bergler (1949) refers to Man's oral sadism as his "basic neurosis." He finds that

What I find is something different. *I claim that "remnants" from the oral phase are not carried around later in life like sentimental baggage, or a souvenir. I claim that that "later"—the anal and phallic phases and what follows in neurosis—is not understandable without taking cognizance of the fact that these phases are but rescue and survival attempts from the oral danger.* [Italics are Bergler's.]

If the concept of morality is to have any meaning, it is fortunate that we have not been born good.[8] Had we been born good, there would be no virtue nor victory in our goodness, just as there is no courage in the man who "knows no fear." And just as courage means *overcoming* fear, so goodness becomes meaningful only if it implies overcoming the temptation of evil. And this can only occur if we are born "evil," if you wish to accept such an unscientific way of saying it. The ants described earlier in this chapter are not "good" even though they cooperated with one another. They had no choice in the matter.

Goodness is of no consequence if it consists only of following the inner directives of the nervous system without a quiver of conflict or ambivalence. Man's whole history reveals that his higher development has been achieved by intensive struggle against hostile forces. It is not meant that the moral values are merely converted displaced aggressive drives, but their existence represents a necessary part of the total picture. Victories won without struggles have failed to yield the satisfactions which human nature requires. In fact, they have not even been "victories." Since morality implies struggle and temptation, any concept of morality which makes it "easy to come by" deprives it of the very characteristic it needs to give Man self-awareness as a moral person.

There can be no morality without a freedom of choice, as I have pointed out earlier. There would be no freedom of choice if Man did not face a continuum of good to bad which stretches from one extreme of moral behavior to another extreme of immoral behavior. The greater the disparity between the phylogenetically rooted "ruthless" tendencies and the culturally rooted inducements for "good" behavior, the greater is the human accomplishment. If two men are identical in their practice of high moral principles, the one who is born with the tendencies

---

[8] "Good" as defined by contemporary standards, i.e. with present day moral values.

of a cannibal is a hero whereas the one born with the inclinations of a saint is, at most, a robot. We should remember that Man is not virtuous because he does not hate but because he does not act on his hate.

THE "HIGHEST" FORM OF MORALITY

Earlier, it was pointed out that there is no hierarchy of moral values except as these are reflected in one's Criteria of Reality. But most people would agree that morality, in its highest form, falls within the Dedications in which there is an identification with all others. "Others," in this sense, is nonexclusive and its dimensions represent the entire human species.

If Dedications represent the highest level of morality, those who dedicate must be free to accept or to reject. Any authority, no matter how well intentioned, that forces people to "dedicate" by using threat and reprisal has, by fiat, made dedication impossible. Other moral values may be, and often must be, enforced to save a society from internal destruction. But Dedication, at most, can be *permitted;* it cannot be demanded.

In looking for an example of this kind of morality, one finds that as a concept it exists and has been visualized by three quarters of the world's population. This concept is generally referred to as the Golden Rule. It appears that though many men are reaching for this ideal, few have as yet actually attained it. This Golden Rule reflects the transcendent nature which sets Developmental Level Seven off from its preceding Developmental Level Six (see previous chapter). A variety of versions of this rule are given below. Note that they all concur in demanding an identification between self and others.

Christianity: "All things whatsoever ye would that men should do to you, do ye even unto them for this is the law of the prophets."

Brahmanism: "This is the sum of duty; do naught unto others which would cause pain if done unto you."

Buddhism: "Hurt not others in ways that you yourself would find hurtful."

Judaism: "What is hateful to you, do not to your fellow men. That is the entire law, all the rest is commentary."

Confucianism: "There is one maxim of loving kindness: do not unto others what you would not have them do unto you."

Taoism: "Regard your neighbor's gain as your own gain, and your neighbor's loss as your own loss."

Zoroastrianism: "That nature alone is good which refrains from doing unto another whatsoever is not good for itself."

Islam: "No one of you is a believer until he desires for his brother that which he desires for himself."[9]

Human values stem from utilizing one's own needs and desires as a basis for understanding and respecting the needs and desires of other persons. Other *modern* moral values can be derived from this primary and universal one. For those who follow the Golden Rule, the question, Is it right or wrong? can be reworded to read, Does it cause anyone *needless* pain? The word *needless* has been inserted to differentiate this kind of pain from the "pain" which parents, in the process of educating their children, may be required to inflict upon them; which in curing, physicians may give their patients; which society, in self-defense, must give those who seek wantonly to destroy it; and which an individual, for self-protection, must sometimes inflict upon those who seek to injure him or his family.

If we, ourselves, represent a moral force, we are obliged to maintain ourselves against those who seek to destroy us, be these individuals, groups, or nations. For, by permitting ourselves to be destroyed, we would be allowing the moral force which we represent to be destroyed. This would be detrimental to moral progress and herein lies the justification of self-defense within a moral society. Unfortunately, however, this line of reasoning is often used as a rationalization for aggressive action.

THE CONSEQUENCES OF NOT BEING MORAL

Why should we be moral? This is a difficult, if not an impossible question to answer. One could refer the question back to the Criteria of Reality. But this would not answer it fully. It is obvious that different people have different reasons

---

[9] Note that the Golden Rule asks that you do to others what you *would* want them to do—not what they actually do. To do to others what they do to you would relegate the Golden Rule to the level of Duties. The *would* places it within the Dedications.

for both being moral or not moral. One line of reasoning for rejecting moral values (as the term is used in this chapter) is that since these differ in various cultures, there can be no right one. Since no value can be shown to be "right," it can be argued that we are not bound by any. Another reason, already touched upon, is advanced by some philosophers who claim that ethical concepts such as the Golden Rule are a falsification of nature which hinders the development of supermen with attributes of brute strength, intellectual cunning, and callousness.

The brute strength superman idea can be identified as belonging to an earlier developmental level than the one in which we are presently involved. If the theoretical concept of Levels of Development described in the previous chapter is accepted, it is possible to consider such ideas as a ruthless super-race as "old-fashioned." Being dedicated, on the other hand, is fashionable, up-to-date, and ahead of one's time within the framework of contemporary development. It may be looked at in another way. One could ask, What would happen if Man were not moral? Perhaps such a question is easier to answer. Let us begin with the Graces.

If a person is ill-mannered and discourteous, he is offensive to others. Some of the Graces vary widely within different cultures and nationalities, while others, such as courtesy, are almost universal. Offense stems from a lack of consideration for another person. If a person is impolite in the presence of some-one else, the latter becomes aware that the Graces need not be cultivated in all cases and that, in turn, makes him resentful that he, himself, feels compelled to maintain them. His own indoctrination to the Graces may have been more effective, or his sensitivities to disapproval may be greater. The tensions and hostilities released by one person's failure to adhere to the Graces would be multiplied if an entire group failed to develop any. Since the Graces disguise our animal natures, they serve as a basis for the development of the Virtues in which repression of primitive emotions takes place.

Sexual regulations and incest taboos are among the few human characteristics which Leuba (1954) has found to be nearly universal among the various cultures of mankind. Repressions, though painful, are a necessary concomitant of living together socially. As far as society is concerned, hermits and recluses need not inhibit their emotions. Though Virtues deal primarily with repression for its own sake, they yield the benefit of enabling a person to feel mastery over himself. Within the Duties, there is repression for the sake of the good of society, which requires that a host of unwritten contractual arrangements be honored between the members of a group. Without these, no society could exist since the Duties represent the structural framework of the society itself. The advantages of the Dedications are more difficult to describe. In order to explore the consequences of Dedications and pseudo-Dedications, let us imagine two large factories, each producing identical pieces of furniture.

An Analogy. Factory A consisted of a brick building at the northern border of the city. Factory B was very similar in appearance to Factory A. It was located at the southern border of the same city.

The two factories were noted for their unusually fine working conditions and the good treatment of their employees. For instance, they both had special facilities for recreation, insurance funds, generous coffee breaks, Christmas bonuses, and whenever an employee had an anniversay, he received a personal letter of congratulation and a gift.

John Smith worked in Factory A but lives in the southern section of the city. He had once lived close to Factory A, but as his family increased he bought a larger house located close to Factory B.

Mr. Smith disliked driving across the city every day to go to work and decided to apply for a position at the more conveniently located Fatcory B. He found an opening with the identical salary at Factory B which would permit him to do exactly the same kind of work he had been doing at Factory A. He carefully investigated the working conditions and the benefits and found that Factory B offered, in every way, the same benefits he had enjoyed at Factory A. So Mr. Smith left Factory A and accepted the position at Factory B. What Mr. Smith was not aware of was that Factory A and Factory B were as dissimilar as any two factories could possibly be. Their apparent likeness was entirely superficial.

The fundamental difference between the two factories was this: the benign personnel practices of Factory A were instituted because they constituted part of the owner's code of moral values. The benefits represented his personal identifications with his employees.

The owner of Factory B, on the other hand, was entirely opportunistic. In periods when workers were in scarce supply, he found that the personnel practices of his competitor—the owner of Factory A—tended to reduce personnel turnovers and increased production, and, therefore, he adopted them. He maintained them only as long as they contributed to increased production.

In time, Mr. Smith learned of the invisible differences between the factories. When conditions changed and there was much unemployment, the owner of Factory B gradually abandoned the benefits. Now the fear of loss of job kept the employees working at top efficiency and other inducements were no longer needed. On the other hand, at Factory A the benefits were continued because they represented an expression of the owner's moral values.

The question which, sometime in his life, every thinking person must ask himself is this, Is the universe in which we live a Factory A or is it a Factory B?

THE MOST IMPORTANT QUESTION

I have digressed considerably, so it seems, from the original question, What are the consequences of the Dedications? The reason for this digression is that the question can be answered only within the context of another question, Is this a moral universe in which we live? Of course, one needs but look around us to answer "No!" Everywhere, injustice can be found and not too infrequently, one sees what in our moral code is called wicked triumphing over good. But that is not the issue. It is rather, must goodness be manifested at all times to prove that it is real?

We see birds flying in the air and dust swirling skyward.

This does not prove that the universe is without gravitational pull. We do know that efficiency and moral behavior are closely linked together. But we do not know with any certainty, as yet, which is the product and which is the by-product. Is efficiency the "reward" for complying with the moral forces, as not falling and hurting oneself is the "reward" for complying with the gravitational forces that exist unseen all around us? Or are we putting the cart before the horse? Is morality only secondary to efficiency . . . an afterthought within the scheme of things?

This question, so abstract and seemingly remote from our work-a-day-world, may be the most important question there is. Not only does our answer decide what kind of lives we should lead but it influences almost everything we do, and it enters into every major decision that we make. Most of all, it determines the kind of relationships we have with our fellowmen. In short, it is the very basis of any morality.

For, if this is not a moral world, or is one in which morality is incidental to efficiency, morality of any kind can be justified only when it contributes to efficiency. In such a world, a rational Man would have to be an opportunist using morality as a means to gain efficiency but discarding it when efficiency no longer appears to require it. Exploitation of man by man would then be perfectly logical, since, as a by-product of efficiency, morality in itself would be meaningless.

On the other hand, if this is a moral world just as it is a gravitational world, a world of atomic particles, a world of specific types of accelerations, and an orderly world in which morality represents an aspect of this order—if it is such a world, then morality can logically be practiced for its own sake. Then, in every decision, we can aim to be consistent with this morality, just as every step we now take is consistent with gravitation. And, by means of consistency, we can explain and justify the adherence to that moral value we have called the Dedications.

The decision of whether or not ours is a moral universe draws upon Criteria of Reality other than empiricism since science has not found the means to cope with such a question. It is, however, a decision that you and I *must* make if we wish to avoid living hit-or-miss, nondirectional, and irrational lives.

But need it be that drastic? Could not Man, if he desired,

simply declare this to be a moral world and act accordingly? As has been found practical so many times in the past, could not he take an "as if" approach? Unfortunately this approach is workable in almost everything with which Man is concerned *except* morality.

Since the moral values always require sacrifice and since, at times, they may slow the path of "progress,"[10] an excellent case can be made (and has been made many times in history) that morality is a delusion from which we must free ourselves as soon as possible. If morality represents something which Man has created by means of culture, he is obligated to weigh its pros and cons. Then, under some circumstances, he may find the cons more to his liking. After all, if morality is merely a figment of the human imagination, why suffer for it? However, if morality is part of a developmental process which is bigger than Man himself but which Man has the freedom to adopt or reject, then the argument in favor of adopting moral values is a powerful one.

SUMMARY

A lack of understanding of the ingredients that comprise morality makes moral values difficult to transmit and causes much confusion. Young people today are trained to ask the question WHY? and are not as prone as the youths of past generations to accept moral values on a purely authoritarian basis.

The moral values were divided into the Graces, Virtues, Duties, and Dedications.

The Graces represent self-control; the Virtues, self-denial; the Duties, obligations; and the Dedications, a relationship with others that goes beyond obligations. These moral values were described as having two other characteristics—dimensions and degrees of freedom. The dimensions pertain to the breadth or narrowness of the focus, i.e. where they are customarily applied in a range extending from a small ingroup to the human species as a whole. Degrees of freedom pertain to the extent that a moral value is applied voluntarily.

The Golden Rule was recognized as within the realm of the

---

[10] As when, for moral reasons, we keep alive the mentally defective, the seriously ill, the insane, the physically handicapped, the old and senile. Obviously it would be more efficient for society to kill them.

Dedications. An analogy between two kinds of factories was offered to illustrate how pseudo-dedication may be used to disguise opportunism. Four levels of cooperation were illustrated. Temptation was seen as necessary to give moral behavior meaning. It was found that Man is not ethical because he fails to feel hate but because he does not act on the hate he feels. The question of whether morality is a consequence of efficiency or whether efficiency is the "reward" of morality was explored.

REFERENCES

BATES, M.: *The Nature of Natural History.* New York, Scribner, 1961.

BENEDICT, R.: *Patterns of Culture.* New York, Houghton, 1934.

BERGLER, E.: *The Basic Neurosis.* New York, Grune, 1949.

BLANC, A. C.: Some evidence for the ideologies of early man. In Washburn, S. L. (Ed.): *Social Life of Early Man.* Chicago, Aldine, 1961.

BRODERICK, A. H.: *Man and His Ancestry.* Greenwich, Fawcett, 1964.

CALDER, R.: *After the Seventh Day.* New York, New Am. Lib., 1962.

CAMPBELL, B.: *Human Evolution.* Chicago, Aldine, 1966.

DART, R. A., AND CRAIG, D.: *Adventures with the Missing Link.* New York, Harper, 1959.

FIRTH, R.: *Elements of Social Organization.* Boston, Beacon, 1963.

HAWKES, J., AND WOOLLEY, L.: *Prehistory and the Beginnings of Civilization.* New York, Harper, 1963.

HONIGMANN, J. J.: *The World of Man.* New York, Harper, 1959.

LEAKEY, L. S. B.: *Adam's Ancestors.* New York, Harper, 1960.

LEUBA, C.: *The Natural Man. Papers in Psychology,* Garden City, Doubleday, 1954.

LISITZKY, G.: *Four Ways of Being Human.* New York, Viking, 1962.

MEAD, M.: *People and Places.* New York, Bantam, 1963.

MORRIS, D.: *The Naked Ape.* New York, McGraw, 1967.

OPLER, M. K. (Ed.): *Culture and Mental Health.* New York, Macmillan, 1959.

SERVICE, E. R.: *Primitive Social Organization.* Studies in Anthropology, New York, Random, 1962.

WASHBURN, S. L. (Ed.): *Social Life of Early Man.* Chicago, Aldine, 1961.

Chapter 13

MAN'S MENTAL HEALTH

"Not who but what
assures a spot—
a master plan
to measure man."

ELIZABETH BARTLETT,
Blueprint for Modern Living

"How can we encourage love and diminish hate? . . . Is it possible to dispose of our aggressions more expediently than by killing ourselves and one another, and to foster and cultivate that tremendous power which draws men together . . . that sovereign remedy which stills the hate that forces men apart?"

KARL MENNINGER, M.D.
Love Against Hate

"We are in the beginning of the greatest change that humanity has ever undergone.

H. G. WELLS,
Smithsonian Treasury of Science, vol. III

MORALITY AND MENTAL HEALTH

CLOSELY ALLIED TO the subject of moral values is the matter of mental and public health. Rogers (1968) asks, "Can the health sciences resolve society's problems in the absence of a science of human values and goals?" Writing on the same subject, Frankl (1963) observes,

Man's search for meaning is a primary force in his life and not a "secondary rationalization" of instinctual drives. This meaning is unique and specific in significance that will satisfy his own will to meaning. There are some authors that contend that meanings and values are "nothing but defense mechanisms, reaction formations and sublimations." But as for myself, I would not be willing to live merely for the sake of my "defense mechanisms," nor would I be ready to die merely for the sake of my "reaction formations." Man, however, is able to live and even die for the sake of his ideals and values!

Frankl is a psychiatrist and his purpose in writing his book is to describe his concept of mental health. He finds that without goals or values Man cannot achieve that condition of adjustment to his environment which we term, *mental health*. If we agree with his view, we may find it regrettable that the converse does not apply. Men who have had both goals and values have succumbed to mental illness, as anyone who has worked in the field of mental health well knows. What, then, is the relationship between mental health and values, and how may this relationship be viewed within the larger conceptual framework of total Man?

There are many answers but, unfortunately, little meeting of the minds. As each expert develops his theories, he attracts a group of disciples who agree among themselves but differ in some essential aspect from followers of other theorists. There is the familiar dualism of Freud's, in which Man's instinctual needs are pitted against the inhibiting norms of society. There is the Adlerian variation with an inferiority-superiority theme, which, in many respects, anticipates the ethological concepts of dominance (Klopfer and Hailman, 1967). There is Jung with his personal and collective unconscious—a phylogenic repository —and his typology of the introvert and extrovert.

With the broadening influence of cultural anthropology, the neo-Freudian deviation from orthodox psychoanalysis took greater cognizance of the culture, society, and the contemporary age. Karen Horney (1937) repudiated Freud's libido theory and placed greater emphasis on social factors as contributing to neurotic trends. Her view is that neurotic needs are patterned by childhood frustrations and reflect how the child has coped with them. She sees neurotic needs as learned needs. Harry Stack Sullivan (1953) stressed that learning takes place through interactions between people and that personality arises from the empathy, or feeling tones, that develop during such interactions. Erikson (1959) considers human nature as shaped by the search for ego identity.

Others feel that dimensions of the personality which contribute to mental health must be identified experimentally and not through subjective analysis or observation. Among these are Eysenck (1962), Cattell (1957), and Guilford (1940). They rely on a variety of experimental situations to ascertain basic personality patterns and statistically analyze these to bring them in the realm of empirically testable hypotheses.

DUALITY-SINGULARITY IN MENTAL HEALTH

It was inevitable that the duality-singularity dilemma should manifest itself in the field of mental health as it has elsewhere (see Chapter 2). Adolph Meyer (1897) first suggested the term *mental hygiene* and emphasized the inseparability of psychological and biological processes. He developed a psycho-biological approach which aimed at understanding all of the factors—biological, psychological, and social. The Gestalt theory, in which the whole person is considered, followed with the writings of Goldstein (1939) and others. Maslow (1954) analyzed this configurational approach and found that certain basic needs have a priority. He arranged these into hierarchy which started with food, sleep, warmth, etc., followed by safety needs. Then came the need for belongingness and love. Esteem needs, such as prestige and success, which develop self-respect, came next. The fifth and final level of needs which Maslow identified, he termed, *self-actualization.* Self-actualization calls for the full development of one's potentialities. Within a hominological context it might be viewed as representing the highest point within the Developmental Level Six (see Chapter 11).[1]

Writers on personality theory explaining mental health are becoming increasingly aware that in order to view the total human personality, they must bring into the picture the role of both social and organic evolution. Menaker and Menaker (1965) observe,

> The introduction of the concept of an inner psychological structuring of personality, arising out of and functioning in a social medium, as an important aspect of human evolution, bridges the gap between organic and cultural evolution. Hallowell (1960) looks to psycho-

––––––

[1] Some elements of Level Seven are also included in self-actualization. Dedication and fulfillment are not sharply differentiated within this concept.

analysis for the model of this structure, making the point that in the phylogenetic understanding of man we owe to the observation of psychoanalysis the realization "that universal dynamic processes are involved which are related to the psychobiological nature of modern man as a species."

Heredity Versus Environment

A review of theories of personality, methods of psychotherapy, and the search for Man's sources of personal values leaves one with the impression that we must deal with four basic factors: Man's phylogenetic history, his individual genetic makeup, his environment, and the interaction between these three. Our problem is that we do not yet know the weight each of these factors exerts and the role each plays in forming either Man as an individual or mankind as a whole. It is not surprising, therefore, that the literature on this subject is controversial and that theories differ greatly. The problem of assessing the different roles that environment and heredity play in shaping Man's nature is one of the most perplexing that the student in the human sciences must face. The pendulum of opinion on this subject swings from one extreme to the other. Not so long ago, it was heredity to which human behavior was largely ascribed. Later, environment bore the brunt of the burden of accounting for human ills. The pendulum is swinging back to heredity again, and now we are beginning to hear that Man's animal nature may be the key to the riddle of his behavior. But controversy persists.

Berkowitz (1967) reviewing two recent books exploring human nature asks, "How can two books on the same subject be so different?" He is referring to Lorenz's *On Aggression* (1966) and Wertham's *A Sign for Cain: An Exploration of Human Violence* (1966). Today, the student in the human sciences will find many examples of such dichotomous views. Fromm (1941) writes,

> The most beautiful as well as the most ugly inclinations of man are not part of a fixed and biologically given human nature, but result from the social processes which create man . . . Man's nature, his passions, and anxieties are a cultural product. . . .

Morris (1967), on the other hand, observes,

Optimism is expressed by some who feel that since we have evolved a high level of intelligence and a strong inventive urge, we shall be able to twist any situation to our advantage . . . that we shall control our aggressive and territorial feelings, our sexual impulses and our parental tendencies; . . . that our intelligence can dominate all our basic biological urges. I submit that this is rubbish. Our raw animal nature will never permit it.

Earlier, it was suggested that the concept of morality I have presented may represent the synthesis of these divergent points of view. Seen in this way, Man is conceived of as neither an an animal nor nonanimal but as a human animal or better, as an animal-human. The question that remains is one that, in our contemporary society, requires an answer. How does Man— the animal-human—relate his moral values to the state of his mental and physical well being? Rogers (1968) notes, "those . . . in the medical and health sciences . . . can hardly be expected to plan and effectuate our programs comprehensively unless we can find a rational pattern." Such a "rational pattern" requires that the relationships between health and Man's moral values be made explicit. For this, some conceptual picture of mental health is necessary.

Mental Health and Satisfaction

The basic idea of mental health is deceptively simple. It is usually expressed in terms of satisfactions. In our society, a person is considered mentally healthy who is able to obtain satisfactions in three important areas of life: home, occupation, and community. A person is generally considered to be "normal" if he is able to carry out his obligations in these areas and derive more pleasure in doing so than irritation or dissatisfaction. Mental health is, then, primarily equated, by current definitions, with ability and pleasure within that moral value we have termed, the Duties.

AGGRESSION AS A HUMAN TRAIT

Within the concept of mental health there is also another element which deals with outlets of aggressions. Whether genetically derived from an animal heritage or generated by an inhibiting culture (all cultures must inhibit to be cultures),

Man, as an animal-human, is known to be aggressive. Anger, hostility, rage, aggression—call it what you will—must be released in order to prevent a psychic explosion. How and in what direction aggression is expressed is the all-important joint concern of morality and mental health.

Even if cultures could be recreated to evoke a minimum of aggressiveness,[2] targets for whatever aggressions remained would still have to be found. Of course we could tranquilize all of mankind and some fear that we seem to be already partially embarked on such a program. But, even then, there would still have to be a few aggressive souls to make the tranquilizers for the rest of us.

It seems that there is no escape in sight from Man's need for outlets for his aggressions. Culture serves its members when it provides targets for hostility which are noninjurious to other human beings. The mental hygiene aspect of the morality-mental health complex concerns the availability of targets; morality's role consists of insuring that the targets consist of nonhuman materials (i.e. things, activities, symbols), or if they must be human, those least apt to feel the brunt.[3]

Writers such as Lorenz (1966) and Morris (1967) have been accused of distorting aggressiveness by giving it a phylogenetic basis. However, aggressiveness need not be equated with destructiveness. It may be viewed as psychobiological energy capable of cultural modification. Destructive behavior has been described as "contagious" because it tends to be imitated. It is, therefore, necessary to study the sources of destructive behavior as well as targets.

Scapegoats and Scape-Elephants

As I write, I am reminded of an event which occurred in

---

[2] This might have to be at the expense of what we call "progress."

[3] Theoretically, the closer the target resembles the original source of the frustrations, the more complete is the reduction of hostile tension. Since many of our frustrations stem from authoritarian figures and rivals (i.e. humans), we tend to use other humans (less dangerous ones) as objects upon which to release our aggressions.

California almost twenty years ago. I was a practicing clinical psychologist then and daily rode to work with a young doctor from another state, who was required to complete two years of training at the hospital.

My colleague was pleasant enough but he had one almost unbearable fault. He had developed a consistent hate for every Californian. It was easy to see that the cause of his hostility stemmed from his unhappiness with his training assignment. Realizing this, I thought that I could endure his daily diatribes, but since the round trips to the hospital were long, I finally tired. The time came when I no longer could stand it.

I was ready to tell him in clinical terms just what his hatred of Californians really represented. But, I caught myself and instead asked him, "How do you feel about Negroes?" He spent some time explaining his belief in equal rights and in increased opportunities for Negroes.

"What do you think of Latin-Americans?" I asked next. He extolled their virtues. I began to be intrigued. "What do you blame the Jews for?" I asked. "Blame?" he echoed, "I think that Jews are among the finest people in the world—just think how much they have contributed to our civilization!"

"Well, Chinese, Japanese, foreigners, Catholics, Protestants, Quakers, Holy Rollers—you must have hostile feelings against some of them—don't you?" I demanded.

He liked them all. "Everyone in our country has the right to choose his religion without being criticized by members of another faith," he said with feeling. He went on to explain how Western Man could benefit from studying the philosophy of the Orient and added that the United States had been enriched by immigrants from abroad.

It dawned on me that my friend had discovered something that could one day prove to be one of mankinds most valuable assets. He had discovered how to project hostile feelings upon individuals who could not possibly suffer from their role as targets. As I contemplated the prosperity, natural resources, and climatic blessings of the sunshine state, I knew its residents would not be hurt by my colleague's disapproval. By channeling his aggressive feelings in their direction, he was not only avoiding racial, religious, and ethnic bigotry, but, no doubt, also sparing the feelings of members of his family and those of his associates. He had wrought the miracle of converting Man's customary array of long-suffering scapegoats into a single thick-skinned and invulnerable scape-elephant!

I turned to my friend, and with emotion, said, "How, very, *very* wonderful it is that you hate Californians!"

As I recall, he gave me a startled look and our relationships were never quite the same thereafter. But my admiration for him has continued unabated through the years.[4]

Ontogenetic Sources of Aggression

In life, almost every stimulus we confront is probed, consciously or unconsciously, for its suitability as a shock absorber for our surplus psychic pressures. In the previous pages, there has been a discussion of some of the phylogenetic sources of human aggression. The ontogenetic factors that contribute to Man's hostile feelings are, perhaps, better understood in current psychological theory and, certainly, they are more readily accepted. It has been mentioned that every society, simple or complex, requires that its members inhibit their behavior to a lesser or greater extent, depending on the nature of the culture. Every society also offers its members a variety of sanctioned opportunities for displacing the hostile emotions which stem, in part, from the requirement to conform to the social norms which it imposes. In a viable society, this input of inhibition is matched by an equal measure of opportunity for approved outlet of frustrations.

Within our culture, the family offers the child his earliest

----

[4] Some will contend that a person who has hostilities towards one minority group tends to be prejudiced against several and perhaps all groups that differ from the one to which he, himself, belongs. Others believe that in having one outlet for displaced aggression, other potential outlets are spared. The research literature appears to be divided on the subject, probably because much depends on the individual personality that is involved. I like the remark of an acquaintance who, when she has a difficult day, exclaims, "I hate *everybody*, without regard to race, religion, or national origin!"

experience in inhibition.[5] Popular contemporary literature has taken full note of frustrations stemming from parental control. Not as much attention has been paid to another source of frustration—one of a different kind which develops when a family fails to provide a child with guide-posts to behavior within a complex society. This more serious frustration manifests itself later in the child's life when he must attempt to live in a world for which the home has inadequately prepared him. He then suffers what may be called the "frustration-frustration," that is, the kind of frustration which develops from not having been frustrated by parent's setting behavioral bounderies and limitations during formative years.

With the declining role of the paternal authority noted in our present culture, a more democratic relationship between the members of the family has become possible. There is no doubt that this is preferable to the sometime tyrannical paternal dictatorship of the previous century, but the new democracy in the home carries with it its own set of dangers.

In his search for dominance clarification and in the exploration of his own relative status position within a dominance hierarchy (which is the adolescent's phylogenetic heritage), the youth of today finds his democratic home a perplexing environment.[6] In the absence of evidence to the contrary, the child may assume that he, rather than his parents, is dominant and when he matures, he is then likely to continue insisting upon this status. To sustain this self-concept requires constant self-reassurance and demonstration that he is "bigger" than any parental symbol which society may provide, such as government, police, law, or society in its entirety.

------

[5] There is considerable cultural variation in the nature and amount of discipline in childhood. The Eskimo culture is often used as an example of parental permissiveness but here the harsh elements of the icy tundra and difficulties of survival may play a role equivalent to parental discipline. There is, however, no known direct relationship between environmental difficulties and parental permissiveness. This entire subject requires further research.

[6] Psychoanalytic psychology has further muddied the water by viewing all intrafamily dominance explorations as "sibling rivalry for mother's love."

Four Kinds of Targets

How the expression of aggression is reflected and helps shape the moral nature of an individual has already been discussed. It has been mentioned that the kinds of targets a child selects are also related to his mental health. Each category of target produces its characteristic symptom complex.

1. Socially sanctioned targets consist of sports, vicarious experiences, and sublimations. These are adopted by those who received acceptance in childhood and who, in turn, are capable of accepting their family and society. The use of socially sanctioned targets is associated with the "normal" personality.

2. Internalized targets are used when a person turns his hostility upon himself or an aspect of self. Such targets are used by those who have predominantly experienced guilt in their attempt to satisfy their basic needs in their childhood. Maladjustments associated with the employment of self as a target are the neuroses, conversion reactions, and somatizations, and the depressive psychoses.

3. The use of other people as targets stems from a discipline that was too harsh or, conversely, from a home where discipline was insufficient. Each of these conditions represents a rejection of the child by the parents. Sometimes this rejection is masked by overconcern. Such home influences may lead to the formation of character-and-behavior disorders and antisocial personalities.

4. A target may consist of the entire universe or *Umwelt*. Such a total rejection stems from a deprivation of childhood satisfactions on a very broad spectrum of basic needs. When this occurs, it may lead to withdrawal reactions and regressive psychoses.

MORAL VALUES AND MENTAL HEALTH WITHIN THE CONTEXT OF DEVELOPMENTAL LEVELS

The idea of geological epochs has served biology and paleontology by providing these disciplines with a framework within which the process of geological changes and organic evolution may be more readily understood. It is proposed that the eight theoretical developmental Levels, described in Chapter 11, be used to conceptualize the developmental history of moral values and mental health. Both the geological epochs and the developmental Levels are man-conceived-of constructs to assist in the classification of events.

The value of such a new format may be seen when we consider the present difficulty in conceiving of the "antisocial" personality. For years, *Psychopath* was used in this connection. It was abandoned when it was realized that the term, literally meaning "mentally sick," was not meaningfully applied to a person having antisocial behavioral traits.

Within a moral historical framework, antisocial personalities are viewed as individuals using the focus of a previous developmental era. The term *hominolopaths* is suggested to describe them within this context. In Table VIII, *hominopathology* refers to a moral culture lag stemming from an abortion of moral values within the developmental schema which the Table presents. Since societies differ in what is considered to be acceptable behavior, the term *antisocial* can not have a universal application. By considering moral behavior developmentally and viewing morally-stunted individuals as hominolopaths, more widely applicable concepts of antisocial behavior may emerge. Admittedly, moral development, like all evolutionary (organic and cultural) developments, is uneven throughout the world. However, the concept of hypothetical developmental foci makes it possible to communicate the meaning of a specific type of behavior without confusing it with the variations that may be contemporary with it.

Table VIII attempts to demonstrate that Menaker and Menaker's (1965) views, taken from the quotation that follows, are not consistent with the hominological synthesis which goes *beyond* fulfillment. The lack of appreciation that fulfillment in today's world is not enough, regardless of how it may manifest itself, contributes to an anxiety growing out of fear that we have reached a dead-end in the road to moral progress. It is not satisfactory to view dedication as simply "a kind of fulfillment" in which one is "fulfilled" by giving. This would be analogous to viewing fulfillment (in the sense that Menaker and Menaker see it) as only a higher form of a survival struggle. Such a view tends to assume that progressive changes alone account for

TABLE VIII

ATTEMPT AT INTEGRATING MORALITY, MENTAL HEALTH, AND DEVELOPMENTAL LEVELS

Developmental Level	Moral Development	Mental Health
Level Eight	Dedications based on maximum self-universe identification	Nirvana? Psychosis? Spiritual mysticism? Maladjustment in terms of present realities
upper	Dedications based on maximum self-mankind identifications	Maladjustment in terms of contemporary social structures (and beyond present bio-social human capacities?)
Level Seven middle	Dedications based on partial self-mankind identifications	Tensions stemming from impatience with society's progress
lower	Dedications within identification bounderies limited to specific groups	Good mental health
upper	Duties relating to fulfillment of talents and capacities°	Satisfactory mental health but some neuroticism
Level Six middle	Self-aggrandizement with desire for power over others. Exploitation with minimum reciprocity°	Certain types of neuroses Hominopathology
lower	Self-gratification with emphasis on maximum expression of instincts and drive	Character and behavior disorders Hominopathology (hedonistic)
Level Five	Ruthless opportunism with uninhibited exploitation of others prompted by the desire for self-aggrandizement†	"Psychopaths" and antisocial personalities Hominopathology (exploitive)
Level Four	Noninvolvement with the external world	Withdrawal psychoses; severe mental deficiency; severe psychologically traumatizing organic illnesses

(left margin, rotated: PRESENT)

° These may assume defensive disguises as Dedications. In that case they are pseudo-Dedications.

† These may assume defensive disguises as Duties. In that case they are pseudo-Duties.

human moral development. Menaker and Menaker see their *highest moral level* as follows:

> On the human level, the struggle for survival has been largely replaced as Huxley would say, "by the struggle for fulfillment." We would say that fulfillment is an essential aspect of psychological survival. For man, the striving towards a harmonious relationship between all aspects of his environment, inner and outer, and his own being—a harmony which would let him feel himself part of the evolutionary stream of life while at the same time experiencing his own individuation.

It is probable that neither Huxley nor the Menakers would argue with the view that dedication is still a higher moral concept than fulfillment, but this should be made explicitly clear and must be developmentally accounted for in order to explain dedication within the context of an "evolutionary stream."

THE CONTEMPORARY CRISIS IN MORAL VALUES

The contemporary crisis that is occurring all over the world, irrespective of national ideologies, reflects the restlessness of today's youth. Perhaps it stems from our inability to provide a coherent framework (or any framework within which moral values can be viewed) which can be realistically applied to the existing world around us.

Roe (1965) reports in *Science* that in her interviews with eminent older scientists, the latter said that the rewards of their work have been "in terms of inner satisfactions and recognition from their peers." However, such "satisfactions" were not enough to give them peace of mind. As they observed the behavior of the newer generation, some of these eminent scientists found that their scientific knowledge did not provide them with meaningful answers to moral questions. This is because, like housewives, shoe-shine boys, lawyers, oceanographers, and everyone else, scientists require a universal framework within which moral values may be viewed. They also require an additional framework such as the Criteria of Reality with which to account for variations of points of view.

Roe quotes one scientist verbatim:

> You know this really is beginning to bother me—I'm having a hard time telling the difference between right and wrong. I always felt I really knew, and now especially for other people I just don't know whether they are doing right or wrong. The frameworks are so different from anything corresponding to the way I used to make judgments for myself, and then I used to make judgments about other people too. But when I look at the different situations in which they live, well, this is kind of upsetting. I've lost my sense of smell, my eyes are kind of feeble, my hearing is a little bit weak—when I can't tell right from wrong, I really had better retire, so it's got me worried.

But there are some of us who cannot "retire" in order to avoid coming to grips with moral problems which demand an answer. The young men and women who are searching for such answers are also a long way from the retirement years. Modern youth has its fingers on the pulse of progress and this includes moral progress. Some of our so-called delinquency stems from youth's inability to feel the beat of that pulse within our contemporary society.

It is characteristic for young people to want to be in touch with "the latest" or to use contemporary slang, "be in" and "be with it." If they are given the opportunity to learn that moral values also have an "in" rooted to a process as old as life itself, they may be motivated to be among the morally up-to-date. Within such a context, being selfish, opportunistic, and exploitive may be equated with being behind the times— the very thing which the young generation of all eras have consistently abhored.

The question, Why adhere to moral values? may, then, be partially answered by explaining that moral values, especially the Dedications, are as modern as Man's exploration of the moon. The older values, Graces, Virtues, and Duties, must remain basic to make it possible for dedication to occur, just as modern space flight still needs the ancient earth from which to take off and draw support. Not to adopt the Dedications is to linger obsolescent and outmoded within a level of development which mankind is now struggling to leave behind.

The argument, however, has not yet been won. In questioning WHY, the young people of today, who ponder such matters as moral values, are especially confused regarding the validity of that group of values I have termed the Virtues. To deny oneself for the sake of self-denial does not convince them. To be virtuous for the sake of self-control alone does not motivate them. Our contemporary moral developmental level, in which dedication is beginning to overshadow fulfillment, seems to make it essential to redefine the role of the Virtues and enlist them within the service of the Duties or Dedications.

This does not apply to those capable of accepting Virtues on the authority of their religion. Society must, however, still concern itself with the sizeable number of today's young people who require additional explanations.

Sexual Morality and Marriage

As an example, let us take a matter on which there is currently a great deal of discussion—the question of youth's sexual morals. It is no longer as easy as it has been in the past to convince the young that behavior such as premarital sexual relations is wrong *only* because it represents a "sin." Those parents who wish to discourage their sons and daughters from engaging in this kind of behavior are more likely to succeed if they are able to offer rational explanations that involve the moral area of Duties, i.e. those values which are necessary for the beneficial survival of society.

A great deal more research is needed in regard to the total role that the Virtues play in such a survival. The Virtues often serve the Duties in a manner that is not easily recognized. Thus, chastity before marriage and non-promiscuity after marriage may strengthen what in zoological language is called the *pair-bonds* between male and female. By restricting the sex act to married couples, the act may become a stronger bond in helping to hold man and wife together in the face of extramarital sexual temptation. Perhaps premarital and extramarital sexual inhibitions tend to reduce a competition for sex partners that otherwise might be disruptive to society (Morris, 1967). A secondary gain which such a virtue may offer is the sense of mastery over self which helps to create a basis for human dignity. Another gain, of course, is that an adherence to Virtues makes it possible to sublimate genetically based psychic pressures and energies to serve society on a higher and more fruitful plane. It is noteworthy when speaking of the Virtues that what is sublimated need not be repressed.

The neurotics who suffer from repressed biological drives have been typically unable to sublimate such drives unto the level of the Dedications. The seemingly "dedicated" neurotic, on the other hand, is actually a pseudo-dedicated individual whose intentions may lie within Level Seven but whose emotional capacity remains within Level Six.

After the marriage ceremony has taken place, sexual fidelity becomes a matter of contractual agreement which is the very essence of the Duties. But the concept of marriage may still be enhanced if its provisions are explained in terms of the Dedications, the core of which is the kind of love in which the needs of another person take precedence over one's own.

From the Sublime to the Ridiculous

The application of the moral hierarchy need not be confined to matters of such importance. Going from the "sublime to the ridiculous" to make the point, let us take, for example, a student dropping a candy wrapper on the campus lawn. He will be serving Duties by picking it up and depositing it in a waste receptacle. If he happens to see another candy wrapper marring the appearance of the lawn, he is not required to remove it within the framework of the Duties since he was not the one who dropped it.

If, however, he wishes to be up-to-date, to really "be in," he may pick up the wrapper even though its presence was not his fault. He may identify with all the others who take pride in the appearance of their campus. He may do this if he feels inclined to go *beyond* the Duties in the way he lives his life. He may have decided to enter the moral realm of the Dedications where, in large ways or in small, he volunteers to give something of himself which neither society nor any authority outside of himself demands. No matter how small or seemingly insignificant such an act of dedicating may appear to be, it will provide the undescribable excitement of participating in the special kind of *approach-avoidance* conflict[7] that is inherent in transcendental change. It will also offer the participant the equally undescribable satisfaction which comes from being among the standard-bearers of Man's most recent developmental advance.

CONSTRUCTION OF HOMINOLOGRAM II

In Chapter 5, the student constructed a hominologram (Hominologram I) as a subjective experience to assist in exploring the nature of the reality which he accepts within a

---

[7] This term is used in psychology to represent a conflict in which something is both wanted and not-wanted at the same time.

psycho-socio-philosophical framework. In Chapter 11, a time-problem chart was introduced in which the student relates the intensity of five current problems with his estimate of how long these problems will persist. Using Hominologram II, the student

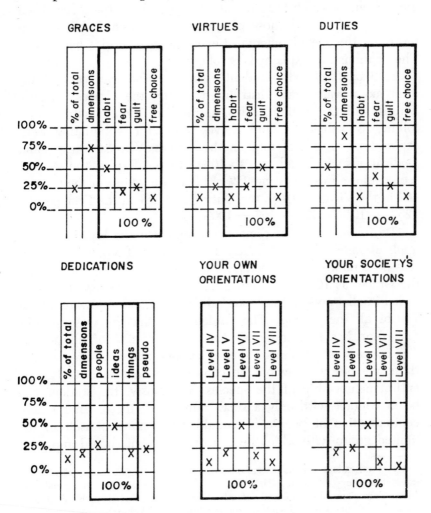

Note: % of total Graces+Virtues + Duties +Dedications should=100%. Also, all of the percentages within each of the heavy-lined rectangles should add up to 100%

FIGURE 22. Hominologram II. Distribution of the Moral Values. A hominology student's self-evaluation.

now utilizes a framework wherein he explores his own moral behavior and analyzes its content.[8]

In Figure 22, such a hominologram is presented. The Graces, Virtues, Duties, and Dedications are shown. Two other boxes are presented which the student uses to indicate the distribution of his own foci and those of the society in which he lives in terms of the Developmental Levels described in Chapter 11. The columns are explained as follows:

1. *% of total:* The student estimates what per cent of his total moral values are distributed among the Graces, Virtues, Duties, and Dedications. This, as in all of the evaluations that follow, is subjective and serves only for stimulating self-exploration. The % of total in the Graces, Virtues, Duties, and Dedications should add up to 100%. In the Figure, the student scored himself as investing 25% of his moral values in the Graces, 10% in the Virtues, 50% in the Duties, and 15% in the Dedications. (25% + 10% + 50% + 15% = 100%)

2. *dimensions:* The dimensions represent the breadth of the application of the moral values. For example, if a person believes that he is polite to *everybody,* he will score his dimensions under the Graces as 100%. On Figure 22, the student believed that he is habitually polite, courteous, and well-manner toward about 75% of all the people. The student felt that he was virtuous (i.e. represses his emotions) towards only 25% of all people. The concept of people is a theoretical one and not only includes those persons with whom he comes into contact but also the entire membership of the species. Obviously, the student can be in contact with only a small number of these. In his conceptualization of people he should not confine himself to the limited group with which he is acquainted but should apply his

---

[8] Moral values are no longer mass-produced by higher authorities to the extent that they once were. They are here to be discovered by individuals like Albert Schweitzer and thousands of others who have found them by dedicating themselves to mankind. Having been self-found, moral values are more meaningful than when they were prescribed like medicine.

Hominologram II was designed to assist the student in the task of self-discovery regarding moral values. Hominology students have dubbed Hominologram I (Chapter 5) "Realogram" and Hominologram II in this chapter "Moralogram."

evaluation also to include those who comprise the total world's population.

In regard to Duties, the student believed that he would be inclined to express his contractual relationships (see definition of Duties) theoretically towards approximately 85% of all the world's people. Dedication, however, would be confined to about 20% of the world's population. When all the percentages of the moral values are added up, they cannot exceed 400% since the maximum dimensional involvement for each of the four moral values is 100%. In the case of the student's Hominologram II in Figure 22, the combined dimensional involvement of the moral values totaled 205%.

3. *habit, fear, guilt, free choice*: The student indicates how the habits, fears, guilt, and free choice are distributed among each of the moral values. These four reasons for adopting a moral value are ranked on a percentage basis to make up a total of 100% for each one of the moral values. For example, if the Graces are adhered to to the extent of 25% because of habits developed through conditioning; 25% due to fear of punishment; 25% because of the desire to avoid guilt feelings (internalized punishment); and, likewise 25% because of a free choice on an entirely voluntary basis (independent of either fear, guilt, or habit), the total investment in the Graces would have been evenly distributed and have added up to 100%. In the case of the student in Figure 22, 50% of his reasons for adopting the Graces is related to habit formation, 20% due to fear of the consequences of not being courteous, etc., and 25% due to guilt feelings which bad manners would have stimulated, and 5% due entirely to free choice (50% + 20% + 25% + 5% = 100%). The Virtues and Duties are evaluated in the same manner. In each case, the distribution of habit, fear, guilt, and free choice should add up to 100%.

4. *people, ideas, things* (Dedications): It is possible to be dedicated to people, ideas (or ideals), and to things. If a person is dedicated to people, he must identify with them and sacrifice for them. But he may also sacrifice for an idea, ideal, or principle which, though it may apply to people, is actually an abstraction like freedom, justice, religion, or universal education.

Persons who are dedicated to ideas may, in actual practice, not really identify with people as individuals but are willing to sacrifice for the abstraction which the idea or ideal involves.

There are also persons who are actually dedicated to things such as their automobile or their home. This kind of dedication is more than a mere love of possession, rather, it is an expression of love (willingness to sacrifice even at the expense of one's own needs) toward a material object *as if* it were a beloved human being which it may, in fact, symbolize. Such dedication endows the material object with an intense sentimental value as is the case in certain heirlooms, for example. The total amount that one is capable of dedicating is ranked by per cent in the heavy-lined rectangle. Since one's entire capacity for dedicating is involved, the distribution of percentages should add up to 100%. In Figure 22, the student believed that his total tendency to be a dedicating person was distributed 30% towards people, 50% towards ideas, 20% towards things (30% + 50% + 20% = 100%).

The student believed, after some self-searching, that about 25% of all of his seeming dedications were actually pseudo-dedications in that they had an opportunistic motive rather than an altruistic one.

5. The last two rectangles in Hominologram II enable the student to evaluate himself and his society in terms of the five Developmental Levels described in Chapter 11. Also, helpful in matching one's own life orientations with Developmental Levels would be a comparison of one's ratings with Table VIII in this chapter.

In Figure 22, the student believed that his own foci were about 10% merely existing in terms of the biological imperatives (Level Four—Struggle for Existence). Fierce competition of the type that could lead to the extermination of rivals involved about 20% of his orientation (Level Five—Survival of the Fittest). Most of his own life orientation was consumed in developing his aptitudes, abilities, and, in general, in obtaining the material and physical comforts, and the status position which was consistent with his millieux (Level Six—Fulfillment). Approximately 18% of his life orientation was seen as directed toward dedication

(Level Seven—Dedication). The student often considered the future of mankind and had done some thinking along the lines of Zen Buddhism, which he equated with a future human development. He rated himself as being involved to the extent of 2% in this kind of preoccupation. His total personal orientations added up to 100% and their distribution with the Developmental Levels was indicated in the first of the two last rectangles.

The student made a similar theoretic distribution of orientation foci for the society in which he lived. This "society" could include any kind of a group and would have to be individually defined by each persons constructing a Hominologram II. In this case, the student used his national group, i.e. the United States of America. A comparison between these two evaluations shows that the student considered himself less involved in the emphasis of simply maintaining himself biologically (i.e. food, shelter, warmth) than the average American. He also thought that he was somewhat less competitive on the "red tooth and claw" level.[9]

In regard to fulfillment, the student estimated that he and the average American were more or less similar in their pursuit of those activities and things which led to a sense of fulfillment. However, he considered himself more dedicated and further advanced in Level Seven than the average American. In his explanatory paper which accompanied his hominologram, he mentioned that his society's Dedications were primarily within the realm of ideas as was true also in his own case. The student did not feel that his society, i.e. the United States, had any involvement within Level Eight other than, perhaps, space exploration. He did not assign this to the category of Level Eight feeling that this, as it was being undertaken, represented primarily a phenomenon that should be classified under Developmental Level Six, fulfillment.

By inspecting his hominologram, the student may now analyze

---

[9] This kind of competition must be distinguished from the "friendly" type of competition which seeks to inspire morale and elicit improved performance but not with the ruthlessness of extermination in mind. The former leads to the destruction or elimination of the competitor, the latter to stimulate maximum effort. These two kinds of competition must not be confused. See Chapter 11 for more on this subject.

the constituents of his own moral behavior and determine to what extent this behavior is genuinely moral, that is, engaged in by either free choice or by habits which have been voluntarily adopted. By means of his subjective appraisal he will gain an idea of how the component parts of his moral values are distributed among the Graces, Virtues, Duties, and Dedications.

The objections to Hominologram I are applicable to Hominologram II. Both represent entirely subjective judgments. But, nevertheless, the experience of constructing them has proven thought-provoking and has stimulated lively discussions.

The simple purpose of the hominolograms are to foster self-exploration leading to self-understanding or at least to the appreciation of the difficulties involved in self-understanding. The search for self-understanding within the framework of the moral values represents the most potent integrative experience to which the student can be exposed to in his search for a glimpse at total Man. This is because the understanding of total Man is meaningful only within the context of understanding the total Self.

SUMMARY

Man's system of values was placed within an evolutionary context together with a concept of mental health. A table was presented which illustrates the relationship between moral values and mental health integrated within the developmental schema described in the previous chapter. It was pointed out that moral values may be transmitted effectively to young people today, only if there are meaningful and convincing explanations. The chapter describes and evaluates a number of such explanations. A hominologram is presented to show how students may explore the concept of moral values and relate these to their own lives.

REFERENCES

BERKOWITZ, L.: Readiness or necessity? *Contemporary Psychology, 12*:580-582, Dec. 1967.
CATTELL, R. B.: *Personality and Motivation Structure and Measurement.* New York, Harcourt, 1957.

ERIKSON, E. H.: The problem of ego identity. In Klein, G. S. (Ed.): *Psychological Issues: Selected Papers by Erik H. Erikson.* New York, Int. Univs, 1959.

EYSENCK, H. J.: Reminiscence, drive and personality: revision and extension of a theory. *Brit J Soc Clin Psychol, 1*:127-140, 1962.

FRANKL, V. E.: *Man's Search For Meaning.* Translated by I. Lasch, New York, Washington Square, 1963.

FROMM, E.: *Escape From Freedom.* New York, Holt, 1941.

GOLDSTEIN, K.: *The Organism: A Holistic Approach to Biology Derived from Pathological Data in Man.* New York, Am. Bk. Pub. Co., 1939.

GUILFORD, J. P.: *An Inventory of Factors STDCR.* Beverly Hills, Sheridan, 1940.

HALLOWELL, A. I.: Personality structure and the evolution of man. *Amer Anthropologist, 52*:164, 1960.

HORNEY, K.: *The Neurotic Personality of Our Time.* New York, Norton, 1937.

KLOPFER, P. H., AND HAILMAN, J. P.: *An Introduction to Animal Behavior.* Englewood Cliffs, Prentice-Hall, 1967.

LORENZ, K.: *On Aggression.* New York, Harcourt, 1966.

MASLOW, A. H.: *Motivation and Personality.* New York, Harper, 1954.

MENAKER, E., AND MENAKER, W.: *Ego in Evolution.* New York, Grove, 1965.

MEYER, A.: A short sketch of the problems of psychiatry. *Amer J Insanity, 53*:538-549, 1897.

MORRIS, D.: *The Naked Ape.* New York, McGraw, 1967.

ROE, A.: Changes in scientific activities with age. *Science, 150*:313-318, Oct. 15, 1965.

ROGERS, E. S.: Public health asks of sociology. *Science, 159*:506-511, Feb. 2, 1968.

SULLIVAN, H. S.: *The Interpersonal Theory of Psychiatry.* New York, Norton, 1953.

WERTHAM, F.: *A Sign for Cain: An Exploration of Violence.* New York, Macmillan, 1966.

Chapter 14

THE APPROACH TO CONTEMPORARY PROBLEMS

"Every year we hear of the progress made by eugenicists, geneti-
cists, statisticians, behaviorists, physiologists, anatomists, biological
chemists, physical chemists, psychologists, physicians, hygienists,
endocrinologists, psychiatrists, immunologists, educators, social workers, clergymen, sociologists, economists, etc. But the practical results
of these accomplishments are surprisingly small. This immense amount
of knowledge is disseminated in technical reviews, in treatises, in the
brains of men of science. We have now to put it together . . . Then,
it will become productive . . . There are great difficulties in such an
undertaking."

ALEXIS CARREL,
Nobel Prize recipient
in physiology and medicine

IN PRECEDING CHAPTERS we have explored Man's role within the
biological and physical universe. In order to locate his own position within this universal human role, the student of hominology
has in previous chapters attempted to identify his philosophical
commitments and moral values. In this chapter we are concerned
with some of the difficulties students may encounter in their attempt to consider some urgent contemporary problems typical of
the industrial society in which they live.

By means of frameworks designed to clarify differences in
philosophical and moral orientations, the communication gap that
exists between different groups of people can be substantially nar-
rowed. Another aid to effective communication consists of the recognition of some of the common pitfalls that contribute to distorted thinking. Students should also be aware of the basic premises that underlie disputes within the social and behavioral sciences. When avoidance of pitfalls and an awareness of underlying
premises are combined with an understanding of one's own and

328

other people's Criteria of Reality, discussions of contemporary human problems become increasingly meaningful and mature.

Before contemporary problems are investigated, the following common pitfalls to logical thinking should be recognized:

THE PITFALLS

1. *Symbol-traps:* Symbols are concepts or objects that stand for or represent other concepts or objects, such as a flag for a country, a word for an idea, an act for a feeling, a gesture for an emotion. Words, phrases, ideas, acts, mores, colors, facial features, clothing, accents, surnames, or national groups may symbolize "good" or "bad" to some people. As we have seen in Chapter 2, the use of symbols has assisted Man in becoming human. But their misuse can dehumanize him. Those who react automatically or illogically to symbols are prone to distortion of judgment and may lose their freedom of thought.

2. *Prejudice:* People often react with fear or curiosity to something new or strange. Some tend to be strongly in favor of, or against, a person, idea, or form of behavior that is "different." Prejudice exists when a premature judgment is made without impartial examination and acceptance of all the evidence. Usually a strong emotional component is present in prejudice that blocks rational thinking.

    It is a mistake to assume that human differences cause prejudice. The reverse is true: because human beings are prejudiced, human differences become significant, and are used as a basis for discrimination. Ethnic, racial, religious, national, class, cultural, physical and sexual differences serve as ready-made "hooks" upon which prejudices may be conveniently hung. In order to avoid discrimination one must rid oneself of the prejudice rather than attempt to do away with the "hooks." If human differences did not exist, prejudiced people would invent substitutes for them since prejudice always requires a vehicle for its expression.

3. *Fixation:* This word is derived from Latin, meaning "to fasten." Persons who are victims of fixation are "fastened" to one or a few aspects of a much broader problem. They tend to ignore relevant factors, and are "tuned out" to all ideas other than their own. Therefore, they cannot consider alternate

points of view. Their narrow outlook distorts the issues with which they concern themselves and their effectiveness for problem solving is proportionally diminished.

4. *Sloganeering:* Slogans or labels can serve as trigger-mechanisms that cause people to discharge emotions which may not be appropriate to the given situation. Slogans tend to block off rational thinking and may cause people to react impulsively either for or against the slogan-loaded cause.

5. *Labeling:* This occurs when a complex phenomenon is given a label or a "name" implying that by attaching the label to the phenomenon one automatically understands it. Labeling is a form of Verbal Structuralism (Chapter 3).

   Sometimes attaching a label to another person serves as a means of expressing hostility. This type of labeling represents an attempt to destroy an idea or an opponent by placing him into a position where he becomes easily vulnerable. This distorts the true image of the person who is being falsely labeled and destroys the essence of the idea or concept to which the misleading label is attached.

6. *Stereotyping:* Stereotyping is uncritical generalization. It may serve as a substitute for thinking and convey a false impression of validity. It leads to inaccurate evaluation and to rigidity of action when dealing with the people who have been stereotyped.

7. *Event-Relationship Confusion:* Two aspects of this pitfall are 1) confusing the cause with the effect of an event, as when a symptom is believed to be the cause of a disease rather than a manifestation of it, and 2) causal-coincidental confusion, which results from the tendency to mistakenly assume that a relationship exists between two completely independent events that occur at the same time and place.

8. *Ethnocentrism: Ethnos* is the Greek word for nation. Ethnocentrism represents a tendency to use the norms of one's own culture to evaluate other groups. People who suffer from ethnocentrism are often unable to recognize the faults of their own group. They fail to realize that differences between people do not necessarily imply superiority or inferiority.

9. *Value Inversion:* This occurs when a member of one group demands improved conditions for himself or his group which,

in turn, he would not grant to another, different group. He may ask for an end to discrimination in the name of social justice but would not hesitate to use another group as a scapegoat were he in a position to do so. This type of behavior represents an inconsistency in expressed values.

10. *Tokenism:* Tokenism is a gesture intended to mislead. An employer, wishing to avoid the reputation of discrimination, may hire a few members of a minority group as a token of equal employment. By using "front-men," noncompliance with moral obligation may be disguised. Tokenism aims to avoid guilt and to diminish outrage by those whose rights are violated.

11. *Uniqueness Fallacy:* Throughout human history a tendency has existed to regard certain human groups as uniquely good or uniquely bad. An impartial study of many different peoples will show that no race, nationality, or ethnic group can legitimately claim that it possesses more desirable attributes than any other. Behavioral differences between human groups can usually be traced to opportunity and to cultural or environmental factors. Furthermore, "desirability" is a subjective concept which lends itself to many different kinds of definitions and interpretations.

12. *Semantic Confusion:* Futile arguments occur when those involved in a discussion use the same words but assign different meanings to them. This results in semantic confusion. The concept of semantics goes beyond the definition of words and includes the meaning of ideas which words express. Semantic confusion involves a lack of clarity in the definitions of words, in basic assumptions, and in the use of Criteria of Reality. Discussions that are obscured by semantic confusion seldom lead to a constructive exchange of ideas.

13. *Mythology:* Massmann (1966) maintains that invalid generalizations may lead to a destructive mythology. He believes that everyone has a mythology and that this plays a major role in the evaluation of events as we observe them in the universe. This personal mythology is often an outgrowth of the generalizations which we make throughout our lives. Massmann believes that generalizations based on insufficient evidence and invalid particularizations from valid generaliza-

tions tend to cause us to make "selfish and unrestrained choices." Massmann claims that the idea that men can live without any mythology is a pitfall and he views all of the pitfalls mentioned in this chapter as aspects of a destructive mythology.

14. *Ignoring Ethology:* Man has had millions of years of experience as a hunter of game and only a bare ten thousand years of experience as a member of an agricultural economy. We are unwilling owners of glandular, metabolic, and neural systems geared to hunting, which became a burdensome physiological handicap after the Neolithic Revolution with its shift to agriculture and animal husbandry. Consequently, we are internally overstimulated if we are living in societies that do not provide sufficient outlet for the excitement and expenditure of energy which men once used to hunt animals with primitive weapons. If a society fails to offer young people constructive outlets for their physiological drives destructive outlets will be utilized.

15. *Ignoring Nature:* Modern Man has changed nature too extensively while changing himself too little in the process. As a result, he finds himself alienated from nature and no longer sees himself as a vital part of it. Modern Man fails to realize that as he alienates himself from nature and the universe, he is inevitably alienating himself also from his fellowman.

This pitfall may be extended to include "human nature." Attempts to reach solutions that ignore human nature are bound to fail although they may be idealistically desirable. Trying to conform to a given social norm at the expense of using originality and creativity represents another pitfall to which modern man is prone. Social pressure to maintain conformity may be viewed as one of the hindrances to mankind's forward thrust along the Developmental Levels which in hominology we have hypothesized as the path of human moral progress.

BASIC PREMISES

Failure to examine basic premises in a given issue or dispute within the human sciences is a common cause of misunderstanding. Intelligent scientists may fail to explore the basic assumptions from which the validity of their conclusions is derived. Different basic premises play a role that is related to the different Criteria of Reality described in Chapter 3. Before considering contemporary problems, it is desirable to learn how to identify basic assumptions that underlie different points of view.

What different premises underlie the following quotations seemingly reflecting conflicting conclusions?

". . . The notable thing about *human* behavior is that it is learned. Everything that a human being does as such, he has to learn from other human beings" (Montagu, 1968).

". . . We prefer to emphasize that there is no cultural development which is independent of man's biology . . . everything man does has an evolved biological component" (Freedman, 1967).

Nature or Nurture?

Different opinions on a wide range of behavioral science subjects may stem from different basic assumptions within the heredity-environment or the nature-nurture continuum discussed in Chapter 13. Such topics include origins of intelligence, violence, crime-proneness, mental illness, racial differences, male-female behavioral differences, cultural variations, and so on.

Ideas regarding human behavior held by those who tend to favor extreme views on the nature-nurture question differ from concepts derived by those who hold eclectic views such as Huntington (1959) who observes that

> . . . biological inheritance, physical environment and cultural endowment . . . all are essential and all play a part in every phase of activity. Any one of the three may acquire predominant importance under special circumstances, although it may not be of greater weight than the others in the long run.

Different premises involving the role of nature and nurture underlie the current controversy among behavioral scientists on the origins of aggression. This may be seen by the following contradictory points of view:

". . . aggression in human society is largely a cultural attribute" (Crook, 1968).

". . . there is so far no convincing evidence that the aggressive response is . . . any less instinctive than the sexual response" (Storr, 1968).

". . . those who speak of 'innate aggression' in man appear to be lacking in any understanding of the uniqueness of man's evolutionary history" (Montagu, 1965).

". . . Human aggression . . . is a deep-seated universal drive" (Carthy and Ebling, 1964).

A better way to examine controversial subjects than taking one-sided views may be to use an analytical approach illustrated by the following example:

1. Possible definitions of aggression.
   a. Psychobiological energy which can be converted into either constructive or destructive behavior.
   b. A determined pursuit of one's interests.
   c. Anger or hostility, controlled or uncontrolled.
   d. A tendency to be belligerent and a desire to fight.
   e. A need to destroy, inflict pain, sadism.
2. Possible environmental sources of aggression.
   a. Frustrations relating to biological, psychological, or social needs.
   b. Indoctrination and conditioning by social precedents.
   c. Imitating aggressive behavior. Aggression is "contagious."
   d. Real or imagined danger; threat to security or status.
   e. Reaction to population density, over-population, crowding.
   f. Territorialism.
3. Possible indigenous sources of aggression.
   a. Hormonal factors such as androgen, adrenalin.
   b. Illness, mental or physical.
   c. Pain, neurological factors.
   d. Physiological reaction to drugs, alcohol, toxins, chemical stimulants, irritants.
4. Possible phylogenetic sources of aggression.
   a. A genetic makeup subject to arousal when exposed to specific cues, signs, or stimuli.
   b. Genetic residuals of a physiology geared for hunting by several million years of natural selection.
   c. Genetically based tendencies for dominance-exploration and establishment.
   d. Genetic characteristics linked to specific chromosomes.

e. Inherited physiological need for stimulation, excitement, challenge.

f. Territoriality.

5. Possible congenital sources of aggression.

a. Constitutional or physiological predisposition of a given individual to irritability.

b. Lack of frustration-tolerance due to congenital, glandular, neurological, or metabolic makeup.

Items 2f and 4f in the foregoing list mention *territorialism* and *territoriality*. Territoriality implies an innate tendency to hold and defend territory. In contrast, territorialism is used here as a culturally determined method for establishing social organization. Territorialism or territoriality (depending on which one accepts as valid) is manifested in the concept of boundaries among nations, states, municipalities, cooperatives, communes, tribes, and in games and sports that people play. It persists symbolically in the human mind as people feud over whether someone has trespassed their professional "territory" or has entered their disciplinary "domain" without proper credentials.

Paul (1967) represents an impartial conclusion on the question of nature-nurture. Although he placed the issue within psychopathology, his comment can be applied generally:

> Do the roots of psychopathology lie tangled in the skein of interpersonal relations . . . that is, in the social processes, or do they reach deeper, originating in hereditary predispositions? Again, the case is necessarily ambiguous in this regard. The data can be so interpreted as to support either view.

EVOLUTION OR REVOLUTION?

In every nation there are people who are keenly aware of the need for social, technological, political, religious, environmental, and other reforms. A basic question with which these people must cope is, Can the desired changes be brought about within the system or is the system too rigid to permit change? Consider the following divergent views on some of the contemporary political systems:

COMMUNISM:

1. Communism is a political system designed to give every worker ownership of the available natural resources and of the eco-

nomic sources of production, thereby doing away with unemployment and ruthless economic competition. It takes from each according to his ability and gives to each according to his need. Thereby, it offers freedom from the age-old exploitation of man by man.

2. Communism fosters violent revolutions making ruthless force and fear the basis of its survival. It cannot function without a secret police which keeps the ruling clique in power. It deprives men of effective incentives for labor and destroys the hard-won freedoms of speech, religion, and personal choice. Thereby, it creates a more brutal exploitation of man by man.

SOCIALISM:

1. Socialism avoids the excesses of communism permitting people to keep most of their individual freedom. It maintains that, legitimately, the industrial resources of a nation belong to all of the people; that government ownership of land will enable every person to receive his fair share of the benefits that a society offers. By discouraging competition for materialistic gain, it raises the quality of human lives.

2. When the government owns and runs everything as it does in socialism, a stagnation sets in that retards progress. Managers gain power by influence instead of merit. Inefficient people become entrenched in jobs that serve no useful purpose. The economy becomes stifled by unnecessary regulations imposed by inefficient bureaucrats who are intent on maintaining their favored position. The quality of human lives deteriorates as people become bogged down by governmental restrictions and regulations which stifle incentive and destroy individual initiative.

CAPITALISM:

1. Capitalism is regulated by the laws of supply and demand. By a distribution of corporate stock ownership, it can meet some of the demands of socialism without its disadvantages. It permits voters to freely elect those who govern them. In modern capitalism, there are government safeguards against exploitation. Individual incentives contribute to maximum efficiency, productivity, and diversification. Rewards are competitively tied to satisfying human needs. In an open market, people are free to buy products and services that they believe fit their needs best. This creates maximum individual freedom and permits a corresponding human dignity.

2. Capitalism is a system aimed at exploiting the working people and the poor. It serves those in power who maintain their positions by financial manipulations and protective laws rather than by genuine contributions to society. Under the guise of

freedom, it permits the financial structure to mold public opinion. Since in-groups operate the educational systems and own the chief communications media, "freedom" is an illusion. Greed and acquisitiveness are rewarded and this destroys human dignity.

When opinions differ on important topics, how can we determine what is acceptable to us? How can the truth be tested? The study of hominology cannot give anyone the answer, but if students apply the Criteria of Reality and the definitions of the Moral Values, they can develop a personal hominological approach which will help them recognize the origins of differences of opinion and enable them to understand why different points of view exist.

How Long Can We Wait?

There is considerable misunderstanding about the role of evolution and revolution in accomplishing change. Evolution *is* revolution enacted slowly. For example, Montagu (1965) refers to the changes which occurred in the last million years as *"The Human Revolution."* Some writers describe evolution as a much slower process than revolution but one that is less apt to trigger off undesirable "side-effects." They point out that as in medicine, side effects may make a cure less desirable than the disease. However, people who are acutely disturbed about the presence of injustice are not willing to wait for evolution to correct what seems to them to be a matter requiring an immediate remedy. The black nationalist leader, Malcom X, once said,

> It's impossible for a chicken to produce a duck egg even though they both belong to the same family of fowl. A chicken just doesn't have it within its system to produce a duck egg . . . it can only produce according to what that particular system was constructed to produce . . . it is impossible for this (political, economic) system (in this country) to produce freedom right now for the black man . . . and if ever a chicken did produce a duck egg, I'm quite sure you would say it was certainly a revolutionary chicken (Breitman, 1967).

But according to the theory of evolution, a chicken could produce a duck egg if the necessary mutations occurred over a long enough period of time. It was by means of evolution that one-celled protoplasm eventually evolved into modern man with over nine billion interconnecting cortical synapses in his brain. According to the theory of evolution, this took at least two billion years. But it represents a much greater "revolution" than changing a chicken into a duck. The question hinges on how long we are willing to wait for change to take place. We cannot blame underprivileged people for not wanting to wait until a chicken lays a duck egg. Much depends on what side of the fence one finds oneself in a society where there are people with advantages and others with disadvantages. As we approach a Level Seven mentality (*Emphasis on Dedication*), an increasing amount of support can be predicted for those who must "swim across the river with a burden of lead on their backs" (see p. 150).

There are some people who are not concerned as much with evolution or revolution as they are with spiritual rehabilitation. They may accept the "good things" that a system provides, but prefer to do without many material benefits if possession entails sacrificing spiritual and creative values. Gonzales (1967), a leader of a Mexican-American group reflects this dilemma in one of his epic poems in which he rejects the current materialistic pattern of modern life with its undue emphasis on affluence and prosperity.

In an introduction to *Understanding Media*, McLuhan (1964) writes, "The mark of our times is a revulsion against imposed patterns." Such a revulsion is consistent with the concept of mankind's movement from one developmental level to another one.

Materialism, however, must not be considered as something modern. In most instances, past historical eras fostered a materialism that may have been different in form but not better in quality than any materialism that exists today. For the vast majority of people the so-called "virtues" of past ages were largely derivatives of fear, superstition, ritual, and rationalizations for conquests. The revulsions that some contemporary people feel towards "imposed patterns" may reflect a rejection of self-centered values associated with a previous behavioral focus on Level Six and a present striving to go beyond this.

However, any change in the acceptance of behavioral patterns must be viewed in the way that Means (1970) describes human development. He points out that

> On the level of man himself, the evolution of the species passes from the banks of Olduvai gorge perhaps two million years ago to modern man, Homo sapiens with all his attendant hopes and weak-

nesses. And in this scope of geological time, man himself has been here but a moment. Since psychologically we have a need for security and uniformity . . . it may be very difficult for us to identify . . . (with) . . . a world of process, of change. . . .

The typical American does not stop long enough to grasp and digest the organic-process view suggested above. If he did, he might think more easily in terms of organic connections between man and nature.

SURVIVAL FOR WHAT PURPOSE?

There are many thoughtful students who are deeply disturbed by the serious problems with which contemporary Man must cope. If questioned why they are concerned they may answer that these problems threaten human survival. However, few of these students have ever asked themselves, Why should the human species necessarily survive? What sound and compelling argument is there to justify our continuing existence as a species?

If pressed, some students might offer the pleasure principle of hedonism as a reason for survival. Some would refer to a natural law of survival or to religious explanations. Others would maintain that an unbiased arbitrator would not be able to find any valid reason against replacing *Homo sapiens* by one of the more than 300,000 species of living plants, or by one of the more than 2 million species of living animals.[1]

If the pleasure principle of hedonism is insufficient (even if it includes the concept of pleasure-through-social-service); if the survival for the sake of survival school of thought is unacceptable; and if religious explanations alone are unconvincing (as they are to some students), what possible basis remains for justifying mankind's continuation? Why shouldn't Man now join the estimated 5 million species that since the dawn of life have become extinct? Is there a rational answer to the question, Survival for what purpose? Or must we all agree with the Persian Poet who wrote nearly a thousand years ago:

> Myself when young did eagerly frequent
> Doctor and Saint, and heard great argument
> About it and about: but evermore
> Came out by the same door that in I went.

---

[1] Approximately three-quarters of this estimated number of species are insects. Thousands of new species of all kinds are discovered yearly. Any of these may be legitimate candidates for mankind's present dominant position on earth.

With them the seed of wisdom did I sow
And with my own hand wrought to make it grow
And this is all the Harvest that I reaped
I came like water and like wind I go.[2]

If the most profound reason for existence is that we must "survive in order to survive," do we have the right to that survival? Is a student really ready to take his place in the world today if, after many years of education, he is completely incapable of giving any logical reason why he or his species should continue to exist?

Beyond Satisfactions

Perhaps part of the difficulty in justifying survival is that hedonistic explanations do not go beyond Level Six (*Emphasis on Fulfillment*). Most of the contemporary "searchers" for Man's basic nature (see Chapter 8) have repudiated the idea that "satisfactions" and rewards alone can justify human existence. Du Noüy writes of a "human destiny." Simpson contributes the idea of nature discovering its potentialities through human evolution. Nogar sees something pertinent to human survival in a "God-centered" universe. Operin seems to envision a cosmic thrust that would justify the survival of an efficient, complex organism such as Man.

The study of hominology suggests that participation in a succession of transcendental changes leading to a developmental improvement in interpersonal relationships gives human life a rational basis for survival. This justification for human survival includes Ewing's (1965) suggestion for making personal behavior "less and less inconsistent by applying the same principle (dedication) more and more thoroughly . . . to more and more people." Whatever the student may eventually adopt as an acceptable reason for mankind's continuation, it should be consistent with his own Criteria of Reality, and it must fit into the historical framework in which he views human development.

Nature's Role in Human Survival

Nature has been described as using a "biological morality" (Fisher, 1970) to help regulate human lives. While most writers may reject such anthropomorphic concepts of nature, some see nature as a teacher "punishing" those who transgress her laws

---

[2] From the Rubaiyat of Omar Khayyam (1942).

(Ardrey, 1970). Such views ascribe a much deeper meaning to current events than is apparent to the casual observer. For example, the high rate of automobile accidents, wars, suicides, and homosexuality is interpreted by such writers as part of nature's plan to reduce human populations. Likewise, women's liberation movements are given additional justification as contributing toward population control by offering alternatives to motherhood. Even drug addiction is seen as representing nature's effort to counteract interest in sexuality, thereby reducing excess breeding. Those who maintain that the exploding over-population is mankind's gravest problem insist no one can really improve any other human condition unless he first solves the problem of population density throughout the world. They claim that if Man fails to do so, nature will restore population equilibrium by war, disease, famine or by mass poisoning through pollution.

To what extent is Man a unique animal and emancipated from nature's laws that govern the breeding behavior of nonhuman animals? This question can be broadened into one that every student of behavioral science must face, To what extent and under what circumstances are man-animal comparisons valid? (Lockard, 1971). Animals have been described as nature's children. Are we humans still members of nature's family and subject to her laws?

GROUP VERSUS INDIVIDUAL IDENTITIES

Would it be more desirable if the world were composed of many diverse groups of people holding fast to their own culture and ethnic identities, or would it be better if a new idea of mankind emerged representing a synthesis of all human cultures and incorporating all human biological variants?

Advocates of cultural pluralism and those who wish to see racial and ethnic identities preserved argue that diversification encourages a broad tolerance toward human differences. They believe that it would be undesirable for diverse groups to relinquish their identity by joining the mainstream of human life to become lost within its flux.

On the other hand, some behavioral scientists believe that the emphasis which has been placed on racial, ethnic, and cultural differences is basically irrational. They insist that minor genetic variations such as skin color, type of hair, eyes, and so on, have been over-emphasized, destroying the concept of human unity and creating artificial psychosocial distances between the peoples of the world.

Throughout history, ethnic and national differences have been emphasized at the expense of human universals and the essential genetic similarity of Man. Advocates of the "melting-pot" idea insist that emphasis on group identities should give way to greater stress on individual identities. They point out that assimilated cultures, while losing one kind of identity, gain a new one which may contribute more effectively to social stability. History offers examples of how people who were absorbed have enriched the population which assimilated them. Rome, Persia, Spain, China, Japan, and India are among the nations whose histories illustrate this. Much depends on one's personal attitude toward the loss or gain of an identity—one mother may say, as her daughter marries, "I have lost a daughter"; another mother may declare, "I have gained a son-in-law."

Historical Aspects of Human Unity

During the stage of Level Five (*Survival of the Fittest*), defeated ethnic or tribal groups were killed off and thus human differences were erased; within Level Six (*Emphasis on Fulfillment*), defeated national or ethnic groups were enslaved and this caused an eventual amalgamation of races; but within the aegis of a Level Seven (*Emphasis on Dedication*), the foregoing methods are obsolete. Instead, each ethnic or racial group must now attain equality, dignity, and self-respect. Some believe that in order to attain this effectively, a temporary cultural isolation may be required.[3] Once equality has been achieved, however, the matter of merging into other larger groups may be just a matter of time.

In writing the story of his sensational trip across the Atlantic in a ship of papyrus reeds with a crew of volunteers consisting of different nationalities, Heyerdahl (1971) observed that "Man is man wherever you find him: I feel he cannot be divided or united according to height, color, or pencil lines on a map." One of the most urgent tasks of our time is to explore and to eradicate the

---

[3] Klineburg, 1971, opposes this point of view.

destructive barriers that today still separate man from man. To accomplish this goal new definitions of Man must be evolved based on new ideas within the human sciences—ideas that would replace those worn-out concepts which in an earlier chapter we have termed *hominolags.*

WHAT IS FREEDOM?

Human beings are deprived of a chance to develop their own unique identities as individuals as long as they are arbitrarily assigned identities and forced to play a prescribed role associated with a given cultural, social, vocational, educational, ethnic, racial, linguistic, religious, national, economic or sexual group. The less rigid such roles are, the greater is the opportunity for individual creativeness and self-actualization. Women, people of advanced age, those physically or mentally "handicapped," persons who have had institutional records, are among the groups who feel that their opportunities in life have been curtailed because of the roles which society ascribes to them.

Obviously, every person is limited to some extent in his ability to extricate himself from the four human environments we have discussed in Chapter 9. But societies differ considerably in regard to the flexibility that they permit their members in expressing their uniqueness as individuals. In evaluating the different kinds of political systems mentioned earlier in this chapter, flexibility and degrees of freedom of choice represent important criteria to consider.

Since every human being has both phylogeny and ontogeny, his uniqueness as a person represents an essential aspect of his wholeness. Personal uniqueness can only be maintained within a social milieu that permits freedom of choice, expression, and movement. Such freedom is necessary to permit each person to establish an individual identity and to make it possible for him to enter into that developmental dimension which we have termed Level Seven.

In studying the whole Man, it is important to be aware of the fact that freedom, or the lack of it, not only pertains to our external environment but also applies to our inner self. External freedom is meaningless without a consideration of internal, psychological freedom. The person who is a slave to his own moods, desires, or to his psychological hang-ups has lost his freedom as much as a person chained to a wall. Both psychological factors within ourselves and opportunity for choice in our environment are elements that contribute to being free.

In considering the matter of freedom, it may be disconcerting to find influential philosophers convincingly arguing that freedom is, in fact, an illusion—an idealization that can exist only within the mind of Man but not in the world as it really is or ever will be. This raises the question of how to meaningfully define freedom. Can we say that freedom consists of the availability of options? Are these options real or illusionary?

If we accept the definition that freedom consists of the opportunity to make choices, we are immediately implying that freedom must be accompanied by responsibility. This responsibility is proportionate to the number of other persons that might be affected and the extent of the affect on each one by the choices we make. Thus a hermit's responsibilities may differ from those of a person whose decisions will affect other people's lives.

Our opportunity of choice between alternative modes of action is likely to be accompanied by ambivalences, anxiety, and even frustration and guilt. Is there any wonder, then, that people are often prone to give up their freedom in order to evade responsibility and gain greater ease of mind? Freedom without responsibility leads to social and personal disintegration and when this occurs we are inclined to have "responsibility" imposed upon us as in a police state. If we do not have the necessary internal strength of mind to handle freedom of choice, we may assign decision-making to someone who will lead our lives for us.

NEW IDEAS

Hoagland (1964) maintains that "Science and purpose are related to man's unique ability as an ethical animal to control evolution." Later, he adds, ". . . new ideas—that is, new insights—are analogous to new mutations of the genes." Analogies of this type are possible only if one is willing to cross disciplinary boundaries to evolve a frame of reference in which different concepts such as mutations and "new ideas" can be compared.

Boring (1964) observes, ". . . man must be content to accept very considerable limitations in the range of his apperception and in the adequacy with which he can scan traces of his past experience." The acceptance of one's limitations is reflected in an open-mindedness to diverse views, which the study of hominology encourages. Diverse views are the rule rather than the exception when it comes to the matter of human nature.

Hirsch (1963), for example, sees that "the effects of experience are conditioned by the genotype." Skinner (1966) takes another view. He considers books such as Lorenz's *On Aggression* (1963) as "seriously misleading if it diverts our attention from the relevant manipulable variables in the current environment. . . ." Skinner concludes:

> Purpose, adaptation, imitation, aggression, territoriality, social structure, and communication—concepts of this sort have, at first sight, an engaging generality. They appear to be useful in describing both ontogenetic and phylogenetic behavior and to identify important common properties. Their very generality limits their usefulness, however . . . .

Where can Man look to obtain a true reflection of himself? Peering into a mirror of interspecies comparisons, Morris (1967) sees Man as a "vertical, hunting, weapon-toting, territorial, neotenous, brainy, Naked Ape, a primate by ancestry and a carnivore by adoption. . . ." Looking at biology, Dobzhansky (1962) concludes, "Man is the last-born, the keenest, the most complex, the most subtle of the successive layers of life . . . Man is the ascending arrow of the great biological synthesis."

On the other hand, Langdon-Davies (1961) considers it "foolish . . . to suggest that man must be higher and more progressive than, let us say, an octopus. It is like saying one boy is better at mathematics than another boy is at Greek." Simpson (1951) has found that "man is much the most knowing animal . . . Man is also the responsible animal." Herzberg (1966) claims that, at the first view, "man is . . . an animal and his overriding goal as an animal is to avoid the pain inevitable in relating to the environment." Later he adds:

> When we look at man in his totality, however, we find that in addition to his avoidance nature there exists a human being—a human being who seems to be impelled to determine, to discover, to achieve, to actualize, to progress and add to his existence.

Simpson (1962) is correct when he notes that evolution which created Man "cannot be understood as a purely biological process, nor adequately described as a history of cultures." He finds that culture and biology are both necessary to explain Man. But the crucial questions that remain unanswered are, to what extent biology?—to what extent culture?—to what extent something more than both of these? It is difficult to give acceptable answers to these questions, not only because sufficient information on cultural patterns and biological drives is lacking, but because the available facts are so complex and controversial that a consensus is not easily obtained. Manning (1967), speaking of animal behavior in general, states,

> The problem of selection and organization is particularly acute for compilers of a textbook on animal behavior. The subject is so diffuse, embracing neurophysiology at one end, and at the other including a good deal of ecology. Everyone will have his own ideas on how best to bring some semblance of order to this vast and diverse material.

In Chapter 8, the work of some contemporary writers who have attempted to integrate knowledge about total Man was reviewed. This review revealed that each of the so-called searchers found answers to the problem of integration which reflected his own unique beliefs, observations, and interpretations. All of these writers used similar considerations of the past, present, and future in their study of the whole Man. But they differed among themselves in regard to how past and contemporary events were incorporated in their final syntheses.

In part, all searchers will omit certain elements because they are human beings with human limitations. But there is also implicit in their work a problem that confronts every student of Man's nature. We tend to add the parts and arrive at a sum total when we analyze and integrate. In doing so, we may forget that the study of the whole Man includes something more—a synthesis and unity which adds other dimensions, qualities, and complexities.

TEN URGENT CONTEMPORARY PROBLEMS

As we arrive at the here-and-now, we find that many of the world's people are facing urgent problems typical of today's industrialized nations. Ten of these contemporary problems have been jointly selected by two Japanese scientists[4] and the author after consultations with a cross-section of people representing the general population in Japan, Europe, and the United States.

The problems were selected on the basis of how universal they seemed to be among societies geared to manufacturing.[5] It is important to identify basic premises, to avoid the pitfalls mentioned in this chapter, to utilize the Criteria of Reality and other hominological perspectives when these are appropriate to the discussions of the following problems:

1. Overpopulation accompanied by the exhaustion and misuse of the world's resources, and the pollution of the air, water, soil, which is disrupting the earth's ecology.

2. The divided world of communism and noncommunism; the rivalry among nations and groups within nations leading to danger of thermonuclear wars, conventional wars, and other forms of violence.

3. The dwindling need for manpower in an automated technology; the problem of unemployment, increased leisure, and lack of opportunity to contribute meaningfully to society by one's labor.

4. The increase in the amount of neurosis, mental illness, and general inability of men to adjust satisfactorily to the institutions of their society.

5. The role of individual freedom and personal choice and its survival within complex, bureaucratic societies.

6. Exploitation of the have-nots by the haves leading to the existence of poverty and the unequal distribution of wealth and power.

7. Discrimination stemming from racial, ethnic, religious, political, class, caste or cultural differences causing social in-

---

[4] The two Japanese scientists are Professor Nobuo Nakanishi, Department of Educational Psychology, Osaka University, and Mr. Masami Onimaru, a clinical and research psychologist, Osaka-Minami National Hospital, Japan.

[5] In a study of these problems within a course of hominology, it may be desirable to divide the class into ten groups and to assign to each group one problem for investigation and discussion. Then group leaders can present a summary of their group's conclusions to the class. Questions and further class discussions may then follow. Of course, smaller classes make it possible to assign the problems to individual students for research and comments.

justice and a failure to accept every human being solely on the basis of what he or she is and does.

8. The increase in crime, violence and drugs by some of today's youth; the rejection of established values and traditional authority by many young people of our society.

9. The role of sex within our culture; the high rate of unhappy marriages, and the search for an acceptable role for the male and female in today's complex world.

10. The ascendency of material values and decline of spiritual ones; the lowering of the quality of human lives; the disappearance of meaning and purpose in human existence.

The hominological approach encourages the student to view these problems in their widest perspectives. For example, a better understanding of problems concerning social unrest may be obtained from world-wide surveys[6] than from news reports describing events occurring in a section of one country. The study of the universal aspects of a problem can help to clarify a local or regional manifestation of the problem. New insights are gained when such problems are viewed in the light of their geographical spread and their historical depth. This permits the use of analogies, comparisons and a "common image" (Ferkiss, 1969).

In such discussions we should also keep in mind philosophical factors such as the difference between legal obligations and moral obligations. Hominology helps define moral responsibility by its description of the four moral values and by presenting the reference points of human moral progress that are inherent in the Developmental Levels.

(See also Introduction pages vii to xiv.)

SUMMARY

Fifteen pitfalls to rational thinking were described. The nature-nurture controversy was explored. Evolution and revolution were compared. The question, Survival for what purpose? was asked and a variety of answers were offered. The problem of group survival versus assimilation was examined. The nature of freedom was discussed. Ten urgent contemporary problems which industrialized societies face were identified on an international basis.

---

[6] Like the one in *U.S. News & World Report,* Vol. LXIX, No. 17, October 26, 1970.

REFERENCES

ARDREY, R.: *The Social Contract.* New York, Atheneum, 1970.

BORING, E. G.: Cognitive dissonance: its use in sciences. *Science, 145*:680-685, Aug. 14, 1964.

BREITMAN, G.: *The Last Year of Malcolm X.* New York, Schocken, 1967.

CARTHY, J. D., AND EBLING, F. J. (Eds.): *The Natural History of Aggression.* London, Academic, 1964.

CROOK, J. H.: The nature and function of territorial aggression. In Montagu, M. F. A. (Ed.): *Man and Aggression.* London, Oxford U. P., 1968.

DOBZHANSKY, T.: *Mankind Evolving.* New Haven, Yale U. P., 1962.

EWING, A. C.: *Ethics.* New York, Free Press, 1965.

FISCHER, J.: Survival U: prospectus for a really relevant university. In DuBell, G. (Ed.): *Environmental Handbook.* New York, Ballantine Books, 1970.

FERKISS, V. C.: *Technological Man.* New York, New American Library, 1969.

FREEDMAN, D. G.: A biological view of man's social behavior. In Etkin, W.: *Social Behavior from Fish to Man.* Phoenix Science Series, Chicago, U. Chicago P., 1967.

GONZALES, R.: *I Am Joaquin.* Denver, privately printed, 1967.

HERZBERG, F.: *Work and the Nature of Man.* Cleveland, World, 1966.

HEYERDAHL, T.: The Voyage of Ra II. *National Geographic, 139*:44-71, Jan. 1971.

HIRSCH, J.: Behavior genetics and individuality understood. *Science, 142*: 1436-1442, Dec. 13, 1963.

HOAGLAND, H.: Science and the new humanism. *Science, 143*:111-114, Jan. 10, 1964.

HUNTINGTON, E.: *Mainsprings of Civilization.* Mentor Book, New York, New Am. Lib., 1959.

KHAYYAM, O.: *Rubaiyat.* In Fitzgerald, E.: *English Verse.* New York, David McKay, 1942.

KLINEBERG, O.: Black and white in international perspectives. *Am Psychol, 26*:119-128, 1971.

LANGDON-DAVIS, J.: *On the Nature of Man.* New York, New Am. Lib., 1961.

LOCKARD, R. B.: Reflections on the fall of comparative psychology. *Am Psychol, 26*:168-179, 1971.

LORENZ, K.: *On Aggression.* Translated by M. K. Wilson. New York, Harcourt, 1963.

MANNING, A.: The inner and outer cause of behavior. *Science, 157*:1159-1160, Sept. 8, 1967.

MASSMANN, S. H.: Myth, Freedom, and Political Thought. Paper presented at the Rocky Mountain Social Science Meeting at Fort Collins, Colorado, May 6-7, 1966.

MEANS, R. L.: *The Ethical Imperative.* New York, Doubleday, 1970.

McLUHAN, M.: *Understanding Media.* Signet Books, New York, New Am. Lib., 1964.

MONTAGU, M. F. A.: *The Human Revolution.* New York, Bantam Books, 1965.

MONTAGU, M. F. A. (Ed.): *Man and Aggression.* London, Oxford U. P., 1968.

MORRIS, D.: *The Naked Ape.* New York, McGraw, 1967.

PAUL, B. D.: Mental disorder and self regulating processes in culture: a Guatemalan illustration. In Hunt, R. (Ed.): *Personalities and Culture: Readings in Psychological Anthropology.* New York, Natural History P., 1967.

SIMPSON, G. G.: Evolution's two components: biological and cultural. *Science, 136*:142-145, April 13, 1962.

SIMPSON, G. G.: *The Meaning of Evolution.* New York, New Am. Lib., 1951.

SKINNER, B. F.: The phylogeny and ontogeny of behavior. *Science, 153*: 1205-1213, Sept. 9, 1966.

STORR, A.: *Human Aggression.* New York, Antheneum, 1968.

ADDITIONAL READINGS FOR CONTEMPORARY PROBLEMS

BINKLEY, L. J.: *Conflict of Ideals,* New York, Van Nostrand, Reinhold, 1969.

DISCH, R. (Ed.): *The Ecological Conscience—Values for Survival.* Englewood Cliffs, Prentice-Hall, 1970.

DUBOS, R.: *So Human an Animal.* New York, Scribner, 1970.

EIBL-EIBESFELDT, I.: *Ethology—the Biology of Behavior.* Translated by E. Klinghammer, New York, Holt, Rinehart, Winston, 1970.

FADIMAN, J.: *The Proper Study of Man.* New York, Scribner, 1970.

FINLAY, J. F. (Ed.): *Contemporary Civilization,* Chicago, Scott, 1967.

FULLER, R. B.: *Ideas and Integrity,* New York, Collier, Macmillan, 1969.

FULLER, R. B. et al: *Approaching the Benign Environment.* New York, Collier, Macmillan, 1970.

HALL, E. T.: *The Hidden Dimension.* Garden City, Anchor, Doubleday, 1969.

TOFFLER, A.: *Future Shock.* New York, Bantam, Random, 1971.

CHAPTER 15

CONCLUSIONS AND APPLICATIONS

In a liberal arts education subjects should be studied from the point of view of how this knowledge can be used to improve or enhance the future of Mankind. This is education in the context of evolution. For now that man is an active agent of his evolution, knowledge of the past must be consciously used to direct the future. The educational institution's function is to produce a good citizen, that is, one concerned with the evolution of Mankind. Without this meaning in mind, the cultural past appears as brilliant fragments of unrelated patterns.

EARL HUBBARD,
The Search Is On

W E HAVE COME to the end of our study of hominology and hopefully it is only a beginning of a continuing search for a deeper meaning of life. Our study of hominology has taught us that contemporary Man is related to all of life—to the entire universe. Dubos (1970) put it dramatically when he wrote:

The humanness of life depends, above all, on the quality of man's relationship to the rest of creation—the winds and the stars, to the flowers and the beasts, to smiling and weeping humanity.

Historically, Man has lacked the intraspecies inhibitions which prevent most other hunting animals from killing their own kind. Contemporary Man is beginning to recognize this lack of inhibition and to feel increasingly anxious about it. In this there is, at least, some basis of hope for our future. Prodded by our anxiety many of us are today attempting to reach a new level of moral improvement which mankind has not, except in rare instances, previously attempted to reach. To do away with contemporary Man's anxiety is to rid him of his present level of morality as well. Today we have crimes, injustice, wars and other serious problems, and their continued existence often leaves us in a state of pessi-

351

mistic despair. We tend to forget that Man's inhumanity to Man is a historical as well as contemporary phenomenon. How much better it is to feel morally anxious about our cruelty as many of us do now, than to boast as an Assyrian king did a few thousand years ago:

> I inflicted a defeat upon them . . . the king of Askelon who did not bow to my yoke. I deported and sent to Assyria, his family-gods, himself, his wife, his children, his brothers, all the male descendents of his family . . . himself I flayed; the rebels I killed in their cities, I have torn out the tongues of those who uttered blasphemies against my God, Ashur. I fed their corpses, cut in small pieces to dogs, pigs, Zibu-birds and vultures. . . . After I had performed this, I removed the corpses whose left-overs, after the dogs fed on them, were obstructing the streets. I beat the warriors to death before the gates like lambs. . . . From some I cut off hands and fingers, from others noses and ears; I deprived many of their sight. . . . I made a pile of the heads. . . . Their young men and maidens, I cast into the fire. I have destroyed the city, devastated it and delivered it to the flames. . . . The harvest, subsistence for its people, and hay, subsistence for the cattle . . . I set alight . . . Over the ruins my shadow rested; in gratification of my wrath I find contentment. The voice of men, the steps of flocks and herds, and happy shout of mirth, I put an end to them. . . .

No foreign aid plan was offered to the defeated nations by such ancient tyrants who typified one aspect of the "dog-eat-dog" conceptional world of Developmental Level Five and the self-gratification characteristic of the early stage of Developmental Level Six. Nor was there anything in those days comparable to an adverse world opinion to such acts of wanton cruelty. In evaluating the present, we must not *only* look forward to where we would like to be, but also backward to where we have been historically.

The study of mankind's historical past may help to explain contemporary events, but it can never justify them. As soon as behavior is justified it is likely to be perpetuated. We should be aware of this danger as through our study of the past we gain a deeper understanding of the present. As we view today's human problems, it is essential that we avoid both typology and the adoption of too narrow a focus. Thiessen (1968) comments on this in his critical review of Ardrey's *The Territorial Imperative:*

> Typological concepts in general are anti-genetic, despite their

biological connotations, as they deny individuals variation and preclude evolutionary change and adaption . . . it is obvious that all
behavior is an *amalgamation . . . of gene action, developmental
gradients and situational circumstances.* Herein lies the escape from
fatalism . . . (Italics are Kahn's).

Hopefully, the study of hominology has contributed a few
ideas to the "amalgamation" that should be considered in the discussion of the problems with which most contemporary industrial
societies are presently struggling. Haydu (1966) believes: "Modern psychobiology confirms earlier notions that man is not seen in
any activity as an unmodified biological being . . . he is . . . a historical creature."

Man, indeed, is a "historical creature" and an understanding of
Man's past is essential so that it can be blended into the "amalgamation" which Thiessen describes. This "blending" is the synthesis which hominology seeks to accomplish. In order to do this, personality and human social behavior must not be viewed as if they
occurred in a vacuum but rather as products of a developmental
spiral. Pattishall (1965) observes,

> The sequence of information and ideas begins on a solid biological
> and biochemical level, progresses into the realm of biosocial, with
> final attention being directed toward personality and social factors.

The attempt to understand what Man presently is and what he
will be in the future requires an exploration incorporating all of
the qualities which Thiessen, Haydu, and Pattishall describe. First,
there must be the sequential analysis of information and ideas,
then the clarification of the operating generic forces, and finally,
the amalgamation of that which Man is and has been since he began with the beginning of all things.

APPLICATION OF HOMINOLOGY

Ultimately the value of the study of hominology lies in its application. Hominology may be applied in three different ways: to
gain self-understanding; to obtain understanding of the behavior
of other people; to acquire insights into the processes that involve
human interactions. The Hominolograms, Criteria of Reality, Developmental Levels, Moral Values, and Pitfalls may be selectively
applied to a wide variety of situations that occur in everyday life.

Let us take the question, "Who is a fit parent?" for example.

We could apply the Moral Values as described in Chapter 12 to this question. The following conclusions might then be derived: fit parents are those whose motivation in having children primarily represent Dedication. Such parents know how to give love, that is, consider the need of their children first, even though this be at the expense of their own needs. It is important to distinguish between Dedication and pseudo-Dedication. Dedication is based on a realistic appreciation of a child's needs whereas pseudo-Dedication may take the guise of permissiveness and overindulgence.

Less fit parents would view their role primarily within the realm of the Duties. They would assume responsibility in preserving the species but also take into account their own limitations in capacity to satisfy their children's needs. Since they have a sense of duty, they would consider the over-population problem in deciding how many children to have. Parents who are themselves duty-motivated tend to teach their children to recognize their duties and obligations. In the absence of Dedication, however, an emphasis on the Duties alone may cause children to rebel neurotically or antisocially against their environment since it has failed to expose them to the experience of receiving and giving love.

Parents whose motivation for having children falls primarily within the Virtues represent still another category. Repression is dominant within such homes. Such parents typically use guilt to obtain compliance. Parents who overemphasize the Virtues at the expense of the other Moral Values may predispose their children to various types of maladjustments. Such children may adopt a fantasy life of sufficient intensity to compensate them for the rejection that is implied in the rigid attitudes of their parents.

Finally, there are people whose parental motivation falls primarily within the domain of the Graces. Their reason for having children is to conform to a convention established by society. For psychological and physiological reasons there may be no desire to have children but they wish to adhere to prescribed social patterns. Children of such parents are prone to become hominolopaths, living mental lives on a Developmental Level lower than that of the society in which they reside. Usually parents utilize a combination of Moral Values in their motivational pattern for having children. However, the distribution of the Moral Values within that pattern is important to the mental health of the child.

Other similar applications of the Moral Values within the Human Sciences may suggest themselves to the student.

Application of the Criteria of Reality

The Criteria of Reality may be used to help explain why it is often difficult for people to communicate with each other when differences of opinion exist. In the previous chapter it was mentioned that some people believe that freedom is a reality whereas others insist that it is an illusion. Differences of opinions on important questions may often be explained by referring to the Criteria of Reality.

Opinions on many vital issues differ because the underlying Criteria of Reality differ. If we examine the factors that cause people to adopt their unique combinations of Criteria of Reality (these factors are listed on page 57) we can understand why they react as they do.

The Criteria of Reality reveal the component parts of a person's basic philosophy of life. Since all of our behavior is colored by our personal philosophy, the Criteria of Reality may be likened to an imaginary pair of tinted glasses that all human beings wear. When people look at the world around them they can never be sure whether the hues they observe are actually there in reality or whether the coloration of facts and events reflect the tint in their own "glasses." As Plato pointed out long ago this tint may be the only reality men are capable of knowing.

The study of the various Criteria of Reality makes it possible for us to recognize the fact that "tints" of many different hues exist and to learn how these various shades and colorations develop through our life's experiences within the Four Environments described on pages 200-202. Some students who have been exposed to hominological insights believe that people who do not have any concept of their own Criteria of Reality will be unable to understand human behavior.

Application of the Developmental Levels

If we constantly evaluate which one of the Developmental Levels we are utilizing in a given situation, we may be able to exercise some control over our position on the developmental scale of human evolvement. The action theme of each Developmental

Level may be symbolized, generalized, or particularized.

Those who have studied how interpersonal relationships take place within the Developmental Levels will observe that people tend to respond on the same level on which they are approached. This does not apply to everyone since some people do not recognize that any higher levels exist than the one which they have adopted. However, there are other people who are more flexible and they will be prone to react to human contact on the same level on which contact was made.

Perhaps, the seeds to both psychotherapy and social improvement are inherent in this concept. Some people may believe that this view of human improvement is too optimistic. Nevertheless, it is known that by adopting a higher level, or a higher stage within the same level than is normative for a given society we can sometimes raise the quality of the lives of the people with whom we interact.

Occasionally we find our environment so structured that we tend to act on a lower level than we would consider desirable. For example, when the driver of an automobile takes the only parking space that is vacant on a busy city street he exploits a very limited ecological niche. By parking his own car there he has effectively eliminated the possibility of other cars parking on the street.

The action theme of Level Five is reflected here; for me to live you must die. Some people live their entire lives with no other thought in mind than to rid themselves of imagined competitors by symbolic—or actual—extermination. Such persons may gain achievements on Level Six but these will only be reflections of their Level Five ambitions. Any concept of a Level Seven may be beyond their grasp.

Provided they are aware of the options that are open to them, many individuals have some control over the selection of the Developmental Levels within which they wish to participate. For example, a vain person who feels threatened by the success of his neighbors may decide to improve the appearance of his house in order to destroy the satisfactions his neighbors have in the appearance of their own houses. This source of motivation places him symbolically within the action theme of Level Five.

If he recognizes the fact that he is in Level Five and is displeased, he can, if he wishes to do so, redirect his motivational drive to fall within the area of Level Six. He can deliberately attempt to utilize a different motivational basis for improving the appearance of his house. He can try to obtain personal satisfactions and fulfillment from the improved appearance of his home without thinking competitively about his neighbors. Or wishing to be on Level Seven he may, instead of improving the appearance of his own house, help to build a house for a handicapped person who needs shelter.

It is largely through our families and our jobs that most of us are able to make our major contributions to society. Yet, since we require the wherewithal to live and to support our families, our daily work cannot be entirely performed within Dedications. Nevertheless, the more our energies are directed toward the emerging Level Seven, the higher we have climbed the ladder of mankind's moral progress.

There are still many people today who restrict their outlook of the world and their daily activities entirely to the action themes of Levels Five and Six. The study of hominology may help us to identify such persons and to understand why their moral growth has been stunted.

How hominology may help us speculate about the future is illustrated by the hypothetical concept of Level Eight. If the world ever reaches a stage where injustice and suffering no longer exist, those living at that time may find themselves in a radical new kind of era beyond Dedication. We have no idea of how many thousands or hundreds of thousands of years in the future that may be. Theoretically, at least, it is possible to postulate a world so well organized that all human needs are met and suffering will have disappeared. Dedication will then no longer be possible and at that time, an existence may be envisioned in which humans will abandon the sense of selfhood and adopt a larger identity—one that merges with the entire universe. This will produce an entirely new kind of human being.

Hominological Algebra

For those wishing to adopt it, the continuation of the ongoing process described as the Eight Developmental Levels (Eight Ages of Man) can represent a theoretical criterion of desirability. Some people believe that in our contemporary era we are now moving from a focus on Level Six to one closer to Level Seven. This implies that in our time, goodness can be defined as an ever increasing emphasis on what in the study of hominology has been called genuine Dedication.

If we are willing to use advancement along the Developmental Levels as a measure of "goodness," the concept of goodness would vary with human development throughout time and with the diverse cultures of Man. However, when the expression of goodness is related to the concomitant level of human capacity for giving it expression, a stable concept of goodness emerges.

This view is analogous to the concept of the IQ which may remain constant even though, with time, the mental age of a child continues to increase. This is because normally the chronological age of the child increases proportionately to the mental age leaving the ratio of mental age to chronological age unchanged.

Similarly, goodness may be viewed as a ratio. In that case *maturity* would represent advancement along the continuum of the Eight Developmental Levels. *Capacity* would denote the estimated capability for giving maturity expression which a person, group, nation, or the entire human species has at any given time in history.

Persons who have reached the highest Developmental Levels within their societies may serve as examples and models of what others can achieve if the necessary motivation and willingness to make the required sacrifices are present. Other guidelines for estimating capacity are the circumstances under which a person or a group of persons live. Obviously people who must struggle fiercely in order to survive will be more goal-oriented towards Level Six than Level Seven and their Dimensions will be correspondingly narrow. On the other hand, circumstances which permit people to live within Level Six make it possible for them to aim for Level Seven. Thus, capacity for achieving maturity depends on the means one has at one's disposal, on motivation, and on the examples of others.

"Goodness" would then be defined as the practice of the maximum developmental maturity which any individual or group is capable of manifesting. Possessing capacity but not expressing it because of inertia, lack of motivation, or because of the adoption of a regressive value system would then be equated with "badness" (or hominopathology as we prefer to call it). The following formula could then be applied:

$$\text{GOODNESS} = \frac{\text{MATURITY}}{\text{CAPACITY}}$$

This is an example of a method designed to make abstractions such as goodness more concrete and easier to visualize. Students have postulated other formulas using the Moral Values. One of these illlustrates to what extent and under what circumstances moral and legal obligations may not coincide. Another one demonstrates how social harmony is equated with equality of opportunity. Some students feel that this type of algebraic approach to human behavior helps them see relationships and consequences of human interaction that would otherwise not be readily discernible. Others see no practical value in it.

Other Applications

Hominological concepts and hominolograms have been used in mental health clinics to aid in diagnosis and therapy. Group dynamic sessions have been centered on the results of hominolograms. In industry hominolograms have been used to explore relationships between salesmen and customers. Employers have used them to ascertain the basis of employee dissatisfaction. Hominolograms have been used in a variety of school and university situations to gauge changes in self-image and attitudes before and after exposure to certain types of courses or experiences. Social workers have given hominolograms experimentally to welfare recipients and reported that they gained a deeper understanding of their clients' needs. In order to understand the attitudes and values of minority groups, students have used hominolograms to explore different philosophies of life and cultural components. In a number of correctional institutions, exposing inmates to the role of the Moral Values as these are defined in the study of hominology created great interest. The Criteria of Reality and the Developmental Levels have been successfully taught to school children of various ages.

THE SEARCH FOR SYNTHESIS

Hominology represents an immodest venture—the integrated study of the whole Man. It has, however, been forced to reach a modest conclusion, namely, that as long as one confines oneself only to scientific methods, it is impossible for such a venture to be entirely successful. This is not because of human limitations alone and not because the "whole Man" is difficult to define, but rather because within science a perfect synthesis of the self, the species, and the universe may not be possible. Individual persons and the human species may be described as any other species within a zoological context, but none of this adds up to the concept of *whole Man* in its widest connotation.

Perhaps mystically, intuitively, and religiously we can unify Man in the universal sense that includes his total environment. But we cannot do this by a purely intellectual effort. In our role as behavioral scientists we constantly fragment Man and put him together again, but always with the hope of approaching closer to his essence. Hominologists as well as other behavioral scientists are like the "king's men" in the nursery rhyme:

> Humpty Dumpty sat on a wall
> Humpty Dumpty had a great fall
>
> All the king's horses and all the king's men
> Couldn't put Humpty Dumpty together again.

Man emerging (Allport, 1955) changes before our eyes even as we observe him. What was true of him yesterday is not true of him today and will not be true of him again tomorrow. Unfragmented Man becomes fragmented and incomplete the moment we attempt to view him. The very tools which we use to study him distort the object of our search. As Herrick (1961) recognizes,

> . . . classifications of behavior are useful devices for systematizing research and clarifying description; but it must not for a moment be overlooked that all of them are artifacts of method. The factors of behavior are so intricately interrelated and so differentially related in every act, that man-made devices may give an unbalanced picture of the actual situation.

The search for a synthesis must be continued, incorporating both physical and metaphysical considerations. Heitler (1963) noted,

> . . . the time is indeed ripe for us to begin to be aware of the metaphysical questions concealed behind the laws of nature, even if in the meantime we cannot answer them, or do not, in our capacity as scientists, intend to answer them.

Even if we cannot grasp the total impact of all that is inherent in Man's nature, the "awareness" of which Heitler speaks will make us reach for a deeper understanding of that which is the heart and substance of the human sciences. As Lee (1959) found after exploring many different cultures, "The way a man acts, his feelings of guilt and achievement, and his personality, are affected by the way he envisions his place within the universe."

MAN'S PLACE IN THE UNIVERSE

The study of hominology offers speculations which may be used in an attempt to locate Man's "place within the universe" (see Fig. 23). It does this by encouraging each student to try to discover for himself the nature and the origins of his own relationships with the universe so that he may better understand "his guilt and his achievement and his very personality." As he attempts to do this, it may be well to recall that the word, "personality," is derived from the Latin word *persona,* a mask worn on the stage by actors in the ancient dramas. The student of hominology who tries to peer behind the mask worn on the collective faces of mankind must first remove the one he himself wears if it distorts his view.

One of the problems which students of hominology and all students who attempt to study human nature must face is knowing how to recognize symptoms of Man's love and hate when these are disguised. It does not matter if they use the idea of Levels of Development or some other system to gain clarification. What is important is that they become a searcher for Man's basic nature and take into account historic perspectives and universals, remembering that in the study of Man, as elsewhere, "the whole is greater than the sum of the parts."

In spite of the turmoil in the world today, contemporary Man's greatest progress has been in the realm of morality and, ironically, this is the very area of human growth which we least understand and in which we seek the least credit for ourselves. For better or worse, this is as it must be since our anxiety at not being morally good enough helps to keep us morally good and tends to make us more so.

Unfortunately, anxiety is not enough to bring about the constructive changes which modern Man requires in order to solve

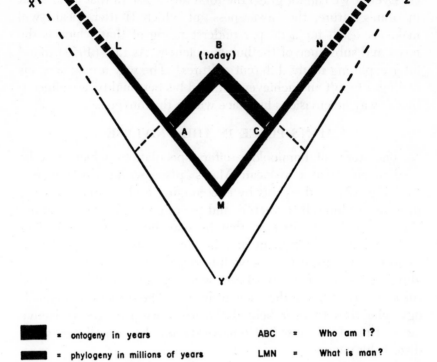

■	= ontogeny in years	ABC	=	Who am I ?
■	= phylogeny in millions of years	LMN	=	What is man?
—	= cosmology in billions of years	XYZ	=	What is the universe?

FIGURE 23. Man's Place in the Universe.

NOTE: To yourself you appear to be a stark and significant reality delineated by years of life. Use millions of years as a divisor when you measure yourself against Man; divide the quotient by billions to measure yourself within the universe. Though this may make you feel insignificant remember that you are the product of all that has occurred since the beginning of time.

his problems. Insight, determination, sacrifice, a sense of direction, an awareness of goals and purposes are also required. Most of all, there is need for love—as we, in the study of hominology, have attempted to define it.

And so, over the millions of years that have passed, Man, the weakest, has become the strongest, and Man, the cruelest, has become the most capable of being kind. That is the power of transcendence. Man has used culture to gain a strength far beyond his natural endowment. This use of culture has made him human. Of greater significance, however, is the hope that in our time, Man will direct more of his efforts toward striving to be not only human—but humane!

SUMMARY OF THE BOOK

Hominology, unlike other social and behavioral sciences does not have 'academic boundaries but uses facts drawn from all the diverse disciplines that deal with Man in order to develop an integrated study of human behavior. Broad area studies within anthropology, psychology, sociology, and biology as a rule use comparative methods to identify human *differences* and behavioral specifics. Hominology, on the other hand, seeks to explore human *universals* using historical and evolutionary perspectives. Increasingly, it is believed that both approaches are necessary in any meaningful attempt to understand what is human about humans.

The study of hominology assists students to explore the component parts of their philosophy of life, their moral values, and their developmental levels within a concept of mankind emerging. Students apply the results of their self-explorations to their search for Man's nature thus avoiding the isolation of the self in their study of the rest of the species.

Unlike the behavioral and social disciplines, the study of hominology is not primarily concerned with uncovering new facts. Instead it attempts to integrate a variety of facts from different disciplines and derive explanations having contemporary applications. Currently there are certain combinations of disciplines that also aspire to study the "whole Man." The means they use in attempting to achieve this goal differ from the methods employed within the study of hominology. This is because hominology is a unified study in a nondisciplinary setting, which combines self-analysis with evolutionary and historical perspectives.

REFERENCES

Allport, G. W.: *Becoming*. New Haven, Yale U. P., 1955.
Dubos, R.: *So Human An Animal*. Lyceum Editions, New York, Scribner, 1970.
Haydu, G. G.: *Reviews, Curr Anthrop*, 7:73-74, Feb. 1966.

HEITLER, W.: *Man and Science.* Translated by R. Schlapp, New York, Basic Books, 1963.

HERRICK, D. J.: *The Evolution of Human Nature.* New York, Harper, 1961.

LEE, D.: *Freedom and Culture.* New York, Prentice-Hall, 1959.

PATTISHALL, E.: Plenteous behavioral science. *Contemporary Psychol, 10:* 418-420, Sept. 1965.

THIESSEN, D. D.: Territory, that's what it's all about. *Contemporary Psychol, 13:*53-54, 1968.

Appendix

TOPICS FOR DISCUSSION BY CHAPTERS

Chapter 1

1. What justification, if any, exists for coining a new term such as "hominology" (pp. 8-9)?

2. Some social scientists believe that the best way to present the total Man concept is to enlarge the focus of one of the social or behavioral sciences rather than to attempt to integrate the study of human behavior outside of traditional disciplines. Others maintain that integration occurs spontaneously in the student's mind as he is exposed to the various disciplines. Discuss these alternatives to hominology.

3. Five characteristics of hominology are listed in this chapter (pp. 5-6). What would be the consequences of omitting any one of them from a study of the whole Man?

Chapter 2

1. Does the structural and physiological similarity that seems to exist between Man and Ape necessarily mean that there is a close phylogenetic or psychological relationship between these two species?

2. Recent experiments suggest that students of Primate behavior have placed too much emphasis on vocalizations and not enough on the idea that gestures and sign language may be used as a means of communicating between humans and apes. Discuss the differences between verbal and nonverbal communication in building a culture.

3. Some scientists believe that social modification and conditioning are the only significant factors molding human behavior. How would these scientists regard ethological tendencies such as territoriality, dominance, and socialization? Would they agree with the opinions expressed on p. 42-43?

4. Assume that territoriality and dominance are inherited characteristics among certain animals but do *not* apply to Man. Give

other than ethological explanations for the existence of human territorial concepts such as boundaries between tribes, cities, states, nations. Explain how hierarchies such as rank and position in government, the military service, industry, and in the professions could have come into being without requiring an ethological basis for dominance. Discuss why you do, or do not, believe that territoriality and dominance are inherited human characteristics.

5. If territoriality is a human characteristic on earth, is Man capable of divesting himself of it as he explores the moon and the planets?

6. What indications are there in contemporary society that we are failing to use our human capacity to delay gratifications (p. 43)?

Chapter 3

1. Some students of philosophy feel that there is only one *right* way of defining reality and truth. How would such persons explain "truth" in the following situation:

Student A is in one corner of a classroom. Student B is diagonally across from him in the opposite corner. The professor walks from student A to student B. Student A states that the professor is "moving away" but Student B insists that the professor is "approaching." The professor explains that both students are right even though they are expressing opposite points of view. Their statements reflect their different spacial positions in the classroom. Is this example analogous to those persons who are in diagreement because they occupy different philosophical positions?

2. Could a measure of harmony be achieved if people recognized that there are different philosophical positions which lead to different perceptions of reality? Discuss this question from the point of view of absolute truth, relative truth, and subjective truth.

3. The pragmatist usually has an *a priori* premise—such as "the greatest good for the greatest number." This premise is often subjective and personal. The empiricist, on the other hand, attempts to avoid subjective premises and search for neutral evidence. Compare how persons with these orientations might react

to such issues as: Should there be capital punishment? What is the best way to reduce taxes?

4. Give some examples of how numerical structuralism (i.e. statistical statements) may be used to yield misleading information.

Chapter 4

1. Are there other life areas that could have been included in the list given in this chapter (p. 85)? What others might have been included? Explain why.

2. Select any one of the Criteria of Reality and describe the typical daily actions of a person who accepts only *this* single Criterion for all of his life areas. For example, assume that a student states he only uses Intuitionism (100%) in his acceptance of Religion, Ethics, Material Goods, Science, Arts, Government, Other People, and Self.

3. Using Figure 6, p. 83, apply the Interaction Complex to the life of an imaginary individual. Write a story about him placing each step in its proper sequence.

4. Select any of the Life Areas and explain how you would like to change its description from the one given in the textbook.

Chapter 5

NOTE: If desired, students may obtain a printed questionnaire and hominologram forms with instructions from Nationwide Press, Ltd., P. O. Box 1528, Pueblo, Colorado 81002. These additional aids can be utilized for the exercises described in this chapter and in Chapter 13.

1. Explain the advantage of using the term "typical" student over "average" student (p. 100).

2. How can the philosophical self-knowledge gained by constructing the hominologram be applied to everyday life?

3. What kind of knowledge of mankind is likely to emerge from a study which excludes a search for self-knowledge on the part of the student?

4. How can one's tolerance and acceptance of another individual be increased by viewing his hominologram?

5. How can "agreeing to disagree" promote harmony between groups or individuals having different political, religious, or ethical orientations?

6. How can the characteristics (personality variables) listed on p. 111 be made statistically acceptable?

Chapter 6

1. Is classification based on how an investigator confronts data clarifying or confusing in comparison with other systems of classification (pp. 122-123)?

2. Discuss the role of the scientist's personality in his selection of the method he will use in investigating data (pp. 136-137).

3. What are the justifications, if any, for the inclusion of intuitive methods in a textbook on hominology (pp. 139-142)?

4. Why and when does Science reject new ideas (p. 142)? Is this justified? What are the consequences of such rejection to creativity?

Chapter 7

1. Why do the lines AB and DC fail to meet at a point at the bottom of Fig. 15 on p. 147?

2. What definition of teleology might be acceptable and what might be unacceptable to modern science (pp. 157-158)?

3. How can the concept of "mankind becoming" be used to retard progress? How can it be used to accelerate progress?

4. What can biology and philosophy learn from each other (p. 158)? What might be the results of combining these two disciplines? What would be the loss and the gain?

Chapter 8

1. The writings of Ardrey, Lorenz, and others who have utilized animal models to explain human behavior have been severely criticized by a number of modern writers. Use the Criteria of Reality (Chapters 3, 4, 5) as a possible explanation of this dispute.

2. Use the following key (p. 171): A = amity; E = intergroup enmity; e = intragroup enmity; h = hazards. Compare the for-

mula $A = E + h$ with $A = E + h$ (if survival is anticipated); and $e = E + h$ (if extermination is anticipated).

3. What are the basic differences between the approaches taken by Walker and Miller as judged by comparing their chapter headings (p. 176)?

4. What are the advantages and disadvantages of combining the three kinds of involvements listed on p. 178?

Chapter 9

1. Fig. 16 on p. 193 implies that in one sense Man began with the beginning of all things (A). How can this concept affect one's attitude towards an individual's relationship with the universe as a whole?

2. What circumstances lead to harmony between Man's four environments and what to conflicts and difficulties between them (pp. 200-201).

3. In the theoretical sequence of Man's cultural development on pp. 206-208, Man's advanced concepts of world wide responsibility follow his venture into space including the moon landing. Discuss possible reasons and significance of this. Why can men land on the moon before mankind has achieved a sense of worldwide responsibility for improving the lives of people on earth?

4. The Birth-Death Phase on p. 214 describes death as a "cessation of potential." How can death be viewed as a transcendental change leading to different kinds of potential, some biological and others nonbiological?

5. What new perspectives on mankind's evolvement can be gained from a study of the varying nature of time?

Chapter 10

The survey conducted by the Gallup Poll on the results of young men participating in the Vietnam war (p. 240-241) leads to the following questions:

1. Assuming the report is correct, is it possible through peaceful means to provide experiences which lead to the same kind of character building that this poll suggests was gained by soldiers

participating in the Vietnam war? Does this poll imply a failure in character building and in teaching good citizenship by current educational methods and home training?

2. Has the poll omitted significant factors that might modify the implications of the results obtained? What are these?

3. Warfare is viewed as a hominolag. In what way could it also be a culture lag? Exploration of the moon and planets has been suggested as an alternative activity to warfare. Can it be conceived of as a modern potlatch (p. 242)? On the other hand, some writers maintain that space exploration is a wasted effort and that our resources should instead be expended on improving living conditions on earth. They feel that space exploration will not create a better world for mankind pointing out that the rash of exploration following Columbus' discovery of America failed to create a better world, but instead accentuated nationalistic acquisitiveness. Discuss this contention in the light of the wording on the plaque left on the moon by astronauts Neil A. Armstrong and Edwin E. Aldrin Jr.:

"Here men from the planet earth first set foot upon the moon, July 1969, A.D. We came in peace for all mankind."

Compare this with the pronouncements made by 15th and 16th century explorers and discuss the differences. Can you explain the reasons for the differences?

4. To what extent are nations now ready and able to use competition based on providing the best life for their citizens as a weapon in ideological warfare? Can this, in the long run, prove to be more powerful than the use of weapons for maintaining national ideologies?

5. How effectively can the so-called "responsibility" (p. 241) learned in war be transferred to use in civilian life?

6. In Fig. 20 (p. 244) the automobile is shown as useful in terms of its original purpose—effective transportation. When cities are so choked with traffic that one cannot get from place to place as well as if one used horses, or so filled with exhaust fumes that there is danger to health, then automobiles, in this particular situation, become culture lags. But in Fig. 20, the implication is that automobile driving has become a method used by drivers

to express ethological residuals suggestive of an earlier phylogenetic level. As we may do in many disguised and symbolic ways, the drivers are depicted as again fighting the battle for survival of the fittest typical of Level Five (Chapter 11, pp. 256-258). When viewed in this way, the automobile may represent a hominolag because it is used in the expression of emotions derived from earlier genetically rooted adaptations which have become maladaptions under changing circumstances and conditions such as are encountered when driving an automobile. Discuss Fig. 20 in terms of aggressiveness, sibling rivalry, need for power, need for feeling important, establishing dominance, regression to Level Five, and suicidal tendencies.

7. What kind of change is envisioned as occurring in death (p. 245) where the dead are buried with food, adornments, and weapons placed with them in their graves?

8. The "Naturalistic Fallacy" is mentioned on p. 247. Discuss the possibility of an equivalent "Culturalistic Fallacy" in which Man is viewed as if he were psychologically molded entirely by cultural influences and environmental condition. If Man's basic nature is constructed by his conditioning subject to cultural manipulation and if hereditary factors play only an insignificant role in making Man what he is, what are the implications of this point of view for rapid cultural change?

Chapter 11

1. In what way may death be viewed as a return to Level Two (p. 255) or Level Eight (p. 269).

2. Compare the Developmental Levels on p. 254 with the ones occurring in geological history: 1) Age of Marine Invertebrates; 2) Age of Fishes; 3) Age of Amphibians; 4) Age of Reptiles; 5) Age of Mammals; 6) Age of Man. Are any of the levels of hominology and the Ages of historical geology formulated on the basis of empiricism, pragmatism, intuitionism, rationalism?

3. How may the Developmental Levels (the Ages of Man) be effectively utilized in the exploration of mankind's ongoing process leading from the past to Man's hypothetical future?

4. The use of drugs and narcotics can be explained as: represent-

ing an escape from self and society, as an act of defiance and hostility, as being caught in an addiction, or as an attempt at self-destruction. Can it also be viewed as an ineffectual effort to reach a state of mind consistent with Level Eight? What fore-runners of Level Eight are currently evident in our society?

5. Could the so-called Hippie phenomenon among some of our youth represent a form of unconscious protest against the values of Level Six?

Chapter 12

NOTE: An exercise in Charting the Self-Image on Fig. 21, p. 288 is available from Nationwide Press, Ltd., P. O. Box 1528, Pueblo, Colorado 81002.

1. Find examples of the moral values in your environment which you can analyze as in the following:

"THANK YOU
FOR LEAVING THIS AREA AS CLEAN AS YOU FOUND IT!"

The above is a sign in a public camping area. Which moral value is represented by "Thank you" (p. 278)? What advantage, if any, can accrue from the fact that "thank you" precedes the suggestion for leaving the area clean (p. 282)? What moral value is inherent in the expectation that campers will leave the camping area as clean as they found it (pp. 279-280)?

2. Discuss the following:

A student spent so much time holding the elevator door open for others to enter that he arrived late to his class. Can he justify his coming late to class on the basis of the graces? Can he do so on the basis of the dedications? Is there merit in participating in one moral value at the expense of adhering to another one? For example, is Dedication justified at the expense of the Duties?

3. Discuss the following:

Manufacturing of goods, sales, and performing services can be done with a focus on several of the theoretical Developmental Levels (Ages of Man). If the owner of a manufacturing company or a firm offering a service to the public operates partially within Level Seven (Dedication), how would this affect the quality of his company's product? How would it affect the morale of his

employees, the guarantees of his merchandise, his customer relationships, his repair and research policies? Compare business
conducted on this Level with one operating solely on Level Six,
or one almost exclusively on Level Five? Discuss this in the light
of the analogy of Factory A and B pp. 300-301.

4. The morality inherent in the Duties represents a two-way
process in all cases. Though true in a moral sense, if not in a legal
sense, if a government fails to do its duty towards its citizens, the
people, in theory, are freed from cooperating with the government provided they are unable to change the unfair government
policies. For example, if a government-owned water company
supplies me with just half of the water furnished to other members of my community, I would not feel morally obligated to pay
the same fee as those who receive more water. This concept
stems from the reciprocity that is inherent within the Duties.

If certain citizens do not receive the same civil rights and
equal opportunities as the rest of the group, can they be expected
to respect the government and its laws to the same extent as
those who receive more rights and greater opportunities? What
are the implications of this point of view for all members of a
society?

5. Often pseudo-dedications are of great value when they convert
impulses that may be undesirable into actions which are beneficial to society. Compare pseudo-dedications and genuine dedications in terms of their potential benefits to society and to the
individual who is dedicating. Can pseudo-dedications lead to the
adoption of genuine dedications?

6. The formula for "goodness" (see Chapter 15, pp. 358-359)
suggests that operationally, "goodness may be represented as a
ratio. According to this formula, the level of "good behavior"
that can be expected in any given case depends upon the capacity
for expressing "goodness." How can this capacity be gauged in
the case of an individual, a society, or for the species, at any
given period within history? Can the lives of those who devote
themselves to human welfare constitute a blueprint of contemporary capacity for acting in a "good manner"? Comment on this
view. In that case, Dedication serves two separate functions—one,
the good that is done; two, the example that has been set for

others to follow. Such examples can be used as suggesting the contemporary level of capacity. Are there other methods of ascertaining capacity for expressing "goodness?"

Chapter 13

1. A person may handle hostile impulses in three basic ways: expressing them negatively on any target immediately available even at the expense of hurting others; using Scape-Elephants (see p. 310); converting them into positive action beneficial to society. What kind of persons and what kind of conditions favor the use of these different methods of handling hostile impulses?

2. A hominolopath (p. 315) is out of tune with his society's level of moral adaptation. His actions represent earlier phylogenetic levels of moral adaptation. What factors may be responsible for his phylogenetic retardation (see Table VIII, p. 316)?

3. The filling out of hominologram II (p. 321) may be facilitated by the use of questionnaires and forms available from Midwest Educational Press. Compare the value of hominologram I (p. 99) with hominologram II in terms of insight and self-understanding derived from participating in these exercises.

4. Discuss the following. A person travelling by automobile may fail to reach his destination because of one (or more) of three reasons.

He has taken the wrong road.
He is on the right road but is stalled by motor trouble.
He thinks, in error, that he has already arrived at his destination.

Discuss these three different reasons for failure to reach a desired goal. (Life's "destination" represents reaching the maximum level of phylogenetic maturity of which the individual is capable.) The "road" is the advancement along the Eight Developmental Levels (see Table VIII, p. 316).

5. Why are you apt to be anxious if you are living beyond the norms of your society in your advancement towards Levels Seven and Eight?

Chapter 14

1. The following abstract is from the *Rocky Mountain News* (Dec. 24, 1970).

NEW YORK (UPI) There are times when blind people think it is the sighted who lack vision. This thought crosses the minds of the sightless most often when those who can see fail to recognize that blind people are individuals.

According to Don D. Nold, a blind magazine publisher, "Some people think that all blind people are the same—that all blind people are musicians, or that all blind people are religious. One man said he wouldn't hire a blind worker because the blind drink too much. . . . Sighted people just don't seem to be able to cope with blindness.

. . . Nold said also, "Blind young people would like to get into the swim of things. They are held back by a lack of communications with sighted. Some blind people are so eager for acceptance that they will do almost anything to get it.

Discuss this article on the blind in terms of pitfalls, basic premises, communications between different peoples, and similarities to racial, religious, and class prejudices.

2. Give examples illustrating each of the 15 pitfalls. These examples may be taken from actual life situations, from fiction, or they may represent imagined situations. Identify the source of your examples and explain how they apply. Estimate how often you are the victim of these pitfalls.

3. In the chapter the various possible definitions and the different sources of aggression were described. Make a similar analysis of definitions and possible sources of: prejudice, fear, love, mental health.

4. Discuss how insights, perspectives, and techniques learned in hominology could be applied in the study of each one of the ten contemporary problems listed in the chapter.

5. List the ten problems in order of their importance and discuss the reasons why you feel this way about them.

6. List the ten problems in order of your personal interest in them. Explain this.

7. If you believe the problems overlap explain this and describe how you might reword the problems in order to prevent this.

8. Make a list of additional human problems that were not represented on the list in the chapter and explain why you think they are important.

9. Do you believe that freedom is an illusion or a reality? Explain why you feel this way about freedom.

10. One may change any society from the top down or from the

bottom up. Changing society from the top down would entail changing the institutions and the government and assuming that this, in turn, would change the people within the society. Changing society from the bottom up would entail changing the people within the society assuming that this would change the institutions and the government. Which method do you think would be most effective? Give the advantages and disadvantages of each of these methods of creating change.

Chapter 15

1. Discuss other possible applications of hominology not mentioned in Chapter 15.

2. Using hominological algebra develop other formulas including at least one that involves the difference between legal and moral obligations.

3. Describe in some detail the kind of lives that are led by persons living primarily within Level Five and compare these people to those who are attempting to live primarily within Level Seven. Perhaps you can write a short story in which you describe how persons from both levels meet, interact and tell what happens to them.

4. Discuss the question of synthesis within the human sciences and explain why such synthesis cannot be achieved by using scientific methods only. Describe what methods you would use in an attempt to achieve synthesis of the whole Man.

5. Give examples of pseudo-Dedications used by parents towards their children.

6. Do you agree that contemporary Man's greatest progress has been in the realm of morality? Explain why you agree or disagree with this statement.

7. What is the best way to motivate modern youth to become involved in activities leading to the kind of Dedication that represents the forefront of Man's ongoing process in our times?

8. In the *Yale Alumni Magazine* (May 1971) Nicholas Johnson writes:

Parents obviously have something to do with the capacity of their children to reach their potential as human beings. The average child will receive more hours of "instructions" from television by the time he enters first grade than the number of hours he will later spend in college classrooms earning his B.A. degree. By the time he is a teenager he will have spent from 15,000 to 20,000 hours with the television set and seen anywhere from 250,000 to 500,000 commercials. It would seem simple common sense to assume that this exposure has its influence.

Describe the possible effects of this influence on the selection of the Developmental Levels, the Criteria of Reality, the Moral Values, and the Pitfalls. What other influences exist in an industrial society that tend to affect the quality of our lives either favorably or unfavorably.

9. Discuss the suggestion that mankind "return to nature" as a means of helping to solve current human problems. Describe the advantages and disadvantages of following this suggestion.

10. Compare the consequences of studying human differences with the possible results of studying human similarities.

11. Use the formula for goodness in this chapter and explain why Society A and Society B are equally "good."

$$\text{SOCIETY A} = \frac{\text{LEVEL FIVE}}{\text{LEVEL FIVE}} \quad \text{SOCIETY B} = \frac{\text{LEVEL SIX}}{\text{LEVEL SIX}}$$

12. Discuss the following kind of speculations and decide on whether or not you find them justified:

One may speculate that people who are hominologically immature, that is, adopt action themes of a lower Developmental Level than they are capable of adopting, are unfit for survival in an age in which the focus of human life is being redirected from Level Six to Level Seven. Nature takes care of this by decreasing their longevity. The more immature people are the less fit they are to survive in today's world and the more subject they are to an early demise.

Thus, people living on Level Four may soon die of boredom. Those living on Level Five tend to be accident prone, develop ulcers and heart attacks. People whose focus is on the self-indulgence of lower Level Six are subject to obesity, high cholesterol, alcoholism, and cardiovascular disease. Those striving hard to gain success on a higher stage of Level Six are likely to succumb to emotional tensions, high blood pressure, and possibly asthma or arthritis.

13. Many religious and political leaders of the world in various different ways have attempted to influence people to leave Level Six and adopt a Level Seven mentality. For example, President John F. Kennedy of the United States, using national Dimensions said: "Ask not what your country can do for you; ask what you can do for your country." Find other quotations from world leaders past or present that similarly urge us towards the goal of Dedication.

14. In this chapter the statement was made that students should learn how to recognize "symptoms of Man's love and hate when these are disguised." Explain why this is important. Why are love and hate disguised?

15. Describe what you believe can be realistically done to make Man more humane.

16. Hominological concepts such as the Moral Values were designed to identify human universals which may be disguised by cultural overlays. For example, the Tasadays of the Philippines and some other nonliterate peoples file their teeth down with sandstone and blacken them with pitch or carbon "so that they will not have sharp white teeth like animals."

This behavior falls within the framework of the Graces and gives it the moral equivalence of "good manners" in literate societies (such as eating with knives, forks, chopsticks, etc.). Provide other examples describing how hominology may be used to identify human universals.

INDEX

A

Acceleration, 209, 217, 259
Action, steps leading to, 61
Adaptation, 149, 257
Aggression, 298, 309-14, 333-5
Agnostics, 106
Amity-Enmity formula, 171, *also see Appendix p. 368-9*
Anthropoidea, 23, 39, 236, 294
Anthropology, meaning of the term, 11-12
Anthropomorphism, 22, 40
Anxiety, 266-7, 351, 361
Apes, 17, 22, 27, 30-4, 38, 236
    comparison of, to Man, 23, 24, *illust.* 25, 42
    fossils of, 225-6
    in human homes, 37-8
Approach-avoidance conflict, 320
Ardrey, R., 42, 169-71, 352
Aristotle, 142, 148
Arithmetic mean, 100
Art
    as a means of understanding Man, 39-40, 45
    in nonhumans, 39-40
Arts, 89
Atomistic school, 148
Attitudes, concepts which shape, 61
Australopithecines, 26, 223
Authoritarianism, 62-3, 111, 194
Automation, 137-9
Average (in statistics), 100

B

Badness, 275, 276, 295, 358
Behavior studies, ideal conditions for, 36-7
Biological imperatives, 35
Biological morality, 340
Biology, 155, 239, 333, 346

Brain, 32-3
    see also Man, brain of
Burial, prehistoric, 216-7

C

Cannibalism, 293-7
Capitalism, 336-7
Challenge, man's need for, 47, 258
Change, 85, 147, 204-5, 245-6, 253-70, 277, 335, 338, 339, 340
    diagrams of, 147, 193
Classification of methods, table, 123
Commitments, 293
Communism, 110, 178, 335-6
Computorized methods, 137-9
Competition, kinds of, 256-7, 325, 357
Configurations, breakdown of, 40-2, 242
Conclusions, why they differ, 185-6, 333, 337
Contradiction, Man as, 45
Cooperation, types of, 290-3
Copernicus, N., 196
Cosmogony, 165, 194
Criteria of reality, *see* Reality
Cro-Magnon Man, 209
Culture, 33, 42, 47, 184, 201, 237, 246, 251, 273, 333, 346, 362
    absorption of, 216
    definition of, 215
    development of, 206-8
    diagrammed view of, 193, 214-6
    gap, 238-46
    humans without, 33-4
    lag, 238-46
Culturology, 183
Cybernetics, 138

D

Dart's baby, 226-8
Darwin, C., 134, 148-51, 154, 155, 156, 159, 161, 167, 169, 170, 171, 172, 247

379

ABOUT THE AUTHOR

Dr. THEODORE C. KAHN has a B.A. from Yale, a masters from Columbia and a Ph.D. from the University of Southern California. In addition to his sociological and psychological training he received a Dr. rerum naturalium (Sc.D.) from the University of Mainz, Germany in anthropology. He is a Diplomate in Clinical Psychology and a Fellow in the American Psychological Association with many years of experience as a psychologist, a counselor, and an educator. He was the founder and first president of the International Society for the Study of Symbols and has written many articles on behavioral science subjects and several books on psychology and behavioral science. For his work he has been honored internationally and is listed in Who's Who in America, Who's Who in the World, and the International Dictionary of Biography. He has taught at the University of Southern California, University of Maryland, Wittenberg University and was recognized as an Outstanding Educator of America. Presently he is a professor of Behavioral Science at the University of Southern Colorado.

Additional Charts, Hominolograms, Questionnaires and the book, AN INTRODUCTION TO HOMINOLOGY - AN INTEGRATED VIEW OF MANKIND AND SELF, Theodore C. Kahn, 1976, may be obtained from Nationwide Press, P. O. Box 1528, Pueblo, Colorado 81002. Also write to this address for information regarding membership in the American Hominological Association and other publications on the subject of hominology.